W.M. THACKERAY AND THE MEDIATED TEXT

W.M. Thackeray and the Mediated Text

Writing for periodicals in the mid-nineteenth century

Richard Pearson

Routledge
Taylor & Francis Group
LONDON AND NEW YORK

First published 2000 by Ashgate Publishing

Reissued 2018 by Routledge
2 Park Square, Milton Park, Abingdon, Oxon OX14 4RN
711 Third Avenue, New York, NY 10017, USA

Routledge is an imprint of the Taylor & Francis Group, an informa business

A Library of Congress record exists under LC control number: 00038988

ISBN 13: 978-1-138-71344-4 (hbk)
ISBN 13: 978-1-138-71342-0 (pbk)
ISBN 13: 978-1-315-19880-4 (ebk)

Contents

The Nineteenth Century General Editors' Preface

The aim of this series is to reflect, develop and extend the great burgeoning of interest in the nineteenth century that has been an inevitable feature of recent decades, as that former epoch has come more sharply into focus as a locus for our understanding not only of the past but of the contours of our modernity. Though it is dedicated principally to the publication of original monographs and symposia in literature, history, cultural analysis, and associated fields, there will be a salient role for reprints of significant text from, or about, the period. Our overarching policy is to address the spectrum of nineteenth-century studies without exception, achieving the widest scope in chronology, approach and range of concern. This, we believe, distinguishes our project from comparable ones, and means, for example, that in the relevant areas of scholarship we both recognize and cut innovatively across such parameters as those suggested by the designations 'Romantic' and 'Victorian'. We welcome new ideas, while valuing tradition. It is hoped that the world which predates yet so forcibly predicts and engages our own will emerge in parts, as a whole, and in the lively currents of debate and change that are so manifest an aspect of its intellectual, artistic and social landscape.

Vincent Newey
Joanne Shattock

University of Leicester

Acknowledgements

I would like to thank all of the people who have assisted my research for this book over a number of years. Library staff at the following institutions have always been helpful: the Pierson Library, University College Worcester; Birmingham Central Reference Library; Birmingham University Library; the British Library, Bloomsbury; the British Newspaper Library, Colindale; the Bibliothèque Nationale, Paris; the John Rylands Library, University of Manchester; Manchester Central Library.

Thanks to the University College Worcester for providing research leave to advance the project to completion.

My special thanks are warmly given to the individuals who have advised and encouraged in many ways: Roger Ebbatson, Sarah Davies, Catherine Neale, Alan Shelston, Barbara Rosenbaum, Joanne Shattock, and all of my friends and colleagues at University College Worcester and elsewhere.

My personal thanks go to Caroline Loughnane, my father, Nick, Kim, Tony, Jo, Mike, Sarah, and all of my friends.

This book is in memory of my mother.

For my mother

Introduction

> I shall not attempt to tell that story of the battle of the 23rd September, which ended in our glorious Captain striking his own colours to our superior and irresistible enemy. Sir Richard has told the story of his disaster in words nobler than any I could supply ... (*Works*, XXIV, 298)

On reading Thackeray's incomplete last novel, *Denis Duval*, left *in medias res* by the processes of mid-Victorian literary production, I was delighted to discover that his last published words were about a namesake of mine, Captain Richard Pearson, and could indulge in the thought that he elevated me to the rank of 'Captain' (a fictitious self-fashioning that several of his characters accorded themselves). Certainly, coming from amongst the 1860s decade of Sensation, it was a haunting moment in my reading. More seriously, it is a testimony to the success of Thackeray's career, and the commercial value of his name-as-commodity in 1864, that the *Cornhill Magazine* could run a serial for its readers knowing (on both sides) that it was only half-finished. The market for Thackeray was strong; his name had pulling power, he *could* supply. This had not always been the case.

This study of Thackeray's writings for the periodical press, and his inscribing of the press into the world of his fiction, aims to demonstrate how the author not only negotiated the commercial marketplace but also explored its nature in symbolic narrative structures. My approach is broadly materialist, placing the text within a network of cultural relationships that shape and define both the 'author' and the reader. However, I do not view the text as a passive product, but, as in the work of Jonathan Dollimore and Alan Sinfield, perceive of it as a site of contention and engagement. I use terminology such as N.N. Feltes' 'commodity-text' to describe the periodical article as a commercial transaction between publisher, editor, writer, and reader. But I also wish to see the writer as able to participate in a symbolic exchange of value in which the reader does not just purchase, say, a newspaper, but a text with added value as able to transgress the readerly assumptions about that purchase. For example, a reader in 1836 may buy the *Constitutional* newspaper and search for its Paris news, and find Thackeray's challenging attacks on capital punishment in the foreign correspondence section. The reader may not choose to return, but their understanding of the medium of Paris correspondence will have altered.

The text as a site of potential transgression within the periodical media poses more cautionary problems. The additional layer of mediation that exists – the editorial and proprietorial policies and politics of the newspaper or magazine – immediately establishes a signifying system that disturbs our conventional view of literary authority. Much critical work has been carried out on how to 'read' the press: consideration must be made of the individual text or article and its intertextual relationship with the periodical as a whole, and within the run of that periodical over time. Furthermore, and something that is often omitted, the journal must be seen in relation to other journals of the period against which it defined its objectives. No launch of a new magazine is unaccompanied by a prospectus that seeks to locate that magazine into a niche or space within the market-place. Magazines create their own identities by distancing themselves from their immediate rivals. Thus, the *National Standard* cited the *Literary Gazette*, the *Atheneaum*, and the *New Monthly Magazine* as indices of its own goals and fashioned its image alongside their existing popularity. Jacques Lacan's theory of the mirror-stage and the reflection of the Other, with its adaptation to postcolonial theory, might seen a long way removed from the Victorian newspaper trade, but it is a model that proves useful. Marketing and image-making establish these structures of dependency on their self-imagined opposition in order to mediate the image of the Self. This process pervades Victorian publishing, and, indeed, is a central theme in Thackeray's writings, as my discussion of *Pendennis* suggests.

Hence we see the text as part of a journal and as part of a culture. However, we must also paradoxically see the text as part of another symbolic configuration – that of the commodity-author. Analysing any modern author with the knowledge of Michel Foucault's 'What is an Author?' generates a constructed and historical concept of authorship. Tracing a model of authorship back to the 1830s when Thackeray began to write professionally (a term suggestive of the shift from describing an author's 'juvenilia' to depicting their 'professional apprenticeship'), we find the definition of authorship itself under duress. Thackeray entered the profession at a moment of significant cultural change in the production, marketing and sale of literature. He is a writer who participates in the emerging mass media and reflects upon the transformation of literary production. As a writer, though, this reflection can only take place within the boundaries of the media itself. Unlike William Blake or William Morris, Thackeray did not possess the means of production and thus the ability to stand outside of commercial publishing. Indeed, his purchase of the *National Standard* might be seen as an unsuccessful attempt to gain a degree of control. His critique, then, his analysis of and engagement with the forces of industrial production, must be situated within the very system being critiqued. It is therefore self-reflexive and deconstructive. But it, in turn, also must be produced, defined and marketed as a product in the same way. Thackeray's writings occupy a space of ambivalence in the periodical press; they demonstrate the limits of authorial autonomy as the man-of-letters gives way to the modern author. As with the boundaries of acceptable taste – the expression of sexuality, for example – Thackeray pushes as far as he can the self-deconstructing of his article's authority, and thus achieves a new level of reader identification beyond the surface mechanics of the modern press. Yet this too is Thackeray's product, his commodification of the author.

An illustration might be found in the theme of male power in 'The Luck of Barry Lyndon', *Fraser's Magazine* (January–December 1844). Two scenes in the novel show how the magazine can be used as a means of imprisoning female desire and fulfilling male appetite within a social framework of male authority operating publicly through the press. Authorship and manipulation become inextricable. The Prince of X murders his wife and her lover in private, whilst controlling the media representation of the story to suggest a more natural series of events. The *Court Gazette* is made to report the Count Magny's 'suicide' and a duplicate copy of the paper, without the report, is delivered to the Princess to maintain her ignorance of her own fate. The newspaper carries reports of the Princess's gradual decline in health, mentally and physically, until, when her death is seemingly imminent, the Prince has her executed (*Works*, XIX, 160-66).

Redmond Barry replicates this tale in his treatment of Lady Lyndon. The Dublin newspapers are persuaded to carry information about him that assists his scheme to marry the heiress. He is presented as a fashionable man-about-town. Wishing to surprise Lady Lyndon in the town, he ensures that the *Dublin Mercury* carries a story of his flight after a duel, and she returns to Dublin believing she is safe only to be caught by him. Lady Lyndon resists the marriage, but Barry has the newspapers announce the marriage and the *Town and Country Magazine* even publishes 'pictures'. When Lady Lyndon attempts to flee Ireland, Barry has the *Dublin Mercury* announce his departure a day earlier and thus counterfeits an appearance that she is chasing him. The ensuing family scandal encourages the Lyndon relatives finally to insist on the marriage. Barry ensnares Lady Lyndon through his access to the Public Sphere and his careful mediation of the news and his wife's image. His actual imprisonment of her is only a furthering of the textual cage he has already built (*Works*, XIX, 187, 195-6, 209, 214-16).

Thackeray suggests in this story, and throughout many of his works, how powerful the creation of a media image can be. The control of the periodical press can confer immense authority as this public domain impacts directly upon the private. Barry-as-writer can inscribe Lady Lyndon's life within a strong net of discourse that enables his masculinity to assert itself. The writer must work with responsibility, but the reader must be cautious of the assumed authoritativeness of the press. A magazine presents only a textual version of the world, a resemblance that is mediated by the ideology behind its surface. The press, then, contains a fascinating possibility of fulfilment, but this is bought at the price of moral reprehension. Such dualism pervades Thackeray's presentation of the periodicals.

We must also consider that a construction of the author has already occurred. The legitimating of an author's identity is historically bounded: the Victorian publishing of Thackeray's *Collected Works* established a canon and a unified sense of his works by taking them out of their original context. For Foucault, this has the effect of the assisting of the making of an image seemingly outside of history, an author 'Thackeray'. The Smith, Elder and Co. collected edition of *The Works of William Makepeace Thackeray* (26 volumes), completes a process of separation between literature and journalism that Thackeray himself was debating. Initially excluded from the 24-volume edition were a series of essays and book reviews and the *Punch* weekly articles which comprise volumes 25 and 26. But even beyond these remain the contributions to the *Morning Chronicle*, *Foreign Quarterly Review*, *Pictorial Times*, *Calcutta Star*, and much more for *Punch* and the *Times*, not to mention several smaller journals and the entire corpus of *National Standard*, *Constitutional*, and *Paris Literary Gazette* writings. The list itself continues incomplete. The 'author' is a selected one, and our construct omits probably the most significant influence on the 'real' author's career – the periodical press itself. Smith, Elder and Co., like their founder, George Smith, privileged the distinguished man-of-letters. This is a symbolic act that is problematized in Thackeray's actual works.

The author is a construct, an image, and we are aware that Thackeray emerged as a writer at the moment when a cultural rift opened up between a Romantic ideal of literary autonomy and a Victorian inscribing of the author into the mechanisms of industrial production. With big money involved, commercial success usually outweighed creative integrity. John Sutherland's work has suggested that the most famous authors, like Dickens and Thackeray, could dictate terms with publishers more favourably. But these 'famous names' are precisely author-products, commodity-authors, too, perhaps even more so than lesser-known writers. Despite this, paradoxically, Thackeray is conscious of his own commodification, and both uses and challenges these commercial mechanisms. Advertising and self-advertising are dominant ideological methods here. The writer might be part of the periodical's corporate identity, part of the journal-product, and subsumed within its contents, but the author is also a product. They can both make use of the branding of the other; the relationship is double-edged. For Thackeray, if the individual writer is to succeed he needs as much marketing as the journal-product. The writer usually wrote for many journals, many publishers and publishing houses. He also stepped outside of the periodical world and published volumes (or serial novels, 'from the publishers of *Punch*', imitating the marketable periodical). Most journal articles went unsigned, thus negating any opportunity for an author to build a discreet audience. However, Thackeray's use of persona and pseudonym assisted the generation of a recognizable identity – a Yellowplush, a Titmarsh, a Pendennis. This was not just a marketing strategy, but recognition by Thackeray of the constructed nature of authorial identity and the changing role of the writer in the production of the text. Thackeray's gallery of fictitious writers – amateurs and journalists, travel writers and novelists – exist as a self-reflexive authorial function of deliberate mediation. They problematize the reader – text relation in order to draw attention to the new media's role in textual mediation.

This study, then, is not about an author's negotiation of the Victorian literary marketplace, the frustrations (and benefits) of having a 'Pegasus in harness'. Instead, it is about how the commodity-text (journal and article) and the commodity-author operate and exchange in a redefining and a resisting of definition in a period of cultural revolution. But it is also about Thackeray, a writer more anxious about than accepting of these turbulent forces. As a subjective writer, his promotion of self and product-text is particularly interesting. His works are filled with symbolic identifications – with characters and narratives – that suggest his desires and guilt about the identity he fashions.

The generation of an author's self-identity is not culturally isolated, but is embroiled in the generation of models of masculinity/femininity and perceptions of racial and class identities. It is not insignificant that, fictionally (and despite the male narrators), Thackeray shows more early identification with female desire (Catherine, the Ravenswing, Becky Sharp) than in later 'male' texts (Pendennis, Esmond, George Warrington). His journalist figures – Wagstaff, Yellowplush, Titmarsh, Spec, Mr Snob, Gobemouche – are entirely male. The journalistic world is symbolically represented as a world of transgressive and illicit desire, of sexual excess, Bohemianism, Parisian *liberté*, and insatiable appetite. Unlike recognizable art, or the careful novel, journalism has no shape, no boundaries, but is repetitive, endless, inexhaustive, and driven by momentary gratification (of payment, of pleasure). Thackeray's consciousness of this begins a line of cultural critique that runs to Jean Baudrillard and Roland Barthes (indeed, Barthes once played Thackeray in a film about the Brontës). Journalism is also part of the world of trade, of profit, of unashamed commercial exploitation. The freedoms of the artistocratic Regency world of gambling, whoring, and dandyism, has been transposed for the male of the 1830s and 1840s to the hand-to-mouth, sensual, appetite-ridden existence of the literary tradesman. Thackeray could get paid to explore Paris, dine out for information, experience and investigate the shadier sides of life, read French literature and cheap licentious magazines, attend the ballet, the theatre, the galleries, and public executions, and peer in through the grill of the Harem, all in the name (but anonymously, without his name) of popular magazinery. There was little moral censorship, only market exclusion. In certain sectors of the press, anything went. Thackeray certainly wrote in the borderlands of propriety at times, but always with ironic self-awareness. To some extent, Thackeray was asking very early in its rise, what sort of maleness, of engenderization, the new literary establishment was preparing.

This study is structured around various kinds of text or genre. The list is not exhaustive and there are no doubt areas of omission – the book review or the comic magazine, for example. Chapters 1 to 3 look at specific journals and roles of the journalist, focusing on the *National Standard*, the *Paris Literary Gazette*, and the *Constitutional*, the editor, magazine contributor, and foreign correspondent. Chapter 4 considers two magazine serials and their direct use of the media as subject matter, as well as their manifestation of the themes of advertising, publicity, and public image. Chapter 5 posits the opposition of Paris and London, and the accessibility of a morally transgressive lifestyle. It looks at how Thackeray plays out in public his emotional traumas, and how desire and death become entwined in his public image at a moment of deep personal anxiety. Chapter 6 considers Thackeray's journalism through his analysis of other journals and his views on the contradictory permanency of ephemeral reporting. Chapter 7 discusses the representation of the journalist in his writings, and suggests his concerns over the power of the reporter. Chapter 8 is a study of *Pendennis* and its sustained inventing of a world of conflict between art and journalism, integrity and profit, gentlemanliness and exploitation of sex and class, the domestic and the erotic. The symbolic parallels in this novel suggest Thackeray's anxieties over the 'dignity of literature' and the needs and desires of the individual. Thackeray largely abandoned the periodicals in the 1850s, but Chapter 9 explores his return, in 1860, as editor of the *Cornhill Magazine*. A process of reinvention occurs as Thackeray refashions himself as a magazine writer through *Lovel the Widower*, *Philip*, and the *Roundabout Papers*. His work exposes all of the old anxieties once more, but also shows an experienced awareness of the commercial tricks of the trade in a new market contest between realism and the sensational.

Chapter 1

Investing in the *National Standard*: representing 'Belles-Lettres'

Thackeray's professional career began at a moment in time that was of great consequence for the cultural development of Britain. The Reform Bill of 1832 generated immense public debate about the state of the nation and the direction of the political parties, and that public debate was fuelled by the growth in newspapers and magazines, itself a consequence of rising literacy levels, cheaper production methods of printing and paper manufacture, swifter distribution and circulation, and a general rise in the prosperity of the market-place.[1] Having left Cambridge behind, and secure in the prosperity of his family inheritance, Thackeray pursued a financially lucrative prospect that would, he believed, make his fortune and enable him to fulfil his writing ambitions. He bought into one of the fastest-growing markets of the day: print. The speculative nature of his first attempted investment is clear in the remark he made to himself in his diary of April 1832: 'My newspaper scheme is done up for want of funds', he wrote, 'perhaps it has saved me £100 perhaps I have lost a thousand by it.'[2] The same day, Thackeray had been present in the House of Commons to hear the second reading of the Reform Bill.

When Dickens was running between Parliament and his newspaper office, reporting on current debates as an occasional contributor for the *True Sun* and *Mirror of Parliament* newspapers, Thackeray was observing the debates at leisure, and negotiating to purchase a newspaper from two roguish proprietors, Gunnell (or Gunning) and Goldshede. His inheritance of approximately £20,000[3] would have been available to him during the summer of 1832 when he reached 21 years of age. He lost his money, and was still searching for Gunnell on 12-13 June 1832.[4] It was a lesson he did not quite learn. Less than a year later, he bought a literary magazine, the *National Standard*, from A.W.N. Bayley, and launched himself on the public, only to fail financially within another nine months. The collapse of the Indian banks in which the family fortune was invested, in the latter part of 1833, deprived him of that background security, and forced Thackeray to move to the cheaper living in Paris and discover an alternative route into the world of literature. Despite this apparent failure, the significance of Thackeray's initial foray into the world of journalism is central to an understanding of his complex response to writing and to the literary profession. Culturally, he emerged onto a faultline between the declining notion of writing as a gentlemanly and aristocratic pursuit, and the modern age of commercial publishing. More than any other writer of the period, he exemplifies a transitional figure, continuously renegotiating between the ideal and the reality of authorship. Though ultimately successful, financially and artistically, he remained deeply ambivalent about the power, image and responsibility of the writer in a world of trade and trade-off.

It is an anomaly of Thackeray criticism, that a magazine owned and largely written by the author should be almost ignored in studies of his career.[5] The formative nature of the experience of owning, editing, and writing the *National Standard* has never been discussed. His knowledge of the marketplace and the processes of literary production are usually overlooked. Thackeray's image, of an often weary genius, aristocratic in taste and manner, and leisurely and conservative (clubbable, Oxbridgean) in his writing, who gambled away his fortune in a late Regency show of cards, and wrote up his world in the satire of *Vanity Fair*, remains in place despite a wealth of evidence to the contrary. What strikes me about Thackeray is his singular determination to understand his profession and to engage intellectually with the rituals of the new commercial market. Thackeray is far more a sociologist of the press than has hitherto been remarked. The *National Standard* was an experiment that failed, but its ideology and the contradictions in its format and design, editorial and content, reveal how Thackeray learned the practices of his trade. The magazine contains the bulk of his early reading, his critical reviewing of this reading, and his initial trials at writing fiction. His hand dominates the contributions.[6] More importantly for the subject of this book, it also contains his initial perceptions of the role of the periodical in contemporary culture, and the function of the writer and editor within that role. As his knowledge of the market developed and he worked to increase subscription to his journal, Thackeray became aware of the advertisorial function of publishing, its place within a network of economic relations, and he took the first steps towards a critique of the commodification of the writer that he was later to maintain. Above all, he became conscious of the ways in which the text within a periodical is subject to the influences of the periodical apparatus that surrounds its reception. In other words, he realized that a text (an article, review, piece of fiction, poem, translation) is not just a free-standing entity, an independent commodity, but is part of a larger product bearing its own market propensities. The text is mediated by the journal, the media, of its promotion. Each item in a magazine contributes to the commercial identity of the whole, and it is this subjugation of the autonomy of the individual writer to the corporate design of the periodical that most concerns him. Never an editor again until he accepted the post on the *Cornhill Magazine* in 1859, Thackeray both negotiates this new relationship of writer to vehicle, of text to metatext, in the movement of his career, and makes it the subject of his writing.

A.W.N. Bayley's[7] magazine, the *National Standard*, was a literary review that had begun publication on 5 January. Thackeray's purchasing negotiations must have begun in May. He was keen to publish reviews almost immediately, and his review of a *Biographical Sketch of Joseph Napoleon Bonaparte* appeared in number 19 (11 May 1833), the first under his editorship, and it is possible that he wrote the review of Archibald Alison's *French Revolution* that appeared the week before.[8] A careful search of the magazine suggests further pieces may have been by Thackeray also. Contributions in March of that year have a Thackerayan style to them, and are similar to pieces he is known to have written later in the magazine's run. Hitherto, he had written only short comic sketches, comic verses, and translations of Latin poets, usually Anacreon.[9] He brought some of these juvenilia into the *National Standard*, and even introduced a comic woodcut into the first few issues of his editorship. The writing of reviews, though, was a new departure for him.

In order to understand Thackeray's editorial ideas for the *National Standard*, it is first necessary to consider the magazine as a whole and see where it came from and how it was situated within the market-place. Thackeray came to feel that he was sold a liability and was duped into paying for a commercial property that was never likely to succeed.[10] It is difficult to assess precisely if this was the case, but it may have been the market competition that would always prove too strong for Thackeray's low-price venture. The 2d. price was substantially lower than that of its middle-class rivals and, although Thackeray made this the central tenet of his advertising, the cheapness proved unsustainable. Dickens succeeded in 1850 with a very different kind of two penny periodical, *Household Words*. Thackeray's early attempt to introduce such was probably squeezed out of a respectably middle-class corner of the literary marketplace.

The *National Standard of Literature, Science, Music, Theatricals, and the Fine Arts* was a weekly Saturday magazine running to 16 pages. It was the sister paper of Bayley's *National Omnibus; and General Advertiser*, that carried the similar reviews and notices, only in lesser quantity and with more emphasis on the commercial advertising product. The *Standard's* advertising was also conspicuous, usually about three pages of the whole, but less so than that of its sister paper. It was the more literary of the two magazines. Initially, it recommended itself with original contributions by well-known authors: William Maginn, Douglas Jerrold, Laman Blanchard, and John Galt. Contributions by Edward Bulwer-Lytton and Tom Hood were pirated from elsewhere. Such authors did not remain with the paper when Thackeray took over, and it may have been this fact, along with a perceptible decline in the amount of advertising after Thackeray's purchase (suggesting some loss of patronage), which contributed to Thackeray's belief that he was gulled. In addition, the magazine contained fiction, poetry and short prose articles, notices of gallery exhibitions, theatre productions, and music concerts, and miscellaneous items of information ranging from 'Meteorology' to 'Voyages and Travels'. The lengthier and more critical reviews of literature and theatre in the *Standard* would undoubtedly have appealed to Thackeray.

Thackeray's journal is part of the commercial stage of periodical publishing identified by Jürgen Habermas as a period when journals were 'released from the pressure to take sides ideologically' and able to 'abandon [their] polemical stance and concentrate on the profit opportunities for a commercial business'.[11] Thackeray promoted the independence of his review, from political party and publishing house. Habermas identifies the 1830s as the period when this process developed, and cites the advance of advertising as one of its central features. 'In a situation of greatly lowered price per copy and a multiplied number of buyers', he writes, 'the publisher could count on selling a correspondingly growing portion of space in his paper for advertisements.'[12] However, though this describes a feature of Thackeray's magazine, beyond the recognised sphere of activity for the writer, the failure of the *National Standard* was likely to have been brought about by the ill-defined nature of the product and its market. Several weeks into his proprietorship, Thackeray began to write editorial addresses to his readership almost as a necessary measure to maintain an understanding of his journalistic goals. As Habermas contends, 'the marketing of the editorial section became interdependent with that of the advertising section',[13] and it was the struggle between the forces of authorial integrity and corporate imaging that generated Thackeray's ambivalence towards the periodical press as a whole. The editorials became self-advertisements as much as vehicles of opinion.

Thackeray bought the *National Standard* presumably on the assumption that it might offer the public an affordable alternative to literary reviews like the *Literary Gazette* (around whose offices Maginn had conducted him) and the *Athenaeum*. It was a risky speculation. Other cheap journals, like the *New Literary Gazette*,[14] failed shortly after their launch. But the *National Standard* managed to survive for nine months. The price was certainly its main attraction to an expanding literary audience frequenting the circulating libraries more often, and subscribing to increasing numbers of magazines and cheap runs of fiction.[15] One surmises that Thackeray was troubled from the start however. He immediately reduced Bayley's three columns per page to two, later returning it to three columns (from issue 27, 6 July 1833). During the summer, he composed the advertising slogan 'And All for Twopence' for his editorials, but by 23 December 1833, he was writing to his mother to tell her of his intention to increase the price from 2d. to 3d.[16] His earlier intention to distribute the magazine in Paris (presumably as a rival to *Galignani's Messenger*, and a precursor to the *Paris Literary Gazette*)[17] had failed by 6 July. He could not find subscribers abroad because the cost of postage was 'so enormous that it quite overbalances the cheapness of the paper'.[18] Thackeray learned an important marketing lesson.

The *National Standard* was one of several journals which failed to break the market strangle-hold enjoyed by the *Literary Gazette* (begun in 1816) and, by 1833, the *Athenaeum* (begun in 1828). These two papers set the style for their imitators, what Hazlitt denoted 'the Weekly Literary Journals, Gazettes, etc.', calling them 'a truly insignificant race – a sort of flimsy announcements of favoured publications – insects in letters, that are swallowed up in the larger blaze of full-orbed criticism'.[19] But they provided a quick review guide to current taste and reading, even if, as Thackeray remarked, they were often the organs of the publishing houses themselves, and 'puffed' the houses' leading authors.[20] Thackeray had some regard for the *Literary Gazette,* and enquired of Jerden in 1837 whether he would be prepared to sell.[21] James Silk Buckingham established the *Athenaeum* in 1828 as a rival, and, when this was purchased by Charles Wentworth Dilke in 1830, its price fell from 8d. to 4d. to increase competitive pressure. Also in 1828, a group of like magazines appeared: the *Edinburgh Literary Journal*, the *Veralum*, Leigh Hunt's *Companion*, the *Literary Journal: A Weekly Review*, and Robert Rintoul's *Spectator*. Others were launched in the early 1830s, some of which were short-lived: the *Literary Guardian and Spectator of Books* (1831-2), Chambers's *Edinburgh Journal* (begun 1832), Leigh Hunt's *Tatler: A Daily Journal of Literature and the Stage* (1830-32), *Bell's Literary Intelligencer* (begun 1834), and Leigh Hunt's *London Journal* (begun 1834).[22]

Walter Graham has described this format of periodical as 'a sixteen-page folio, issued on Saturdays, and containing reviews of various lengths, poetry, letters of contributors, and gossip of books and authors'.[23] The *National Standard* was precisely of this kind. Thackeray clearly intended to capitalize on an existing and successful formula, but made his paper lighter and more satirical in tone, and promoted its low price. However, his editorship of the magazine was also of its kind. Richard Altick, in a discussion of Chambers's *Edinburgh Journal*, surmises that 'none of these short-lived cheap papers had any definite plan; they consisted for the most part, as William Chambers wrote, "of disjointed and unauthorized extracts from books, clippings from floating literature, old stories, and stale jocularities"'.[24] In contrast, the established organs such as the *Literary Gazette* insisted on their quality and resourcing to provide up-to-date material. Keeping an eye on the market-place, and just five days after Thackeray had written of his price increase, the *Literary Gazette* commented:

> The novelty of our pennyworths of compilation has worn off, and as the supply of ready materials has become more scarce, those things which were at best but hetrogenous and aimless medleys, misleading instead of informing the mind, are now as dull and tiresome as they always were smattering, erroneous, and inefficient. In another year we shall hear little of the folly; and, whether in books or journals, the public will have generally discovered, what is pretty well and widely understood at this time, that unless talent and learning are fairly remunerated, there will be but trash in the market, which cannot be cheap at any price.[25]

Thackeray's paper was not to last for two more months before being wound up.

However, the *National Standard* was probably a victim also of the monopolistic business practices of such papers as Jerden's. The larger circulation papers had the interest of the major publishing houses, too. Indeed, the publisher Henry Colburn ran the *New Monthly Magazine* partly as a mechanism to promote his authors. As Thackeray complained in his opening editorial address, his paper did not receive the 'early copies' of newly published books that were sent to the press for 'advertising' reviews (or 'puffs'). The major reviews helped to sell books and so they were 'as much the property of the booksellers as the books themselves, and the oracles speak by the inspiration of those who own them'.[26] Thackeray pronounced the independence of his reviews for the *National Standard* and situated them outside of this industrial relationship. However, he recognised the ambiguity of his own editorial practice; the desire to promote the paper was in itself a mechanism of the market-place, and it is therefore caught in the net of commerce. Integrity is, ironically, a selling point, a form of commercial exploitation. Reviewing could never be without motive, especially the profit motive. Thackeray qualified his opening editorial address thus:

> The world of books is all before us where to choose our course. Others boast that they are perfectly independent of all considerations extraneous to the sheet in which they write, but none we know of reduce that boast to practice: we therefore boast not at all. We promise nothing, and if our readers expect nothing more, they will assuredly not be disappointed.[27]

The complicated and double-edged humour of the final sentence here signifies the caution with which readers should approach the literary magazine. No-one, not even Thackeray, is 'independent of all considerations extraneous to the sheet'; the interconnectedness of profit, commerce, writing, authorship, integrity and self-advertising ensured that the literary property of the 1830s was a new and complex phenomenon. Throughout the run of the *National Standard*, and beyond through Thackeray's career as a whole, one feels that he was always anxious about the powerful influence of the press and the difficulties of authorial responsibility. The writer appears to have access to truth and the text appears to be a conduit between author and reader. But, in fact, the text in the new world of commercial periodicals is a mediated text, that is, a text filtered through a new medium. It is always part of the processes of production and circulation of the magazine or newspaper itself, part of a new market. There are forces acting upon the text that emerge from 'considerations extraneous to the sheet', from economics, from business. Although Thackeray champions unbiased reviewing, for instance, he remains locked into the reviewing system. Something of this is felt in *Pendennis*, when Pen declares to Captain Shandon (the William Maginn figure of the novel) that the important feature of any review is to 'tell the truth' and that he objected to the conventions of attacking books from a rival publishing house merely because of that rivalry.[28] One senses that Pendennis is right, but naïve.

Thackeray learned much about the publishing of a literary magazine in the 1830s from his ownership of the *National Standard*. He moved from an enthusiastic literary idealist, keen to make his mark on the literature of the nation, to set the 'standard' of taste, to a more realistic and cynical commentator on the practices of the press. There are, I would argue, four stages to the development of the *National Standard* as a product. Analysing it with an eye to the editorial decisions made by Thackeray reveals a periodical adapting and reshaping its identity in an effort to create a market for itself and survive in the rapacious business world of the early 1830s. The opening numbers, from 19 to 25, show Thackeray continuing the comic and sketchy style of his undergraduate productions, whilst beginning to learn the trade of book reviewing. From no. 26, Thackeray adopted a more Continental outlook, introducing himself as a Paris correspondent (which only lasted for four issues) and beginning a series of reviews of French books. This lasted until no. 36, but continued more or less until the ending of the magazine. For number 35, and then 37 to 46 and 48 to 53, Thackeray adopted a more aggressive editorial policy and began to market his journal with a distinctive voice and a process of self-advertising through the 'leader items' or editorial addresses. Finally, the last stage, marking the magazine's decline, ran from no. 54 to the last edition, no. 57 (1 February 1834), during which period it is clear that the editorial policy has vanished and that the paper is simply being produced from habit. These stages of the development of the magazine are further defined by the physical changes which took place: the increase from two to three columns from no. 27 (6 July 1833), and the increase in price from 2d. to 3d. from no. 53 (4 January 1834). Such an experience for the young writer made him far more aware throughout his career of the changing nature of literary publication and the ambivalent status of the writer in the industrial world. The leisured man-of-letters had become the fractured figure, half tradesman, half professional, part producer, part product, that negotiates the commercial necessities of modern capitalism.

An examination of the reviews in the *National Standard* leads one to conclude that many were indeed written by Thackeray himself. Critics have tentatively suggested this in the past, but have shied away from the implications.[29] It seems improbable that an ambitious young writer such as Thackeray clearly was, aiming to break into the literary world, and now owner of a literary review, would write little for it. The costs would also have been substantially less for a magazine written by the proprietor. The identified pieces reprinted in Spencer, Melville, and Saintsbury's volumes demonstrate a bibliographical desire to increase the canon of reprinted matter from the magazine, but still do not provide the full picture.[30] A careful noticing of echoes of later known Thackeray works, as, for instance, in the mentioning of Indian place names, Bundlecund and Futtyghur, conjoined in the *Paris Literary Gazette* and the *Adventures of Major Gahagan*, in the reviews of the *East India Sketch-Book* and *Aurungzebe; or, a tale of Alraschid*,[31] can show his likely authorship of certain reviews, and these in turn can be shown to express opinions mirrored in other reviews in the journal. In fact, a simple assessment of the kind of works noticed, fiction, biography, and travel books taking precedence, suggest those interests which he maintained (and continued to review) throughout his journalistic career. I would surmise that Thackeray wrote upwards of two reviews or contributions to each number of the magazine, and often a lot more (as for example when he complained to his mother of being left by his sub-editor to produce a whole number – that for 28 December 1833).[32] This suggests a substantial body of work of well over a hundred items.

Thackeray's reviews for the *National Standard* set the pattern for his subsequent reviewing and parodying of contemporary fiction in *Fraser's Magazine*, the *Times*, and *Punch*. His interest is often not solely in the text itself, but in matters 'extraneous to the sheet'. He connects texts to other parts of the chain of production: the reader, or the editor, or the author, for instance. In his review of John Galt's *Eben Erskine; or, the Traveller* (1833), he caricatures the reader's boredom with the text in a manner familiar to readers of his later fiction.[33] Readers have expectations and the commodity does not always fulfil these. Here, female readers from the opposite ends of the social spectrum are imagined in their reception.

> Lady Slipslop, when she receives this work from the library, will most likely yawn over the first chapter, and never have the courage to attempt the second. The butcher's ladies in Whitechapel will be disappointed with it, for it does not say a word about Almack's, or the fashionable world.[34]

In the same issue of the magazine, in his review of Sarah Austin's *Characteristics of Goethe* (1833), Thackeray introduces the figure of the editor. 'Have our readers any curiosity about Goethe's Walpurgis sack?' he asks. 'If they had ever had the management of a periodical, they would not be ignorant of its use and importance.'[35] The Walpurgis sack is the bag into which the editor flings poems and fictional contributions sent to his office by would-be writers and via which they travel straight to hell never to be seen again. Thackeray reveals similar such editorial dilemmas in the *Roundabout Paper*, 'Thorns in the Cushion'.[36]

Thackeray does not delimit the boundaries of the text as the controlling parameter of his reviewing. He is interested in reception, authorship, and the technical processes of literary production. But he is also concerned with the integrity of the medium of writing itself, especially that writing which is produced within the new business of the periodical. For Thackeray, modern writers do not enjoy the same kind of authorial autonomy present in the eighteenth century. Literary periodical precursors, like Addison and Steele, created and controlled the voice of their magazines; they sold to a specific and educated market. In the new democratic reading world, periodicals respond to the market-place, they do not set the standard but rather seek to exploit public preferences. By introducing the figures who write, edit and read the texts he reviews, Thackeray suggests a qualification of the authority of media discourse. The personae who emerge from behind his reviews and display their human failings are representations of the processes of mediation that complicate the signification of a text. Meaning is distorted, made impure, by the presence of the moneyed author. Thackeray's awareness of the filtration of meaning through mediation is first projected in the *National Standard*. The 'critical profession', he notes, contains within it a 'plurality' of voices, and within his own reviews, he adopts many '*propriis personis*'.[37]

One example of the magazine's playfulness in this regard comes in an early art review he wrote for the 'Fine Arts' column on the 'Somerset House Exhibition' and a new painting by David Wilkie of the current monarch. The piece is a precursor of the Michael Angelo Titmarsh art criticism for *Fraser's Magazine* (1838-47), and of the work for the *Pictorial Times* (1843-4).

> Availing ourselves of the privilege of cats to look at kings, and little dogs to bark at lions, we ventured last week to attack Mr. Wilkie's picture of William IV. No doubt, if Raphael himself were to return to earth, and send pictures to the Royal Academy, some sagacious twopenny critic would call his painting a daub, and his ideas common-place. The painter employs genius, skill, and labour; muses for months on his subject; carefully considers every variety of light, shade, and colour, and then tremblingly exhibits his picture. The critic raises his glass complaisantly for half a minute, and is satisfied; his judgement is formed; his catalogue is marked; and if, on a future day, he condescends to look further at the condemned picture, though he may alter his opinion, he cannot, for consistency's sake, recall his words. In a week's time too, (that is, in papers of enormous circulation like ours,) these critical remarks are read and adopted in all the cities of the kingdom. Three hundred thousand persons at least, by a moderate calculation, have seen the account of Mr. Wilkie's picture of William IV. Our reporter (whom we have turned off in consequence,) called it a failure; whereas, it seems, it is one of the finest portraits that ever was laid before the public.[38]

The new editorial stance that condemns the art critic's view of the preceding week is placed in such a way as to appear to be asserting the truth, but is intentionally unconvincing and ironic. Opinions in the ephemeral press are maintained 'for consistency's sake', for the corporate image, and not honestly revalued after reflection. Although self-denigrating in the image of Thackeray-as-art-critic 'rais[ing] his glass complaisantly for half a minute' (Thackeray wore a monocle at this time) and producing an authoritative view of the picture which will influence the readership (exaggerated, of course, for publicity's sake), the apology undermines the newly authoritative picture by its eulogistic tone ('whereas, it seems, it is one of the finest … '). Thackeray most likely wrote the earlier article, and then, in response to external criticism of or differing opinion on his views, wrote the mocking apology to demonstrate, firstly, how infrequently magazines proffer a change of heart and, secondly, how his acceptance of an altered opinion is bought at the cost of a reporter's job, who failed to respond to the market's popular opinion. Thackeray as a proprietor is not interested in the Wilkie painting; he is more intrigued by the relationship between the magazine and its public. The circulation figures are a clear indicator of this. The article has not quite attained the tone of familiarity that he was later to develop in his magazinery and fiction, but it has introduced the technique of locating in the text a trace of the author as a character and embodying an image of the profession itself within the narrative discourse of that selfsame profession. The effect is a form of deconstruction in which authority is replaced by a structure that, like Browning's dramatic monologues, provides both persuasive statement and idiosyncratic voice. However, in a press noted for the unambiguity of its corporate voice, this effect is also one of defamiliarization. Thackeray was to develop this technique later in his career.

It is perhaps the misfortune of Thackeray's magazine that it was bought and produced at a period when the literary world lacked genuine talent. Wordsworth had ceased to produce much beyond occasional poems; the other romantic poets were dead or at the end of their careers; Tennyson had not achieved recognition for his earliest poems; Dickens had not arrived; Carlyle was perhaps the most significant writer of the moment, with *Sartor Resartus*, hardly a popular read. The novels that Thackeray found himself reviewing were not of the highest order. He is confronted with works such as '*Gale Middleton; a Story of the Present Day*. By the Author of "Brambletye House". 3 vols. London: 1833. Bentley.'[39] A particularly facile passage in the novel prompts Thackeray's remark: 'Now, did Mr. Smith write this passage, or was it the production of his kitchen maid?' Then, in a foreshadowing of his later essay, he adds, 'where is, after this, the dignity of literature … ?'[40]

The formulaic nature of much writing of the time comes under constant criticism. Thackeray turns to French fiction to extend his magazine's interest (and market), but finds similar formulaic productivity.[41] The 'Silver-Fork' school of fiction appears several times; in a review of *Struensee; ou la Reine et la Favori* by Fournia and Augusto Arnould, he writes:

> … besides this principal character, there is a pretty little background of intrigues, debauchery, wicked queen-mothers, conspiracies, and northern scenery, which a skilful hand might easily fill up: and puff! There is a flourish of trumpets at Bentley's, and three handsome volumes, price one pound eleven shillings and sixpence, in boards.[42]

Elsewhere, he comments on the system of publishers' puffing of their own novels, perpetuating the poverty of ideas in modern romance. For example, in his review of '*The Coquette*. By the Author of "Miserrimus". London: 1834. Hookham', he complains:

> The only thing remarkable in "Miserrimus" was the extreme absurdity and pretension of the book, and the great skill and energy employed by the publisher in puffing it. As for the author's present

> performance, we do not hesitate to pronounce it as foolish, as flippant, and as vulgar a production, as ever was sold for a guinea and a half.[43]

The mercantile relationship between writer and reader again features prominently. Such literature is priced at a very high rate and appeals to a very small purchasing readership and library system. The great difference between this kind of literature and the growing body of magazine productions generates the tension in Thackeray's ideas about authorship. In the early 1830s, he was confronted by poor and formulaic fiction on the one hand, and a ruthless commercialism in the magazine market on the other. The 'puffing' of fiction demonstrated the nature of writing as a trade. It was led by advertising.

Where he does tackle better quality literature, Thackeray's reviews form the basis of his aesthetic convictions developed in his fiction during the late 1830s and early 1840s. In his review of '*Notre Dame; A Tale of the Ancient Regime*. From the French of Victor Hugo ... By the Translator of Thierry's "History of the Conquest of England by the Normans" ... (London: Wilson, 1833) (from an English translation)', Esmerelda, the gipsy heroine, is criticized for lacking realism. 'She has been brought up amongst vagrants, prostitutes, thieves, and cut-throats,' he argues, 'yet she is a miracle of purity, delicacy and truth.'[44] His later criticism of Dickens' Nancy in 'Going to See a Man Hanged', and the basis of his character, Catherine Hayes, in *Catherine, A Story*, derive from this opinion. How can 'such a character' have been 'formed under such circumstances', Thackeray asks? While the novel 'is one which no female can read, except the young ladies who take the evening air in Fleet Street' (a euphemism for prostitutes).[45] Several other reviews also suggest that, through his reading for the *National Standard*, Thackeray formed his opinions of literary art. 'More historical romance!' he declared in despair on reading '*Sir Guy de Lusignan: A Tale of Italy*. By E. Cornelia Knight, Authoress of "Dinarbas", "Marcus Flaminicus", "Latium", & c.', adding, 'When will this end?'[46]

Thackeray opened issue no. 35 of the *National Standard* (31 August 1833) with an announcement by 'Our Leader', the first editorial he had written since the inception of his proprietorship in May. No editorial appeared for no. 36, but from no. 37 (14 September 1833), the editorial feature appeared in the first column of the front page until no. 53 (4 January 1834). The new column established a direct communication between magazine and reader, and inducted a critical attack on certain aspects of the journalistic profession. At times, he used it to defend the magazine against rumours circulating of its demise (probably circulated in an attempt to hasten its end). In 'Our Leader' of 30 November 1833, he joked about the location of the paper's offices in St Paul's Church-yard (close to the publishing centre of Paternoster Row), saying: 'We confess that we do haunt a churchyard, but ... there is nothing else to affect our vitality.' He continued, 'we are ... active and energetic in making all sorts of new arrangements for opening the new campaign [for 1834] with re-doubled strength and quintupled resources'.[47] The public was not convinced.

'Puffing' and 'fishing', discussed in Thackeray's editorial 'Puffing and Fishing', 12 October 1833, are terms which relate to the construction of a literary identity for both the individual and the magazine. As Laurel Brake has noted, puffing was a financial necessity for many early magazines. In its most basic form, this was printing favourable reviews of recent publications on behalf of publishing houses.[48] These could be provided by the House (a puff) or by a friendly critic or editor. Several publishing houses owned their own journals which favoured their books. Thackeray satirized this system in *Pendennis*; his rival publishers Bacon and Bungay represent figures like Colburn and Bentley. In 'Puffing and Fishing', 12 October, criticizing both Colburn and Bulwer-Lytton, his editor on the *New Monthly*, Thackeray writes:

> ... every book in which Mr. Colburn had any interest was lauded in the *New Monthly*, because it was the publisher's; and every book written by a gentleman or lady who gave Mr. Bulwer a dinner, received similar attentions, in honour of the feeding of the editor.[49]

In addition,

> ... we could, without giving ourselves much trouble, write down a list of persons whose books, when they publish any, are duly buttered and puffed in the *Athenaeum*...We do not wish to mention names, but we recommend the curious in such matters to refer to the review in the *Athenaeum* of Allan Cunningham's 'Maid of Elsar' ... [50]

The *National Standard*, however, attempts to remain beyond this commercial duplicity:

> We do not puff anybody – not even ourselves – we have one standing ground of approbation, and that we print every week. Like our stately neighbour, St. Paul's, we are accessible for TWOPENCE ... [51]

In definition, then, 'puffing' is promoting the work of another for your own gain (usually money or status). 'Fishing' is generating a self-image that will attract and catch the target-audience: a market.[52] Both are a form of advertising.

Thackeray's usage of these words in commercial terms was simultaneously linked to his view of individual human relationships. In 'A Lecture on Humbug', the editorial for 2 November, he sets out a thesis which will become the *Book of Snobs* a decade later. Vanity, snobbery, showing a front which is less than honest, cutting a figure, creating an image: these are forms of self-advertising which correspond to the market system of the day. The noisiest, the most visible, those with access to the organs of the day, will be advantaged. Human weakness is open to easy exploitation where 'humbug loudly trumpeted forth is the finest thing in the world':

> There exists no human being on the face of the earth who cannot be humbugged, if the humbugger takes care to try him on the proper vein. Every man, says the proverb, has his weak side – the proverb is too lenient. Every man has his profusion of weak sides – he is, in that respect, a perfect polygon.[53]

Thackeray remarked on how the professionals and the petty thieves in the world live by the same principles (connecting together stock merchants, manufacturers, shopkeepers, and newspaper editors): 'They get on by showing as good a front as they can – by displaying an appearance of credit and consideration at all times, even when they have not a farthing in their coffers ... '[54] Translating this into the literary market-place, Thackeray notes how the act of puffing authors is part of a similar process of deception: the merits of a book are 'bawled forth' by author, bookseller, reviewer and critic, to give the impression of a writer as 'the greatest man of the month'. The new author is 'set down as destined to last for ever'. The success is due to a textual construction of identity: the press colludes to launch a new commodity, a new author or book. The truth, Thackeray says, is eventually realized and the success fades: 'but what of that? the object has been attained ... The author has been the lion of the allotted minute, and the hoax, for such it is, has succeeded for its time'.[55] The book has been advertised and sold.

Thackeray implies throughout his editorials that the economic principles of the day, the commodification of all saleable goods including literary texts, made authorial integrity difficult. The advertising function forced a writer, or producer of any goods, to look at market taste and suit his wares accordingly. Competition was pervasive and pernicious. In his discussion of an advertisement in the magazine, the *Age*, for the firm of Messrs Hall and Allen, whose premises were also located in St Paul's Churchyard, he deconstructs the language of the modern advertisement.[56] It is written, he says, in a 'circumlocutory mood', which describes St Paul's locale as 'this great medium of conjunction and communication of valuable resources'. Without actually commenting on what goods the store sold, Thackeray attacked the modernity of its attitude to retail. But his only counterpoint to this commercialism is nostalgia:

> ... when we look at their shop, in spite of all the fine and astonishing things which we see there, we cannot help breathing a sigh over their predecessors. For generations it was the hold of Carrington Bowles, the seller of those wondrous prints that grace all the country public-houses.[57]

The proximity of the shop to the *National Standard* offices in St Paul's Churchyard makes one aware of a connection between the two. The notion of 'communication' was, of course, central to Thackeray's magazine writing, and one might suppose that his criticism of Hall and Allen's is tangentially a criticism of his own practices on the *National Standard* itself. The opposition of modernity and nostalgic retreat might also have been felt in the difference between the old ideals of authorship that Thackeray held and the new consciousness of precisely what authorship now entailed. Indeed, this opposition is felt later in Thackeray's novels where he imaginatively returns to the days of Johnson and Goldsmith in *Barry Lyndon* and *The Virginians*, and to those of Dick Steel in *Henry Esmond*. *Pendennis* confronts this even more directly.[58]

Elsewhere, Thackeray's editorial column tried to understand and make understood the processes and structures of the contemporary press. He tried to provide a portrait of the commercial and market-orientated aspects of publishing for a readership that had little experience of the new industry of print. In 'Solitude in September', for example, Thackeray discusses the quietness of the city during the Parliamentary recess, a period thought of as an off-season month when the upper and middle classes tended to leave for the countryside or the Continent. For the literary review, this period heralded a dearth of new publications; for the newspaper, it meant little in the way of official, government news.[59] 'Solitude in September' is a comment on modern newspaper sensationalism and the public interest in the grotesque. In an earlier piece of Paris correspondence for the *National Standard*, he discussed and translated portions of a newspaper story by the French journalist, Jules Janin, which described the visit of a group of Paraguayan Indians to Paris. This was a 'strange tale', but one 'more truthful and moving than all the dramatic fictions of Paris'.[60] With Janin's work, the newspaper demonstrates more humanistic concern than he saw amongst the Gothic absurdities at the French theatre. The English press, on the contrary, with space to spare during the recess, was becoming adept at spinning a tale over a number of days and thus creating its own narrative sensationalism. During Parliament, he says, 'the columns of the newspapers are so blocked up by it that they cannot move in any other direction'. In the vacation, however:

> What a field is opened to the ingenuity of the caterers and purveyors of news of a more miscellaneous and soul-subduing character! A good murder is a great godsend. Light be the stones on Thurtell's bones; – he was the best friend the penny-a-line men had for many a day ... [61]

The newspaper must sell itself in the commercial age, and sensational narratives were beginning to sell copies. In the 1840s, Thackeray was to criticize French newspapers for their publication of serial stories, 'feuilletons', as cheap, if compelling, gimmicks to retain readers.[62] In the *National Standard* editorials, he criticizes instead the desire to commodify, to turn literature and news into goods for a marketplace. In 'A Fog on the Town', he denounces the practice of creating a 'fog' to cloak these tradesman's techniques. The public remains in a 'fog' regarding the real nature of the periodical press because of this disjuncture between the persuasiveness of the media to generate its own version of the truth and the public's misrecognition of the game being played. For many, a magazine or newspaper is a source of contemporary history, a recording of the truth of the times. But for Thackeray it was also enmeshed in contemporary economic discourses and the language of publicity, advertising, and trade. 'A Fog on the Town' considers the difference between earlier magazines (showing Thackeray's knowledge and thinking on such) and the present publications, to the detriment again of the latter.[63] The 'fog' concerned 'is on the centre of the town', he says, slightly misquoting Byron, and is a symbolic 'commodity', 'so very English ... so thoroughly Cockney', consisting of poorly written but commercially viable books.[64] The 'fog' is a metaphor for the dearth of good books and magazines in the market, 'the stagnant state of literature'. But in the past, he suggests, this 'fog' was recognized and called by its name. In Walpole's day, Thackeray remarked, there existed a journal entitled 'Fog's Journal', whereas in the 1830s, it was a sign of the cynical commercialism of the age that what was being sold to the public was, instead, proclaimed as the *True Sun*. Thackeray did not believe that the mass press was necessarily a good thing for the public; indeed, his involvement with the *Constitutional* newspaper suggests he was dissatisfied with the Tory and Whig domination of the press.

Coningsby (1844) notes how, in 1832, 'Evening Journals and Quarterly Reviews, were continually proving that this was the best of all possible governments', but, by 1844, Disraeli felt more comfortable with *his* press:

> To us, with our *Times* newspaper every morning on our breakfast table, bringing on every subject which can interest the public mind a degree of information an intelligence which must form a security against any prolonged public misconception, it seems incredible that only five and twenty years ago the English mind could have been so ridden and hoodwinked, and that too by men of mean attainments and moderate abilities.[65]

The Thackeray of 1833 conceived of this power of the press as mediating between public and private realms. But he felt that the mediation itself was bounded by commercial practices which, though a necessity, were also demeaning to the integrity of authorship.

Thackeray's critique of the periodical press in these editorials, and elsewhere, is the precursor to his continued analysis of the state and art of publishing in nineteenth-century Europe. The *National Standard* was the seed bed for many of his later ideas on the state of the arts in Victorian England. Although the magazine failed, and left Thackeray somewhat disillusioned with journalism (he moved to Paris in 1834 and took up training as an artist), nevertheless, it proved a significant training ground for his literary ideas. At the end of December 1833, his penultimate editorial gave to the readers a retrospective comment on the *National Standard*'s achievements, a testimony which might be taken as a description of his own gains as a proprietor and editor.

> We have, at no great cost to him [the reader], and at small profit to ourselves, made him acquainted with *some hundreds* of books, pleasant and dull: we have praised, with him, when we found genius or merit; and laughed, with him, at dullness and pretension.[66]

Financially, the magazine might have failed, but the 'profit' in the longer term was the recognition of a subject matter central to the rapid transformation of culture in the Victorian age. The *National Standard made* Thackeray, even though it contributed to his early monetary misfortunes.

Notes

[1] See K. Tillotson, *Novels of the Eighteen-Forties* (Oxford: Clarendon, 1954); J. Sutherland, *Victorian Novelists and Publishers* (London: Athlone Press, 1976); L. Erickson, *The Economy of Literary Form: English Literature and the Industrialization of Publishing, 1800-1850* (Baltimore: Johns Hopkins University, 1996).
[2] Gordon N. Ray (ed.), *The Letters and Private Papers of W.M. Thackeray*, 4 vols (Cambridge, Mass.: Harvard University Press, 1945-6), I, 191.
[3] *Letters*, I, 162-6; *Letters*, I, appendix 4, 506-8.
[4] *Letters*, I, 189, 191.
[5] The only recent study is Donald Hawes, 'Thackeray and the "National Standard"', *Review of English Studies*, 23 (1972), 35-51; see also Richard Pearson, '"The public likes light literature and we write it": W.M.Thackeray and the Periodical Press, 1833-46' (PhD thesis, University of Manchester, 1994), chapter 1.
[6] See Appendix 3 for a bibliography of probable contributions.
[7] Bayley was later to write for the first few numbers of *Punch*, as did H.P. Gratton of the *Original*.
[8] *National Standard*, 18 (4 May 1833).
[9] H.S. Gulliver, *Thackeray's Literary Apprenticeship: A Study of the Early Newspaper and Magazine Work of W.M. Thackeray* (Georgia: Valdosta, 1934), 1-6; Ray, *Uses*, 106 rejects most of these attributions; Pen's early career might be seen as a version of Thackeray's own, however, *Pendennis*, *Works*, III, 28-9.
[10] *Lovel the Widower*, *Works*, XXIV, 18; Ray, *Uses*, 161.
[11] Jürgen Habermas, *The Structural Transformation of the Public Sphere: An Inquiry into a Category of Bourgeois Society* (Cambridge: Polity Press, 1989), 184.
[12] Habermas, ibid.

[13] Habermas, 185.
[14] A copy of this journal in the British Library runs to only two issues, priced 4d., 27 December 1833 and 22 February 1843, each under a different proprietor.
[15] For information on library subscriptions and reprints of popular works, see Erickson, 142-6, 146-55.
[16] *Letters*, I, 270-71.
[17] See Chapter 2 for Thackeray's involvement in just such a venture in 1835.
[18] *Letters*, I, 262.
[19] William Hazlitt, 'The Periodical Press', *Edinburgh Review*, 38 (May 1823); reprinted Walter Graham, *English Literary Periodicals* (New York: Thomas Nelson, 1930), 314.
[20] 'Puffing and Fishing', *National Standard*, 41 (12 October 1833).
[21] Lionel Stevenson, *The Showman of Vanity Fair: The Life of William Makepeace Thackeray* (London: Chapman & Hall, 1947), 76.
[22] Graham, 279-80; 315-30.
[23] Graham, 315.
[24] Richard D. Altick, *The English Common Reader: A Social History of the Mass Reading Public, 1800-1900* (Chicago: University of Chicago Press, 1957), 319.
[25] *Literary Gazette*, volume for 1833 (28 December 1833), 817.
[26] *National Standard*, 19 (11 May 1833); reprinted in W.T. Spencer, *Mr. Thackeray's Writings for the 'National Standard' and 'Constitutional'* (London: W.T. Spencer, 1899), 2.
[27] Ibid.
[28] *Pendennis*, *Works*, III, 390.
[29] Hawes, 45-6, suggests that Thackeray contributed frequently, but lists only four certain reviews and four possible ones; Ray, *Uses*, 160-61, notes that Thackeray 'and his subeditor James Hume seem to have been responsible for most of the paper's contents'.
[30] In total, 21 items have been reprinted (18 in George Saintsbury (ed.), *Works of William Makepeace Thackeray*, Vol. I (London: OUP, [1908]); Edgar F. Harden, *A Checklist of Contributions by W.M. Thackeray to Newspapers, Periodicals, Books, and Serial Part Issues, 1828-1864* (Victoria: University of Victoria, 1996), 14-15, lists the 21 items and shows that only 3 have external verification.
[31] *National Standard*, 54 (11 January 1834). and 57 (1 February 1834)
[32] Letter to Mrs. Carmichael-Smythe, 23 December 1833; *Letters*, I, 270-71.
[33] Compare Jones in his club armchair in *Vanity Fair*, *Works*, I, 6.
[34] *National Standard*, 21 (25 May 1833); in Lady Slipslop we have a forerunner of Lady Smigsmag in 'Fashnable Fax and Polite Annygoats' (1837), and of the Countess Otillia von Schlippenschlopp in *Fitzboodle's Confessions* (1843); Mrs Slipslop is a character in Fielding's *Joseph Andrews* (1742).
[35] *National Standard*, 21 (25 May 1833).

[36] One of the many examples of Thackeray reusing old periodical material; 'Thorns in the Cushion', *Cornhill Magazine*, 2 (July 1860); *Works*, XXII, 43-4.
[37] 'Our Own Leader', *National Standard*, 43 (26 October 1833).
[38] *National Standard*, 20 (18 May 1833).
[39] *National Standard*, 50 (14 December 1833).
[40] Ibid.; 'The Dignity of Literature', *Morning Chronicle*, 12 January 1850.
[41] In his reviews for the *Foreign Quarterly Review* in 1842-4, he frequently alludes to the French novel industry and sees Frédéric Soulié as a writer who 'publishes circulating libraries at once'; 'French Romancers on England', *Foreign Quarterly Review*, 32 (October 1843), 226.
[42] *National Standard*, 32 (10 August 1833).
[43] *National Standard*, 53 (4 January 1834).
[44] *National Standard*, 35 (31 August 1833).
[45] Ibid.
[46] *National Standard*, 33 (16 August 1833).
[47] *National Standard*, 48 (30 November 1833).
[48] Laurel Brake, *Subjugated Knowledges: Journalism, Gender, and Literature in the Nineteenth Century* (London: Macmillan, 1994), 20.
[49] *National Standard*, 41 (12 October 1833).
[50] Ibid.
[51] Ibid.
[52] The initial illustration of Becky fishing in *Vanity Fair*, chapter 4, Works, I, 26, is a coded reference to this form of advertising.
[53] *National Standard*, 44 (2 November 1833).
[54] Ibid.
[55] Ibid.
[56] 'Messrs. Hall and Allen's Work', *National Standard*, 38 (21 September 1833); Thackeray called the *Age*, 'that ojus *Hage* newspaper' in 'Fashnable Fax and Polite Annygoats', *Fraser's Magazine*, 16 (November 1837); *Works*, XXV, 4.
[57] Ibid.; Andrew H. Miller, *Novels Behind Glass: Commodity Culture and Victorian Narrative* (Cambridge: CUP, 1995), 1-6, discusses an observation of Allen & Son, Drapers, St Paul's Churchyard, made in 1851, whose plate-glass window displays offered a 'world of show' – this is clearly the same shop.
[58] See my discussion of literary nostalgia in this novel (in Chapter 8).
[59] 'Solitude in September', *National Standard*, 37 (14 September 1833); Thackeray's *Calcutta Star* column also describes the quiet summer season, see 'Letters from a Club Arm-Chair', d. 7 July 1845, *Calcutta Star*, 21 August 1845, H. Summerfield (ed.), 'Letters from the Club Arm-Chair: William Makepeace Thackeray', *Nineteenth-Century Fiction*, 18 (December 1963), 230.
[60] 'The Charruas – Paris Correspondence', *National Standard*, 28 (13 July 1833); Spencer, 35-6.
[61] 'Solitude in September', op. cit.

[62] 'Thieves Literature of France', *Foreign Quarterly Review*, 31 (April 1843), 233.
[63] *Thackerayana: Notes and Anecdotes* (London: Chatto & Windus, 1875) reprints extracts from eighteenth-century magazines held in Thackeray's library at the time of his death, including literally hundreds of marginal sketches scribbled in the magazines by Thackeray himself; details of his library holdings can be found in the reprint of Christie's sales catalogue of his house auction, 18 March 1864; J.H. Stonehouse (ed.) *A Catalogue of the Library of William Makepeace Thackeray* (London: Piccadilly Fountain Press, 1935).
[64] 'A Fog on the Town', *National Standard*, 40 (5 October 1833).
[65] Benjamin Disraeli, *Coningsby; or, The New Generation* (1844) (London: Dent Everyman, 1967), 58-9.
[66] 'Address', *National Standard*, 52 (28 December 1833).

Chapter 2

Echoes and Narcissisms: repetitions and structures of self across the periodical lines – signature and persona in the *Paris Literary Gazette* and *Fraser's Magazine*

When Thackeray's *National Standard* collapsed in 1834, the efforts to construct a corporate identity for a magazine product were freshly channelled into the development of an authorial identity for the commercial writer. Hitherto, little has been known of Thackeray's career during the two-year period between the demise of the *National Standard* and the launch of the *Constitutional*, with Thackeray as Paris correspondent, in mid-1836. He is usually described as a Bohemian art student, registered at an atelier, and resident with his maternal grandmother in Paris.[1] He had lost his inheritance through the collapse of the Indian banks and the failure of his magazine venture.[2] Regarding his literary career, biographers have tended to see him as neglecting writing, and turning to art, and generally uncertain of his future;[3] however, despite the patchy evidence, enough now exists to suggest that, on the contrary, Thackeray remained committed to journalism, and continued to contribute to periodicals. Indeed, far from abandoning the pen, he advanced into new literary fields and broke new boundaries in his creative development. These early magazines are important but neglected in Thackeray studies: the *National Standard*, the *Paris Literary Gazette*, and the *Constitutional* played as significant a part in Thackeray's career as the later *Cornhill Magazine* – more so, in fact, as they provided the formative experiences of his professional writing life and established his attitude towards the periodical press.

Thackeray contributed to the *Paris Literary Gazette* between October and December 1835.[4] He wrote three distinct types of letter-press for the magazine: four reviews and an 'editorial' item, signed 'W.M.T.', a comic book-review and a short story, signed 'Augustus Wagstaff', and a piece of comic fiction describing characters gathered at a country house, signed 'By One of the Guests'. These articles raise interesting questions about the problems of signature in the early nineteenth-century periodicals, and reveal how Thackeray manipulated the principles of anonymity and signature to complicate and intensify his ideas of magazine writing. The creation of a persona to mediate between text and reader, or, rather, between the object of textual attention and the reader, exposes the fragility of periodical authority. As Laurel Brake has argued, 'the complex relations of author to text, of text to other texts, and author to other authors are problematised by the periodical form'[5] and this is further confounded by the contrived or indiscriminate use of signature or pseudonym. Thackeray's personae both establish a periodical identity for the author (whilst paradoxically concealing the real identity of the writer), and draw attention to the artifice of periodical authority.

This early experimentation led to Thackeray's development of distinctive personae in *Fraser's Magazine* during the period of 1837 to 1841. His earliest work for *Fraser's* saw the simultaneous creation of Charles Yellowplush and Michael Angelo Titmarsh, two author-figures representing different sides of his critique of the periodical press. These figures of mediation are a direct continuation of the work for the *Paris Literary Gazette*, and suggest how Thackeray both tackled the problem of authorial anonymity in the magazines, and challenged the sense of unproblematized magazine authority. These personae simultaneously offer coherence to Thackeray's identity, and dissolve the verbal omniscience of the writer. They are and are not Thackeray himself, and provide a profoundly ambivalent response to periodical writing that later informed the characterization of his novelistic narrators.

The Paris Literary Gazette, or Weekly Reportery of the Belles-Lettres, Arts, Sciences, and Literature of Great Britain, America, and France was launched on Tuesday, 27 October 1835 and continued weekly publication from 34, rue Notre-Dame-des-Victoires, Paris.[6] The file of the magazine in the Bibliothèque Nationale runs from 27 October 1835 to 19 April 1836 (25 numbers), when, unless further issues have failed to survive, it would appear to have folded without warning. Three months subscription to the paper cost 10 francs in Paris, in France 11 francs, and 12 francs elsewhere. Subscribers to its proposed sister paper, the daily *London and Paris Courier* (advertisements for which ran for the first eight numbers of the *Gazette*), received a 10 per cent discount. The *Gazette* consisted of the journal of 'belles-lettres' format of 16 pages of three columns per page, and carried four pages of advertisements. It was a similar vehicle to the *National Standard*. Thackeray worked for the magazine from October 1835, contributing to its first number, until at least 29 December 1835.[7]

The magazine was geared towards and sold to the English-speaking 'colony' then residing in Paris, many of whom had drifted to the Continent after Waterloo and Napoleon were forgotten, attracted by the high society glamour and the cheapness of living. Thackeray depicted Becky Sharp and Rawdon Crawley settling in Paris for the Winter of 1815, in *Vanity Fair*.[8] An advertisement for the *London and Paris Courier* claimed that

> ... there are not less than 100,00[0] English at present residing all the year round, in France, Switzerland, and Belgium. There are besides

> these, great numbers in Germany, Italy, Holland, and, generally speaking, there are not fewer than from 40 to 50,000 English travellers, who visit France and other countries of Europe during the Summer months.[9]

The magazine had, therefore, a defined market and could operate as an advertiser for London and Paris businesses, a newspaper and gazetteer of English events and Paris entertainments, and a review guide to new French books. It also offered a platform for poetical and fictional talents from the 'colony' itself. Thackeray's involvement was undoubtedly connected to his experiences on the *National Standard* and his desire to make that magazine more European.

The editors of the magazine are unknown. Jean Guivarc'h argues plausibly that G.W.M. Reynolds was the editor, listed as 'Reynolds' along with two others called Fallon and Lees.[10] These three are mentioned as editorial staff in an advertisement for the *London and Paris Courier*, a sister paper to be launched by the proprietors of the *Paris Literary Gazette*. This would seem to contradict the understanding of Henry Reeve, who, in his diary of 16 January 1836, described Thackeray as 'at the present moment editing an English paper here, in opposition to Galignani's' (i.e. *Galignani's Messenger*).[11] However, in a letter to Fitzgerald in November 1835, Thackeray wrote:

> I have been making German translations for this new paper here are two of the best I think though they have been cut out by that Jackass the Editor.[12]

The article referred to was eventually published on 29 December 1835. Thackeray was not the editor of the *Paris Literary Gazette*, and from the evidence of the magazine, it seems Thackeray's association with the *Gazette* ended with the last number of 1835. He may have moved on elsewhere. Since he began contributing to the magazine from its first number, he must have known, or been known to, the editors; his likely role was probably that of literary reviewer, employed on the strength of his *National Standard* criticism and his knowledge of French culture.

The *Gazette*'s main Paris rival was not *Galignani's Messenger* (begun in 1814), but *Galignani*'s weekly sister paper, the *London and Paris Observer* (1825-48).[13] The *Observer* was a Sunday weekly, more expensive than the *Gazette* at 14 francs for a three-month subscription, and did not include any advertisements (the payment for which clearly subsidized the *Gazette*). The *Gazette* targeted the *Observer* in its first issue calling it (like a parson), 'a tall, gawky creature, of much less standing in society, which is seen once a week on a Sunday morning'.[14] Advertising the paper meant identifying the opposition and defining the product against it. The main serious argument against the *Observer* was that, because published on a Sunday, it had not time enough to receive and analyse the London dailies from the second half of the previous week; it was therefore, the *Gazette* claimed, a week behind in its news. This creation of a binary opposition as a means of advertising the self is a continuous feature of Thackeray's works, from the polarities of Becky and Amelia, Pendennis and Warrington, or the Virginian brothers, to the dualism of the publishers Bacon and Bungay or magazines like the *Dawn* and the *Day* in *Pendennis*.

The *Gazette* further differed from these papers in both its composition and aims. Whereas the *Messenger* and *Observer* were 'scissors-and-paste' compositions, comprising mostly cuttings of news and reviews from the English press, the *Gazette* hoped to attract greater attention by writing its own articles, concentrating on the French culture around the 'colony', and drawing on articles from within the fraternity itself. The advertising discourse was new, too. Not only did the magazine offer what it liked to call a service to the 'colony', showing their readers what goods were available from London retailers,[15] but it also carried a series of comic prose dissertations on the cultural importance of advertising.[16]

The evidence of the numbers surviving would seem to suggest that the public were not so receptive of change, and probably remained loyal to the Galignani library. The *Gazette* possibly was sold to a new proprietor in March 1836. The type-face of the magazine alters from number 18 (1 March 1836), the print becoming larger and clearer, not always a sign of wishing to improve accessibility and quality but sometimes simply revealing the need to fill out space. The contents of the magazine became hackneyed and stale, less innovative, and less literary based. It still included reviews, gossipy news items, and readers' poetry, but poor in quality. The new style turned itself over to shorter items of local smalltalk at the expense of fuller articles, and omitted most fiction.

For Thackeray, the *Paris Literary Gazette* was familiar territory. It was, like the *National Standard*, a light-hearted miscellany, consisting of a wide range of articles. It included extracts from the London *Literary Gazette* (the *National Standard's* main rival) and *The Spectator*, but mostly provided its own material: book reviews, fictional pieces, poetry, and news items. It openly requested contributions from its readership. Through its pages, Thackeray was able to develop areas of his art which his writings for the *National Standard* had suggested, and more. He continued book reviewing, coping with similar genres to those he analysed in his own magazine, but seems to have been limited to one item per week. More significantly, he began to compose articles which were not either reportage (such as his foreign letters), derivative (such as his translations), or directly parodic. He produced his first pieces of sustained narrative and created the prototypes for several later works.[17]

The new magazine required something of a change of emphasis. The historical, cultural, political, and even literary discourses that framed the Paris 'colony' were very different to those that operated in London. The *Gazette* could not relevantly engage in a debate with the London journals, nor could it, given the still delicate situation between Crown and parliament and press in

Paris, really attack French journalism in the manner to which London had become accustomed.

In this environment, Thackeray's work became more concerned with establishing self-identity and exploring images of England, particularly in the form of advertisement – one might say, self-advertisement and patriotism. Also, possibly due to his flowering relationship with Isabella Shawe (whom he married in August 1836), he began to explore the literary themes of romance and love, undermining them with dashes of self-parody and anti-Romance. His writing gained in self-awareness; the figure of the critic, for instance, becomes a married man and metamorphoses into a narrator and autobiographer. Thackeray also examined his attitudes as an Englishman abroad, simultaneously deriding the spread of commercial materialism and patriotically affirming Britain's superiority (a line of argument reflecting the magazine's own advertising policy). In addition, he revealed an awareness of writing for different effects, and used the magazine's procedures of signature and pseudonym (signing articles with initials, or with a disguised or expressive name) to move from self to persona and combine the dialectics of criticism and fiction.

Of the five books which he reviewed for the *Paris Literary Gazette*, three were treated to serious-minded appraisals, one was displayed in a comic and moral light, and the fifth was used by Thackeray as a foil for his elaboration of a new comic technique. The reviews rely on the English knowledge of the readers, referring, for example to Astley's, part of the London entertainments scene.[18] He does not suppose that any but the middle-class English 'colony' will read the *Gazette*. Further, he assumes that the 'colony' was as English as he, and adopts a tone of familiarity and comradeship, 'tuning our harp in a strange land', as he put it.[19]

Thackeray's literary identity accorded with the direction of the magazine. He helped to set out the editorial principles of the *Paris Literary Gazette* in his article 'England'. Written for the third number of the magazine, it is 'editorial' in its tone, and speaks on behalf of the magazine with the editorial 'we'. The tenor of the piece makes Thackeray's association with the paper appear much closer than other evidence indicates. However, despite the collective identification, the article is also an expression of Thackeray's personal feelings and self-understanding, scarcely matched by the other contributions to this magazine. The article sets out to introduce the 'thirty thousand English people in this city, chiefly of the higher and educated classes' to the aims of the journal. Both the paper and Thackeray wish to provide the readership with a familiar voice, published from amongst themselves, 'By One of Themselves', as it were.[20] The tone had its counterpart in the 'Leader' items written for the *Standard* nearly two years before.

> We were desirous that our journal should be a companion for the stranger here, a chronicle of such light matters as would be likely to interest him in this country, and a summary of the literary news of his own.[21]

Thackeray went on to sound a note familiar to readers of the *National Standard*, commenting '[t]he heavier business of politics will be treated by other hands in another journal; our aim is humbler and easier'.[22] He asserts that the *Gazette* will not be 'a literary scrap-book', a description befitting the other publications available to the English market in Paris (*Galignani's Messenger* and *Observer*), but would instead provide 'entertainment of a nature somewhat more lively and original'.[23] The 'editorial' voice is distinctly Thackerayan, stressing the companionship between writer and reader, the periodical as a chronicle or historical record, its literariness and non-political bias, and, above all, the magazine as a form of 'entertainment'.

Thackeray has been accused of xenophobia in the past,[24] and certainly the essence of patriotic pride fills 'England', echoing the magazine's pro-English discourse and pandering to English insularity and bigotry. It seems little wonder that Thackeray kept his association with the paper quiet in later days, when he had become, as Ray put it, 'at least as well known among publishers and editors for his ability to deal with French topics as for his fiction'.[25]

The article begins with *Punch*-like humour:

> There never was a man so eminently patriotic as an Englishman, when he happens to be out of his country. He may have been grumbling all of his life against tithes, taxes, fogs, or other evils which exist there; but place him on this side of the channel, and he straightway forgets the ills of which it has hitherto been the business of his life to complain ... It is, we confess, with this feeling of love and reverence, that we, who are tuning our harp in a strange land, are disposed to consider all things connected with our own birth place.[26]

Thackeray combined an image of the self-conscious Englishman abroad, such as he was to evolve more completely in the self-mocking humour of *A Journey from Cornhill to Grand Cairo* (1846) and parody in the comic persona of the 'Fat Contributor' in *Punch* (1845), with a genuine homesickness. He invoked nostalgia for London fogs and bygone coaches though he knew they were uncomfortable, unable to bear their absence, or at least the disappearance of them as ideals. But he makes these allusions with a knowing smile, focusing on what would be important to an English audience (most notably a male version of this, emphasizing taxes and business), to what he would miss the most, and creating almost a caricature of an Englishman.

By the end of 'England', the patriotic discourse is uppermost; the comedy is maintained, but the hint of self-parody has gone and the caricature of the Englishman is not portrayed or developed so much as defiantly asserted. Thackeray flaunts the egotism of the English, with humour but without mockery, and affirms Britain's industrial supremacy and pride:

> The French press and people in those days spoke continually of the effects of English influence in Europe. – Yes, there was English influence – the influence of good men writing good books, which, in

> their peaceful progress through the world, establish kingdoms and overturn them, and win more battles than are enscribed on Nelson's victory-roll! Foreigners may flout us as they will: abuse us for our pride, sneer at our roving dispositions; it is true that we are proud, and we have reason – it is true that in every corner of Europe you may see English faces, and English wealth. – Is not this another reason for pride? Our people travel, for they have money to support this luxury, and yet money does not grow on trees, or in our pockets. – We have no gold in our mines, no rare fertility in our soil; we occupy but an insignificant island, that makes no figure by the side of the mighty European continent; and yet what name is heard so much as England's? What power is felt so much, what rights and institutions are praised so much as ours? – Guiness's porter is drunk in the wilds of Siberia, the King of Timbuctoo wears British broad cloth, and Birmingham buttons; and the thirty centuries which look down from the Pyramids on the name of Napoleon, may see Warren's Blacking inscribed underneath it.[27]

The last sentence shows just how far British mercantile commercialization had spread by 1835. Twenty years after Waterloo, the French hero and leader, Napoleon, had been replaced in the world order by, as Thackeray superciliously states, a British shoe-polish. Commercial advertising was now more powerful than military prowess. In 1844, Thackeray comically returned to this image, having visited the Pyramids for himself, and gave a rousing 'three cheers for *Punch*' from the summit of the largest structure.[28] In later writings, as his understanding of foreign cultures increased, he came to regard the spread of English commerce as essentially boorish, destructive and hypocritical. He disliked the tourist, the uneducated traveller, for his lack of sympathy, tolerance, and understanding; he became cynical about the spoliation of national characteristics through the spread of English, and other, exports. But his response to the foreign was always complex and ambivalent.

The alteration of concerns experienced in moving from the *National Standard* to the *Paris Literary Gazette*, the sudden inappropriateness of engaging in satirical combat with other rival magazines, forced Thackeray to develop new narrative strategies for his writings. A study of Thackeray's contributions to this small magazine compared to Thackeray's other known writings of the 1830s, gives a greater sense of continuity to the development of his ideas and the evolution of his narrative techniques than has hitherto been accepted. His experiments with persona and with forms of criticism and fictionality began here. Knowledge of his subsequent work reveals his readiness to return to these early pieces when searching for ideas, and even names of characters, for his later journalism and novels.

Although there are only a handful of contributions by Thackeray in the *Gazette*, they display a broad range of narrative techniques. He moves from reviews and 'editorials', to a book review incorporating fictional devices (his review of Sir John Ross's travelogue), then writes a fictional first-person story of Augustus Wagstaff, the fictitious critic of Ross's book, and finally contributes a social satire based on a house-party and its 'guest'. The book review, the social satire, and the narrative, are all given the extra dimension of a persona-narrator who directly addresses the reader. From the basis of a book-review, Thackeray fictionalized the critic as a distinct character, 'Augustus Wagstaff', a character who the reader could identify with, could accept as 'a man and a brother',[29] to be agreed with, or argued with, or laughed at. The unassailable position of the critic was assailed on behalf of the reader; the critic's absolute authority in his field was undermined. In 'A Passage in the Life of Augustus Wagstaff', Thackeray uses the same character again, only alters him into an egotistical story-teller, a fraudulent adventurer. The narrative revolves around Wagstaff's unashamed, perhaps unaware, exposure of his own true character. In the final piece of fiction, the 'Guest' at 'Willowford Hall' is allowed to mock the pretensions of her friends, creating a social satire on upper-middle-class stereotypes, but is simultaneously attacked as an example of the hypocritical gossip. She is a critic who is also criticized; the article is an early description of 'Snobs', 'By One of Themselves'.

The 'Wagstaff' pieces are interesting for the light they cast on the use of signature in the magazine. For his serious book-reviews and his 'England' item, Thackeray signed his own name, 'W.M.T.', one of the few times in his career when he did so.[30] Since the 'Wagstaff' pseudonym was used between numbers including the 'W.M.T.' signature, the effect was to distinguish the 'serious', the corporate, the editorial voice, from the dissonant, critical, irreverent voice. 'Wagstaff' is a burlesque of the authoritative critic, as well as a narrative persona. In 'England', Thackeray adopted an editorial responsibility that did not permit him to offend his readership. But as 'One of the Guests' in 'The Party at Willowford Hall', he wrote under a signature which could be that of an 'outsider'; certainly, this latter piece was written as by a female approaching the male editor with a potential new series for the magazine, and not as from the pen of an established member of the team. The 'Party at Willowford Hall' ridicules the type of person one imagines read the *Gazette*: comfortable middle-class with the means (or needs) to travel or emigrate.

The name 'Wagstaff' was a pseudonym used by Thackeray elsewhere. As with the later 'Titmarsh' appellation, he used it with several first names.[31] *Floré et Zephyr* appeared in March 1836, only a few weeks after the *Gazette* articles, under the pseudonym, 'Theophile Wagstaff'. This enabled Thackeray to authenticate his own signature 'W.T.', signed in the corners of the illustrations presumably before he determined to adopt a *nom de plume*. Further, it linked the little volume, published in Paris as well as London, with the magazine contributor. In 1840, Thackeray intended to publish what eventually became the *Paris Sketch-Book* under the pseudonym of 'Wagstaff'. He appeared again during the middle of the 1840s, this time as 'Lancelot Wagstaff', the gourmand of four *New Monthly Magazine* articles published between May 1844 and August 1845.[32] There is also a 'Major Wagstaff' who was an officer of the engineers in *Vanity Fair* (1847-48). As early as 1835, then, Thackeray was experimenting with processes of publishing that were to build up his distinctive narrative voices.

In the *Paris Literary Gazette*, Augustus Wagstaff is the ill-fated critic burdened with having to review an 'unfortunate book' of travel memoirs by Sir John Ross, and who then, a month later, becomes both narrator and character in a tale drawn from his own life. He begins by casting himself as a disappointed literary reviewer:

> I confess that I expected to have commenced my labours in your journal, either with a profound metaphysical paper, or a touching article in poetry, or a brilliant historical essay; – why, then, did you (entertaining those sentiments regarding me which you have been so pleased to express) send me the unfortunate book which figures at the head of this letter?[33]

Moreover, as with Yellowplush, the comic ridicule deployed against Ross's book operates by suggesting the ordinariness of the critic and the lack of appeal that the volume held for the average household.

> Sir, I occasionally read the *Morning Chronicle* newspaper; I have perused Lord Brougham's last article in the Edinburgh; I have actually read Mrs Trollope's new novels; but I declare to you, that Sir John Ross's work, in desperate and undeviating dullness, infinitely exceeds them all three.[34]

The review continues with an image of everyday domestic existence:

> On the members of my household it has acted like a dose of laudanum. Since its perusal, Mrs Wagstaff has been in a perpetual doze; – that most lively of women lies in a state of torpidity, which astonishes her servants, accustomed to her eloquence, and her husband, who misses cruelly that ceaseless flow of language, for which you know she was remarkable.[35]

The interruption of the critic's argument by the realities of his home life inaugurates Thackeray's technique of fusing criticism and fiction that later became so effective. It is subsequently complicated in the review by introducing the language of newspapers themselves, in a parody of the 'Court Circular' of the *Morning Post*.

> I suppose the Esquimaux Court Journal must have contained a blazing paragraph on the business: – 'Yesterday some of our fashionables were invited to a party, by the commander of the English ship stationed here, and a repast consisting of all the delicacies of the season was provided by the hospitable captain. The train-oil went gaily round, and dancing was kept up to a late hour ...

> The lovely Z-gl-sh had a necklace of seals intestines, one end of which she kept continually in her mouth – "Why do you wear that necklace," said Bl-gch. "Because I chews it," was the lovely creature's ready and elegant reply. Our gentlemen vied with each other in bolting slices of blubber to the King of England's good health – and much curiosity was excited concerning the Prince of Whales.'[36]

The parody of gossip columns is, in effect, a parody within a parody, which helps authenticate the subtler comedy of Thackeray's 'Wagstaff' voice. As with the humorous tone of the *National Standard*, the refusal to adopt a serious and sober discourse, and the strict resolve to remain independent of publishing houses and treat all books on their merits (or otherwise), the 'Wagstaff' review punctures the surface of the magazine by revealing, for satirical impact, the realities of life and the artificialities of the periodical monologue. Both 'Court Circular' and critic are undermined, and Wagstaff himself is a hen-pecked husband who draws his critical authority from the effect of a book on his servants. And yet, the review as a whole does what it sets out to do: demolishes the credibility of Sir John Ross's memoirs.

'A Passage in the Life of Augustus Wagstaff' does not make consistent use of the character of the narrator as suggested in the first review. 'Wagstaff 2' is much less tolerable or likeable, and is more akin to Barry Lyndon than Charles Yellowplush. He is a rogue, who plays on the hearts of three Irish women (Lady Barbara, Wilhelmina, and Arabella Grady), allows them to keep him in idleness for several weeks as a result of their mistaken apprehension of his love for one of them (each believes herself to be the lucky person), and finally, called to duel by each of three male rivals or relatives, and escaping the shot by displaying the women as foolish and denying his responsibility for their delusions. The tale of one man, a mother and her two daughters, in an isolated boarding house, reminds the reader of Gordon Ray's comment about Isabella's family, the Shawes, in Paris: 'the family was Irish and consisted entirely of women, though there were male relatives lurking in the background'.[37]

Wagstaff's appearance is a comic and exaggerated version of Thackeray himself. In this, he is the forerunner of Titmarsh, Spec, and Pendennis:

> When I lost my nose at the battle of Bundlecund, I gave up all claims to be considered a handsome man. The previous poking out of an eye at Futtyghur was a trifle, for I had a very handsome glass one blown by a travelling chokeybader or tinker, which quite cut out the other ball in lustre, expression and general appearance ... But still I don't know – although, as I say, with but one eye, a stiff knee (shattered by the bursting of a baggage wagon at the affair of Ferruckabad), and a large piece of sticking-plaster covering the spot where once had grown a goodly nose, there was a something about me which won the hearts of the dear creatures ... [38]

The persona then proceeds to tell his tale which shows the influence he certinly seems to possess over the 'dear creatures', and how his character is crafty enough to escape final justice. He is a schemer: more cunning than the naïve and blustering Gahagan, but not as sharp as Deuceace, or as developed as Barry Lyndon.[39] If Mrs Wagstaff of the review is perhaps a fledgling version of Pendennis's wife, Laura, Wagstaff himself, in his active role, is the first of a line leading through Becky Sharp.

There is continuity here in the evolution of Thackeray's writing. The review of '*Narrative of a Second Voyage in Search of the North-West Passage* ... By Sir John Ross' and the 'Passage in the Life of Augustus Wagstaff', taken together, form an intriguing parallel to Thackeray's development of the more famous Charles Yellowplush, who first appeared in *Fraser's Magazine* in November 1837. Previous biographers and critics of Thackeray have given the impression that Thackeray had a sudden surge to fame when forced to write for his living in the London periodical market, after the collapse of the *Constitutional*. His initial idea was a brilliant off-the-cuff response to an absurdly bad book, John Skelton's *Anatomy of Conduct* (1837).[40] Having created the character of the footman, Charles Yellowplush, to ridicule the book by acting the role of reluctant reviewer from the position of authority behind the tables of fashionable life, Thackeray went on to utilize Yellowplush as the narrator of a series of adventures in which he plays a part.

If the Wagstaff papers have their counterparts in those of Charles Yellowplush, then 'The Party at Willowford Hall' also has its offspring. The subtitle, 'By One of the Guests' is echoed in the 'By One of Themselves' of *The Book of Snobs* (1846); however, the content and structure of the piece are certainly regenerated in the Christmas book, *Mrs Perkins's Ball* (1847). The *Gazette* item is a prototype for this latter, the 'Guest' being replaced by the, by then, well-known figure of Michael Angelo Titmarsh. Titmarsh comments satirically upon a number of guests at a high society ball, taking each in turn, drawing several, and completing a set of middle-class stereotypes. 'The Party at Willowford Hall' similarly describes the characters present at a country house weekend: Sir Thomas Smith Willowford, Mrs Thomas Smith (now Lady Willowford), Master Henry, and Mr Colon, whilst certain traits of the 'Guest' herself are also revealed. The end of the article indicates the author's willingness to continue the account and describe further characters, but the offer was never taken up.

This repetition and transformation of articles from the *Paris Literary Gazette* indicates the strength of Thackeray's early ideas, if not always their execution. They form the embryonic subject matter at the beginning of a long continuous growth towards his mature work. In later years, Thackeray could turn back and re-work these earlier outlines, knowing they could be refined. It is, of course, possible to suggest with a touch of cynicism, that, at times, when producing a large number of different articles, Thackeray occasionally found it simpler and more economic to re-vamp an old idea than think up a new one. But it is preferable to believe that Thackeray immersed himself so completely in his fictional world, and wished to foster an impression of realistic cohesion between diverse compositions, that he continued to repeat the names of characters, companies, and places, once he had invented them.

Continuity in personae was matched by continuity within the narratives themselves. His fictional world had a stability about it that could not help but repeat the form and content of earlier work. This was a stability missing from contemporary reality, both in the devastating events of his own life, and in the rapidly changing historical continuum. Thackeray made it possible, therefore, for the briefest mention of a family like the Kickleburys in a *Punch* article, 'The Persecution of British Footmen', Part 1 (1 April 1848), to be transformed into a full-blown narrative about the whole family, *The Kickleburys on the Rhine* (written 1848, but published 1850), and for members of that family to continue to wander through the pages of his work for some years to come.[41]

'A Passage in the Life of Augustus Wagstaff' is littered with names and places that occur elsewhere in Thackeray's works.[42] He draws mostly on Indian and Irish backgrounds, reflecting the people in his own life: his own Indian Civil Service birth and ancestry, military members of his family, the Irish hack writers he knew like Maginn and Mahony, and his wife's family coming from the County of Cork and her birth also in India). 'Bundlecund' (the battle site) becomes a regiment of 'Invincibles' in 'The Tremendous Adventures of Major Gahagan', *New Monthly Magazine* (1838-39) and a bank in *The Newcomes* (1853-54). As already noted, the towns of Futtyghur and Ferruckabad are also in 'Major Gahagan', as is the small town of Stoke Pogis,[43] which has its own newspaper, the *Sentinel*, and a Marchioness of Stoke Pogis in 'Codlingsby', from '*Punch*'s Prize Novelists' (April-May 1847). There are a family of O'Grady's in *The Newcomes* and a Captain O'Grady in 'Bluebeard's Ghost' (*Fraser's Magazine*, October 1843). From the family of Fitz-Agues, there are Lady Blanche and Lady Rose in *The Book of Snobs*. 'O'Toole' is a character in *The Kickleburys on the Rhine* and in the parody 'Lords and Liveries' from '*Punch*'s Prize Novelists' (June 1847). Finally, one of the best examples, the firm of solicitors, 'Higgs, Biggs, and Blatherwick', operate in *The Bedford Row Conspiracy* (1840), *Cox's Diary* (1840), *Samuel Titmarsh and the Great Hoggarty Diamond* (1841), and, reduced to 'Higgs and Blatherwick', in *Vanity Fair* (1847-48). Thackeray clearly did not forget his Parisian scribblings.

In 'The Party at Willowford Hall', the parallel names are not as conspicuous. There are no other Willowfords in Thackeray's writing, as far as I know; the nearest derivatives of the name are Lord and Lady Willowbank in *Pendennis* and, interestingly, Tom Willoughby in *Mrs Perkins's Ball*. A Thomas Smith Dawkins (using the same 'ordinary' double-barrelled fornames) is fleeced by Deuceace in the *Yellowplush Papers* (1838). The name of 'Mr Colon' is not repeated either, but it is mirrored in Thackeray's continued giving of pieces of punctuation as names for his characters – for instance, the 'Reverend James Asterisk' and the 'Duchess of Dash' in *The Paris Sketch-Book* (1840). These latter characters are so-called for reasons of comic disguise, taking literally the magazines' habits of hiding identities behind asterisks and dashes, but the former is part of Thackeray's concern to see better writing amongst his contemporaries. He was always quick to ridicule a writer whose poor punctuation led to a confusion of meaning, as, for instance, in the *National Standard* review of Montgomery's *Woman: The Angel of Life.*[44] A second parodic connection to the *National Standard* can be found here in the reference to the 'European, Asiatic, African, American, and Australian Quarterly', recalling the list of macabre journal titles in an article on French popular newspapers,[45] as well as half-mocking the complete titles of the *Paris Literary Gazette* and other such miscellanies.

The *Paris Literary Gazette* contributions permit a balanced survey of Thackeray's abilities and ideas at this early stage in his career. His articles for periodical markets, whilst often seeming spontaneous, or to happen upon unpremeditated ideas, in fact show a continuous nurturing of similar concepts and techniques from the very first publications to the very last. The *Gazette* offered Thackeray the opportunity to experiment with fictional techniques for the first time, and the hybrids of journalism and fiction which he created remained his popular medium for many years. From the standard book-review, he developed the sense of the critic as an entity, not beyond the reach of everyday life, but part of it and affected by it just as much as everybody else. His combining of critical and fictional discourses enabled Thackeray to suggest the fallibility of men of letters; like anybody else they belonged to a profession, and like anybody else they were human. Thackeray's personae provide a layer of irony between the author and the reader, and between the narrative and the reader. They function as an integral part of Thackeray's literary world: a world that portrays not only scenes and characters, books and magazines, but also the writers themselves.

The character of Augustus Wagstaff, in his small way, enabled continuity across periodical articles and even across media lines. Thackeray was clearly conscious of the need to overcome the disadvantage of anonymity and construct a litereray identity for himself that would be recognisable and memorable. The writer was a commodity and needed a brand image with which the audience could identify. The repetition of place and character names in his works also functioned as an advertisement of identity. Edgar Harden has argued that Thackeray's serial novels suggest 'a continuous recurrence of birth' in their reintroduction of personages from previous novels,[46] but this process had begun in the earliest writings for magazines and operated more as self-advertising and image-branding than narrative theory. Thackeray produces an aesthetic of the marketplace that makes realism out of the realities of nineteenth-century publishing.

Charles Yellowplush and Michael Angelo Titmarsh were created at approximately the same time for *Fraser's Magazine*, on Thackeray's return from Paris, and were the first of several more rounded writer-personae. They are distinctly of the 1830s, and different from the more modern journalist-personae of the 1840s and beyond. They are also less complicated narrator-personae than Pendennis or Esmond. Yellowplush and Titmarsh are amateur figures in keeping with the traditional image of the man-of-letters, a dilettante figure who writes for himself as an outlet for his feelings and desires. Both have other professions: Yellowplush is a footman, a satire on the society novelist; Titmarsh is a painter, a satire on the failed artist-turned-judge. They engage with the literary and artistic world of commercial production: through Yellowplush, Thackeray examines writers like Bulwer-Lytton and their relations with publishers; through Titmarsh, he considers the function of the reviewer. Yet both also operate as observers and commentators in their own right. They are vehicles for Thackeray's literary and art criticism and fiction, as well as being used to draw attention to the new writing practices. As mediating voices, they expose the moral ambiguities of periodical publishing; they are personalities who satirize the pretensions of magazine authority.

The initial conception of Charles Yellowplush followed the pattern of Thackeray's first attempts at fiction in the *Paris Literary Gazette*. In that magazine, Thackeray used the comic persona of Augustus Wagstaff, first of all as a literary critic and then as a narrator and participator in a tale about his own experiences. In *Fraser's Magazine*, Thackeray introduced Yellowplush as the comic reviewer of John Henry Skelton's *My Book; or, The Anatomy of Conduct*, in 'Fashnable Fax and Polite Annygoats',

> My Dear Y. – Your dellixy in sending me 'My Book' does you honour; for the subjick on which it treats cannot, like politix, metafizzix, or other silly sciences, be criticised by the common writin creaturs who do your and other Magazines at so much a yard. I am a chap of a different sort.[47]

Thackeray continued with his footman-character as narrator of a series of tales relating to his life and profession. It is possible that Yellowplush's success in *Fraser's Magazine* owed something to the cult following that Dickens had attracted with Sam Weller two years before and to the growing popularity of fiction depicting characters from the 'lower' urban social orders.[48] Also, the pun was the popular comic style of the period and Thackeray's success with Yellowplush (and Jeames de la Pluche for *Punch*) lies in the clever punning on Cockney dialect. The readers of *Fraser's Magazine* were used to writing of this kind.

'Fashnable Fax and Polite Annygoats' advances on a stage from the Wagstaff review of Ross's *Memoirs*, in that it imagines a reviewer who is more learned than the author he critiques, but who is from a different class. The grotesque language Yellowplush employs explodes his writerly pretensions but is problematic as a version of a lower-class writer. Thackeray makes fun of working-class ignorance. But the language is simultaneously a clever way of generating comedy through pertinent puns. Skelton's rules of etiquette are blasted by a character who is equally ridiculous, yet who carries more 'common sense' in his common-ness. The book recorded rules of etiquette such as '28. Vulgar abbreviations, such as gent for gentleman, or buss for omnibus, & c., must be shunned' and '31. Be especially cautious not to drink while your plate is sent to be replenished'.[49]

Fraser's advertises Yellowplush as an authentic observer of the upper classes. His role is as a counter-Skelton, more knowledgeable and more penetrating. Thackeray was also attacking the popular mode of the 'Silver-Fork' novel, popularized by Bulwer, Disraeli, and Catherine Gore. As the 'editor' of *Fraser's* remarked in a post-script to the article (probably by Thackeray himself):

> There is a luxury of fashionable observation, a fund of apt illustration, an intimacy with the first leaders of the ton, and a richness of authentic anecdote, which is not to be found in any other writer of any other periodical. He who looketh from a tower sees more of the battle than the knights and captains engaged in it; and, in like manner, he who stands behind a fashionable table knows more of society than the guests who sit at the board.[50]

Yellowplush, *Fraser's* says, will 'be able to present the reader with the only authentic picture of fashionable life which has been given to the world in our time'.[51] There is plenty of comic exaggeration in these facetious claims for absolute integrity, yet they demonstrate precisely the ironic reader response that Thackeray was aiming at. He is using the contrast between the ridiculous character of Yellowplush and the *Fraser's* editorial remarks to satirize the tendency in other magazines to make absurd claims for their contributors. Yet, on another level, the article does have a more persuasive integrity than Skelton's *Anatomy* or the novels of the 'Silver-Fork' school.

In addition to the satire on Skelton, the article reveals some of the apparent realities of the reviewer's life and working method. The reader discovers little vignettes of town house life, supposedly located at 'No. – , Grosvenor Square'.

> Ever since you sent me the volum, I have read it to the gals in our hall, who are quite delighted of it, and every day grows genteeler and genteeler. So is Jeames, coachman; so is Sam and George, and little Halfred, the sugar-loafed page: – all 'xcept old Huffy, the fat veezy porter, who sits all day in his hall-chair, and never reads a word of anythink but that ojus *Hage* newspaper.[52]

Here, the influence of literature and the new magazines on the lower classes of the household is described in comic terms. The signifiers of popular culture – the *Age*, and reading for betterment – suggest a genuine belief in the power of print media, combined with a sense of its purposelessness. Thackeray was never a believer in the Society for the Diffusion of Useful Knowledge or a supporter of the argument that literacy brought personal improvement as a matter of course.[53] But equally comical is Yellowplush's own particularity for the '*Sat'rist*' newspaper, with its 'Raddicle principils'. The reader is never quite permitted to occupy Yellowplush's position. Elsewhere, the details of high society life assist the persuasiveness of the article. Although he fictionalizes anecdotes of a bishop choking on a lump of fat, and Lady Smigsmag losing her false teeth, he is able to suggest something of the actualities of dining with the wealthy. Lady Smigsmag's false teeth, for instance, turn up in 'them blue water bowls which are brought in after dinner' to rinse the mouth.[54]

Charles Yellowplush is also used as a means of critiquing the processes of 'puffing and fishing' that concerned Thackeray elsewhere. The *Yellowplush Papers* are a burlesque of Bulwer-Lytton's style of self-advertising and the publicity of personality.[55] In places, Thackeray imitates Bulwer's *England and the English* (1833)[56] by using dramatic scenes to discuss issues, only here using Bulwer himself as one of the participators. Referring to him as 'Sawedwadgeorgeearllittnbulwig', Yellowplush innocently asked 'Bulwig' why he had been created a Baronet, and Bulwer is made to reply:

> Ask the histowy of litewatuwe what faw? Ask Colburn, ask Bentley, ask Saunders and Otley, ask the gweat Bwitish nation, what faw? The blood in my veins comes puwified thwough ten thousand years of chivalwous ancestwy ... on the thwone of litewature I stand unwivalled, pwe-eminent; and the Bwitish government, honowing genius in me, compliments the Bwitish nation by lifting into the bosom of the heweditawy nobility, the most gifted member of the democwacy.[57]

The passage makes explicit Bulwer's reliance upon the publishing-houses (Colburn, Bentley, and Saunders and Otley). It continued his campaign begun in the *National Standard*. The attack was quite malicious and personal, something which Thackeray apologized for in later years.[58] Bulwer is also brought up for his practice of explaining and defending his works in a 'Preface'. Thackeray never defended his own writings, except to defend his right to write as he chose to and leave the public to decide the value of his work.[59] Bulwer used the preface of a published work as a means of justifying what the critics disliked. Thackeray found this practice deplorable; it was a form of self-advertisement that attempted to anticipate objections to certain elements in the writing.

> What the juice does the public care for you or me? Why must we always, in prefizzes and what not, be a-talking about ourselves and our igstrodnary merrats, woas, and injaries?[60]

The attack was part of his campaign against the denigration of the author's status in early Victorian culture. Thackeray remained ambivalent in his attitude: regretting the loss of the gentlemanly author, but recognizing the need for the writer to be honest about the contemporary commercial world.

Thackeray's training as an artist in the ateliers of Paris in 1834 and 1835, and during his period on the *Paris Literary Gazette*, was the foundation of his capability as an illustrator and his aptitude as an art critic. The experiences provided the background for *The Newcomes*, which fictionalized both the life of an emerging artist (Clive and J.J.) and the network of magazine art critics who promote the artists' work. More significantly here, the persona of Michael Angelo Titmarsh provided an ambivalent figure, at once a vehicle for Thackeray's views on contemporary painting, and a satire on hack journalism in the new magazines. Titmarsh is also a device of continuity in periodicals and volume publications. Although initially created specifically for the art reviews, Titmarsh was to continue as a *nom de plume* for Thackeray well into the 1840s. Robert Colby refers to the persona as 'Thackeray-Titmarsh' to emphasize their identification.[61] However, the fissure between the author and his voice is evident in the early Titmarsh pieces. Titmarsh is a caricature of the self-publicizing and amateurish journalist, a regular contributor to the journals of the 1830s. But Thackeray also makes him a comic version of himself. His reviews also provide a critique of press practices of the day, and a critique of the system at work in the art world for the promotion of new painters (a system focused exclusively on the Royal Academy). Titmarsh gradually became more than a caricature (more so than Yellowplush or Wagstaff), and became the voice for Thackeray's French articles as well. The character stepped beyond a satirical role to enable Thackeray a more complex device for distancing himself and examining his own personal anxieties and emotions. Titmarsh moves from being a comment on the problems of authorial integrity in the publishing industry to a figure representing Thackeray's psychological traumas.[62] In this multi-faceted role, he is an early version of Pendennis.

Thackeray had been innovative in his introduction of articles and reviews of French culture in the *National Standard*, and indeed had also produced accounts of the art exhibitions.[63] In *Fraser's* in 1838 he began a series of writings on art at a time when hardly any other popular magazine carried such items. Amongst the rivals of *Fraser's* in the press, only *Blackwood's* took regular notice of the Royal Academy, and other, exhibitions, with reports by such writers as John Eagles, W.F. Deacon and David Scott. There were, of course, more specialist papers, such as the *Art Journal* and the *Athenaeum*, and the buoyancy of the market can be seen in new, if short-lived, ventures like *The Probe* (1839).[64] Previously, during the early 1820s, the middle-classes had been treated to a critical debate on art by Hazlitt and P.G. Patmore through the pages of the *London Magazine* and the *New Monthly Magazine* respectively.[65] But the shilling satiricals, 'Maga' and 'Regina', did not provide Exhibition notices until Michael Angelo Titmarsh appeared in 1838 with 'Strictures on Pictures' (though some newspapers gave exhibition reports).[66] With the plans to build a new National Gallery in Trafalgar Square (1833-37) and the moving in of the Royal Academy collection to share the premises in 1837,[67] both of which opened in 1838, a fresh interest in the fine arts flourished in the press, and Thackeray clearly recognized this. *Fraser's* enthusiasm was reflected in their eagerness to publish Thackeray's reviews up to two months ahead of their rivals at *Blackwood's*. Each review was written to coincide with the opening of the Royal Academy exhibitions, the highlight of the London fine art season (April – August[68]), and reckoned by many to be the finest art that Britain had to offer.[69] After Thackeray's final contribution to *Fraser's* in 1847, their interest in the exhibitions waned.

Titmarsh provided Thackeray with a signature that was recognizable and distinctive. Imaginatively, he hovered between an authentic world of genuine signifiers and a parodic world of comic exaggeration. His name is highly referential. There are resonances of broken noses (which both Michael Angelo and Thackeray had)[70], and was possibly suggested by the character of Michael Angelo Pops in Douglas Jerrold's 'Isaac Cheek; or, "The Man of Wax"'.[71] There was also an MP and magistrate called Michael Angelo Taylor (1757-1834), caricatured by Gilray at the turn of the eighteenth century, and responsible for the 'Metropolitan Paving Act, 1817'.[72] Further, the surname 'Titmarsh' might have come from the headstone of a grave just inside the gate of Kensal Green cemetery: a cemetery that Thackeray certainly knew, and in which he is buried.[73] However, his resemblance as a character to Vasari's characterization of Michael Angelo serves to reinforce the early idea of him as a literary creation and not an alter-ego.[74]

The articles carry occasional self-references to Thackeray's career, too. These would be missed by the readership of his day, but are also a feature of his later writings as he strives to draw attention to his other productions whilst seemingly dismissing someone else's. This self-advertising is yet another product of Thackeray's consciousness of the need to develop marketing strategies for the author in the commercial age. In 'A Pictorial Rhapsody', he comments: 'Mr Webster has the bump of a philoprogentiveness (as some ninny says of George Cruikshank in the *Westminster Review*).'[75] As this item was published anonymously under the signature of 'Ø' it is unlikely that anybody outside of Thackeray's circle of publishing friends and personal acquaintances would know of his authorship of 'George Cruikshank', which had appeared the previous month.

Thackeray also projected his own position in the periodical world onto the character of Titmarsh, but again not without a degree of mockery external to the immediate article. Titmarsh's landlady, Mrs Barbara, provides a description of the last evening on which her household saw the critic, and exposes the drunken egotist in the persona:

> After dinner he was a sitten over his punch, when some of our gents came in: and he began to talk and brag to them about his harticle, and what he had for it; and that he was the best cricket in Europe; and how Mr. Murray had begged to be introjuiced to him, and was so pleased with him, and he with Murray; and how he'd been asked to write in the *Quarterly Review*, and in bless us knows what; and how, in fact, he was going to carry all London by storm.[76]

Thackeray's affectation of despair at never being accepted to write for the *Quarterly Review*, released through the creation of a position of acceptance for his rogueish persona, may be his way of dealing with disappointment. The reader receives no clues in the article as to Thackeray's humorous intention in bringing in the magazine editor, Murray. *Fraser's* readership would surely have seen this as an ironic dig at Titmarsh's presumption to be 'pleased' with Murray, yet perhaps Thackeray also intended the inference to be that Murray and the *Quarterly* had been cajoled by Titmarsh's fashionable popularity into 'begging' for the favours of a braggard and drunk. Whatever the full meaning behind these words, Thackeray cannot help adding another piece of self-mockery in a footnote to the word 'cricket' from the above passage. The footnote reads: 'Critic, Mrs. Barbara means, an absurd monomania of Mr. Titmarsh.' Thackeray laughed at his own habit of mispronunciation and phonetic spelling, significantly at a word that he enjoyed playing with even in his letters.

As a character, Titmarsh is boastful and self-promoting. He is also something of a rogue and leads a rake's life whilst contributing his reviews. Like Wagstaff and Yellowplush, he represents the pompous critic who believes, probably more than anything else, in his own superiority to the artists he discusses. Titmarsh assured the reader that 'there is nobody like Titmarsh: you will learn more about the arts in England from this letter than from anything in or out of print'. In other artists, he would like to see what he feels Mulready possesses, the 'inspiration' of 'majestic and pious harmony': 'I know no-one else who possesses it, except, perhaps, myself.'[77]

These audacious and self-important statements contrast sharply to the impressions that the reader is given of the critic by the ordinary people who cross his life. For instance, he is described as ridiculous in appearance by his landlady, Mrs Barbara, when she notes his arrival in a new set of clothes at the end of 'A Pictorial Rhapsody':

> Mr. Mike Titmarsh came into our house in a wonderful state of delarium, drest in a new coat, a new bloo satting hankysher, a new wite at, and polisht jippannd boots, all of which he'd bot sins he went out after dinner ...[78]

And none of which, of course, had been paid for.

In the peripheries of the reviews, the editorial and framing paragraphs that appear 'outside' of the reviews themselves, Thackeray invented a rather dissolute and unflattering life for his persona. The first two reviews were addressed to 'Monsieur Anatole Victor Isidor Hyacinthe Achille Hercule de Bric-a-brac, Peintre d'Histoire', a detail reflecting Thackeray's knowledge of the pretensions of the Bohemian art world in nineteenth-century Paris, and meant to indicate Titmarsh's travelled bachelorhood. The letters were written from, initially, 'Lord's Hotel, New Street, Covent Garden', and then, 'Jack Straw's Castle, Hampstead' – implying a descent from fashion to notoriety, caused, it is assumed after Titmarsh's exploits at the Lord's Coffee House owned by Mr. Moth.[79] At the end of 'Strictures on Pictures', Oliver Yorke describes how the unfinished article just read was found in a gutter at the end of St Martin's Lane, 'whence a young gentleman had been just removed by the police', having been found drunk asleep. This young man (M.A.T.) had not paid his bill for, amongst other items, 'thirteen glasses of gin-and-water'.[80] The erratic behaviour of the critic suggests a disaffection in his life which in turn might be a result of his failure as a painter. There is an impotency about Titmarsh, who certainly represents Thackeray's sense of the difference between the ideals of high art and the realities of commercial writing. Titmarsh exhibits his own paintings as 'pretty well known in Paris already, as I flatter myself'. But his works are typical of the day, and mediocre in their derivative and stylized nature. He describes:

> ... my historical picture of 'Heliogabalus in the Ruins of Carthage,' or the full-length of Sir Samuel Hicks and his Lady, – sitting in a garden light, Lady H. reading the 'Book of Beauty,' Sir Samuel catching a butterfly which is settling on a flowerpot.[81]

In addition, as a criticism of contemporary artists, Thackeray is outlining the absurdities of genre painting.[82] Titmarsh's transformation from artist to writer, supported by a livelihood that began as a sideline to his desire for artistic fame, is completed at the end of 'A Pictorial Rhapsody'. We learn that, despite his apparent death, 'Peace to his ashes! A couple of volumes of his works, we see by our advertisements, are about immediately to appear.'[83] These volumes return us to Thackeray's own career, and could either be *The Paris Sketch-Book*, which was published at the end of 1840, or the *Comic Tales and Sketches*, which appeared in 1841, both under the Titmarsh pseudonym.

The Titmarsh art reviews also operate as a critique of the magazine industry's casual approach to reporting. Far from being organs of truth and realism, many newspapers he felt were using ignorant journalists to write on topics of which they knew little. The corporate authority of the journal was a sham. Thackeray felt that art critics in particular were generally ignorant of art, beyond their smattering of terms from the 'Painters' Cant Dictionary'. Titmarsh, though, is given Thackeray's knowledge.[84] In a comment on the lack of expertise in the newspapers to deal with intellectual subjects and the multiple roles of the hack journalist, Titmarsh says:

> I know of newspapers in this town, gentlemen, which send their reporters indifferently to a police-office or a picture gallery, and expect them to describe Correggio or a fire in Fleet Street with equal fidelity.[85]

Thackeray's art criticism introduced techniques of fiction to illustrate the criticism of other contemporary reviewers and further to create a fictional version of the magazine world for his readers. To extend this world beyond Titmarsh, Thackeray introduced, in 'A Pictorial Rhapsody', the comic sparring team of Dash, Blank, and Asterisk – a journalist and rival painters whose actions are intended to show up the corruption inherent in a system built, like the literary world of Yellowplush, on personal preferences and subtle bribery. The power of the Royal Academy members to hold public attention over their non-Academician competitors, and the power of the newspapers to perpetuate this domination, did not make for a flourishing impartiality amongst reviewers. The same point was made by Thackeray in his reviews of novels and illustrated Annuals noticed favourably in magazines owned by the same publishing house.

In the 'real' contemporary press, a forlorn young painter complained in the *Morning Post* in 1840 to Sir Martin Archer Shee, the President of the Royal Academy, that the process of selection for the Academy Exhibition was purely one of privilege; 'What chance can there be for strangers?', he asked.[86] The unlucky artist, who signed his article 'John Smart', had two of his paintings rejected despite praise by independent judges. The artist argued that he was the victim of the Royal Academy's fear of raising outside talent against their own position. He complained that the 'most mediocre' artists had been favoured 'for party purposes', whilst with other newcomers, the RA 'cooly assist in blighting their prospects, and covering them with ruin'. The emotion in this public letter to the *Morning Post* runs away with the writer at times, but his deep anguish at his own future prospects is plain to read.

Fraser's art reviewing, whilst essentially conservative, maintained the magazine's open declaration of impartiality. Thackeray felt strongly that such must be the aimed-for standard. It is known that Thackeray's criticism of certain artist friends was considered to have gone too far and caused offence.[87] His attacks on Daniel Maclise, for instance, were blunt and forthright, and did not attempt to shirk what Thackeray felt ought to be said. However, the advice was perhaps unfair and too personal in the public media:

> What might not this man do, if he would read and meditate a little, and profit by the works of men whose taste and education were superior to his own.[88]

Less convincing was a comment by the *Morning Post* about the first part of 'A Pictorial Rhapsody'. Declaring that 'the present number of Fraser is of no great attraction', the writer went on to single out Thackeray's piece for specific abuse:

> Among other papers in the magazine is what is called a 'Pictorial Rhapsody' upon the Royal Academy, in which great personal favouritism and general bad taste in the criticisms is boldly and unscrupulously indulged. The absurdities of this notice are plenty, and *parmi les autres*, the writer defends Mulready and the postage covers![89]

Thackeray's retort to this was one of typical humour, and is a good specimen of the interplay between periodicals that complicates the impartiality of an article and shows Thackeray's awareness of his role as principally a *Fraser's* critic. In the second part of 'A Pictorial Rhapsody', Titmarsh is so distraught at being 'rejected' by a newspaper like the *Morning Post*, renowned for its attentions to the illustrious and fashionable of the day, especially as he did believe they thought him a 'fashnable chap', that he fled his hotel without paying his bill or concluding his article. His career, the character bewailed, was in tatters.[90]

Thackeray was able to use effectively the device of the *Fraser's* editor to ridicule the journalist by exaggerating the *Morning Post's* influence. His merging of fiction and criticism protected the position of the writer behind his persona. A common editorial device was borrowed to end the article, extending the idea of the fictionality of the article. Nol Yorke, the *Fraser* 'editor', concluded Thackeray's review with the words:

> It appears that, on the 1st of June, the *Morning Post* published a criticism upon him [i.e. Titmarsh], accusing him of ignorance, bad taste, and gross partiality. His gentle and susceptible spirit could not brook the rebuke; he was not angry; he did not retort; but *his heart broke*![91]

Although the criticism here is comic and slight, it is worth remembering that Thackeray fought for all of his writing career against the habit of malicious and unjust attacks, indulged in by other sections of the press. He was accused of such attacks himself, but felt that, though a little severe at times, he had never been unfair.[92]

Wagstaff, Yellowplush, Titmarsh, and others, are ways for the reader into the world of art and literature, as well as ways into the world of newspaper criticism itself. Perhaps when Ruskin talked about newspaper writers on art continuously trying to meet the needs and feelings of their readership, he had things of the Titmarshian nature at the back of his mind.[93] But Thackeray mediates not just between the painting and the reader, translating the picture into print, but also between the periodical and the reader. His personae integrate his texts into the medium of the literary journal or newspaper – reflecting its practices and inscribed into its modes of production – and they exist outside of that medium, commentating and reflecting upon those practices. The *Paris Literary Gazette* was a learning platform for Thackeray's understanding of the commercial nature of writing just as much as the *National Standard*. Their different contexts demanded different responses from the writer. But in each case, Thackeray recognized a rupture between the ideals of the gentlemanly writer and the profit-based economies of the periodical. He devised the figure of the writer-persona to signify his unease at the schism in the mass periodical age between the print medium and the writer. Authority rested with the journal it seemed and not with the individual. The text could not be a free signifier where it was so dependent on the signification of the context. Indeed, the context was a text itself, and this inculcated further fractures. Thackeray's personae present both a method of holding together the dissipating of the author's identity in the ephemeral confusion of the press, and a deliberate fracturing of the integrity and reliability of the corporate periodical tone. They do this, however, within the parameters of a journal, *Fraser's Magazine*, well known for just such fracturings, and they are thus bounded or contained by the readers' expectations of satire. Where Thackeray tried to write beyond the boundaries of reader expectation, he was less successful, as is evident from his contributions to the *Constitutional* examined in the next chapter.

Thackeray had given some sort of shape to his periodical world by 1841 in the varied but coherent mixture of fictional, critical, biographical, historical, and travel writings that he produced. The frontispiece to *Comic Tales and Sketches*, which is reproduced in Saintsbury's Oxford edition of the *Works* (p. ii), creates an image, drawn by Thackeray, that makes visible his sense of position in relation to his fictional creations. It shows Charles Yellowplush and Major Gahagan on either side of Michael Angelo Titmarsh, each linking an arm, and all three walking towards the edge of a cliff. Titmarsh explains in the preface that 'they are supposed to be marching hand-in-hand, and are just on the very brink of immortality'.[94] What Titmarsh does not, and implicitly *cannot*, describe is that the picture of the three 'editors' hangs, as on a sandwich-board, on the back of a fourth figure: the figure of the costumed fool, or jester, with his eared jester's-hat, holding a staff with a miniature of his own head as its knob. This is the masked Thackeray in one of his favourite pictorial disguises, later used as the original title-page character for *Vanity Fair*. He is a Thackerayan equivalent of Mr Punch, and a caricature that Thackeray had drawn since his earliest school-days and seemingly reserved as an image for special association with the writer. Thackeray does not here choose to be identified with any one of his personae – most specifically, not with Titmarsh. This is the playful Thackeray. It is also the subtle Thackeray; once again he hides his true self, or another version of his true self, behind the public character whose name he appends to the periodical sketches, whilst simultaneously denying that persona's omniscience.

Notes

[1] Catherine Peters, *Thackeray's Universe: Shifting Worlds of Imagination and Reality* (London: Faber and Faber, 1987), 62-3.

[2] See Ray on Thackeray's inheritance, *Letters*, I, Appendix 4, 506-8.

[3] See, for instance, W. Elwin, 'Thackeray in Search of a Profession', *Monthly Review*, vol. 17 (October 1904), 104-5.

[4] The articles signed 'W.M.T.' were first identified as Thackeray's in J. Guivarc'h, 'Deux Journalistes Anglais de Paris en 1835 (George W.M. Reynolds et W.M.T.)', *Etudes Anglaises*, 28 (1975), 203-12; Guivarc'h

tentatively suggests the two 'Augustus Wagstaff' articles as Thackeray's, which I confirm here; I have further added the 'Party at Willowford Hall' as Thackeray's. Guivarc'h reprints 'England', *Paris Literary Gazette*, 3 (10 November 1835).

[5] Laurel Brake, 'Production of Meaning in Periodical Studies: Versions of the English Review', *Victorial Periodicals Review*, 24: 4 (Winter 1991), 169.

[6] These facts are presented from my own examination of the magazine, a file of which is in the Bibliothèque Nationale in Paris; Guivarc'h provides some of this information.

[7] Guivarc'h, 209.

[8] *Vanity Fair*, *Works*, I, chapter 34.

[9] *Paris Literary Gazette*, VI, 94, col. 2-3; Thackeray gave the figure of 30,000 English residents in Paris in his article 'England'.

[10] The magazine does not, however, offer the radical stance of Reynolds' later career; Thackeray was critical of his role in the Chartist movement in 1848, see G.N. Ray, *W.M. Thackeray: Contributions to the 'Morning Chronicle'* (Urbana: University of Illinois Press, 1955), 194-6.

[11] Ray, *Uses*, 184.

[12] *Letters*, I, 297.

[13] Thackeray had a copy of the *London and Paris Observer* for 1842 in his library at his death; see J.H. Stonehouse (ed.), *Catalogue*.

[14] 'Prospectus', *Paris Literary Gazette*, 1 (27 October 1835), 1.

[15] Ibid.

[16] See, for instance, the article, 'A New Class of Writers: For the Lovers of Light Reading', *Paris Literary Gazette*, 9 (22 December 1835), 141, which argues for the critical analysis of advertisements and suggests to book-sellers the commercial potential of a volume entitled 'The Rise and Progress of the Art of Advertising, with the Advertisements of the Present Age now first collected'. The cynicism was perhaps premature.

[17] Thackeray's *Paris Literary Gazette* reviews, all signed 'W.M.T', were: 'La Verité sur les Cents Jours, par L. Bonaparte, Prince de Canino, Paris, 1835', 1, (27 October 1835), 3-5; 'Souvenirs d'Antony, par Alexandre Dumas. Paris, Dumont, 1835', 2 (3 November 1835), 19-21; 'England', 3 (10 November 1835), 33-4; 'Servitude et Grandeur Militaires, par Le Comte Alfred de Vigny. Paris, 1835', 5 (24 November 1835), 65-7; 'German Songs,. Schwab. Mustersammlung Deutscher Lieder – Leipzig, 1835. Schwab's Specimens of German Songs. Paris, Heidelhoff and Campe', 10 (29 December 1835), 145-7; and see Appendix 1 below.

[18] Review of Alexandre Dumas, *Souvenirs D'Antony*, Paris Literary Gazette, 2 (3 November 1835)...

[19] 'England', *Paris Literary Gazette*, 3 (10 November 1835), 33; reprinted in *Etudes Anglais*, 28 (1975), 210.

[20] Thackeray's sub-title for *The Book of Snobs: By One of Themselves* (1846).

[21] 'England', 33; *Etudes Anglaises*, 211.

[22] Ibid.

[23] Ibid.
[24] See especially J.Y.T. Greig, *Thackeray: A Reconsideration* (Oxford: OUP, 1950), 75-8.
[25] G.N. Ray, 'Thackeray and France: Being an Account of the part played by Thackeray's life in France and his reading of French Literature in the Formation of his Mind and Art', PhD thesis (Harvard University, 1940), 99.
[26] 'England', 33; *Etudes Anglaises*, 211-12.
[27] Ibid., 33; *Etudes Anglaises*, 212; compare this to his mockery of the French nation in 1847: ' ... for all that it's admiral to see how the French gents will swagger – how they will be the scenters of civilization – how they will be the Igsamples of Europ, and nothink shall prevent 'em – knowing they will have it, I say I listen, smokin my pip in silence. But to our tail' ('Punch's Prize Novelists. Crinoline. By Je-mes Pl-sh, Esq.', *Punch* (28 August, 4 and 11 September 1847); *Novels by Eminent Hands*, *Works*, XV, 78).
[28] See Chapter 7, below.
[29] *Vanity Fair*, chapter 8, *Works*, I, 84; this was the abolutionists' slogan, as identified by John Sutherland in the Oxford edition (1983), 905.
[30] He was not to use his own name again until his 1840 item of social journalism, 'Going to See a Man Hanged', in *Fraser's Magazine*.
[31] Titmarsh was both Michael Angelo and Samuel.
[32] These were, 'The Partie Fine' (May 1844), 'Greenwich-Whitebaits' (July 1844), 'The Chest of Cigars' (July 1845), and 'Bob Robinson's First Love' (August 1845).
[33] *Paris Literary Gazette*, 4 (17 November 1835), 52.
[34] Ibid.
[35] Ibid.
[36] Ibid., 54.
[37] Ray, 'Thackeray and France', 71.
[38] *Paris Literary Gazette*, 8 (15 December 1835), 116.
[39] The connection to Major Gahagan is increased by Thackeray's calling Gahagan, 'Goliah O'Grady Gahagan', and the Major's presence at Futtyghur and Ferruckabad; Gahagan is also a striking character, 'with blazing red hair, six feet four in height' (*Works*, XV, 269).
[40] See 'Fashionable Fax and Polite Annygoats', op.cit.; see, for instance, Peters, 82, and Ray, *Uses*, chapter 8.
[41] They also appeared in 'A Little Dinner at Timmins's', *Punch* (May-July 1848), *Pendennis* (1848-50), chapter 22, 'Mr Brown's Letters to his Nephew', chapter 12, *Punch* (11 and 18 August 1849), and then later in *The Newcomes* (1853-5) and *The Wolves and the Lamb* (1855).
[42] I am indebted to I.G. Mudge and M.E. Sears, *A Thackeray Dictionary* (London: Routledge, 1910), for several references here.
[43] Probably intended for Stoke Poges, near Slough, where Thomas Gray wrote the 'Elegy in a Country Church-Yard'; the name is spelled 'Stoke Pogis' in *Little Travels and Roadside Sketches*, *Fraser's Magazine* (May and October

1844, January 1845), where the town is characterized as politically volatile (*Works*, XVI, 311).

[44] '*Woman; The Angel of Life: A Poem*. By Robert Montgomery. London: 1833', *National Standard*, 24 (15 June 1833); discussed in Hawes, 48-9.

[45] 'Paris Correspondence', *National Standard*, 27 (6 July 1833).

[46] Edgar F. Harden, *The Emergence of Thackeray's Serial Fiction* (London: George Prior, 1979), 324.

[47] *Works*, XXV, 3.

[48] John Carey, *Thackeray: Prodigal Genius* (London: Faber & Faber, 1977), 58, suggests that Thackeray's Yellowplush was intended as a more realistic portrait of a servant than Dickens's Weller.

[49] *Works*, XXV, 10.

[50] Ibid., 11-12; Thackeray had a good working knowledge of fashionable life from acquaintance with such friends as Edward Fitzgerald.

[51] Ibid., 12.

[52] Ibid., 4; the *Age* was a scandalous rag, somewhat lewd, to which Maginn contributed.

[53] See his article 'Half-a-Crown's Worth of Cheap Knowledge', *Fraser's Magazine*, 17 (March 1838), considered below.

[54] *Works*, XXV, 7.

[55] Bulwer's 'On Art in Fiction' appeared in the *New Monthly Magazine* in March and April 1838; Eigner and Worth suggest that Bulwer's ideas were very much intended to enhance the reputation of the novels that he was working on and had already published; a portion of Bulwer's article is reprinted in E.M. Eigner and G.J. Worth (eds), *Victorian Criticism of the Novel* (Cambridge: CUP, 1985); the citation is from J.P. Runzo, 'Aspects of English Criticism of the Novel, 1830-1850,' dissertation, Indiana University, 1970, cited Eigner and Worth, 4; many of Bulwer's works were published anonymously, which made is easy for him to describe his own novels as examples of good practice, see Thackeray's correct assumption of Bulwer's authorship of *Alice; or, The Mysteries* in *The Times* (24 April 1838), Gulliver, 214-17; and his correct attribution of *The New Timon* to Bulwer in the *Morning Chronicle* (21 April 1846), Ray, *Contributions*, 128.

[56] Reviewed in the *National Standard*, 30 (27 July 1833).

[57] 'Mr. Yellowplush's Ajew', *Fraser's Magazine*, August 1838; *Works*, XVII, 126.

[58] Preface to Appleton and Co.'s edition of *Thackeray's Minor Works* (New York, 1852-3); Thackeray apologized to Bulwer in 1861 for the two scathing attacks in the *Yellowplush Papers*; see Lewis Melville, *The Life of William Makepeace Thackeray* (London: Caxton, 1906), 77-8; however, he appears to have forgotten other personal criticism – in the *Morning Chronicle* review of Bulwer's *The New Timon*, 21 April 1846, Thackeray mocked Bulwer's vanity over the smallness of his feet (Ray, *Contributions*, 132).

[59] See, for example, 'An Essay on Thunder and Small Beer', preface to *The Kickleburys on the Rhine* (second edition, 1851).

[60] 'Epistles to the Literati', *Fraser's Magazine*, January 1840; *Works*, XVII, 142.
[61] Robert A. Colby, *Thackeray's Canvass of Humanity: An Author and his Public* (Columbus: Ohio State University Press, 1979), chapter 2.
[62] See my discussion of *The Second Funeral of Napoleon* (1841), Chapter 5 below.
[63] See nos. 19, 20 and 23 of Appendix 3.
[64] This magazine attacked its rivals on the first page of the first number, singling out the *Athenaeum*, *Art Union* (later, the *Art Journal*), the *Parthenon*, and the *Torch*.
[65] See Maryanne C. Ward, 'Preparing for the National Gallery: the Art Criticism of William Hazlitt and P.G. Patmore', *Victorian Periodicals Review*, XXIII, no. 3 (Fall, 1990), 104-10.
[66] *Fraser's Magazine*: 'Strictures on Pictures', 17 (June 1838), 'A Second Lecture on the Fine Arts', 19 (June 1839), 'A Pictorial Rhapsody', 21 (June 1840) and 22 (July 1840), 'May Gambols', 29 (June 1844), 'Picture Gossip', 31 (June 1845); in addition, 'M.A.T.' contributed 'An Exhibition Gossip', *Ainsworth's Magazine*, 1 (June 1842), and a series of articles for the *Pictorial Times*, March–May 1843; Thackeray also wrote art criticism for *Punch* and the *Morning Chronicle* during the 1840s.
[67] Paula Gillett, *The Victorian Painter's World* (Gloucester: Alan Sutton, 1990), 97.
[68] Gillett, 274, n.96.
[69] For a summary of Thackeray's main artistic concerns in these articles, see Colby, *Canvass*, 60; Helene E. Roberts, '"The Sentiment of Reality": Thackeray's Art Criticism', *Studies in the Novel*, 13: 1-2 (Spring-Summer 1981); Judith K. Fisher, 'The Aesthetics of the Mediocre: Thackeray and the Visual Arts', *Victorian Studies*, 26 (1983), 65-82; Laura Fasick, 'Thackeray's Treatment of Writing and Painting', *Nineteenth Century Literature*, 47 (1992-3), 72-90.
[70] This was also used in the description of Augustus Wagstaff, see above.
[71] See Douglas Jerrold, *Men of Character* (London, 1838), illustrated by Thackeray.
[72] *Dictionary of National Biography*, XIX, 453-54; Thackeray referred to him in a review in his review of *Waltzburg. A Tale of the Sixteenth Century*, *National Standard*, 29 (20 July 1833).
[73] Gordon Ray suggests the source was the name 'Samuel Tidmarsh' on a 17th-century pamphlet in Thackeray's library; Ray, *Uses*, 198.
[74] See 'Michael Angelo' in Georgio Vasari, *Lives of the Artists*, Vol. I (Harmondsworth: Penguin, 1965/1987), 431.
[75] 'A Pictorial Rhapsody: Concluded', *Works*, XXV, 152.
[76] Ibid., 166.
[77] 'Strictures on Pictures', *Works*, XXV, 101, 107.
[78] 'A Pictorial Rhapsody', *Works*, XXV, 163-4.

[79] 'Jack Straw's Castle' was (and still is) a pub on the outskirts of Hampstead, North London, notorious in the eighteenth century as a stopping post for robbers on the highways in and out of the capital (like 'The Spaniards' a little further down the road where Mrs Bardell was arrested in Dickens's *Pickwick Papers*).
[80] 'Strictures on Pictures', *Works*, XXV, 111, 112.
[81] Ibid., 101-2.
[82] Colby, *Canvass*, 62-3; see also the list of Gandish's genre paintings, *The Newcomes*, *Works*, V, 193-5, and Sandy M'Collop's Scottish paintings, ibid., 197.
[83] 'A Pictorial Rhapsody', *Works*, XXV, 168.
[84] Helene Roberts compares Thackeray's knowledge of artistic techniques and aesthetics to the other more famed art critics, Hazlitt, Haydon, and Ruskin; Roberts, op. cit., 21-39.
[85] 'A Pictorial Rhapsody', *Works*, XXV, 127-8; Thackeray repeated this point in 'May Gambols', *Fraser's Magazine* (June 1844), *Works*, XXV, 194, but praising 'now' 'the *Times*, the *Chronicle*, and the *Post*' for the professionalism of their new art criticism (though Thackeray himself was art critic for the *Chronicle* at this time!).
[86] *Morning Post*, Friday, 29 May 1840, p. 2, col. 4; Shee is included in *The Newcomes* as Andrew Smee, R.A.
[87] Judith Fisher, op. cit., 67.
[88] 'Strictures on Pictures', *Works*, XXV, 108.
[89] *Morning Post*, Monday, 1 June 1840, p. 6, col. 3; printed in Melville, *Life*, 86-7.
[90] Thackeray's feud with the *Morning Post* continued into the 1840s, see Chapter 4.
[91] 'A Pictorial Rhapsody', Works, XXV, 168.
[92] See, for instance, *Pendennis*, *Works*, III, 387-8, where Pen is described as writing 'like a gentleman'.
[93] John Ruskin, Preface to the second edition of *Modern Painters*; Vol. I (London: George Allen, 1897), xix.
[94] Preface to *Comic Tales and Sketches*, George Saintsbury (ed.), *Works*, I (Oxford edition), xl.

Chapter 3

The foreign correspondent: writing across borders in *The Constitutional* and *The Adventures of Philip*

There have been a number of recent studies of Thackeray in relation to the Otherness of non-English cultures. Books on Thackeray and Jewishness, and Germanisms, and American and Oriental slavery, as well as articles on his travel writings, have posited the writer as an essential Englishman, carrying a sense of exile whenever abroad, and speaking as the colonist and outsider.[1] As Robert E. Lougy comments, referring to the travel book, *A Journey from Cornhill to Grand Cairo* (1846), the narrators of the text are both 'Michael Angelo Titmarsh, an overweight, slightly jaded, and opinionated humorist and observer of human nature' and 'a voice that is variously aggressive, sensitive, self-denigrating, racist, or insightful and moving.' He is 'the exile or alien visiting strange lands'.[2]

The Englishness of the traveller is a very conscious trait in Thackeray's writings.[3] Dealing with the intermingling of English and French in *The Adventures of Philip* (1861-2), he writes, 'British Trojans and French Trojans take their Troy everywhere' and in New Orleans, there 'are French cafés, billiards, estaminets, waiters, markets, poor Frenchmen, and rich Frenchmen, in a new Paris – shabby and dirty, it is true – but offering the emigrant the dominos, the chopine, the petit-verre of the patrie'.[4] Likewise, 'British Trojans, who emigrate to the continent of Europe, take their Troy with them':

> We have numerous Anglo-Trojan doctors and apothecaries, who give us the dear pills and doses of Pergamus. We go to Mrs. Guerre or kind Mrs. Columbin, and can purchase the sandwiches of Troy, the pale ale and sherry of Troy, and the dear, dear muffins of home. We live for years, never speaking any language but our native Trojan; except to our servants, whom we instruct in the Trojan way of preparing toast for breakfast ... I am sure there are many English in Paris who never speak to any native above the rank of a waiter or shopman. (*Works*, XI, 17)

This notion is not, however, wholly Anglo-centric. As the above passage denotes, other races have a similar desire for home and a need to find the commodities of home when abroad. Trade for the major European countries has made this possible, and certainly, as with the *Paris Literary Gazette* articles, Thackeray sees trade as the domineering fact in modern international society. But Thackeray too was not wholly an unequivocal Englishman. Born in Calcutta, he had roots and relatives in the East. His love of Paris saw him travel to the French capital every year of his professional life.[5] From his early reading, Thackeray saw the possibilities of writing on French culture, and he gradually made himself an authority on such. His break into the newspaper world, into newspaper journalism, came with his step-father's involvement of the purchase of a daily London newspaper, *The Public Ledger*. Thackeray sought a post as Belgian correspondent initially, but was appointed as Paris correspondent (which, one imagines, he found far more appetising). He had previously, though, looked to write from Paris, and made his own experience whilst writing four Paris letters for the *National Standard* and reviewing several recent French novels. In 1835, prior to working on the *Paris Literary Gazette* from October of that year, it seems probable that he filled in as Paris correspondent for his friend, Eyre Evans Crowe, on the *Morning Chronicle*, and certainly applied to that newspaper for the post of Constantinople correspondent.[6] With the *Constitutional*, Thackeray added a daily London newspaper to his textual and commercial experience; he had then a thorough grasp of the operating mechanics of a weekly literary magazine, a weekly foreign magazine, and a daily newspaper, but in each case he demonstrated an interest in locating himself within an international framework. Nearly thirty years later, when writing *The Adventures of Philip* for the *Cornhill Magazine*, Thackeray returned to the life of a newspaper foreign correspondent as the background to Philip's history. The boundaries that structure that novel are also present in his earlier writing – the borders between the past and the present, between fiction (or art) and journalism, between the private life and the public life, between love and work, and between cultures and races or people. This chapter will traverse a few of these important borderlands by juxtaposing Thackeray's work across a gulf of nearly thirty years.

Thackeray held ambivalent views on France and the French. In a letter to Edward Fitzgerald, 8-9 September 1831, he concluded that 'there is something manly & straightforward & independent in the French'.[7] By the time he had experienced writing his Paris correspondence for the *National Standard*, however, he could say to his mother that the French had 'always an absurd imitation at being chivalrous'.[8] Nevertheless, Thackeray clearly wished to involve himself in the opening up of Europe to English travellers, and, in particular, to examine the cultural relations between England and France. In his review of Victor Hugo's *Notre Dame de Paris*, he suggests that Hugo's descriptions of the French capital are inaccurate, and that the author:

> … forgets that it is a time of peace, and that the English think little more of a trip to Paris than of a jaunt to eat white-bait at Greenwich. Every third person who takes up the book will be qualified, by his own observation, to contradict this falsehood.[9]

This was not true a decade before, and Thackeray was well aware of the changes in European traffic.

The magazines and newspapers of the day were beginning to develop a Continental eye generally. Thackeray ought to have read the 'Sketches of Parisian Society, politics, and literature' by Stendhal in the *New Monthly Magazine* from 1826 to 1829; Thackeray and his Charterhouse friends read the magazine at school.[10] The main literary magazine devoted to European culture was the academic *Foreign Quarterly Review* (1827-46), for which Thackeray wrote in the 1840s (and, indeed, applied for the editorship). In 1836, John Kemble, an acquaintance of Thackeray's, founded the *British and Foreign Review; or, European Quarterly Journal* (1835-44), to which Thackeray contributed two articles, but felt that it lacked a 'lightness' of tone.[11] In the daily newspapers, there were regular columns provided by foreign correspondents, themselves a growing breed in the late 1820s and 1830s. Letters arrived from Paris and other European cities taking two to four days by the regular postal service.

When Thackeray declared to his mother that, on the *National Standard*, 'it looks well however to have a Paris correspondent',[12] he was reflecting the innovativeness of his journal and the current literary context, and not, as Peters suggests, simply providing a lame justification for his absence in Paris.[13] His sequence of four Paris letters lasted from 29 June to 20 July 1833, and covered literature (fiction), periodicals, society (and newspapers), and politics. They were not daily news reports, but cultural analyses, taking, for example, a newspaper item by Jules Janin (whose 'J.J.' signature possibly influenced Thackeray's 'T.T.' signature in the *Constitutional*) and translating and assessing it as social commentary. Whilst in Paris, Thackeray also worked through material for later in the magazine, telling his mother that he had enough done for ten months.[14] When he returned to England, Thackeray began to publish a series of reviews of French novels (in a sections headed 'Foreign Article'), and translations of French stories and poems (and even, in the 'Science and Art' section, an article from a French newspaper entitled 'Description of the Salt Mines of Wieliezka'). This interest continued right until the last number of the magazine, when he reviewed Hugo's *Etude sur Mirabeau*.[15]

In the last chapter, I discussed the contributions Thackeray made to the *Paris Literary Gazette* during late 1835. Like the work for the *National Standard*, these items were magazine orientated and essentially 'literary'. In April 1836, Thackeray made his first direct connections with the newspaper industry, discussing the 'Brussels business' with the editorial board of the forthcoming *Constitutional, and Public Ledger*[16] and the successful launch of the share issue for the paper.[17] With the prospect of full-time employment in hand, giving an annual income of £400, Thackeray married Isabella Shawe on 20 August 1836. On 24 August, the *Public Ledger* began to run advertisements of its impending alteration of proprietorship and new title. The date of the first issue was to be 15 September 1836, the day on which London newspapers expected the Stamp Duty on news, then currently 4d. per copy, to be reduced or even abolished.

The *Constitutional* was launched as part of a growing context of radicalization in the press, just as the *National Standard* was part of a movement to make available (or develop the market in) lower-priced literary reviews.[18] Much critical work has been done on the illegal unstamped press of the period, the press of the working-class movements, but the *Constitutional* was an example of how far a Radical agenda had permeated into middle-class society.[19] It was also a marketing venture, intended to take advantage of a cheaper press free from taxation. The general opinion of such abolition was that it would make legal newspapers available to the working classes (magazines were not taxed as they did not carry news), and this would aid the spread of democracy as well as literacy. However, most of the daily papers did not support the change.[20] Paralleling the *Literary Gazette*'s argument against cheap reviews (discussed in Chapter 1), the dailies reasoned that cheaper newspapers would lead to lower standards and the growth of shoddy, and even revolutionary, journalism. The magazine press, generally in favour of the reduction, was vocal in its criticism of the newspapers and saw their lack of enthusiasm as betraying an anxiety about competition, loss of circulation, and reduced profits. The actual reduction was from 4d. to 1d., and most of the dailies cut their cover price from 7d. to 5d. (and thereby pocketed the extra penny reduction themselves). The *Constitutional* was launched at 4½d. However, it was soon in financial trouble. On Wednesday 1 March 1837, it was forced to raise its price to 5d. in line with the rest of the press, although it increased its number of columns from six to seven. This fell back to six again from 5 June, and on Saturday 1 July 1837 it ceased trading without prior warning.

Before dealing with Thackeray's Paris correspondence and his role as a foreign correspondent, I want to consider how the *Constitutional* related to the newspaper market-place of 1836. Aled Jones has referred to the 'Press' which emerged at this time as 'capitalized and with an aggressive and self-assured collective identity'.[21] Certainly, the power of news editors, such as Thomas Barnes of the *Times*, and their party orientation, has been the subject of several studies.[22] But it is also true that the newspaper industry in 1836 was a very static and surprisingly uniform one in terms of content and style.[23] The *Constitutional, and Public Ledger*, although to be a Radical paper, was created from a Tory newspaper called the *Public Ledger*. *Fraser's Magazine*, itself conservative, called it:

> ... a high and rising authority in the commercial world; and in politics [it] supports the English party. Its influence is most important, circulating, as it does, among the wealthy and educated classes of the commercial world.[24]

Its politics, like those of its contemporaries, were located primarily in the editorial column. For the rest, the *Public Ledger* was a shipping journal, containing merchant and maritime information. Its columns of economic and market information, police reports, and accounts of sensational murders and suicides reprinted from the provincial press were typical of all the daily London newspapers.

Newspapers of the mid-1830s had a close physical and economic resemblance. Their price, broad-sheet size and shape, number of pages (four) and columns (six per page), and even general layout, were identical. They all carried advertisements on the front and back pages, an editorial in the middle of page 2, court briefs and police reports on the back page. Articles of news circulated across all of the papers. For example, on Thursday, 1 September 1836, an article entitled 'Detection of a Gang of Coiners and Receivers of Stolen Goods' by a 'Liverpool Correspondent' appeared in four dailies: the *Morning Chronicle*, *Morning Herald*, and (evening) *Standard*, published precisely the same piece, whilst the *Morning Advertiser* reparagraphed and shortened the text and gave a name as 'Mr. Cave' rather than 'Mr. Crewe' as in the others. The evening paper would have pirated the morning editions, but the three morning newspapers must have acquired the same story. In this same edition for 1 September, articles entitled 'The Late Fire', 'Church rates – St. Luke's, Chelsea', and 'Another Fatal Steamboat Accident', appeared in more than one newspaper, often with the same heading. 'Court Circulars', 'City Intelligences', bankruptcy and police reports, were all much the same as well. In size, the *Times* occasionally ran to an eight-page special edition, and the *Globe* had only five columns per page, but otherwise the newspapers were four-page broad-sheets, and therefore remarkably uniform. It is hardly surprising that the profession of journalism was held in such low esteem at the time, and that the editor remained the main power in a newspaper, presiding over sub-editors (who cut and pasted news from elsewhere) and co-ordinating free-lance work.[25]

Foreign correspondence in the newspapers was similarly structured.[26] The 1830s press had two basic methods of collecting foreign news: a letter from a correspondent (free-lance or employed by the paper) was printed in full; or foreign correspondence and translated passages from the foreign newspapers were paraphrased in reported speech in the editorial section. Less prominent newspapers would print translations made directly from daily foreign newspapers. Others, such as the *Standard* and the *Globe*, would pirate news from the previous day's or that morning's editions. There were no political boundaries here. The Tory *Standard* would usually pirate the Tory *Morning Herald*, but would also extract the Whig *Morning Chronicle*.[27] The *Globe* would mostly use the Whig *Chronicle* or *Morning Advertiser*, but sometimes too the Tory *Morning Post*.[28]

The foreign correspondent was a recent figure in the press of the 1830s. The *Morning Herald* and the *Morning Advertiser* made a point of suggesting that having writers *in situ* in foreign capitals meant that they had no need to pirate other newspapers, and they kept regular reporters at certain centres of news interest – in 1836, these were the Spanish Civil War, Ireland, and

Constantinople. But they did not have extensive financial resources.[29] The dispatches would always take at least two days to arrive and were thus slightly out of date. The *Advertiser* had a Paris correspondent, whose 'Express from Paris' appeared almost every day.[30] The *Advertiser* took its foreign news seriously, and even refers to the Canton Papers from China and news from 'Our Correspondent' in Barbados.[31] Other foreign-minded papers in 1836 included Albany Fonblanque's *The Examiner*, a weekly Sunday newspaper.[32] The *Standard* professed to its 'Own Correspondent' in Paris, but used him little beyond providing a summary of political stories in *La Paix* and *Le Constitutionnel*.[33]

The most important foreign correspondent in Thackeray's career was Eyre Evans Crowe, Paris correspondent for the *Morning Chronicle* from 1830.[34] During 1836, Crowe introduced Thackeray to several significant politicians as well as providing a model of the journalist abroad.[35] Thackeray had known the Crowes in April 1835, when Crowe had assisted Thackeray's unsuccessful application for post of Constantinople correspondent for the *Morning Chronicle*.[36] The family remained close to him for the rest of his life, Crowe's son, Eyre, acting as Thackeray's amenuensis and secretary on the American tour of 1852-3, and Thackeray helping another son, Joseph Crowe, to the post of Crimean correspondent in 1854.[37]

The *Constitutional* represented Thackeray's initiation into the world of newspaper journalism. The correspondence was his first attempt at a continuous transmission of daily news and politics. The journalistic world provided the imaginary material for *Pendennis* and *The Adventures of Philip*, in particular, and Thackeray's descriptions of the newspaper hacks of the day were very different to the usual impression of newspaper writers.[38] Amongst the Paris and London hacks he discovered something very different from the ideal of the gentlemanly man-of-letters; the reality was a form of literary promiscuity. Shortly after commencing the *Constitutional* letters, he wrote to Edward Fitzgerald:

> I am sorry to say that I like the newspaper work very much, it is a continual excitement, and I fancy I do it well, that is very sarcastically, and though we agreed about literature, sarcasm does no good either to reader or writer, I think in politics were all are rogues to deal with (yr. hble. Servt. among them) a man cannot sneer and scorn too much, and bring the profession into disrepute – but the poor picture-painting is altogether neglected; and for this neglect I can give you no better illustration, than to tell you that it seems like quitting a beautiful innocent wife (like Mrs. T. for instance) to take up with a tawdry brazen whore.[39]

The polarity created here of angel and whore as metaphors for art and journalism indicate Thackeray's concerns for the status of his new profession. But the delight in the newspaper's energy and vitality suggests how attractive this world was to Thackeray. The ideas here underpin the narrative of

Pendennis and will be elaborated in Chapter 8. His comments about sarcasm show how much he was thinking about the nature of journalism in comparison with 'literature', and the desire on his part to make his writings comic and satirical and not merely mechanical. Such a design complemented the editorial direction of the *Constitutional* (which boasted Laman Blanchard as editor, Douglas Jerrold as literary editor, and Leigh Hunt's son, Thornton Hunt, as political editor – Blanchard and Jerrold later working with Thackeray on *Punch*). The editorial of the first number of the new regime announced:

> We shall rarely adopt – never where it is needless – a loftiness of style or a solemnity of tone. When we are dull it will not be by design, but because we cannot help it. Instead of wearing a visage ever rueful, in season and out of season, we shall be cheerful while we can – in the conviction (a wise one for the world, and the world is fast coming to it) that although there is much to mourn over, there is infinitely more to hope for and rejoice in.[40]

The light-hearted note was, for Thackeray, a continuation of his policies on the *National Standard* and *Paris Literary Gazette*, and his criticism of the *British and Foreign Review*. In addition, the *Constitutional* held moderate views about criticism directed at public figures, and rejected the growing contemporary practice of publishing personal invective motivated by personal and political bias. The newspaper's journalists would evaluate politicians, actors and artists in the same way:

> These discussions will perhaps assume an unfashionable tone, for they will not be so freely sprinkled with fierce invective or coarse personality, as the taste of the day, in the higher circles, seems to require.[41]

In fact, Thackeray later took the editorial column of his paper to task for their attack on Louis Philippe; Thackeray disliked the Citizen King, too, but felt that the editors had attacked him too personally and that he was not 'naturally cruel and unjust', as had been suggested.[42]

In employing a Paris correspondent, the *Constitutional* undoubtedly aimed to follow the trends of the market-place. However, it could not afford the networks to transmit the correspondence quickly across Europe, and so Thackeray's column was at a disadvantage to those of other foreign journalists. Established newspaper dailies had secure postal routes for their mail that rushed correspondence and continental journals to the main office within two days. A letter dated from Paris on 1 September could be in print for the edition of two days later. Thackeray's letters appeared two or three times a week, and, initially, they competed with this two-day rate. However, by December 1836, for an unknown reason, the letters were taking at least three and mostly four days to appear. This irregularity meant that the *Constitutional* was not able to produce foreign news as up to date as that of many of its contemporaries. Thackeray would inevitably have to alter the manner in which he wrote about Parisian events, and, indeed, he tended towards a more light-hearted review than a daily political analysis. It may even have been his attitude towards the Paris letters that resulted in this delay in publication.

C.P. Johnson, an early biographer of Thackeray, remarked in 1888, regarding the *Constitutional* writings, that 'the importance of his letters, and of the position and type allotted to them, increased as time went on'.[43] There is no evidence, however, that this was the case. Unlike Eyre Evans Crowe, Thackeray was almost continuously published on page 3 at the top of column 3, and, although typefaces did change, there is no sense of a gradual improvement. Larger print was often a sign of a paucity of news. In December 1836 and January 1837, the letters rose to columns 1 and 2 of page 3, but then returned to their old position by the end of January. They moved to page 4, columns 1 and 3 in February. By June 1837, when Thackeray was recalled to London to assist with the financial problems of the paper and deal with creditors (presumably using his experience as a bill discounter and magazine proprietor),[44] and his column was taken over by 'H.',[45] it had returned to the original position of columns 2 or 3 on page 3.

Despite the average position his work occupied, Thackeray's foreign reporting was unusual in the newspapers of the day. He was not simply imitative of other approaches. Even Crowe's columns of political analysis, amongst the best of the day, have a completely different style and method. But there does exist a clear tension in Thackeray's correspondence, indicative of a writer forced into a medium with which he is not entirely at ease. The blend of humour (his 'sarcasm') and analysis does not always work. The complex interplay of irony, cynicism, apology, and pleasantness make his letters more like essays than regular political correspondence, and two letters in particular stretch the format into directions unique amongst other foreign reporters.

Alongside the political reportage, Thackeray indulged in discussions of a wide range of subjects, such as constitutional monarchy, public executions, the ideals of gentlemanly (chivalric) behaviour, and ceremony and festival in French life. He did not remain within the boundaries of the political, but would turn discussions towards the moral and social. I do not intend to discuss Thackeray's political ideas here. He was broadly liberal in views, uncomfortable with the absolute power of monarchy, but fearing the violence of the democratic revolutionaries. He is not a radical in the sense that, perhaps, Jerrold would have been in coming to the new newspaper. If there is any movement in his series, it is towards humanism and away from politics (Crowe's analyses of human nature offered a pointer, perhaps). It is something of an irony that, eschewing politics in the *National Standard*, he should become a political commentator for the *Constitutional*. But his intentions in this new post may always have been to create a space for his digressions on humanity, whilst fulfilling the obligation to report on daily events.

Two topics towards the end of the series are the most interesting from this perspective. Thackeray can be seen crossing the boundaries between factual journalism and a comic and literary commentary on people. The first of these concerns a revolutionary plot against Louis Philippe, instigated by Prince Louis Napoleon Bonaparte (later Napoleon III) and involving two young apprentices. The ministerial reaction was severe against the perpetrators when the coup failed; the two apprentices were sentenced to execution for treason, but the Prince was banished from the kingdom in a well-provisioned ship, reputedly stocked with champagne, and directed to America. Thackeray was highly indignant at the government's hypocrisy. The French authorities declared that, due to his youth, Napoleon could only be considered as the tool of the plot. Thackeray noted that the Prince was nearly thirty years old and had often spoken out against the monarchy. It was, he wrote, like *Tom Jones*, where Thwackum punishes Jones to correct Blifil.[46] The apprentices were to be hanged as a lesson to Napoleon. He was also pleased to announce that a ministerial journal 'hinted that the Constitutional was leagued in the Buonaparte plot!' (perhaps this is a touch of impromptu advertising).[47] On 1 December, Thackeray alleged:

> A young prince may play pranks and excite rebellion – it is his Royal Highness's nature to do so; he is excusable, from his rank and royal blood ... but woe be tide to the low-bred ruffians who attempt to create revolutions! When will the ignorant rabble learn, that the law was made by princes and not for them? When will they see what is only good sport for their masters is often death to them?[48]

It was a question of class. The implicit radicalism here is tempered by Thackeray's real concern, however: a renunciation of capital punishment, a view that he expressed at other points in his life.[49] He manifested both a fear of revolutionary violence, and a disgust at the violence the state uses against the individual.[50] The comments he made were not entirely in keeping with the radicalism of the newspaper. By mid-November, he had to apologize for his 'tone', noting 'Perhaps, from having resided so long in this country, I have caught the tone of French feeling rather than of English ... '.[51] His social conscience led him into more moralistic statements than political ones, a stance in keeping with the philosophies of his previous periodicals. The revolutionary nature of France, he suggests, leads youth into dangerous incendiary actions:

> ... two disreputable boys, whose foolish heads were turned by Marat and Robespierre, and by the insane vanity so peculiar to this great nation. When Fieschi died, he said: 'all the world will speak of me'. The ruffian Lacenaire, and the madman Alibaud uttered the same foolish sentiment; and it goes so far in this country as to reach even these two silly apprentices – to find two regicide-ragamuffins, who leave their pegtop and marbles, to meditate assassination, and become the heroes in 'strange stories of the deaths of kings'.[52]

The narrative of the fate of the two apprentices ran through Thackeray's correspondence until January 1837. His dealing with the case brought out a number of different literary approaches that challenge the regular direct reporting of the other newspapers. On 19 December, he begins with a metaphor:

> ... justice (according to law) is like an ogre in a fairy-tale, he lurks in hidden caverns, invisible to all eyes, but now and then he issues from his hiding place, seizes and slays his victim, drinks his blood, and retires content.[53]

Explaining the image, he continues, 'Justice ... is made only for the people, not for their masters'. Once again, the message becomes humanitarian and not confined within the borders of France. Thackeray is not even generating a sense of the movement of modern history through his reports. He is, rather, insisting on the universality of his ideas.

Following the metaphor, the letter of 19 December develops a comic conceit, familiar in Thackeray's later works, of a youth's letter home (from school) to his guardian uncle.[54] It purports to be a letter from Prince Louis Napoleon to his uncle in America (once King of Spain). Although only a short digression into comic farce, it nevertheless demonstrates where Thackeray's creative energies were tending, and how much they were restricted by the assumed seriousness of the Paris correspondence format.

> My dear Sire, – You will be surprised to hear of my late 'lark' at Strasburgh – it was a glorious piece of fun. Vaudrey will be hanged. Have you any land to sell cheap? I cannot help them cutting off poor Parquin's head – but what is the price of oats at New York! – Ever, my dear Majesty, your affectionate Royal Highness – L.N.B.[55]

A post-script was added to the Paris letter of this week in the style of a playbill: 'Paris Preserved, or the Plot Discovered', and records the acquittal of the two sixteen-year old apprentices. The sudden dramatic movement into burlesque in this letter goes a small way to puncturing the surface uniformity of the paper, and disturbs the homogeneity of anonymous journalistic writing. It is a momentary Bakhtinian reversal of power rituals, an invasion of Carnival. Although other newspapers, such as the *Morning Chronicle*, which ran Dickens' *Sketches by Boz* in 1834-5, blended fiction and factual reportage in their pages, it is unusual to find a newspaper thus incorporating satirical humour into the actual news column. The brief experiments anticipate *Punch*.

The Napoleon story is finally concluded in Thackeray's letter for 28 December 1836, which was delayed and published (with a second for that date) on 2 January 1837. Here, he makes a more overt claim for the universality of his moral vision. His condemnation of social intolerance spreads to the English as well as the French. No longer hiding behind the journalist's persona, Thackeray speaks with vehemence and decisiveness in unmediated speech. The passage carries with it the same openness as caused him to drop his anonymity when he wrote 'Going to See a Man Hanged' for *Fraser's Magazine* and appended his signature, 'W.M.T.'

> You boast in France and in England that you are the most civilized people of the world, among whom freedom is best understood, and justice most enlightened, and yet the axe and the gallows are always at work; you show the superiority of your laws by making them as bloody and ruthless as the wretches you kill; your vaunted system of justice is little better than a system of public revenge, quite powerless to correct men or even to deter them ... it only familiarizes men with the idea of killing, and lessens, by the cruel nature of the retribution, the general horror for the crime.[56]

This may have suited the *Constitutional*'s radical aims in that it implicitly attacks both the royalist French government and the Tory English one, but it speaks more directly to the reader and appeals beyond the level of politics.

In January 1837, Thackeray's letters begin to introduce comic flashes and mocking asides that again move beyond the normal tone of regular foreign reporting. On 10 January, Prince Louis Napoleon's manifesto is described as having 'the weight of an oration of Mr. Ducrow to his soldiers on the eve of a battle at Astley's ... '.[57] On 21 January, the French politician, Berryer, is 'not unlike the poor knight of La Mancha ... with exactly the same share of reason'.[58] Whilst on 24 January, Thackeray derided those in the French Ministry who would, he believed, vote for anything which helped them: 'royalist, republican, regicide, any side, it is all one to them ... '.[59] The humour of these brief sentences are not typical of the tone of the letters as a whole, but they suggest an author who needs to introduce something beyond the plainness of his contemporaries. These jokes support the *Constitutional*'s claims to offer 'lightness', but they also puncture the surface illusion of objective and authoritative reporting that the newspaper is normally perceived to represent. Perhaps one might best describe these asides as the infiltration of Thackeray's magazine-mentality; certainly, they have more of the style of the *National Standard* Paris letters than of newspaper correspondence. But they do further indicate how Thackeray was concerned to set a new tone in newspaper journalism. The unmediated speech against capital punishment, standing beyond the politics of his newspaper, the satirical mockery of all players in the Napoleon episodes, the comic sentences, all contribute to a form of journalism ill at ease with the established style used in the other daily papers. Quite how successful Thackeray's approach actually was is perhaps another matter.

Probably the most interesting passage in the whole of his Paris correspondence for the *Constitutional* comes in a letter dated 8 February 1837, and published three days later. In the middle of an uninspiring account of 'Dupinism' and M. Fonfrede, a newspaper editor, Thackeray introduced a description of the French festival of the 'Boeuf Gras'. In effect he moves out of his study and the newspaper reports and on to the streets of Paris. He produces a light-hearted and evocative piece that is the forerunner of numerous articles and fictional passages produced later in his career. Indeed, it is his first foray into travel writing.[60] Thackeray was always sceptical of outward displays of pageantry and festival; he always wished to expose the paste and sticky-tape behind all of the glitter. But he was also fascinated by the human vanity on display, and the surface comedy remains in tension with a deeper sensual response.

> To-day all the world seemed mad and out of doors. The Boulevards were thronged with carriages containing hundreds of children and grown up babies in various dresses, Turks, Spaniards, postillions, bears, harlequins, punches, and fools, who were very predominant, both in masquerade and out. The unhappy ox destined to bleed with tomorrow's dawn was paraded through the streets with a saddle of scarlet and gold, and his horns elegantly tipped with gilt paper. Before him marched a troop of Turks and 'salvage men', and between his horns was seated a little bandy-legged Cupid in a tight garment of wash-leather or nankeen, followed by a huge gilt car containing a score of musicians, and a whole regiment of disguised butchers of the metropolis, whose annual duty is to follow this ox through the town. This was the last promenade of the poor creature, who looked sadly worn-out by his fatigue; he paused successively at the houses of all the ministers and dignitaries of state, the little Cupid got down from his seat between the horns, delivered a complimentary oration, and received a bank note in return.[61]

Thackeray concludes his account with a swipe at Louis Philippe. The King, as in all things, collected the fattest cut of the ox for his dinner.

Once again Thackeray extends his commentary on French news and politics to incorporate social and cultural observation. The 'harlequins, punches, and fools ... both in masquerade and out' prefigure Thackeray's most famous motifs: the jesters on the cover pages of *Vanity Fair* and the figure of Mr Punch himself. The theme of the vanity of all of us, drawn to the festival/fair to parade our frailties under a disguise of 'gilt paper', turns not just against the French but against all such fairs. In addition, the immediacy of the account here, the use of the present tense ('To-day'), and the evocation of the visual, distance this letter, this section of a letter, from the context of the political reportage expected. The 'correspondent', whose title emphasizes the textual nature of his activity – letters, writing, commenting on news reports and speeches, translating – has suddenly become the 'observer'. Great statesmen are forgotten for an account of ordinary revellers and the fate of an ox. There is humour here too, but not of the sarcastic kind such as was seen in the Napoleon letters. Thackeray moves suddenly towards the position of the humorist.

Thackeray's brief career as a newspaper journalist ended in February 1837. It had brought him to a new point of maturity in his writing, and, although not fully tested, he was to capitalize on his progress during the next four years as a writer for the magazines and a newspaper reviewer for several important London periodicals. Harold Gulliver has remarked that Thackeray's 'genius lay in what his admirers call a fine display of the personal ego'. The *Constitutional* letters fail, he argues, because they 'appear to be straight reporting with almost no glimpse of the deep and rich personality behind them'. He continues, 'the subjects treated kindled no spark of self-expression, but extinguished it almost completely'.[62] However, as I have tried to demonstrate, Thackeray's attitude towards his Paris correspondence was not to make it 'straight reporting' but to extend the boundaries into comedy, satire, social morality, and cultural observation. He was limited, perhaps, in the amount of such material he could produce in a political column of a daily newspaper, but in places he succeeds in challenging the generic form of the Paris letter from 'Our Correspondent'.

In 1861, Thackeray returned to the role of foreign correspondent in his creation of Philip Firmin, the central figure in *The Adventures of Philip*, serialized in the *Cornhill Magazine*. The novel was the third of his novels on 'contemporary' life, following *Pendennis* (1848-50), which dealt with the rise of a magazine writer and novelist, and *The Newcomes* (1853-5), which was set in the art world and contained characters working for the art reviews. Both of these novels, like *Philip*, were set in the 1830s and early 1840s. Even as a novelist, Thackeray was drawn back to the excitement and difficulty of his period as an emerging journalist.

The Adventures of Philip is a problematic novel that causes critical consternation for its seemingly racist overtones. Joseph Baker, John Sutherland, and, most recently, Deborah Thomas and John Peck, have all tackled the issue and all found Thackeray wanting in tact, if not even in humanity. John Peck's recent contribution, which cites Thackeray as clearly racist in his attitudes towards the mulatto Woolcomb – his 'racism is incidental', 'offensive', 'unthinking', and notes that '*Philip* is the only novel of the period that sinks to the level of racist taunt'.[63] Describing a writer who had an Irish wife and several close Irish friends (such as the Crowes), and who worked across so many periodicals with an international focus, these blunt assertions appear incongruous. Indeed, Peck seems rather gudgingly to acknowledge several useful points that he refrains from pursuing: the character of Philip, 'is incapable of self-fashioning', 'the sense of a threat from an other always co-exists with self-doubt', 'what is most fearful in a stranger is the quality we do not want to recognise in ourselves', and finally that the novel offers the reader 'a revelation of what lies behind one version of racism rather than being just an expression of racism'.[64] Peck and Thomas provide interesting discussions of Thackeray's last complete novel, but both follow the conventional line of Baker and Sutherland, that Thackeray's racial attitudes became less tolerant (but presumably only towards Afro-Americans?), and that *Philip* cannot really be condoned. No critic, however, has considered why

Thackeray should make Philip Firmin a foreign correspondent and whether a novel about 'truth'/realism might not be concerned in its margins (where the 'racism' is located) with media manipulation of the trope of foreignness.[65]

Pendennis is usually seen as a broadly autobiographical figure, and he acts as the writer/narrator for both *The Newcomes* and *Philip*. Beside him is the voice of Laura Pendennis, his wife, whose personality/persona offers a different, feminine perspective on the characters and story. The status of Philip himself is thus complex: his life contains elements of Thackeray's own, but he is described as a unique character, and his personality, not always likeable, is distinct from that of Pen/Thackeray (as indeed Pen's voice is equally problematic). Moreover, unlike earlier novels which contain generous foils against which to remark the central figures (Dobbin in *Vanity Fair*, Warrington and Laura in *Pendennis*, Rachel in *Esmond*, the Colonel in *The Newcomes*), Philip has no such foil. The Little Sister is the nearest such figure, but her constant worship of Philip makes her position more unsighted. I would contend that, as Juliet McMaster has indicated,[66] *Philip* is a darker novel, akin to Dickens' *Our Mutual Friend*, and that through Philip, Thackeray explores the apparent paradox in his own personality that a writer so bound up with representing the Other should feel so uncomfortable in its presence. Thackeray is not Philip, but nor is he against Philip; Philip (character and novel) is a realist text. The textual slippage of the slogan 'AM I NOT A MAN AND A BRUDDER' used in *Philip*, a slogan used many times by Thackeray previously, not least in *Vanity Fair* and *Pendennis*, is the clearest indication of a self-reflexive writerly act. The slogan suddenly loses its innocence in a quite deliberate act. When the Miss Pinkertons charge the mulatto Miss Swartz a double fee to attend their academy, it is the condoning of such exploitation by an English society that is the target and not an implicit racism in the author which is at fault. So, in *Philip*, one might look at the role of the media in the Woolcomb-Firmin ending and consider whether Thackeray might not be implicating his newspaper-reading readers in the production of racial hatred.[67]

The newspaper world surrounds the novel, and provides both characters and plot devices. It is also present as a signifier of cultural trends in a historical period. Whereas in *Pendennis* and *The Newcomes*, the period of the 1830s was not so far removed, in *Philip*, there is a greater sense of history, although this is confused in places by Thackeray's anachronistic references to, for instance, *Punch*. Woolcomb, the hated half-caste in the novel, has a barracks'-friend, Nixon ('doosid funny and witty fellow, Nixon is') who 'sent a thing once to *Punch*', which places the incident sometime after 1841, although at that point in the text we are clearly back in the mid-1830s.[68]

Newspapers affect the lives of many of the characters in the novel, at different levels of interaction. At the lower end of the scale of involvement are such characters as Old Ridley (the father of J.J. Ridley, the painter, of *The Newcomes*) who 'liked to have the paper read to him' (X, 168). He was, Thackeray notes, 'never quite easy with print, and to his last days, many words to be met with in newspapers and elsewhere used to occasion the good butler much intellectual trouble' (X, 168).[69] Tufton Hunt, a disreputable and malicious force in the novel, confesses to a series of employments and opportunities, including 'school-mastering, bear-leading, newspapering, America, West Indies' (X, 189), and signifies the low status of the periodical profession. As he begins his way in the world, Philip takes lodgings in the Inns of Court, and resides in Parchment Buildings with Mr Van John, 'a betting-man', and Michael Cassidy, 'a newspaper reporter'. Philip's father, a quack doctor and (semi-)bigamist, displays his moral fibre by condemning the latter person: 'Dr. Firmin had a horror of newspaper-men, and considered they belonged to the dangerous classes, and treated them with a distant affability' (X, 159). Finally, Laura, Pendennis's wife, shows her consideration for the newspaper profession when she spends 'a great deal of unprofitable time, bread, butter, cold beef, mustard and salt, in compiling a heap of sandwiches, which were tied up in a copy of the *Pall Mall Gazette*' (X, 335). The newspaper has become part of the culture of mid-Victorian society very quickly.

The stages of Philip's career are the most detailed account of the newspaper business in the novel. We are given little of Pendennis's writing career; Thackeray finished with that in *Pendennis*, and the narrator's literary background remains invisible here, although we see glimpses of his comfortable life established as a contrast to Philip's poverty. Phil describes Pen's morals as 'genteel atheism' (X, 324), and accuses him of bourgeois complacency. Indeed, in terms of the narrative, the energy in the book lies with Philip and his uncontrollable anger and passion, and not with the calm deliberations of the omniscient narrative voice. Philip's career is interesting. Making his way in the world, he begins by writing reviews of travel books in the *Pall Mall Gazette*, work he obtains through Pen and his friends. 'You should just see, sir, how I polished off that book of travels this morning', he says, indicating that, like the young Thackeray, he gives himself airs and postures as an authority (X, 324). Like Thackeray, too, Phil's entry into the world of journalism comes from the necessity of obtaining work: it is one profession open to a person who, in their gentility, has learned no other trade. Phil's fortune is squandered, not by banking collapse, but by the corruption of his father. Without a patrimony, he becomes Paris correspondent for the *Pall Mall Gazette*.

First, though, he idles away his time. He intends to study for the Bar, but 'necessary duties', rowing on the river, drinking beer, sleeping, eating, and learning 'the quotidian history of his country' by reading the newspaper (X, 300-301).[70] His attachment to the *Pall Mall Gazette* comes largely through the Irish hacks he consorts with, including his room-mate, Cassidy (the *Gazette*'s 'fashionable correspondent'), and his friend Finucane who is the *Gazette* editor. Thackeray advances time, in *Philip*, by suggesting that Pendennis's days as writer for the *Pall Mall Gazette* have been superseded by a new group of writers. Shandon has passed away and Finucane is the editor.

However, Thackeray firstly describes the old version of the paper at some length:

> When Pendennis and his friends wrote in this newspaper, it was impertinent enough, and many men must have heard the writers laugh at the airs which they occasionally thought proper to assume. The tone which they took amused, annoyed, tickled, was popular. It was continued, and, of course, caricatured by their successors. They worked for very moderate fees: but paid themselves by impertinence and the satisfaction of assailing their betters. Three or four persons were reserved from their abuse; but somebody was sure every week to be tied up at their post, and the public made sport of the victim's contortions. The writers were obscure barristers, ushers, and college men, but they had omniscience at their pens' end, and were ready to lay down the law on any given subject – to teach any man his business ... (X, 301)

Pen describes the irony of becoming the butt of a new generation's jokes in a sharp review received by one of his new books in the *Pall Mall Gazette*; 'the victims who were immolated by the editors of to-day were very likely the objects of the best puffery of the last dynasty', he suggests. The newspaper world is bordered by fashion, taste and popularity. It is also transient, and the status of writers within that world can and does change: Pen is no longer the newspaper man, but the 'author' – 'let us turn away from the author's private griefs and egotisms', he says (X, 302). 'A reporter to a newspaper remains all his life a newspaper reporter' is another phrase used here, but the actuality for Thackeray was different, and he was one of a few writers who did succeed in transcending the trade (X, 350). Phil does not: he fails. Before the novel is half-way through, Thackeray has told the reader that Philip 'has seen the errors of his ways, and divorced with the muse whom he never should have wooed' (X, 302). His career as a newspaper writer and Paris correspondent is not going to be a success; Phil is a hack writer and never grows beyond that. His fate is to inherit part of the Ringwood fortune and return to the easy gentility of his youth. He gets back by birth right what Thackeray regained by writing. Indeed, his entry into journalism in Mugford's *Pall Mall Gazette* is largely due to the influence of his friends whom Mugford, the proprietor, greatly admires. Mugford accepts Phil's slashing review of a volume of poems, despite recognizing that Phil cannot write well and believing that he 'had better stick to the law, and leave writing rubbish alone' (X, 304).

Phil's role as Paris correspondent is conjoined with his love for Charlotte Baynes, whose family must live on the Continent for the cheapness of the living, and from Baynes being responsible for the loss of Phil's fortune (and personally liable – Phil, however, will not accept any money). The life is one of rough and ready Bohemianism, skirting poverty and drinking and smoking cheaply in the cafes. Phil's friends are medical students, impoverished artists, and 'the newspaper correspondents, whose houses and tables were open to him' (X, 349). The life he leads is likely to be based on Thackeray's own experiences in the 1830s. His position is a marginal one; we are told that he is not feted like the correspondents of the major newspapers and occupies a more comical situation, suitable for the tone of irony employed. Thackeray is never wholly serious about the employment of Philip; the world he inhabits is a sham, built on inadequate knowledge and weak philosophy. Much of it seems façade, without real substance. The press coverage of Europe is derived from the comedy of human existence, its loves and pecuniary needs, and not from any altruistic or intellectual desire to know the European Other. This was Thackeray's comment on the commodification of foreign news in the 1830s and beyond.

> It was wonderful what secrets of politics he learned and transmitted to his own paper. He pursued French statesmen of those days with prodigious eloquence and vigour. At the expense of that old king he was wonderfully witty and sarcastical. He reviewed the affairs of Europe, settled the destinies of Russia, denounced the Spanish marriages, disposed of the Pope, and advocated the Liberal cause in France with untiring eloquence. 'Absinthe used to be my drink, sir,' so he was good enough to tell his friends. 'It makes the ink run, and imparts a fine eloquence to the style. Mercy upon us, how I would belabour that poor King of the French under the influence of absinthe, in that café opposite the Bourse where I used to make my letter! Who knows, sir, perhaps the influence of those letters precipitated the fall of the Bourbon dynasty! Before I had an office, Gilligan, of the *Century*, and I, used to do our letters at that café; we compared notes and pitched into each other amicably.' (X, 349)

The opinionated self-importance of Philip (who, at times, has as much bluster about him as his fraudulent father) is punctured by Thackeray's assessment of his world.

> Gilligan of the *Century*, and Firmin of the *Pall Mall Gazette*, were however, very minor personages amongst the London newspaper correspondents. Their seniors of the daily press had handsome apartments, gave sumptuous dinners, were closeted with ministers' secretaries, and entertained members of the Chamber of Deputies. Philip, on perfectly easy terms with himself and the world, swaggering about the embassy balls – Philip, the friend and relative of Lord Ringwood – was viewed by his professional seniors and superiors with an eye of favour, which was not certainly turned on all gentlemen following his calling. (X, 350)

Phil's class background, his aristocratic connection, gains him access to the drawing-rooms of Paris and the kind of information he seeks to enliven his correspondence. Certainly, Thackeray gained something of this himself, possibly through Eyre Evans Crowe and possibly through his own connections. The hack-writers, of lower-class and non-university background, are mere penny-a-liners, watching the European histories from the café tables.

Philip is intended as an unusual character here. He mediates between classes and responds as well in the tavern as the ballroom, that is, equally fiery and often lacking in control of his temper. Unlike his contemporary Philip Pirrip, Pip, in *Great Expectations*, there is no snobbery about Phil. He is an anti-Snob. However, his prejudices are based around race and not class.

Philip is classless, or, rather, like Thackeray, Becky Sharp and Clive Newcome, he crosses class boundaries throughout the novel. Promised the life of a gentleman, he loses his inheritance, and accepts with equanimity the life of work now required. Establishing his household with Charlotte Baynes on a minimal income, and continuing to pay off the bad debts of his unscrupulous father who draws bills on his son continuously, Philip makes a tolerably happy life for himself and his family in the lower, shabby genteel world. But the wealth he obtains at the end of the novel through the ludicrously melodramatic accident of Woolcomb's coach – the negro target of much of Philip's resentment in the novel – in which Woolcomb discovers the will that legitimizes Philip, is a shift which destabilizes the values of Philip's character and signification. 'And was the tawny Woolcomb the fairy who was to rescue Philip from his grief, debt, and poverty? Yes', we are told (XI, 334). This reversal of fortune removes Philip from the world of journalism and he quickly leaves his colleagues behind. The newspaper world remains outside of the sphere of comfortable gentility. Papers are read by the wealthy and assist in constructing their fashionable status, but the writing of them is marginalized. The family also excludes the press, as it does the threat of interracial usurpation. At the end of the novel, the three societies of Thackeray's three modern novels come together for dinner at Clive Newcome's; Pendennis, Clive and Philip, Laura, Ethel and Charlotte, sit down and plan marriages between their own children. Just as the worlds of the Esmonds and Warringtons entwine in the historical novels of *Henry Esmond* and *The Virginians*, so Thackeray's modern characters shelter each other in a close world removed from the rigours of the public sphere in which they work, write, and paint. Cassidy and Gilligan, pressmen of Irish race, are forgotten. Yet Thackeray's own marriage was cross-cultural and he was re-embracing the periodical world as he wrote *Philip*.

The newspaper press in *The Adventures of Philip* is international in outlook and sphere. Where the earlier novels tended to use the London newspapers as reference points,[71] with the occasional mention of *Galignani's Messenger* when the characters were in Paris, *Philip* develops more of the world press. As Thackeray did in his own career, Philip finds himself working for a variety of newspapers, in different countries, and frequently changing his post. Several of his opportunities are temporary chores. He writes Smith's 'letter' for the *Daily Intelligencer* for ten francs a day, while he takes a month's holiday (XI, 7). Subsequently, the connection made, he works as a translator for the London daily: 'Phipps, of the *Daily Intelligencer*, wanting an assistant, Philip gladly sold four hours of his day to Mr. Phipps: translated page after page of newspapers, French and German; took an occasional turn at the Chamber of

Deputies, and gave an account of a sitting of importance, and made himself quite an active lieutenant' (XI, 39). Later in the novel, Tom Glazier of the *Monitor* does Phil's work for two weeks whilst he visits Charlotte in London: 'All the designs of France, Spain, Russia, gave that idle "own correspondent" not the slightest anxiety' (XI, 138). On his return, Philip continues his arduous work in between his ardour of love, and writes for one day in the week retaining the other six for his love-letters to Charlotte (XI, 140). He 'composed his eloquent "own correspondence"' at his Paris café (XI, 152). But, remarks Thackeray, 'no doubt Philip's political letters became, under this outward pressure, very desponding and gloomy' (XI, 141). Once again, he hints that the personal world invades the public sphere in a manner of which the newspaper reader will not be aware. As he would comment elsewhere, the serial writer is at the mercy of his illnesses and emotions; the pen cannot stop when the body or mind is weak, as income depends on the sheets supplied.[72] But throughout all of Philip's foreign work, there seems to be no genuine investment in or empowerment of the Other.

Next, we hear of Michael Cassidy, Philip's Irish friend and colleague, who departs from the sub-editor's post on the *Pall Mall Gazette* to become the editor of a new Dublin paper called the *Shamrock*. Thackeray comments on the advertisements for this new paper and recalls the political tensions of the day: issued on St Patrick's Day, it boasted 'the most famous pens of the national party in Ireland', 'illustrious advocates, whose manly voices had ever spoken the language of hope and freedom to an &c. &c ... ' (XI, 155). Thackeray clearly sounds unimpressed by the Irish movement of the time, but has only a sardonic view of Irish nationalism in the period after the famine as Philip, of course, is written in 1861. Cassidy intends his post to go to one of 'scores of gentlemen of his nation, who would not object to take the Saxon's pay until they finally shook his yoke off, and would eat his bread until the happy moment arrived when they could knock out his brains in a fair battle' (XI, 155). Cassidy, though, is a comment on Philip, who is also exploiting the foreign. The ideal and the mercantile real are divided throughout.

Cassidy's departure heralds Philip's promotion to the post of sub-editor on the *Pall Mall Gazette*. This was another post Thackeray held in the 1830s. The employment shows just how imitative and plagiaristic the press of the day could be, as summarized earlier. Philip is described by a laughing Pen as:

> ... installed in the sub-editor's room, with a provision of scissors, wafers, and paste-pots, snipping paragraphs from this paper and that, altering, condensing, giving titles, and so forth; and, in a word, in regular harness ... When his paper was completed at the week's end, he surveyed it fondly – not the leading articles, or those profound and yet brilliant literary essays which appeared in the *Gazette* – but the births, deaths, marriages, markets, trials, and what not. (XI, 163)

Although Philip is attracted by his own domain, 'fondly' overseeing it, this is a familiar Thackerayan view of the newspapers. As he comments earlier in the novel, the kind of historical material that the newspapers will provide the scholars of the future is not to be found in the 'authoritative' editorials, but in the miscellaneous business further down the pages. 'A score of years hence, men will read the papers of 1861 for the occurrences narrated – births, marriages, bankruptcies, elections, murders, deaths, and so forth; and not for the leading articles', he writes (XI, 2).

There is a simple rule of house in the work for the *Pall Mall Gazette*: be faithful to your own. Philip's duties begin on a Tuesday, we are told:

> ... snipping and pasting paragraphs for the ensuing Saturday's issue. He cut down parliamentary speeches, giving due favouritism to the orators of the *Pall Mall Gazette* party, and meagre outlines of their opponents' discourses. If the leading public men on the side of the *Pall Mall Gazette* gave entertainments, you may be sure they were duly chronicled in the fashionable intelligence; if one of their party wrote a book it was pretty sure to get praise from the critic. I am speaking of simple old days, you understand. Of course there is *no* puffing, or jobbing, or false praise, or unfair censure now. Every critic knows what he is writing about, and writes with no aim but to tell truth. (XI, 167)

Of course, the irony is clear here. Thackeray is both describing a past historical period of the press, and also questioning whether the press of his day is really any different. Despite a more professional approach to journalism in the 1860s, Thackeray finds the same human weaknesses present.

Philip's career covers many of the less exciting occupations of the early Victorian newspaperman. His future is not bound into writerly success, and thus he can represent periodical drudgery and the average journalist rather than the prospective success of Pendennis. Indeed, Thackeray's constant reminder to the reader that Philip is happy in the future and has none of the cares described in the book, suggests how Phil's life is seen as a trial of his strength of personality and not a middle-class trade. Looking back from the prosperity of the 1860s, Thackeray enjoys the energy of the journalistic world once again, but also depicts its poverty. Of course, the contrast with the periodicals of the 1860s is also present in the text. It is worth remembering that newspapers had greatly increased in circulation by the time Thackeray wrote *Philip*, and the profession was on firmer footing than ever before. His association with younger magazine writers like Sala and Yates must have made him conscious of the difference in standing that the profession held in just those few years. For a periodical like the *Cornhill Magazine* to have a circulation of 100,000 was unheard of in the 1830s and early 1840s.

Another international aspect of *Philip* is cultivated through the New York papers introduced in the second half of the novel. These operate on a principle which is more personality orientated than the English papers, but clearly intended to suggest the direction of news reporting in some parts of the London media. Thackeray comments on the publicity element in the

American press: he had experienced this himself whilst touring the country with his lectures in the 1850s and written a satirical piece for *Fraser's Magazine* on the art of American reporting.[73] Thackeray juxtaposes *Galignani's Messenger*'s report of a fight at a ball between Philip and Twysden Ringwood with the same in an American paper called the *New York Emerald*, 'one of the most brilliant and influential journals of the city' (XI, 88). Phil's father sends Philip the report and suggests:

> ... the correspondent of the *Emerald* makes some droll blunders regarding you in his letter. We are all fair game for publicity in this country, where the press is free *with a vengeance*; and your private affairs, or mine, or the President's, or our gracious Queen's, for the matter of that, are discussed with a freedom which certainly *amounts to licence*. (XI, 88)

The London correspondent who writes the 'Letters from an Attaché' is more interested in celebrity and gossip than genuine reporting. But his work is only one step away from the personal reviewing of literature and stage that Pen exposes elsewhere. Thackeray clearly also has in mind the various pieces dealing with himself over the years: including the Garrick affair in the late 1850s. 'In this way, history is written', he writes. 'I dare say about others besides Philip, in English papers as well as American, have fables been narrated' (XI, 89).

It is an irony of the text, and an indication of the desperation of newspaper journalists, that Philip's next appointment is as London correspondent for another American periodical, the *Gazette of the Upper Ten Thousand*. Its class arrogance shows how far Philip's morals have been compromised. Immediately following the censure of modern critics for their puffing of personalities, and the *Pall Mall Gazette's* partisan politics in the sub-editor's choice of material, Thackeray introduces Philip to the American press. Philip's father, Dr Firmin, is exiled in America and pursuing a quack livelihood of more or less illegitimate speculations. He hears of Phil's 'drudgery of the press' and adds in a letter:

> It has been despised, and press-man and poverty were for a long time supposed to be synonymous. But the power, the wealth of the press are daily developing, and they will increase yet further. (XI, 174)

An indication of the potential of the press for profitability is felt in the Doctor's own move into the arena. His friend has established the *Gazette of the Upper Ten Thousand*, and the reader is led to suspect that the Doctor has more than a friendly helping hand in mind when he suggests Philip should become the London correspondent (indeed, he asks his friend the proprietor to pay *him* on Philip's behalf, XI, 202). The proprietor of the American paper eventually flees with the profits and Philip is never paid (XI, 210).[74] The proposed employment is as London fashionable correspondent; 'Political treatises are not so much wanted as personal news regarding the notabilities of London ... Suppose you were to trust a little to your imagination in composing these letters? ... Anecdotes of men and women of fashion – the more gay and lively the more welcome ... ' (XI, 175). This is not really Philip's way, although he takes the post. His friends help him to gather (and create) material for the column: 'We happened to overhear the most remarkable conversations between the most influential public characters who had no secrets from us' (XI, 197). They remain good-natured and 'nobody was wounded' by their remarks. However, the material is not wholly suitable. Dr Firmin writes again to his son to inform him:

> ... your Philalethes' letters are not *quite spicy* enough ... They are *elegant and gay*, but the public here desires to have *more personal news; a little scandal about Queen Elizabeth*, you understand? Can't you attack somebody? Look at the letters and articles published by my respected friend of the *New York Emerald*! The readers here like a *high-spiced article*: and I recommend P. F. to put a little more pepper in his dishes. (XI, 202)

Thackeray had written for an American paper, the *Corsair*, in the late 1830s, and the *Gazette* here may be a parody of that newspaper. But the only Club-land gossip column of a comparable kind known in Thackeray's writings so far is his work for the *Calcutta Star* in the early 1840s.

At the death of the *Gazette of the Upper Ten Thousand*, after six months, Philip is fortunate to become involved with another foreign venture: the *European Review*, founded by Sir John Tregarvan, a Cornish MP. The editor's aim for the review is to:

> ... expose the designs of the Great Power which was menacing Europe. He would show up in his proper colours a Minister who was careless of the country's honour, and forgetful of his own: a Minister whose arrogance ought no longer to be tolerated by the country gentlemen of England. (XI, 210)

Such sentiments demonstrate the tensions in European culture of the time. But it also shows how strongly a magazine can be founded on negative principles, as a pro-English and anti-French mouthpiece. Francophobia sells. Philip becomes the sub-editor and a contributor. In later years (in the context of the novel), Philip tells Pendennis about his writing for the *European Review*. Reading it:

> I came upon an article of my own, and a very dull one, on a subject which I knew nothing about. 'Persian politics, and the intrigues at the Court of Teheran.' It was done to order...the facts (we will call them facts) and papers were supplied to me, and I went home to point out the delinquencies of Sir Thomas [Nobbes], and the atrocious intrigues of the Russian Court. (XI, 213)

This is the paper that Philip is left with after a temperamental argument with Mugford of the *Pall Mall Gazette* that loses him his sub-editorship. Towards the end of the novel, he is reinstated by Mugford, but finally released from this catalogue of periodical workmanship by the recovery of his aristocratic fortunes.

It is an interesting feature of *The Adventures of Philip* that it should polarize gentlemanliness and journalism in the manner that it does. However, unlike *Pendennis* which proffers a similar binary, *Philip* also creates a binary between Englishness and foreignness which equates to this other polarity. Although Philip gains in manliness by his writerly 'poverty', there is never any doubt that his final reward will be a more aristocratic one. In addition, despite his assumed Parisian Bohemianism and intercontinental literary productions, in the final chapters of the book it is his racial intolerance that comes to the fore. The textual dealings with foreign news and history tend to have a falsity about them present in the newspaper and magazine because of the interplay between public and private spheres. The journalist creates as much as he reports; politics and ideology, necessity and gain are all bound up in the industrial production of writing. The *Shamrock*, the *Gazette of the Upper Ten Thousand* and the *European Review* hold basically racist attitudes and promote their image of 'worldliness' only to extend their readership by baser ideologies.

The ambivalent status of the journalist is a good example of the intricacies of textual authority. Many of the characters in the book hold themselves up as models and as representatives of current important taste and thought. Mugford and Tregarvan are both magazine proprietors who have airs about them of their own importance. The Colonel of the *Gazette of the Upper Ten Thousand* uses his magazine for his own unscrupulous gains. None of these characters, Pendennis included, would see themselves as lower class in their profession. Dr Firmin's comments about the current rise in status of the writer hides a deeper anxiety about the reality of this rise. Philip, on the other hand, retains a sense of himself as a worker in a new industrial process. He shows how his work provides bread directly, as a direct result of his labour, and not via the labour of others. Pendennis/Thackeray comes to recognize the point:

> Ah! how wonderful ways and means are! When I think how this very line, this very word, which I am writing represents money, I am lost in respectful astonishment. A man takes his own case, as he says his own prayers, on behalf of himself and his family. I am paid, we will say, for the sake of illustration, at the rate of six-pence per line. With the words, 'Ah, how wonderful,' to the words 'per line,' I can buy a loaf, a piece of butter, a jug of milk, a modicum of tea ... (XI, 238)

Philip has no snobbery about his profession, and accepts the labour it requires. Indeed, the reviewer in the *Saturday Review* found the 'candour of authorship' was pushed to an extreme in the novel.[75] Philip's position is that of the worker, his expectations are no higher than the finding of a basic wage. The

Little Sister has higher ambitions for him, however, and cannot accept the inherent poverty of the life of a journalist for her Philip even though her own life offers a parallel to his. The gulf between gentlemanliness and journalism finds an affirmative voice in Caroline's; the reader is left to feel that she is right:

> 'Suppose you quarrel with your newspaper masters, and your reviews, and that, you lose your place. A gentleman like Mr. Philip oughtn't to have a master. I couldn't bear to think of your going down of a Saturday to the publishing office to get your wages like a workman.'
> 'But *I am* a workman,' interposes Philip.
> 'La! But do you mean to remain one forever? I would rise, if I was a man!' (XI, 238)

Any implied democracy in Thackeray's views of the profession are unclear. He sees Philip's position as that of worker, and subject to the exploitation of the worker. Philip cannot assert himself and his own personality. As soon as he does, he loses his post (XI, 304).[76] But Thackeray also sees the profession as low, the province of the failure. Philip makes more of himself when he begins to take on law cases as an advocate. His role in the local elections as a speech maker for the opposition to Woolcomb's campaign offers another dimension to the character and suggests again a more dignified status for Philip. However, the speeches he makes, and their implicit racism, are an uncomfortable ending for a novel of foreign affairs.

The main slogan of Philip's anti-Woolcomb campaign, an ugly satire based on his mulatto colour, is 'Are you white slaves to be sold to that fellow?' (XI, 303). It is Tregarvan of the *European Review* who proposed Woolcomb as candidate for Whipham, and the connection makes an obvious parallel to the 'slavery' of the journalist, only based on bigotry and racism rather than realism. The election becomes a racial one promoted by the newspapers. Phipps of the *Daily Intelligencer* places a placard in the window of the 'Ram' public house: 'no WEST INDIAN, no CASTLE FLUNKEY, but a TRUE ENGLISH GENTLEMAN' is needed to challenge Woolcomb (XI, 323-4). The candidate found is Philip's old schoolfriend, Mr Hornblow. The campaign is fought on the grounds of English purity: Woolcomb is caricatured by J.J. Ridley as a 'dusky charioteer', and described as a man 'who could not spell or speak two sentences of decent English' (XI, 327). It is his personal character which is emphasized beyond this, however; he is impudent and mean, and brutal to his wife (Philip's old flame, Agnes). Throughout the book, he is seen as the 'Black Prince' and 'Othello'. Philip's final triumph is to launch a cart and effigy of Woolcomb, driven by a negro bearing a placard announcing: 'VOTE FOR ME! AM I NOT A MAN AND A BRUDDER?' (XI, 331). The words parody Thackeray's own usage of the phrase as a call for equality in *Vanity Fair*, and perhaps raise the colonial issue in relation to the American Civil War of 1861.[77] But the aggression shows the brutal and Anglo-centric side of

Philip. Indeed, the narrator refers to Philip's own basic primitiveness: 'there was no reasoning with this savage [i.e. Philip] when in wrath' (XI, 328). Pendennis also claims the authenticity of his portrait to include the flaws in Philip's character: 'I don't set [Philip] up for a moment as a person to be revered or imitated; but try to draw him faithfully, and as nature made him' (X, 294).

The pantomime finale, with Woolcomb's upturned carriage breaking open to reveal the will that re-establishes Philip's fortunes, closes the narrative in an awkward manner. Philip's fortune comes about as a result of his opposition to the foreign Other, where his work to promote truthful representation in the press comes to nothing. Yet this textual representation is itself parodied in the newspaper sloganism of the campaign run by Phipps of the *Daily Intelligencer*. Woolcomb wins the election, as he knows he will, having already secured the majority of the votes, and the anti-black campaign appears rather an aggressive gesture than a critique. The novel is not ready for a hero of foreign journalism; Philip's future lies in the casual gentility of the moneyed English gentleman.

For a writer who began with so many hopes and desires to establish a cultural understanding of the French, it is a rather poor ending. *The Adventures of Philip*, in the end, has lost sight of the 1830s and the grand designs of the *Constitutional*. The journalist, a slave to his financial desperation, cannot be the paragon of Englishness. An understanding of foreignness is not to be found in the experiences of the foreign correspondent. Foreignness is as much a mediated discourse as any other in the media; Thackeray tries, in *Philip*, to deconstruct its authority and to expose the media influence on popular racism. But, unable to escape his own mediation, the novel does not quite dispose of the polarity of self and Other.

Perhaps Thackeray's last completed novel fails for this reason more than any other. Its roots lie in the expansion of the press in the 1830s, and in particular in the opening up of European and American cultural exchanges during the 1830s and 1840s. But it needs to engage with the attitudes of the 1860s, in a context of Indian mutinies and the American Civil War (almost prophesied by Thackeray in *The Virginians*). The final irony of this novel is that its novelistic status seems to be established above the lower-class forms of journalism depicted within its pages, whilst its own status as a magazine serial economized at a penny-a-line is not problematised. It may be the anxieties of Thackeray's return to the *Cornhill Magazine* and the magazine serial that produces the ambiguities towards journalism seen here. It may also be the nature of the *Cornhill* readership that dictates something of the ending of Thackeray's novel. These problems, however, surface throughout Thackeray's career. He is never at ease with the journalistic voice, and his continuous endeavours to negotiate the new forms of production in his professional career demonstrate his uncertainties. The confused 'candour' in his attitudes towards race, particularly black America, is distracting and has certainly, in today's context, distracted critics, but this should not eclipse the author's innovative endeavour to deconstruct press authority regarding the representation of the Other.

Notes

[1] S.S. Prawer, *Israel at Vanity Fair: Jews and Judaism in the Writings of W.M. Thackeray* (Leiden, New York: E. Brill, 1992); Deborah S. Thomas, *Thackeray and Slavery* (Athens: Ohio University Press, 1993); S.S. Prawer, *Breeches and Metaphysics: Thackeray's German Discourse* (Oxford: Legenda, 1997).
[2] Robert E. Lougy, 'The Dynamics of Exile and Desire: Narrative Form and Meaning in Thackeray's *Notes of a Journey from Cornhill to Grand Cairo*', *Modern Language Quarterly*, 50 (1989), 228.
[3] Thackeray distinguished between the 'tourist' and the 'traveller' ('Europe is abandoned to the mere tourists') in his review of Puckler Muskau's *Egypt under Mehmet Ali*, *Morning Chronicle* (27 March 1845); Ray, *Contributions*, 65.
[4] *The Adventures of Philip*, *Works*, XI, 17 [references in the text are to this edition].
[5] Gordon N. Ray, 'Thackeray and France', 283-4.
[6] Undated letters attributed to 1835, *Letters*, I, 502; to John Payne Collier, 2 April 1835, *Letters*, I, 281; letter to Edward Fitzgerald, May 1835, *Letters*, I, 287-8; see Richard Pearson, '"The Public likes light literature"', for further comments on this.
[7] *Letters*, I, 159.
[8] Letter to Mrs. Carmichael-Smyth, 22-30 October 1833; *Letters*, I, 268.
[9] *National Standard*, 34 (24 August 1833).
[10] Ray, *Uses*, 88; P. Collins (ed.), *Thackeray: Interviews and Recollections*, 2 vols (London: Macmillan, 1983), I, 11-12.
[11] Letter to John Mitchell Kemble, 13 December 1836; *Letters*, I, 325; Ray, *Uses*, 189.
[12] Letter to Mrs. Carmichael-Smyth, 6 July 1833; *Letters*, I, 262.
[13] Peters, *Universe*, 61.
[14] Letter to Mrs. Carmichael-Smyth, 6 July 1833; Letters, I, 262-3.
[15] *National Standard*, 57 (1 February 1834).
[16] Letter to Isabella Shawe, 10 April 1836; *Letters*, I, 301.
[17] Letter to Isabella Shawe, 14 April 1836; *Letters*, I, 302-3.
[18] Little study has been devoted to the *Constitutional*, but general accounts are in Ray, *Uses*, 184-5, 190-3; C.P. Johnson, *The Early Writings of William Makepeace Thackeray* (London: Elliot Stock, 1888), 28-34.
[19] See, for example, Louis James, *Fiction for the Working Man, 1830-1850: A Study of the Literature Produced for the Working Classes in Early Victorian*

Urban England (Oxford: OUP, 1963) and *Print and the People, 1819-1851* (London: Allen Lane, 1976).

[20] For the arguments, see William E. Hickson, 'Reduction, or Abolition, of the Stamp Duty on Newspapers', *London Review*, 2 (January 1836), 336-55, and 'Proposed Reduction of the Stamp Duty on Newspapers', *London and Westminster Review*, 25 (April–July 1836), 264-70; for 'persecutions' by the Stamp Office Agents see the columns of reports of such in, for instance, *The Working Man's Friend and Political Magazine*, 1 (22 December 1832), and following weeks.

[21] Aled Jones, *Powers of the Press: Newspapers, Power, and the Public in Nineteenth Century England* (Aldershot: Scolar Press, 1996), 4.

[22] See A. Aspinall, *Politics and the Press, c.1780-1850* (London: Home and Van Thal, 1949); Lucy Brown, *Victorian News and Newspapers* (Oxford: OUP, 1985); G.A. Cranfield, *The Press and Society: From Caxton to Northcliffe* (London: Longman, 1978); Derek Hudson, *Thomas Barnes of 'The Times'*, With Critical Essays edited by Harold Child (Cambridge: CUP, 1944); Joel H. Weiner (ed.), *Innovators and Preachers: The Role of the Editor in Victorian England* (Westport, CT.: Greenwood Press, 1985).

[23] Thackeray commented on this in 'French Romancers on England', *Foreign Quarterly Review*, 32 (October 1843), 226, 'when you are once at the conclusion of the debates in the "Times", you are not called upon to peruse the same orations in the "Post" or the "Advertiser": which each luckily contains precisely the same matter'.

[24] 'The Morning and Evening Papers', *Fraser's Magazine*, 13 (May 1836), 631.

[25] Joanne Shattock, *Politics and Reviewers: The Edinburgh and the Quarterly in the early Victorian age* (Leicester: Leicester University Press, 1989), 15-20.

[26] For a general introduction, see Brown, *Newspapers*, who deals mostly with the later nineteenth century.

[27] See an item on Turkey, 1 September 1836, p. 2, col. 1 and an article on p. 3, col. 3.

[28] See 'The State of Spain', 8 September 1836, p. 4, col. 2.

[29] James Grant, *The Newspaper Press: Its Origins–Progress–and Present Position*, 3 vols (London: Tinsley Brothers, 1871-2), I, 321, 324; Grant was editor of the *Morning Advertiser*.

[30] Thackeray subbed for one Battier, Paris correspondent for the *Morning Advertiser*, and a contributor to *Galignani's Messenger*, in March-April 1838; letter to Mrs. Carmichael-Smythe, 15-17 March 1838; *Letters*, I, 119.

[31] *Morning Advertiser*, 6 September 1836; 7 September 1836.

[32] A. Sullivan (ed.), *British Literary Magazines, Vol. II: The Romantic Age, 1789-1836*; *Vol. III: The Victorian and Edwardian Age, 1837-1913* (Westport, CT.: Greenwood Press, 1983, 1984), II and appendix to vol. III; John Forster was the literary editor.

[33] *Standard*, 1 September 1836, p. 2, col. 1.

[34] See my preface to Eyre Crowe, *With Thackeray in America* (London: Routledge/Thoemmes Press, 1996), v-vii.

[35] *Letters*, I, 325 and n.
[36] *Letters*, I, 283.
[37] See Chapter 7 below.
[38] Kathryn Chittick, *Dickens and the 1830s* (Cambridge: CUP, 1990), 3-4.
[39] September 1836; *Letters*, I, 322-3.
[40] *Constitutional*, 15 September 1836, p. 2, col. 5; reprinted in Gulliver, 54.
[41] Ibid.
[42] *Constitutional*, 9 November 1836, p. 3, col. 2.
[43] Johnson, *Early Writings*, 29.
[44] *Letters*, I, 341-2.
[45] John Sheehan; letter September 1836, *Letters*, I, 320-21; Sheehan later worked for the *Morning Herald* with another *Constitutional* journalist, Dudley Costello – the latter also worked for the *Daily News*.
[46] *Constitutional*, 16 November 1836, p. 3, col. 3.
[47] Ibid.
[48] *Constitutional*, 1 December 1836, p. 3, col. 4.
[49] Notably in 'Going to See a Man Hanged' and 'The Case of Peytel'.
[50] Contrast this with Dickens' views, who tended to oppose *public* executions, and capital punishment generally, but remained 'moderate' in his overall opinions; see Philip Collins, *Dickens and Crime* (London: Macmillan, 1962), 220-49.
[51] *Constitutional*, 14 November 1836, p. 3, col. 2.
[52] *Constitutional*, 8 December 1836, p. 3, col. 4.
[53] *Constitutional*, 19 December 1836, p. 3, cols 1-2.
[54] An early hint of 'Mr. Brown's Letters to a Young Man about Town', *Punch*, 24 March 1849 - 18 August 1849.
[55] *Constitutional*, 19 December 1836, p. 3, col. 1.
[56] *Constitutional*, 2 January 1837, p. 3, cols 1-3.
[57] *Constitutional*, 10 January 1837, p. 3, cols 2-3.
[58] *Constitutional*, 21 January 1837, p. 3, col. 3.
[59] *Constitutional*, 24 January 1837, p. 3, col. 1.
[60] See the writings discussed in Chapter 5; see also Richard Pearson, 'W.M. Thackeray: An Uncollected Paris Letter from the *Constitutional* (1836-37)', *Notes and Queries*, 238: 4 (December 1993), 474-7.
[61] *Constitutional*, 11 February 1837, p. 3, cols 5-6; reprinted in Pearson, ibid.
[62] Gulliver, 53; the view persists in Edgar Harden, *Thackeray the Writer: From Journalism to 'Vanity Fair'* (London: Macmillan, 1998), 10.
[63] Joseph E. Baker, 'Thackeray's Recantation', *PMLA*, 77 (1962), 586-94, retitled '*The Adventures of Philip*' in A. Welsh (ed.) *Thackeray: A Collection of Critical Essays* (New Jersey: Prentice-Hall, 1968); John Sutherland, 'Thackeray as Victorian Racist', *Essays in Criticism*, 20 (1970), 441-5; Deborah A. Thomas, *Thackeray and Slavery* (Athens: Ohio University Press, 1993); John Peck, 'Racism in the Mid-Victorian Novel: Thackeray's *Philip*' in Gary Day (ed.), *Varieties of Victorianism: The Uses of a Past* (Macmillan, 1998), 127, 129.

[64] Peck, 131, 134, 136, 137.
[65] Thomas, *Slavery*, places the racial theme within a debate about 'truth', which is seen as the central subject of the novel, 169-87; Baker makes a telling point, again not furthered, when he comments on Philip's attachment to the *European Review*, arguing 'Philip is for sale and takes the job gratefully, without any thought as to the damage such journalism might do to the nation', 167.
[66] Juliet McMaster, 'Funeral Baked Meats: Thackeray's Last Novel', *Studies in the Novel*, 13 (1981), 133-55; this point is followed further in Chapter 9 below which considers the novel's 'sensational' context.
[67] Peck suggests, in a quite contradictory manner I believe, that, with Miss Swartz, Thackeray has a 'particular animus' for 'a black character with money', 127.
[68] *The Adventures of Philip*, *Works*, X, 210 [references in the text are to this edition].
[69] Ibid., 258 he is 'slow at his reading'; this continues from *The Newcomes*, *Works*, V, 137.
[70] The notion of the 'seasonality' of the press reflects another aspect of its commercial design.
[71] See R.D. McMaster, *Thackeray's Cultural Frame of Reference: Allusion in 'The Newcomes'* (London: Macmillan, 1991).
[72] See, for example, chapter 36 of *Pendennis*, *Works*, III, 392.
[73] 'Mr. Thackeray in the United States: John Small to the Editor of *Fraser's Magazine*', *Fraser's Magazine*, 47 (January 1853).
[74] Thackeray's relationship with N.P. Willis of the *Corsair* was similar, see Ray, *Uses*, 200; Peter L. Shillingsburg, *Pegasus in Harness: Victorian Publishing and W.M. Thackeray* (Charlottesville: University Press of Virginia, 1992), 38; Shillingsburg, 56, also notes that Thackeray contributed to an Indian paper (possibly the *Calcutta Star*) and an unidentified American paper owned by Henry Wikoff in January and February 1844.
[75] [Anon.], *Saturday Review*, 14 (23 August 1862), 223-4; reprinted in G. Tillotson and D. Hawes (eds), *Thackeray: The Critical Heritage* (Routledge and Kegan Paul, 1968), 311.
[76] Philip loses his *Gazette* and his *European Review* posts after quarrels; his idealism does not suit the profession.
[77] Thomas, *Slavery*, 159-61.

Chapter 4

Journalistic metamorphoses: women, sensationalism, and periodical fiction – *Catherine: A Story* and *The Ravenswing* in *Fraser's Magazine*

There have been several studies of Thackeray's portrayal of women and female characters, including the recent book-length analysis by Micael Clarke.[1] In this chapter, I intend to focus on two early serial tales from *Fraser's Magazine*, *Catherine: A Story* (May 1839-February 1840) and (from the series *Men's Wives*) *The Ravenswing* (April-September 1843), both of which deal in some way with the media representation of women and, more specifically, Thackeray's deconstruction of this. I do not intend to follow the lines of investigation pursued by Clarke, into the relationship between Thackeray's work and the women's movement or women writers of the period. Instead, I wish to emphasize the theme of the mediation of the female by the male-dominated media, and how this has a bearing on Thackeray's sense of the imprisoning of the female in social and literary structures of his time. Although *Catherine* is a historical novel, set in the period of Queen Anne, between 1705 and 1726 (it is carefully dated), as Clarke has noted, it deals with several issues relating to the condition of women in the 1839-40 period in which it was written. Indeed, the narrator, Ikey Solomons, writes from his male prison in 1840.

Thackeray was interested in 'mediated visibility', or the 'managing of visibility' in the emergent public sphere.[2] This is part of a series of themes, such as the creation and manipulation of the female image in the magazine text, the transforming of materials from 'rawness' into culturally commercial commodities, and the gratification of pleasure and desire through the manipulation of others (readers/sexes). In *Vanity Fair*, an association might be perceived between Becky Sharp and the author, as manipulators of self-images, an important consideration for my arguments about Thackeray's perception of a market.[3] Such a theme in his work has its origins in the early fiction, where it is also closely associated with the media and how public personae may be generated through text. Thackeray's writing in the late 1830s and early 1840s began to take his critique of the press into areas that subsequently inform his fictional processes in the major novels. The closeness between the magazine form of publication (here, *Fraser's Magazine*) and the story, further increases this sense of Thackeray's conscious engagement with the new structures of literary industry. Commerce and trade are central themes, too, transposed into the realm of romance and marriage, but in a more subtle way than in the writings of Dickens, for example. Thackeray's work within the world of magazinery and journalism pervades his sense of cultural semiotics and how they affect our appearance in contemporary life.

Catherine and *The Ravenswing* position the central female (identified in the title of the first, and, in the second, inscribed as an image which is itself symbolic of her commodification) within a network of male controllers and shapers. The first story is a parody of the Newgate school of fiction, represented by such contemporaries as Bulwer-Lytton, Harrison Ainsworth, and the Dickens of *Oliver Twist*. It centres upon the seduction and betrayal of a young inn maid, Catherine Hall, by an aristocrat, Count Maximillian von Galgenstein. Based on a report in the *Newgate Calendar*, the plot follows Catherine's attempt on the Count's life, her married life to a childhood suitor, John Hayes, and the misery of this, her reclaiming of the son she had produced by the Count, his reappearance on the scene, and her murder of Hayes in order to free herself to marry the Count. The Count has no real intention of marrying her, however. In the final scene, the lovers' tryst in a churchyard is interrupted by the sight of Hayes' head on a pole (so placed by the local sheriffs to assist in identification), and the Count falls into madness and Catherine is doomed to be burned at the stake. Thackeray attempts to mock the reader's predilection for violent crime fiction and his contemporaries' tendencies to romanticize the criminal world, by showing the reality of this world and the unpleasantness of the people who inhabit it. As critics have noted, he felt the attempt was a failure as he retained 'a sneaking kindness for his heroine, and did not like to make her utterly worthless'.[4] However, the story shows much more than this, and represents a significant step in Thackeray's development as a writer of fiction. In particular, he dramatizes themes that will remain as distinct concerns in the later writings.

There are three main areas of interest here. History, for Thackeray, is composed of text. In *Catherine*, he makes use of contemporary newspapers and magazines as 'realistic' interventions in the Romance narrative. In the figure of Corporal Brock, later Captain Wood and later still the Rev. Doctor Wood, he creates an author-figure who manipulates the action for his own pleasure. And, finally, he brings together the serial form and the theme of desire to explore the excitement of delay and deferral in terms of character and reader psychology. Micael Clarke has compared the figures of Catherine and Caroline Gann in the unfinished *A Shabby Genteel Story* (1841), and one might add to this point that the sensationalism of the story and its interest in the grotesque are later to be expanded in *The Adventures of Philip*, a novel which derives in part from the narrative of *A Shabby Genteel Story*. As elsewhere in his writings, Thackeray frequently returns to earlier magazinery in order to furnish the inspiration for later works.

As well as being a response to romance writers, *Catherine* forms part of a tradition of magazine parody and satire which was in keeping with the editorial ethos of *Fraser's Magazine*. Indeed, the most immediate precursor of the story, and one which Thackeray probably knew, was William Maginn's parody, 'Elizabeth Brownrigge: A Tale', which appeared in *Fraser's Magazine*, August-September 1832. Thackeray has been attributed with the authorship of this tale, but it was not his.[5] Another comparison is with comic fiction. Thackeray illustrated Douglas Jerrold's series of moral tales, *Men of Character* (1839), which included 'Isaac Cheek: the "Man of Wax"', a tale about a proprietor of a failing wax-works exhibition:

> The present wax-seeing people, sir, require excitement; their bowels are only to be come at through blood ... my figure of Mrs Brownrigg brings showers of shillings ... while the Venus de Medicis takes never a farthing.[6]

Jerrold's tale uses Maginn's Newgate heroine to suggest the difficulty of high art competing with popular sensationalism in the current market. Jerrold also used the name 'Brownrigg' for a series of stories in the *New Monthly Magazine* in 1838-9. He was accused of a similar means of profiteering; some years earlier, Samuel Warren had complained to the editor of *Blackwood's* that 'Jerrold was marring the respectability of that distinguished periodical by his "vulgar" stories'.[7]

Maginn's parody is simpler and more direct that Thackeray's. He claims a similar intention, but the execution is more straightforward and unambivalent in its morality.

> I had attempted to excite the sympathies of the audience in favour of the murdered apprentices, but your novel has disabused me of so vulgar a prejudice, and, in my present version of her case, all the interest of the reader and all the pathetic powers of the author will be engaged on the side of the murderess.[8]

Bulwer-Lytton and his novel, *Eugene Aram*, were the main targets; indeed, Bulwer appeared in the *Fraser's* 'Gallery of Literary Characters' in his capacity as novelist and editor of the *New Monthly Magazine* in the same month's edition (August 1832). In the story, the foppish Alphonso Belvidere is 'distinguished among literary men as the editor of a new monthly magazine'.[9] But this story also gives a hint to Thackeray about the powers of newspaper reporting in the field of crime. Maginn uses the press to parallel the public response to crime; newspapers generate circulation by the reporting of sensational stories and exaggerating the grim details of crime. Ironically, they are not so pleased to report the truth that often lies behind such initial censorious reactions:

> ... the newspapers, had declared that both children were found covered with bruises, beaten to death, and tied up with the same rope to a large beam in the roof of the coal-cellar...a very striking and impressive story indeed ... The succeeding post-day, on the other hand, brought intelligence altogether as disappointing ... Two *sick* children in a poor-house, desperate as their case was reported to be ... was a sad falling-off from two *dead* girls in a coal-cellar.[10]

Nevertheless, for Maginn the real purpose of his story is to demonstrate how the Newgate novelist manipulated the reader into more favourable opinions of the criminals depicted than he felt they deserved. The romancing of crime was inappropriate, even if the truth was sometimes complicated.

'Elizabeth Brownrigge' belonged to the periodicals of the 1820s and early 1830s, and made no attempt to portray the eighteenth-century narrative as anything other than a nineteenth-century parody. Thackeray, on the other hand, as well as exploring different styles of narrative, such as the Gothic romance, the adventure romance, and the sentimental love story,[11] explored his own methods of historical representation.

The ending of *Catherine* is an interesting example of Thackeray's early experimentation with the relationship between the press and the writer of fiction. Robert Colby describes the denouement as a purely historical interpolation; it is also a textual one. Thackeray copied the details of Catherine Hayes' murder of her husband and her public execution from the *Daily Post* of 3 March 1726 and the *Daily Journal* of 10 May 1726. The media narrative interrupts Thackeray's parody of Gothic melodrama, in a scene where Catherine and Galgenstein discover Hayes' head on a pole in a churchyard. The newspaper report was intended to distress the reading public, a manipulative act related to Brock's treatment of Catherine. Ironically, the passage was removed from the version of *Catherine* in the first edition of Thackeray's *Works* (Smith, Elder & Co., 1867-9), for precisely the reasons that Thackeray wished the extracts to be included. The unidentified editor noted:

> The details of the crime are simply horrible, without one touch of even that sort of romance which sometimes gives a little dignity to murder. As such they precisely suited Mr. Thackeray's purpose at the time – which was to show the real manners and customs of the Sheppards and Turpins who were then the popular heroes of fiction. But now-a-days there is no such purpose to serve, and therefore these too literal details are omitted.[12]

The notion that 'romance' could add 'dignity to murder' reverses Thackeray's parody. But his purpose was not just to expose false heroes; indeed, Thackeray developed a heroine that he felt some sympathy towards. His use of the newspaper material has the direct effect of reducing the substance of his narrative to its first principles, and of exposing to the public how a writer shapes fiction from factual details. Yet the 'real' here is also textual, itself a mediation.

John Loofbourow acknowledges the cleverness of the effect Thackeray achieves, but dismisses the supplanting of artistry by journalism. He says:

> This insertion of a lump of unassimilated journalism is a crude device; it represents an early phase in Thackeray's integration of 'realism' with allusive parody ... [the story] ceases to be a novel and becomes an essay skilfully woven of random fragments.[13]

The disintegration of Thackeray's narrative, the 'novel' becoming 'random fragments', is, however, precisely the point. Earlier in the narrative, Thackeray was at pains to show that certain elements in his work had their basis in historical text. When Brock, disguised as a pressgang agent, imprisons Hayes for money, he does so by way of an item in the *London Gazette* of 1 April 1706. The newspaper, Thackeray says, gave notice of 'a proclamation by the Queen for putting into execution an Act of Parliament for the encouragement and increase of seamen'. The Act 'which occupies four columns of the *Gazette* ... caused a mighty stir throughout the kingdom at the time when it was in force' (XX, 57). Making money from press speculations has its counterpart in Thackeray's life. From this piece of information, Thackeray is able to suggest the state of life in the early eighteenth-century without trying to 'strive too feverishly for the antique effect'.[14] As Colby suggests, Thackeray believed that:

> ... the novelist, no less than the historian, builds upon fact, not fancy, upon the world as it is, not as one would wish it to be. Consequently, [Thackeray] always valued primary sources – records, documents, letters, memoirs – for the texture of actuality that they conveyed ... His demonstration of how the novelist-historian-philosopher can draw instruction for mankind from the fleeting records of the day went generally unappreciated.[15]

In *Catherine*, then, Thackeray is being consistent, not with what Loofbourow believes should have been a greater narrative continuity, but a much wider view of the substance of history and its reflection in contemporary periodicals and novels. But their usage is not just for verisimilitude.

However, whilst many of his other articles reveal a distrust of magazine writers, Thackeray does not here take issue with newspaper reporting. Maginn's exposure of the sensationalism inherent in the reporting surrounding the Elizabeth Brownrigg case is ignored in Thackeray's account of Catherine Hayes. He relies explicitly on the veracity of his sources. He was prepared to accept such early accounts as authoritative. They suited his shock-tactics. The issues that he took against political bias, for instance, against the 'bigotry and wicked lies of that abominable old *Times*',[16] were not a concern when he sought source material in the periodicals and newspapers of the previous century.

In the final words of the convict-narrator, Ikey Solomons, in *Catherine*, Thackeray justifies his inclusion of journalistic narrative as the climax of his tale:

> … the 'ordinary' narrative is far more emphatic than any composition of his own could be, with all the rhetorical graces which he might employ. Mr. Aram's trial, as taken by the penny-a-liners of those days, had always interested him more than the lengthened and poetical report which an eminent novelist has given of the same … We very much doubt if Milton himself could make a description of an execution half so horrible as the simple lines in the *Daily Post* of a hundred and ten years since, that now lies before us … as bright and clean as on the day of publication. (XX, 167)

Thackeray's interest is derived from those same ballads and cheap periodicals that he was examining, in their nineteenth-century versions, in 'Half-a-Crown's worth of Cheap Knowledge' and 'Horae Catnachianae', the second of which appeared a month before *Catherine* began. At the heart of his first major piece of fiction, his longest sustained narrative of the 1830s and rightly considered his best work of that period, is his interest in the periodicals and their interpretation of life. The historical novel or article could not be said to enhance an understanding of the past if all it could do was reduce first-hand records into the mush of romance. Thackeray could easily value an old newspaper above a modern novel. Additionally, *Catherine* demonstrates the mediation of violence, showing how representations have changed. Catherine Hayes herself is subject to male control just as she is eventually subjugated within the historical press.

Peter Brock is a character similar in type to Augustus Wagstaff in a story in the *Paris Literary Gazette*, and to Deuceace in the *Yellowplush Papers*, as well as Barry Lyndon, and other male and female manipulative rogues. He is also another example of a character able to live on his wits and rise and fall and rise again as his fortunes change. Brock's fashionable campaign in London's high society sees him acquainted with Addison and Steele, part of the parody against Bulwer whose historical name-dropping was renowned, and a treatment of one of Thackeray's favourite historical periods returned to in *Esmond*.[17] Brock is initially a Corporal, then Captain Wood, and finally, the Rev. Doctor Wood. His changes of identity enable him to remain socially successful, although he does suffer a period of seven years' transportation to the plantations in Virginia.

Brock is another side of the writer's ego. He stands with Yellowplush and Michael Angelo Titmarsh as part of Thackeray's early exploration of the processes of writing and creativity in the nineteenth-century market-place. He is a manipulator of others for his own pleasure, operating on them like a puppetmaster. Self-gratifying pleasure seems to be the difference. The narrator (more Thackeray than Ikey, and, in truth, the latter does not have much of a distinct personality) attracts the reader with promises of gratification of readerly desire for the grotesque and violent. The story will be in the current 'fashionable style and taste', and is 'agreeably low, delightfully disgusting' and therefore 'eminently pleasing and pathetic' (XX, 4). It contains only 'vice, agreeable vice', which 'is the only thing which the readers of romances care to hear' (XX, 7). The promise made by the narrator is to pleasure the reader and to supply the reader's desires: 'We give the reader fair notice that we shall tickle him with a few such scenes of villainy, throat-cutting, and bodily suffering in general, as are not to be found, no, not in – ; never mind comparisons, for such are odious' (XX, 5).[18]

Brock, on the other hand, is versed in self-advertising and the managing of others for his own delight. When we first see him, he is making use of a pair of horses to attract the locals' admiration as he runs an illegal press-gang with Count Galgenstein. The horses 'were only placards or advertisements for the riders', we are told (XX, 9-10). He is successful in obtaining recruits, just as Galgenstein is successful in obtaining love in the shape of Catherine Hall, 'a slattern and a minx' (XX, 10). Both are described as 'conducting operations with perfect success' (XX, 22). Through the first half of the tale, he is able to maintain a powerful, self-made presence, but largely remains unfulfilled. Initially described as a man of appetites, he lives in the shade of Galgenstein whose class position enables him to satiate his desires. Galgenstein takes Catherine – Cat – and makes her pregnant; Brock offers marriage to her when the Count deserts her, but is refused. He flees with the Count's money and by changing his identity is able to baffle the newspaper advertisements for his capture. These appear in the *Daily Post*, *Courant*, *Observator*, and *Gazette*, and form part of the texture of historical realism. They are also symbolic of the way newspapers seek to define individuals. Brock, now called Wood, manages to elude this newspaper closure in a way that Catherine does not. He then enjoys a fashionable London life, but is exposed when he accidentally removes his eye-patch and reveals that he has a good eye. He is finally caught on the road with Ensign MacShane, another kind of rough Becky Sharp who lives on nothing, and transported for theft.

The transportation is an important moment in Brock's life; the narrator remarks how, in the prison colonies, he loses all of his appetites for drink, gambling, and women. This symbolic social castration ironically mirrors Thackeray's own state after his wife's insanity becomes known in 1841, a year or so after *Catherine*. Here, it frees Brock from the drive for the fulfilment of desire that engenders the downfall of the other characters. Hayes loves Cat 'with a desperate, greedy eagerness and desire of possession' (XX, 17). His decapitation by Cat – signified by the two references to the story of Judith and Holofernes (XX, 41, 143) – is a symbolic castration, again repeated in the image of the head attached to the top of the pole. Galgenstein becomes a wreck of a nobleman, reduced to pure pleasure in a bloated and useless state. He then loses his sanity through the obsessive desire for Cat that her refusal to gratify his lusts produces (significantly this is arranged at the directions of

Brock). Catherine herself is destroyed by her desires for Galgenstein, which lead her to murder her husband in a bid for the freedom to remarry.

Brock's loss of appetite frees him from the bondage of desire that drives the other characters and the narrative itself. He becomes a kind of surrogate reader in the text, watching the violence and lusts of the other characters and deriving his satisfaction from their torments. He is both writer and reader, and also, significantly, the only one who seems to gain from the story. He vanishes at the end, and we are not told what happens to him. The family fights between Cat, Hayes, and Tom Billings (Cat's son by the Count), are fuelled by Brock. We are told:

> He felt an indescribable pleasure ... in watching the storms and tempests of the Hayes menage. He used to encourage Mrs. Catherine into anger when, haply, that lady's fits of calm would last too long; he used to warm up the disputes between wife and husband, mother and son, and enjoy them beyond expression: they served him for daily amusement ... (XX, 111; see also 139, 145)

The entertainment provided by the violence of the household is enacted in a serial format almost. Brock stirs up the trouble in periodical moments of ennui. His pleasures are provided with plentiful satisfaction. 'There was mean malice, and fierce scorn, and black revenge, and sinful desire, boiling up in the hearts of these wretched people, enough to content Mr. Wood's great master himself', the narrator notes (XX, 146).

Brock is an important figure in the text as he demonstrates an early Thackerayan exploration of the theme of male power over female image. In the male-dominated media of the 1830s and 1840s, this might be seen as a symbolic representation of the media control of public discourse in the gender debates of the time. Brock it is who seems to play upon Cat's passions and tip her towards the murder that she seems to have the potential to commit. From the beginning of the tale, Cat is transformed by the male figures who enter her life. Initially, however, she is commodified by the landlady who keeps the Bugle Inn and sees Cat as an asset to attract customers. As a woman, however, Mrs. Score keeps a protective eye on Cat, and denies the Count further opportunity to ruin her maid. In an interesting phrase, Cat, she says, 'would not be visible that day' (XX, 22).

Visibility is an important concept for understanding Thackeray's attitude towards the media and the public image of himself and his characters. It is a recurring theme in his work. In both *Catherine* and *The Ravenswing*, Thackeray deals with women who move outside of the private world of the home and into a public arena, and in each case this move is as a consequence of male interference in their lives. The woman is forced into a public sphere and then subjected to male manipulation and control whilst there. Micael Clarke sees *Catherine* as essentially about economics. 'From Catherine on', she suggests, 'Thackeray's works reflect the reality that marriage provided social, sexual, and economic advantages for men, whereas it was the only profession open to women and, furthermore, a lottery in which they had little or no recourse if they bought a losing ticket.'[19] Catherine and Becky Sharp are both types of destructive women, who destroy as part of their rebellion. Catherine is 'pressured by economic and political powerlessness to marry where she does not love'.[20] The outcome of this unequal relationship is, as George Eliot later suggested, a kind of deformity of mind. Clarke sees Catherine as both a 'metonym for female rage and mental derangement' and a 'satire on literary representations of women'; the novel 'provided implicit commentary on the social system in which Thackeray found himself mired'.[21]

Thackeray's interest in the transformation of image complicates the more straightforward gender question analysed by Clarke. Catherine is established as the perpetrator of crime in the text; symbolically, she, as woman, is blamed for the Fall. On one level, her desire can be read as the central force in driving the narrative towards its catastrophe. As Linda Hughes and Michael Lund have noted of romance serials, '[t]he eroticism in romance fiction ... consists of the feminine desire of being desired, and the impetus toward, yet prohibition of, desire for a male erotic figure.'[22] The decapitation of the male/husband at the end of *Catherine* is a form of castration, but it is also a site of phallic exchange – the husband for the lover in a churchyard tryst – and as such has a conventionality about it. Cat's exchange is to embrace a perverse desire, typical of Gothic fiction, and which is signified by the simultaneous 'decapitation' of the Count, who loses his head at the sight (literally, in a sense, as he has an epileptic fit and loses his mind).

The reader is also presented with two competing versions of closure. The first is the 'Gothic' ending, in which we are not permitted to know much of the actual crime Catherine commits; it is hinted at merely in the allusions to Judith's murder of Holofernes, and a stumbling of feet on the ceiling coming from Hayes' bedroom. Parts of the body are disposed of, we assume, by Brock and Tom Billings, but we are not made acquainted at first with Catherine's part in the murder. Her shock on seeing the severed head could be mistaken for innocence as to what had actually occurred, though we are in no doubt that she is an accomplice. This takes place in 'The Last Chapter'. In 'Another Last Chapter', we are presented with the record of the *Daily Post*, 3 March 1726 (the passages cut by the editor of the Smith, Elder *Works*). This asserts a kind of authoritative newspaper realism into the story and shows the real nature of Catherine's crime in all its gory details. The fragmented ending perhaps represents a concern on Thackeray's part about the final fixing of a male-orientated identity onto Catherine Hayes. It also suggests, but leaves unsatisfactory, the parodic alternative ending of newspaper realism. Clearly, this ending forms the 'tyranny' of the ending that the reader feels bound to accept. But the media manipulation of female character, and the final metamorphosis of country girl into murderess, via abused mistress and abused wife, remain awkward subtexts in the narrative. If we are being presented with alternative versions of Catherine, in some ways, both versions of the woman are the same – she is a murderess. However, if we remain concerned about the male 'creation' of Catherine Hayes, then we perhaps find both endings deconstructed by the presence of figures like Brock and Ikey Solomons as mediators of image in the text. It is interesting that Ikey describes the human condition as one that pertains, in the end, to media print. In death, we all become newspaper type, as the announcement of our death is published; it is not the Ferryman who waits, but 'yonder stands the compositor at his types who shall put up a pretty paragraph some day ... ' (XX, 167).

Ikey Solomons leaves the reader with a puzzling paradox, which suggests that Thackeray had perhaps not fully determined his position on newspapers, parodies, and realism. Yet it does also suggest something of the ambivalence which dogs his life as a magazine and newspaper writer. Solomons says he prefers the writings of the newspaper 'penny-a-liners' of such publications as the *Daily Post* as they are more genuine and truthful. In his other works, Thackeray is not so certain of the veracity of periodicals. However, here he also comments on the contemporary newspapers' attacks on *Catherine*, and thus making *Fraser's* engage with the contemporary debates about magazine fiction and 'vulgarity'. Certainly, in *The Ravenswing*, this kind of media exchange was repeated, as Thackeray strove to assert the need in fiction to tackle all aspects of human life and the human condition. His work was causing unease in other sectors of the press.

The Ravenswing was published between May and August 1843, in *Fraser's Magazine*, part of a connected series of tales entitled *Men's Wives*. It is the longest of four tales of 'wives', narrated by George Fitz-Boodle (an indistinct narrative voice).[23] The story marks a development in Thackeray's career; it is steeped in his knowledge of the periodical press and makes use of this broad cultural context in locating the characters and stimulating the narrative. For the first time, Thackeray extends his narrative to form a complex relationship with other journals and newspapers (both real and fictitious), and transforms these into signifiers of behaviour. Further, he establishes a reading of the periodicals through his readers' knowledge of characters, thereby simultaneously adding realism through his portrayal of these everyday articles, and forming a critique of these as commodities. As in *Barry Lyndon*, the periodicals become open to misuse and thus form an unreliable public discourse removed from the private domestic realities of life.

Engaging directly with the world of newspapers makes more explicit the fabrication of the world in texts and exposes the growing notions of public and publicity that inform Habermas's formation of the public sphere. History and parody diminish this. *The Ravenswing* is Thackeray's first sustained exploration of the themes that are to find their greatest success in *Pendennis*. It is perhaps this novel, rather more than *Vanity Fair* as has previously been suggested, to which the tale is a precursor, although there are certainly elements of both.[24] The figure of Becky Sharp owes more to Brock than to Morgiana Crump; Morgiana the Ravenswing is in fact more like Amelia Sedley. The contemporary dating of the tale enables Thackeray to be more specific and immediate in his press indicators. This is 'realism' rather than parody, and as such the central figures are not overshadowed by the parodic intent, as happens somewhat in *Catherine*. Furthermore, the interplay between serial magazine tale and other periodicals in the present foregrounds a level of contemporary critique that *Catherine* obscures. For any study of Thackeray's relationship with the press, this text is seminal.

To some extent the story is a burlesque of the 'Silver-Fork' novel; it deflates with bathos a lower-middle-class society of tavern clubs, theatres, gambling dens, social climbers and debtors, aping the fashionable world, and being shown up for its shallow pretensions. This is what Tillotson calls the story's 'moral commentary'.[25] However, as the generic title suggests, the tale also explicitly explores power relations in gender politics.[26] The tautology of the term, 'Men's Wives', shows a conscious associating of marriage with male ownership. Like Catherine, Morgiana is a young woman seduced by the promise of wealth and male power in the figure of Hooker Walker, a flash self-promoter and society rake. She abandons her home and the rather bland attentions of a tailor and hairdresser (symbols of her vanity, and shapers of her image in an unconscious way) to marry Walker. But their marriage is an unhappy one, and Morgiana's life becomes much like that of a mistress, kept in a modern mansion in Maida Vale.[27] Walker's gradual abandonment of her is inverted by her gradual increasing success as a singing sensation on the stage. Her coterie of male admirers assist in creating a public image for her in the press and, despite her relative ordinariness of voice, the publicity promises a glittering launch for her professional career. Walker, in the Fleet debtors' prison, takes control of his wife's career by refusing her permission to sing unless his creditors settle their bills, and plans a 'sting' himself using the newspapers. The launch is eventually successful, but the marriage anulled, and Morgiana marries her faithful tailor and settles down to an ordinary life as a wife and mother. She is a figure very much trapped by her contemporary circumstances, both in terms of the prospects of a woman in public life and the prospects of a woman in private marriage. As Thackeray says of Amelia in *Vanity Fair*, during one of her happier chapters:

> I like to dwell upon this period of her life, and to think that she was cheerful and happy. You see she has not had too much of that sort of existence as yet, and has not fallen in the way of means to educate her tastes or her intelligence. She has been domineered over hitherto by vulgar intellects. It is the lot of many a woman.[28]

Like Catherine, Morgiana is shaped by the network of males who surround her. Where Catherine was courted by the Count, Hayes, Brock, Thomas Bullock and Thomas Trippet, Morgiana attracts Walker, Eglantine and Woolsey, and is admired in her portrait on the walls of the local undergraduates. Her name, 'The Ravenswing', refers to her waves of black hair that attract men like Walker, but which effectively commodifies her as an image rather than a person. She is sold on the stage, advertised and 'puffed' like any other commodity. Thackeray makes the point that this is also the process behind modern publishing, and we see in Morgiana a representative of the writer himself. Indeed, the manipulation of both Catherine and Morgiana might be seen to replicate the commercial management of the writer's public identity.

The manipulation of public images, of writer or businessman or *femme fatale*, became a key theme in Thackeray's fiction. Advertising processes of 'puffing' and 'fishing' become Thackeray's metaphors for the means by which we gain worldly success above our rivals; they are also intimately connected with sexual and gender relationships in his fiction.

The Ravenswing, which appeared in *Fraser's Magazine* from May to August 1843, articulates Thackeray's analysis of the complex interaction between public and private spheres.[29] In addition, the story demonstrates the power of the press to construct public identities, to generate self-rewarding publicity. Thackeray creates a gallery of literary characters familiar in essence to the readers of Yellowplush and 'Reading a Poem'. These are the forerunners of the literati, Bungay and Bacon, Captain Shandon, Pendennis and Warrington. They create Morgiana's public image and commercial success in a number of magazine caricatures: 'I don't know how it was, but before the *début* of Morgiana, the English press began to heave and throb in a convulsive manner, as if indicative of the near birth of some great thing'.[30] The newspaper men consist of Bludyer, Squinny, and Mulligan.

First, there is Bludyer, whose 'sallies in the *Tomahawk*' (an aptly named Saturday weekly paper) are 'wicked, but oh! so pleasant' (XX, 270). Bludyer writes 'slashing articles'; 'he would not only write, but fight on a pinch; was a good scholar, and as savage in his manner as with his pen' (XX, 272). It is dangerous to refuse Bludyer money, but, we are informed, even more dangerous to lend it him. Bludyer is a portrait of William Maginn: Thackeray's dubious tribute perhaps, to the man who helped him into his profession and who had recently died on release from the Fleet. His is the 'slashing' review style of the 1830s, which Thackeray parodies in an account of Thrum's forthcoming opera: 'The opera will do much more than compete with the infernal twaddle and disgusting slip-slop of Donizetti, and the milk-and-water fools who imitate him ... ' (XX, 281).

Squinny is the editor of *Flowers of Fashion*, a foppish production characterized by its bad French and affected appreciations. Bludyer calls it 'filthy flattery' (XX, 281). He praises Morgiana in the following manner: 'We have just heard the lovely *élève*, whose rare qualities the cavalier has brought to perfection ... a creature more beautiful and gifted never bloomed before *dans nos climats* ... ' (XX, 280). He is 'as delicate as milk and water', but 'in his journal mildly malicious' (XX, 272). He is a political man, a sycophantic yet self-interested figure, and an ancestor of Tapeworm in *Vanity Fair*.

The third journalist is an Irishman, Desmond Mulligan. He is a poet and reporter for a morning newspaper; in his 'political enthusiasm', he 'lives and writes in a rapture' (XX, 273). He resides in the Inns of Court and is training for the Bar. He 'quitted his country [Ireland] on account of a quarrel with Government regarding certain articles published by him in the *Phoenix* newspaper' (XX, 273). In his professional capacity, he is the political correspondent for 'that famous Munster paper, the *Green Flag of Skibbereen*' (XX, 274).

Between them, with some coercion from Sir George Thrum and Woolsey, the tailor, these periodical hacks launch Morgiana's career. Her Messianic launch is helped by *The Moon, Albion, Flowers of Fashion*, and the *Tomahawk*. These hacks puff Morgiana in a manner set out in an article in *Ainsworth's Magazine*, July 1842, which offers comic suggestions for the puffing of writers. Thackeray almost certainly knew this article. *Ainsworth's* describes those contemporary advertising practices which follow the dictum 'no publicity is bad publicity': the author of *FitzHenry Fitz Hildebrand* is given a 'puff preliminary' which lauds his work, a 'puff negative' which denies sensational rumours (whilst making them), a 'puff mysterious' which rumours that passages in his novel refer to real personages and events in aristocratic life, and, finally, a 'puff deprecatory' asking the public not to believe reports that the author is not the real author but to judge for themselves.[31]

Thackeray repeats these ideas, describing five different kinds of puff used on a fictitious author, Blazes, to launch his career (XX, 278-9): the 'management of visibility'.[32] Blazes is reported in the local press as passing through Windsor intending to give readings; a second paper questions this and suggests he is in fact suffering from chickenpox; a London paper ridicules the provincial press coverage; Blazes writes to the London papers to defend himself as having no control over press reporting; and the editor of the paper apologies to the worthy gentleman – thus obtaining five publicity notices! Thackeray's moral is set out at the beginning of Chapter 8:

> ... some country readers not acquainted with the class of persons by whose printed opinions they are guided ... are simple enough to imagine that mere merit will make a reputation on the stage or elsewhere. The making of a theatrical success is a much more complicated and curious thing than such persons fancy it to be. Immense are the pains taken to get a good word from Mr. This of the *Star*, or Mr. That of the *Courier*, to propitiate the favour of the critic of the day, and get the editors of the metropolis into a good humour, – above all, to have the name of the person to be puffed perpetually before the public. Artists cannot be advertised like Macassar oil or blacking, and they want it to the full as much; hence endless ingenuity must be practised in order to keep the popular attention awake ... (XX, 278)

As Thompson indicates, publicity is the means of exercising power over the new public of the capitalist era.[33]

Newspaper reports play a number of roles in the story; in the main, they hold the power to either destroy or create personalities. They reveal the hierarchies and fortunes of the world to be largely textual; real people, like Thackeray's view of historical personages, are replaced by their textual equivalents, revalued according to the preferences of the newspaper. Walker holds a certain notoriety fostered by the press; his fight with Lord Doublequits 'went the round of the papers' as a 'paragraph' entitled 'Affair of Honour in the Fleet Prison' (XX, 253) – the 'honourable' nature of the event being established by the paper and exposed in Thackeray's text. Walker's career has a history: 'There is no use in raking up old stories, and hunting through files of dead newspapers, to know what were the specific acts which made the Commissioner so angry with Captain Walker' (XX, 257). Sir George Thrum's house is an archive in itself; its decor reflects the age of George III when Thrum was at his height, and his book cases retain 'the newspaper which contains the account of his distinguishing himself at the siege of Seringapatam' (XX, 265). Each of these characters find their public selves defined by the papers: Morgiana's singing triumphs, Walker's bankruptcy and the account of his duel, Sir George's collection of clippings about his past military campaigns. The newspapers can support an individual's public persona or expose it.

In the tale the press is shown as a platform for personal gain. There is a clear connection between finance and journalism. Morgiana's singing career is carefully reported in order to keep her and Sir George (the opera composer) in the public eye. Thackeray sets out the campaign in the following order: firstly, Thrum throws a dinner to gain the confidence of Bludyer, Squinny, and Mulligan, as well as Slang of the theatre. By introducing them to a member of the nobility, he ensures that they are deeply moved in his favour. The press canvassing begins with the Mulligan's historical anecdotes about George III in *The Moon*, in which he reminds the readership of the 'famous' English composer, Thrum. Next, the *Flowers of Fashion*, describes the 'Ravenswing' as part of the select world. The *Albion* mocks the French nation and declares itself a fan of Thrum's Patriotic anthems sung at recent military victories. Finally, Bludyer attacks the opposition, Miss Ligonier (Morgiana's singing rival), in the *Tomahawk*, and brings a comic, critical, and worldly readership (like *Fraser's* own) onto the side of Morginana. Her favourable reception is guaranteed. The launch of a new talent (whom even Fitz-Boodle describes as 'an ordinary singer', XX, 277) thus becomes partly a matter of press pressure, generating rather than reflecting public taste. The 'authority' of the press is manifest. From historical anecdote to national pride, from cultural snobbery to worldly cynicism, all of the tricks are deployed to sway opinion. The image of the 'Ravenswing' is quite evidently a literary construct, sold and bought.

In order to make the process clearer and the criticism stronger, Thackeray paralleled this rise to the salvation of Walker. Despite his wife's progress, Walker has remained in the Fleet prison, beset by creditors, and seemingly lost to the world. It is here that he learns, through the newspapers, of his wife's growing fame and impending riches. Immediately, he launches a 'sting' through the press. As Morgiana's husband, he forbids her to go on the stage and has reports circulated that she has a sore throat. Unless Thrum and Slang agree to pay off his debts, he will not allow Morgiana to sing. He realizes that his wife's teachers and managers stand to make a fortune out of her career. Not content with this blackmail, he writes letters to the press praising Miss Ligonier, and continues to authenticate stories that his wife's illness is so severe that she may not sing at all. The newspapers are filled with regrets and sentiment at this tragedy. Walker's creditors have been holding off from reaching any settlement in expectation of reaping some of his wife's earnings; realizing now that nothing may be gained at all, they settle at a low percentage of his debts. Once settled, the press re-bolsters Morgiana's reputation and her opening night, with a rigged audience to throw flowers, is an outrageous triumph. The 'sting' is completed. The press becomes an instrument by which the unscrupulous and the mediocre gain wealth and fame at the expense of the public. Controlled by humans fraught with human failings and foibles, run by snobs and social climbers, Thackeray's press cannot be trustworthy, objective, or detached, cannot, in short, be the repository of truth he would like. History evident from his periodicals is the history of vanity fair.

The untrustworthiness of the press is inherent in the plot and structure of this tale as well as thematically. Newspapers made Morgiana, they made Walker, and they made Fitz-Boodle and Thackeray. They are the site of authority and power in his fictional world – more powerful than the Lords who read them and the tradesmen who buy them. They are advertisers of people. Journals become the instruments of con-tricks of differing degrees, replacing the decks of cards of Barry Lyndon and Deuceace (eighteenth-century and Regency), the 'fairy-tale' diamond of Samuel Titmarsh, and heralding the economic speculation of the Industrial age and the railway gambling of the mid-1840s.

Morgiana's public success on the stage represents a reversal in gender roles between husband and wife (Walker and Morgiana) in the story – a reversal of the normal genderization of the public sphere. When Morgiana begins singing lessons, Thackeray opens a discourse on the lack of female opportunities in private domesticity: like Dickens' prisoners in solitary confinement, he says, women have 'a sad life' and 'Women's fancy-work is of this kind often – only prison work, done because there was no other exercising-ground for their poor little thoughts and fingers' (*Works*, XX, 251). Prison becomes an actuality for Walker, who finds himself constrained (though happily) to the private, even domestic sphere, whilst his wife comes out on the stage (visualized in the initial letter to Chapter 8). Such a process ironically leads to a second engendering of public image, again detrimental to the now 'public' Morgiana. Released from the Fleet, Walker gains public recognition as a suffering and abandoned husband whilst Morgiana, surrounded by male admirers at the opera, becomes the subject of moral condemnation (XX, 289). Predictably, it is actually Walker who keeps a mistress.

Thus, whilst on one level we read Morgiana's triumph as female empowerment – her obtaining of access to the construction of a mediated public identity – she actually remains dependent upon the males in her life and defined by their image of her. Her hair, which, with its thick raven tresses gives her her name, operates as a symbol of this: Morgiana initially uses the letting down or freeing of her hair as a means of attracting Walker (her fishing), and it generates her visibility; later, when her husband languishes in the Fleet, she cuts off her tresses and sells them for his benefit and he gambles the money away, symbolically living on her identity.

Having transgressed into public life, Morgiana is re-inscribed into the private sphere at the end of the story by the narrator's postscript: symbolically transformed from 'Mrs Ravenswing' into, this time, 'Mrs Woolsey', the wife of the faithful tailor. She has left the stage and her voice is supplanted by Woolsey's as he talks about her with Fitz-Boodle. In some ways, she is only permitted to live up to her fairy-tale name: Morgiana, from *Ali-Baba and the Forty Thieves*, is the slave who pries into forty jars and finds a man in all but one. She kills them all with the boiled oil from the last jar and gains 'freedom' in the marriage to her master's son.

Thackeray's own career is covertly echoed in the tale, too, albeit beyond his reader's comprehension. For instance, an account of a famous Astley's 'dying-horse' routine comes from a *National Standard* review, as does the name 'Roundtowers'.[34] The roles of the editor and sub-editor described return the reader to the world of journalism of Thackeray's own apprenticeship in the 1830s:

> It is only the business of the great man who writes the leading articles which appear in the large type of the daily papers to compose those astonishing pieces of eloquence; the other parts of the paper are left to the ingenuity of the sub-editor, whose duty it is to select paragraphs, reject or receive horrid accidents, police reports, & c.; with which, occupied as he is in the exercise of his tremendous functions, the editor himself cannot be expected to meddle. (XX, 281-2)

This aspect of *The Ravenswing* brings to life the public side of the profession of which Thackeray (and *Fraser's*) are clearly a part. When Eglantine, the hairdresser, remarks 'I'm not...a tradesman, I'm a hartist' (XX, 180), we recognize the absurd ostentation of the ordinary man trying to reach his zenith, the desire for fame, the hack masquerading as a philosopher. But this is also precisely those terms in which Thackeray's battle for the 'Dignity of Literature' was fought out during the *Pendennis* controversy. The Ravenswing attains the fame her mother almost achieved but can only acknowledge in others through her collection of prints of famous singers which hang on the walls of the 'Bootjack Hotel'; the daughter's portrait hangs on the walls of the chambers of undergraduates. But even the Ravenswing's mythological status is to be exploded, fate replacing her on the show-bills with 'Snooks, the rhinoceros-tamer, with his breed of wild buffaloes' (XX, 288).[35]

Morgiana's 'managed visibility' is mirrored in the story's inscribing of its own reception. *The Ravenswing* establishes the relationship between Thackeray's fictitious story and the real press of his day. Fictitious and actual journals are mentioned in the story – some of which the readers will know: for instance, the *Morning Post*, here as elsewhere in Thackeray's works, is a cultural signifier of foppishness and vanity, read by the hairdresser Eglantine (XX, 246). In addition, as in his *National Standard* editorials, Thackeray directly engages with the critical opinions of newspapers partly as a justification of his work and partly as an advertising strategy with a deliberately ironic self-reflexivity. Only the magazine serial can effect this. The press accounts of 'the Ravenswing' as singer-character are fictional; but the accounts of *The Ravenswing* as commodity-text are genuine and actually circulate in London society. Trying to avoid the impropriety of directly referring to Morgiana's pregnancy, Thackeray notes:

> Mrs. Walker's mother was about to become a grandmother. There's a phrase! The *Morning Post*, which says this story is vulgar, I'm sure cannot quarrel with that. I don't believe the whole Court Guide would convey an intimation more delicately. (XX, 256)

In evading 'vulgarity', Thackeray is mocking the literary censorship of his day, whilst simultaneously defending his work, and continuing his satire against the *Morning Post* and the Court Guide.

Thackeray's sustained engagement with the *Morning Post*, fuelled by attacks from both sides, is symbolic of their competing media ideologies. Thackeray's 'vulgar' realism and the *Post's* romantic portrayal of the world of wealth and fashion are diametrically opposed. On 4 March 1843, in its review of *Fraser's*, the *Post* noted succinctly, '"Fitzboodle" makes a further fool of himself'.[36] On 1 April 1843, they were more considered: 'A continuation of Fitz-Boodle's Confessions, in *Fraser*, is equivocally indistinct, as the author is not even apparent through the article, and it might have been written under any other nom de guerre that author thought fit to assume.'[37] Next, on 4 May 1843, having attacked at length Jerrold, A'Beckett, and 'the Jerrold clique' (including Albert Smith and Mark Lemon), the *Post* notes: 'Fitz-Boodle's Confessions begin to wax vulgar, and with all our liking for the style of their commencement, we protest against the fashion of their continuation.'[38] Thackeray countered in *The Ravenswing*, as cited above. The June review continues:

> *Fraser* has suffered Fitz-Boodle to get very ungentlemanly in his 'Confessions'. The 'Ravenswing' is a terrible falling off from the commencement of these papers, and in addition to their want of freshness, which was so singularly apparent a virtue in their first numbers, seem to have little or no connection with the fortunes of the hero.[39]

In July, the narrator's absence was criticized: '"Fitzboodle" does not continue his confessions.'[40] Finally, in August, having referred to the *Post* in his story, Thackeray found himself attacked for this very engagement. The *Post* literary columnist answers him dryly:

> *Fraser* also shines in the kicking line against criticism. 'Fitz-Boodle', it is of no use, you are a vulgar fellow, although sometimes irresistably amusing, and we cancel not our verdict because you show fight upon the question. A meek, well-bred, and gentlemanly spirit would have listened to us without growling.[41]

The debate reveals how close journals could be to each other at this period; that the *Post* should speak directly to an anonymous writer in another magazine is evidence of how small was the circle of readers. *Fraser's* and the *Post* have an assumed commonality of readers, and both lay claims to being the teachers of public manners and morals. Perhaps, too, the influence of the *Post* might add to the success or notoriety of Thackeray's reputation. Thackeray's singling out of the charge of vulgarity serves a double purpose for him: it challenges the contemporary standards of moral censorship which he always found too strict and hypocritical, but it also establishes his story as a transgressive and subversive text, perhaps thus attracting readers as Morgiana's hair and Becky Sharp's licentiousness do men. It provokes the *Post* into a further response, thus obtaining another advertisement. Elsewhere in *The Ravenswing*, Thackeray displays further examples of his presupposing his own readers reading habits: he mentions 'this morning's leading story in the *Times*' and 'the rush for the evening paper' in the clubs (XX, 233).

Through a negotiation between the magazine or newspaper and the reading public, described in the story, the creative artist can achieve fame. As he describes:

> ... to have the name of the person to be puffed perpetually before the public ... endless ingenuity must be practised in order to keep the popular attention awake. (XX, 278)

Thackeray's tale deals directly with the realities of commercial life in the 1840s and the recognition that Victorian capitalism did not secure a meritocracy. His story is a comic exposé of this to a readership still relatively naïve about mass circulation journalism. His attack is paradoxically self-advertising and self-critical; it is underpinned perhaps with a note of bitterness that his own ability continued to wear itself away largely unrecognised and unappreciated in the bread-and-butter columns of the magazines. By drawing his readers' attention to the review in the *Morning Post*, Thackeray may be responding to a detractor of his literary style. But he is also demonstrating the extent of his visibility in the world of 1840s letters. This is *his* advertising, his visibility, a monthly mention of his progressing work. The circulation of the *Post* must increase the fame or notoriety of Thackeray's reputation. The deliberate act of self-justification, is, in the light of this story, an ambiguous additional exposure of the private face of the press. This is puffing and fishing of a subtly inverted and morally ambivalent kind.

Notes

[1] Micael M. Clarke, *Thackeray and Women* (DeKalb: Northern Illinois University Press, 1995).

[2] See John B. Thompson, *Ideology and Modern Culture* (Cambridge: Polity Press, 1990), 247.

[3] Barbara Hardy, *The Exposure of Luxury: Radical Themes in Thackeray* (Pittsburgh: University of Pittsburgh Press, 1972), 68-79, sees Thackeray and Becky as both performing for profit; Chrétien Maurice, 'Miroirs de *Vanity Fair*', *Etudes Anglaises*, 45: 4 (1992), 424-31, sees Becky as a manipulator of others in her reflecting of their desires; Robin Gilmour, *The Idea of the Gentleman in the Victorian Novel* (London: Allen & Unwin, 1981) sees both Thackeray and Becky as paradoxically subversive and conforming.

[4] Letter to Mrs. Carmichael-Smyth, March 1840; *Letters*, I, 432-3.

[5] Reprinted in Lewis Melville (ed.), *Stray Papers By William Makepeace Thackeray, Being Stories, Reviews, Verses and Sketches (1821-1847)* (London: Hutchinson, 1901), 424-92.

[6] *Men of Character*, III, 24-5; the waxwork proprietor possible also influenced Dickens' *Old Curiosity Shop* (1840-41).

[7] Richard M. Kelly, *Douglas Jerrold* (New York: Twayne, 1972), 117.

[8] *Fraser's Magazine*, 6 (September 1832), 67-8.

[9] Ibid., 74.

[10] Ibid., 136-7.

[11] See John Loofbourow, *Thackeray and the Form of Fiction* (Princeton: Princeton University Press, 1964), 19-22.

[12] *Catherine: A Story*, *Works*, XX, 166 [references in the text are to this edition].

[13] Loofbourow, *Form*, 22.

[14] Robert Kiely, 'Victorian Harlequin: The Function of Humour in Thackeray's Critical and Miscellaneous Prose', in Harry Levin (ed.), *Veins of Humour* (Cambridge, Mass.: Harvard University Press, 1972), 165.

[15] Colby, *Canvass*, 165.

[16] Letter to Mrs. Carmichael-Smyth, March 1840; *Letters*, I, 434.

[17] See Lidmila Pantuckova, *W.M. Thackeray as a Critic of Literature*, *Brno Studies in English*, 10-11 (Brno: Universita J.E. Purkyne, 1972), 141, who also refers to Colby's chapter on *Catherine* in *Canvass*. Brock's London life is described in *Works*, XX, 63-6, where the character, now Captain Wood, recounts his adventures and embellishes the incidents; the format of this story was reused in *Barry Lyndon*, but the historical period was altered to Dr Johnson's London.

[18] The comparison is, of course, to the novels of Bulwer, Ainsworth, and Dickens.
[19] Clarke, *Women*, 16.
[20] Ibid., 49.
[21] Ibid., 38.
[22] Linda K. Hughes and Michael Lund, 'Textual/sexual pleasure and serial publication', in John D. Jordan and Robert L. Patten (eds), *Literature in the Marketplace: Nineteenth century British Publishing and Reading Practices* (Cambridge: CUP, 1995), 157.
[23] For general discussions, see Carey, 109-12; Peters, 103-5.
[24] See Carey, 109-10; Ray, *Uses*, 336 suggests that Morgiana is a precursor of the Fotheringay in *Pendennis*.
[25] G. Tillotson, *Thackeray the Novelist* (Cambridge: CUP, 1954; London: Methuen, 1963), 211.
[26] Thomas, *Slavery*, 20-23, discusses the four tales as a group of interrelated explorations of marital exploitation and slavery, a hint picked up from Peters, 103-5.
[27] Her status reminds me of the William Holman Hunt painting of *The Awakening Conscience* (1852).
[28] *Vanity Fair*, chapter 62, *Works*, II, 298.
[29] Jürgen Habermas, *Transformation*, 22-3.
[30] *The Ravenswing*, *Works*, XX, 279 [references in the text are to this edition].
[31] D. and G. Hindley, *Advertising in Victorian England, 1837-1901* (London, 1972), 92-3.
[32] Thompson, *Ideology*, 247.
[33] Ibid., 238, 242-3. Thackeray repeats this advice in a letter of December 1843 to a young author, Richard Bedingfield, stating, 'A laudatory paragraph here and there will do you no earthly good, unless the name of your book is perpetually before the public' and noting that the *Paris Sketch-Book* (1840) had 'some thirty pounds of advertisements'; cited in Shillingsburg, 54; *Letters*, II, 136-7.
[34] 'Drama; Drury Lane, Olympic', *National Standard*, no. 53 (4 January 1834), 14; review of '*Phoenician Ireland*. Auctore Doctore Joachimo Laurentio Villanueva ... Translated by Henry O'Brien' (London, 1833), *National Standard*, no. 36 (7 September 1833), 141-3.
[35] For an account of Ethel Newcome as an example of woman in the market-place and her reinscribing into Patriarchy, see Donald Hall, *Fixing Patriarchy: Feminism and Mid-Victorian Male Novelists* (London: Macmillan, 1996).
[36] *Morning Post*, 4 March 1843, p. 6, col. 4.
[37] Ibid., 1 April 1843, p. 6, col. 1.
[38] Ibid., 4 May 1843, p. 6, col. 1.
[39] Ibid., 9 June 1843, p. 3, cols. 5-6.
[40] Ibid., 7 July 1843, p.. 3, col. 4.
[41] Ibid., 8 August 1843, p. 3, col. 4.

Chapter 5

Confronting the French: *The Paris Sketch-Book* and travelling French letters

In his recent book, *Heathcliff and the Great Hunger*, Terry Eagleton comments that, through the nineteenth and twentieth centuries, 'Ireland figured as Britain's unconscious'.[1] The notion of a 'mirror' country, against which the national characteristics of the home country are defined, has become a central tenet of postcolonial critical theory. Lacan's theory of the mirror self has been translated into the racial arena and the Other (black, or, here, Irish) occupies the site of the reflected self.[2] Whilst culturally a country might be described as discovering its own features in the glass of its colony, and whilst it is accepted that the relationship between colonizer and colonized is inextricable and an interface, for the nineteenth-century middle-class Englishman, the mirror-image was perhaps not to be found in the colonies or the occupied. Marxists situate the workers as the Wellsian Morlocks of the Victorian middle classes; Thackeray, on the other hand, found the working-class and popular culture of the 1830s and 1840s to be derivative and similar to that of his own. Moreover, he recognized that few of his class had much knowledge of the working-class districts close by their own. Elsewhere, however, the interconnection of cultures was more pronounced and complex. For much of the first half of the nineteenth century, Britain looked to the east for its uncomfortable opposite, to France – the country that best exemplifies the fascination–repulsion syndrome of the mirror-image.

France was the country of difference, moral, economical and political. It was close to London and gradually more accessible. Moreover, it was a place of moral transgression: Paris was a by-word for youthful indiscretion and sexual licentiousness. For a woman to be associated with Paris was fatal; Becky Sharp has a Parisian mother, for instance. France was a refuge for the financially strained English middle class. Thackeray spent time there with his grandmother after the collapse of his fortunes and his magazine in 1834. He met colleagues in France who had fallen on difficulties, including writers in positions similar to his own, such as Jerrold and Maginn. It was acceptable to be living in Paris, and yet everyone in English society knew that it was a place of secrets, of hidden disgraces and hardships. I have already discussed the English community in Paris, of which Thackeray was a part. But Paris was important for the insular English culture, too. It offered a region of cultural exchange that was not present from elsewhere – Ireland was not fashionable, India was too remote, Italy and Germany too fragmented and diverse. France was the closest in terms of nationhood, identity, and assimilation. And it was to France that Thackeray turned as a source of material, both observational and imaginary. Gordon Ray describes Thackeray during the period from 1837 to 1846 as 'a rising man of letters, using the knowledge he had acquired to such effect in his writings as to establish himself as a recognized expert on the humane aspects of French civilization'.[3] Moreover, Ray adds, Thackeray's 'reputation among editors and publishers was higher as a specialist in things French than as a humorist or writer of fiction, [and] he found it desirable to keep intimately in touch with his material'.[4]

Paris is a symbolic place of value to Thackeray's sense of self-identity, and his notion of the writer in the modern age. One of the ironies in his life is that he found both his wife and, probably, his sexual illness, in Paris. Paris was a place of desire. It was a holiday city where Thackeray spent part of every year of his adult life.[5] It contained, but released, sexual excitement and decadence; in the artists' ateliers, he could observe painters drawing human nudity from the life and share a bohemian world impossible in London. The freer culture was appealing to him; the fiction and the periodicals were, whilst more controlled in political matters, more explicit in depictions of violence and sexuality. *The Paris Sketch-Book* (1840) intellectualizes the English response to France, and describes something of the fascination for the darker side of desire present in the French capital. Darker for the English, that is. Part of the energy of Thackeray's reaction to Paris culture is the sense of guilt and uncertainty that is always present. Paris life is also about isolation and dislocation. It rarely invokes images of family and unity. It is an ambivalent place, and thus perfectly represents the drive of appetite and the fear of excess and loss of self that characterizes his relationship with journalism too.

In this chapter, I want to explore the themes of desire, loss and absence, as they manifest themselves in Thackeray's periodical writings about France. His articles on Paris, I would contend, frequently focus on pleasure as the basis for assessing Parisian life and values, and respond to the seduction of guilty pleasures, such as gambling, feasting, drinking, eating, sexual encounters, and experiences which emerge from the French streets, as well as topics covered in the London articles, such as periodicals, paintings, and more controversial subjects like public hangings and sensation fiction. Variously, his Paris articles are about appetite (as, indeed, are many of his other writings), but the perceived openness of French culture enables the fulfilment of such appetites. David Musselwhite, in his study of *Vanity Fair* and *Cornhill to Grand Cairo*, argues that:

> ... the journey to the Orient marked a break with the constraints and taboos of the West but while, on the one hand, that break meant the freedom to indulge in an excess of pleasure, on the other it courted the risk of the lack of all control: over and against the serpentine

> arabesques of desire must be set the inertia and catatonic arrest of the body without organs. That schizophrenic polarity of excess and lack, of desire and inertia, of delirium and death is to be found figured in the bewitching bohemianism of Becky Sharp and in the turgid Regency buck, Jos Sedley.[6]

The shift in argument here from Orient to Becky, from West to Regency, signifies more than Musselwhite intends. Indeed, it is Becky's Parisian bohemianism that marks her out as seductive. Whilst Jos's sexual exhaustion, symbolized by his transfer of desire from Becky to food and drink (the curry dinner and the Vauxhall rack-punch) casts him as another version of the replete and repentant mid-1840s Thackeray. The movement from desire to inertia is precisely that movement characterized by Thackeray's Paris writings between 1838 and 1841.

Thackeray's awareness of this makes his analysis of French culture also a self-exploration. The relationship between traveller and subject is internalized far more in the French articles than, for instance, the travel books to Ireland or Cairo. *The Paris Sketch-Book* and the articles for *Fraser's*, the *Corsair*, and *Britannia* during 1841 offer an intriguing insight into the transforming image of the magazine writer at a significant moment in his life and career. *The Second Funeral of Napoleon* (1841), a small volume publication that Thackeray called 'the best book I ever wrote' even as late as 1845,[7] marks a rupture between desire and attainment and introduces a new internal scrutiny to Thackeray's work. After 1841, Thackeray's writings on France are subsumed into his work for *Punch*, or used as background to his novels. One might ask whether the writer undergoes a loss of appetite which makes French culture less problematic to the man, or whether he finds other structures more appropriate for the channelling of his desire.

Between the years of 1837 and 1841, the periodicals in England continued to raise the reading public's consciousness of alien cultures by publishing many accounts of the experiences of travellers abroad.[8] *Fraser's Magazine*, *Blackwood's*, the *Literary Gazette*, the major quarterlies, and other journals, all carried frequent reviews of travel books, weekly and monthly serials dealing with a particular country or the wanderings of a certain writer, single articles ranging from assessments of the state of Ireland to descriptions of Tibetan monastries, and short fiction and novels set in foreign locations, both contemporary and historical. The newspapers matched this with reviews of travel books and continuous coverage of world events significant to England – such as, in the mid-1830s, the Spanish Civil War and the political struggles after the restoration of the French monarchy. Alongside these, novel writers kindled interest in foreign places and characters by creating a genre of travel novels.

The popular periodicals bred different kinds of travel writers. The free-lance contributors, often used by the magazines as column-fillers, vary greatly in the quality of their articles; few are particularly memorable. But some established free-lancers, such as Thackeray, found themselves in the position both to criticize contemporary travel writing and to produce articles describing their own observations and opinions. For the language expert, there was also the opportunity of translating, not only the foreign newspapers (as Thackeray had done for the *Constitutional*), but also Continental novels and short stories.[9] G.W.M. Reynolds' career, for example, extended into translating the popular French novelists Victor Hugo and Paul de Kock, from 1836 to 1840, as well as writing derivative travel novels, such as *Pickwick Abroad; or, The Tour in France* (1839). Reynolds, like Thackeray, sought to correct the biased opinions of the English press and public towards French writing; he published translations of several contemporaries, previously unavailable in English, in *The Modern Literature of France* (1839), including Eugène Sue and George Sand.[10] Thackeray's work as a translator in this field, whilst not prolific, also helped to stimulate public interest. Donald Hawes repeats George Saintsbury's remark that Thackeray's summary of *Jérôme Paturot* was better than the original, and suggests that the same can be said of his version of Soulié's *Le Bananier*.[11]

Thackeray's confidence as a travel writer grew enormously during this period. The publication of 'the immortal Paris Sketch-Book'[12] was more important to him than the reception of *Comic Tales and Sketches* a year later. He put more effort into his French writing than into any other form at this time, and hoped to gain some recognition for his abilities.[13] His work was continuous. In mid-1838, he was temporarily employed by the *Morning Advertiser* to cover the foreign correspondence of a sick friend, a Frenchman called Battier, also undertaking his post of sub-editor on *Galignani's Messenger*.[14] In the same year, Thackeray completed his illustrations for Charles G. Addison's *Journey to Damascus and Palmyra* – a task that he found almost beyond his powers.[15] Elsewhere, possibly around this time, he was working in some capacity as a correspondent for a foreign newspaper.[16]

Against this background Thackeray wrote his various chapters for the *Paris Sketch-Book*, many appearing first as individual articles or stories in *Fraser's* or the New York magazine, the *Corsair*. His conception of the art of travel writing had been formed whilst working upon a series of reviews for the *Times* in 1838. His first full article on Paris was published in the *London and Westminster Review* of April 1839,[17] whilst his series of French articles for the *Corsair* and *Fraser's*, which provided the basis of the travel book, were written shortly after this, over a period of six months. Thackeray's idea of producing a travel book detailing his impressions of the French capital, supplemented by a series of his own drawings, was born as early as January 1837, before he left the *Constitutional*. He offered the book to the minor London publisher, John Macrone, with whom he had dealt regarding an aborted project to edit the memoirs of Colonel Maceroni. Thackeray's letter referred to the prospective work as 'a book in two Wollums with 20 drawings entitled Rambles and Sketches in Old and New Paris by WMT – I have of course not written a word of it.'[18] Macrone initially bought the rights to publish the final version of the *Paris Sketch-Book* some four years later, only to pull out of the business at the last minute, the travel book finally being published by Hugh Cunningham, though under Macrone's imprint.[19] The initial idea of the travel book as a genial 'ramble' around the capital was soon to be replaced by the broader concept of a magazine-style miscellany, consisting of light-hearted descriptions and commentaries, diverse fictions, and intelligent articles on all subjects. Although the shift was practical in that Thackeray had already published several periodical articles that he could reuse, it was also meaningful; the miscellany helped to conceal the voice of the author and associated the ideas with the 'lower' journalism. Thackeray could suggest the eroticism of Paris without subjecting himself to the personal criticism he might have received had he stepped out in his own voice.

Thackeray could be cynical about the contemporay vogue for travelogues:

> A man may step into an omnibus in Piccadilly, and at such a trifling expense of time, money, and personal fatigue, voyage down the Strand and Cheapside to Billingsgate-market and thence to Cadiz, and from Cadiz to Gibraltar, and thence to Malta and Alexandria. So many have gone through this simple and easy journey, that the accounts which they bring back of their travels can hardly be expected to differ from the personal narratives of the hundreds of predecessors who have made the same tour.[20]

Although he was to undertake a similar tour to Cairo himself in 1844, this early criticism led him to attempt something different in the *Paris Sketch-Book*. In its magazine format, the book suggests something which could be read, like a newspaper, during leisure time, and which was not aimed specifically at helping the traveller find a path around the city. The book is not a personal account of a single journey, but the fruits of several years of experience and scholarship. It introduces the reader to a selection of areas of cultural importance in France. The best description of the book is as a miscellany:

> A collection of clever and smart papers, of the better kind of light magazine articles, and half of which have already appeared in periodicals; consisting of sketches and stories descriptive of Parisian life and character, with discussive remarks on French novels, dramas, and pictures.[21]

The *Paris Sketch-Book* was not a guidebook in the traditional sense, this reviewer said, nor a sustained travel narrative. It contained 'the flippant touch-and-go style of magazine writing', which was 'not fit ... for continuous reading'. It was meant, therefore, to be dipped into at leisure, but taken cautiously, because the 'descriptions' were 'exaggerated'. Robert Colby points out that the book deliberately avoided giving the kind of details about places which would have been found in *Baedeker's* or *Galignani's*,[22] yet it does rely on such descriptions in places.[23] His intention as a traveller was to describe and come to terms with the whole of human society. He wanted to educate the tourist and inform the traveller. The English tourists were not well liked abroad; even the usually unprejudiced George Sand passed a comment that springtime in the Alps was beautiful because 'it is possible to walk between hedges of hawthorn and wild plum for a whole day without meeting a single Englishman'.[24] In his review of 'Dumas on the Rhine', Thackeray himself noted that 'we have obtained for ourselves the hatred of Europe, by our contemptuous assumption of superiority in our frequent travels'.[25]

However, the most interesting aspect of the *Paris Sketch-Book* is its generic cross-dressing. As both magazine miscellany and volume publication, it seems in its dualism to partake of the doubleness of its cultural outlook and its morality. It translates the French into English and places the Englishman in France. Morally ambivalent, it revels in the freedom of Parisian extravagance whilst remaining deeply anxious about the exposure of the English self. Several of the chapters generate a tension between the determination to retain the gentlemanly demeanor and a sense that Parisian culture excites emotions not wholly expected in the English gentleman's character. On the other hand, for Thackeray, a 'gentleman' must contain such desires and energies as are natural in all men. The honest writer must contend with all sides of his own personality. Symbolically and directly, the Paris writings engage with facets of the self that expose the solid, gentlemanly persona to disintegrating forces and the threat of moral dissolution. They are a confrontation of the self in the Other.

The first chapter of the book is entitled 'An Invasion of France', a title that resonates in *Vanity Fair* as the chapter 'In Which Amelia Invades the Low Countries' (Chapter 28), and the initial letter of Becky as Napoleon (Chapter 64).[26] Thackeray both invades the Continent and is invaded by it, just like his many confreres in the Rue de Rivoli. As he leaves London, Thackeray leaves behind the cares of writing. He hears 'the bell of the packet … tolling a farewell to London Bridge' and 'warning off the blackguard-boys with the newspapers, who have been shoving *Times*, *Herald*, *Penny Paul-Pry*, *Penny Satirist*, *Flare-Up*, and other abominations, into your face … '.[27] The traveller passes beyond print, news, the pry of the media, and into a foreign space governed by no such public sphere. Again, the volume itself might be seen to enact this movement; the travel writer is his own moral master and reveals overtly only so much of what he wishes to reveal.

During the book, Paris is established as a place of vitality and energy, and contrasts with the deadness of London. The Faubourg St Denis is 'a strange contrast to the dark uniformity of a London street, where everything, in the dingy and smoky atmosphere, looks as though it were painted in India-ink – black houses, black passengers, and black sky'. In Paris there is 'a thousand times more life and colour' (XVI, 10). Later, in 'Madame Sand and the New Apocalypse', we are reminded:

> When a man leaves our dismal, smoky London atmosphere, and breathes, instead of coal-smoke and yellow fog, this bright, clear,

> French air, he is quite intoxicated by it at first, and feels a glow in his blood, and a joy in his spirits, which scarcely thrice a year, and then only at a distance from London, he can attain in England. (XVI, 225)

This passage offers several readings. Its focus on the experience of the 'man', and the obviously sexual 'glow in his blood', shows just how phallocentric is Thackeray's version of Paris. Paris gives potency where London stifles such. Even in England, the author can only attain such power away from London (where the press makes visibility an off-putting problem?). Moreover, the economic base of London is a depressant. London is industrial and its very modernity is choking. In 'Meditiations at Versailles', the industrial age, in the shape of the railway, has spoiled the journey between Paris and Versailles, 'the cast-iron Frankenstein of an engine' turning the passengers into 'stone figures ... cold and silent'. This invasion of the industrial prevents the fleshly excitement and vitality found in the carriage (the 'coucous') of old: 'the age of horseflesh is gone – that of engineers, economists, and calculators has succeeded; and the pleasure of *coucoudom* is extinguished forever' (XVI, 278). The symbolic language here is not heavily veiled. The writer finds fresher air in the arcane gentility of Paris. It is no surprise that Samuel Pogson in Chapter 2 of the *Paris Sketch-Book*, 'A Caution to Travellers', carries his copy of *Don Juan* with him and mistakes the pronunciation of his lady-friend's title (Madame la Baronne) for 'Madame la Byron' (XVI, 16). Paris enables the forgetting not only of moral strictures but of class antagonisms too. It is an escape back into the Regency – to gambling, whoring, drinking, eating, and the assumed excess of an aristocratic life.

John Carey characterizes Thackeray's response to France as ambivalent, having a 'frustrating doubleness', but in an unflattering way: the 'artist and Bohemian in him, plainly aroused, keep struggling with a prissy conformist and Francophobe'.[28] I think it is more pertinent, however, to see Thackeray as pushing beyond what was more commonly expected in the 1830s: the middle-class conformity and suspicion of the French is continually displaced by the obvious seduction of Parisian pleasure. Thackeray forces his fellow countrymen to confront their prejudices and their own uncomfortable desires. He brings into the public arena, the private drives of the individual. This is clear enough in *Pendennis*, but it is present throughout the earlier journalism too. 'A Caution to Travellers' confronts a variety of social and sexual taboos and warns the inexperienced male of the dangers that his exhilarated and liberated libido will face in Paris. The initial-letter illustration for the chapter shows a man falling into raptures over the reflection of a mermaid in her looking-glass (XVI, 14).[29] The narrator explains that 'his own experience ... painfully ... acquired' can help to teach others to avoid the dangers of the foreign (XVI, 14). Samuel Pogson is a commercial traveller with a drugs company. Young and naïve, nevertheless, his 'only fault is too great an attachment to the fair'; as he remarks 'the sex ... will be his ruin' (XVI, 15). Pogson is a comical figure, but his situation is a real one. On arriving in France, he is immediately attracted to a skilful older woman (who admits to 32 but is nearer 45). Her attractiveness is a mixture of her aristocracy ('the extreme pink of the nobility') and her commodified beauty. His knowledge of cosmetics makes him aware of the 'finest Chinese rouge' and 'ruby lip salve' that she wears (XVI, 15). Thackeray hints at the sexual nature of Pogson's desire; he spends time alone with her at an inn and squashes between her and her maid in the coach to Paris. He 'began enumerating her attractions, as a horse-jockey would the points of a favourite animal', we are told (XVI, 21). In a circumstance again reminiscent of *Vanity Fair*, Pogson discovers that his lady-friend is married and that her husband, the Baron, is keen to acquaint him with billiards. Other friends, such as the Honourable Tom Ringwood (whose namesake the Earl of Ringwood appears as the Lord Steyne figure of *Philip*), entrap Pogson at play. The story moves away from the sexual overtones of its opening and the intimacy of the *ménage à trois* to focus on the risk of card-playing, but the worldly narrator and the caricature, Major British, who extricate Pogson from his debts, hint at their familiarity with this *risqué* society. And it is Pogson and not the raffish world that bears the brunt of Thackeray's condemnation. British remarks, 'what right has a bagman to gamble? ... tradesmen, sir, have no business with the amusements of the gentry', whilst his downfall is deserved for 'making love to other men's wives' (XVI, 28, 29). Pogson is a tradesman who aped the Regency aristocrat. That is his crime in the eyes of British. The narrator is more circumspect and does not offer a judgement.

Pogson's weakness is a human one, as we discover elsewhere in the *Paris Sketch-Book*. In 'French Dramas and Melodramas', Thackeray talks of 'the hideous kind of mental intoxication' produced by brutal dramas and the monsters of Dumas-père and others. Thackeray outlines here the seductive nature of such entertainment; pleasure in Paris is of the baser sort for the English gentleman, and generates guilt whilst it feeds the sensual side of man.

> After having seen most of the grand dramas which have been produced at Paris for the last half-dozen years, and thinking over all that one has seen, – the fictitious murders, rapes, adulteries, and other crimes, by which one has been interested and excited, – a man may take leave to be heartily ashamed of the manner in which he has spent his time; and of the hideous kind of mental intoxication in which he has permitted himself to indulge. (XVI, 258)

In 'The Case of Peytel', this sensual delight is problematized by its association with public execution. Thackeray was very much against public hangings and spoke out several times against them. In the *Paris Sketch-Book*, his attendance at an execution is an attempt to see for himself and analyse his own feelings. The event was cancelled and he had to wait until François Benjamin Courvoisier was hanged in London on 6 July 1840, when he saw the whole spectacle.[30]

The basis of this chapter, written especially for the *Paris Sketch-Book*,[31] is the accounts of the trial of Peytel, presumably taken from the newspapers.

Thackeray was convinced that an English jury would have acquitted Peytel of double murder, and believed that the sensationalism of the prosecution's statement, 'as turgid and declamatory as a bad romance; and as inflated as a newspaper document, by an unlimited penny-a-liner', was to blame (XVI, 232). Thackeray rewrites the defence statement and suggests how a servant might have committed the crime. His final part of the chapter argues against capital punishment on the grounds that it does not deter and only degrades the public audience. He says, 'people make a holiday of a killing-day'. Likening the spectacle of an execution to the sexual tease of the ballet, he adds:

> Do we crowd to see Mr. Macready in the new tragedy, or Mademoiselle Elssler in her last new ballet and flesh-coloured stockinnet pantaloons, out of a pure love of abstract poetry and beauty; or from a strong notion that we shall be excited, in different ways, by the actor and the dancer? And so, as we go to have a meal of fictitious terror at the tragedy, of something more questionable in the ballet, we go for a glut of blood to the execution. The lust is in every man's nature, more or less. (XVI, 252-3)

Although the passage condemns French and English onlookers alike, as the criticism of the same had done so in the *Constitutional*, it also further commits the author to a confession of delight in the 'questionable' morality of modern pleasure and entertainment. Desire for sexual gratification and the blood-lust are acknowledged in every man. In Paris, Thackeray recognizes, not an escape into unmediated pleasure and sin, but the common nature at work in all of us. It is not a pretty sight. After the execution of Lacenaire, to which Thackeray arrived too late, a small group of children dance around a pool of ice tinged with red from the blood of the decapitated man. It is a startling image of corrupted innocence. But it is not Paris that does this; the remarks he makes are universal and not confined to France. 'Was any man,' he asks, 'who saw the show, deterred, or frightened, or moralized in any way?' The answer is blunt: 'He had gratified his appetite for blood, and this was all' (XVI, 254).

The suicide of Jack Attwood in 'A Gambler's Death' is equally stark in its brutal human honesty. Attwood is an old Charterhouse friend of the narrator and his story is based on an actual incident in 1835.[32] Attwood, a professional gambler, loses heavily at cards and borrows a pair of duelling pistols from a group of drunken and aggressive rakes to which the narrator belongs. Summoned to a breakfast, Titmarsh is told of the suicide of his school friend by the cynical Fips, whose 'mouth was full of bleeding beef as he uttered this gentlemanly witticism'. The author is surprised at his own feelings of indifference to the death of Attwood. He 'had not a tear or a pang', and muses that friendship bought over drink is not of any depth: 'it only entices men and ruins them; it is only a phantom of friendship and feeling, called up by the delirious blood, and the wicked spells of wine' (XVI, 111). The men attend Attwood's funeral, '*almost drunk*' from a night's drinking to stay awake for the early morning burial, and then go home 'to a warm and comfortable breakfast' and later to Frascati's, a notorious gambling den (XVI, 114). It is hard to imagine a harsher pair of stories in a volume which begins so brightly and comically, and promises to sketch France for the traveller.

Thackeray's portrait of Paris is not straightforward travel journalism. It can shock the reader with its frank exposure of male desires and lusts. Even in its pronouncements on art it can be erotically suggestive; thus in 'On the French School of Painting', Thackeray turns away from the beauty of Claude and Poussin, for the simpler pleasures of Watteau. But his judgement connects together drinking and art, outlining the 'hidden analogy between liquors and pictures'. Once again we are confronted by a sensual response to pleasure. For Thackeray, 'the eye is deliciously tickled by these frisky Watteaus, and yields itself up to a light, smiling, gentlemanlike intoxication'. There is a sexual enervation in the attractiveness of 'light' art that equates to the constant delight Thackeray finds in the periodical press. With Poussin, we are told, 'the luscious odour almost sickens you ... you feel as if you had been drinking hot blood' (XVI, 55). The argument is turned into an aesthetic one appropriate to a writer turning magazinery into a volume:

> I think in my heart I am fonder of pretty third-rate pictures than of your great thundering first-rates. Confess how many times you have read Béranger, and how many Milton? ... Let us thank heaven, my dear sir, for according us the power to taste and appreciate the pleasures of mediocrity. I have never heard that we were great geniuses. Earthy we are, and of the earth ... (XVI, 55)

The parallelism that draws together sensual titillation and minor, mediocre art, is the same as that equating of whoring to journalism seen in a letter of the mid-1830s. Paris excites Thackeray; journalism excites Thackeray; and the prospect of writing Paris journalism is the most exciting of all. But Thackery does not turn away from an exploration of his own sensual distractions. Paris reveals Thackeray to himself, confronts him with the truth of his own inner drives and uncomfortable attraction to the 'delightful, savage spectacle' of human pleasures ('The Case of Peytel', XVI, 253). The world of *Vanity Fair* emerges from this confrontation, but for Thackeray it is a world that does not last.

The French articles written after the *Paris Sketch-Book* establish more extensive links in the narrative between the author and his readership. As travel narratives, they combine a greater fictionality with a self-awareness on the part of the narrator. The descriptions look inward as much as they portray the outer world. In addition, the articles continue and develop the trend in Thackeray's work of contrasting the nostalgic appeal of family happiness and the worldly, intellectual response to modern society.[33] In a small book, *The Second Funeral of Napoleon* (1841), and in the two descriptive articles written for the *Britannia*, 'A St Philip's Day at Paris' (15 and 22 May 1841) and 'Shrove Tuesday in Paris' (5 July 1841), Thackeray cast himself in the role of a wistful, rather sad, observer. At the same time, in 'Memorials of Gormandising', *Fraser's Magazine* (May 1841), he was, as Michael Angelo Titmarsh, the wry and witty observer of good eating on the Continent. But all of these pieces contain significant allusions to the personality of the author and the erotic drives within him. They are all about appetite; not just the gormandizer's guide to Parisian gastronomies, but the celebrations of St Philip's day – the apostle who asked Jesus if the available bread would be enough to feed the 5,000 – and Shrove Tuesday – a day of eating before the fast. All of these articles place the author in relationship to the physical body and its generation of human needs.

Paris is no longer a place of companionship for Thackeray but an ironic comment on his isolation. The individual, cut off from discourse and familiarity in a foreign country (although Thackeray himself could speak fluent French, it is noticeable that his narrators rarely, if ever, make use of languages), and from companionable society, became introverted and self-absorbed. The intensity of his personal problems forced its way through into the pages of his magazine articles as though he was working out his anxieties in public. The immediacy of the magazines clearly encouraged this. Thackeray was forced from sheer necessity to write regularly for the periodicals despite great personal tragedy, and he confronted his emotional traumas by deliberately colouring the public discourse of the foreign correspondence with the personal voice and private memories of the narrator. The magazines thus became, for a time for Thackeray, the mirror of his personal agony. The characters inspected and memorialized on his travels became reflections of aspects of himself – kings and emperors, poor students and artists, gay family men and solitary, ridiculed outsiders – and represent facets of the human personality attempting to construct a new identity in the face of disintegration. These personages surround the isolated observer as apparitions of his dreams and losses. The very miscellaneousness of the magazines, the possibility of a kaleidoscope of images in different modes, enabled Thackeray to visualize through language the tensional forces in his own imagination at this moment. Thackeray effectively acts out a kind of psychodrama in the genres of magazine writing he had come to know well.

The self-characterization of the narrator as an old man is central in Thackeray's response to the breakdown of his marriage. Two distinct themes new to Thackeray's writings emerge here: the solitariness of the traveller and his sentimental attachment to family life, and the wisdom and good sense that come with age and experience. Moods of weariness, exhaustion, and inertia suggest a decline in desire that points to a loss of sexual appetite and an expulsion of the pleasures of France.

The illness of Thackeray's wife, Isabella, was a turning point in his fiction and criticism, creating the need for more sustained self-analysis than had previously affected the writer. In his foreign writings, this focusing upon the self became more overt because of the solitary nature of his Continental travel, reclusive despite the circle of family and acquaintances around him. In

December 1840, Thackeray was staying with his mother, step-father, half-sister, grandmother and daughters in Paris. It had only been three months since Isabella had attempted suicide during the ferry crossing to Ireland. As Gordon Ray indicates, Thackeray's life in the interim had been fraught with anxiety about his wife, and not helped by a terrible reception at Isabella's family home in Cork, a general poverty induced by the expense of the journey and the inability to work because of having to nurse his wife, and the final trial of a dreadful journey to Paris. The move was intended to release Thackeray from the nursing which Isabella required and to reduce their expenses in the cheaper climate of France and family. Ray summarizes that 'the relief and gratitude that Thackeray felt at finding himself once more at home, among people who would give him affectionate and unquestioning help, can hardly be exaggerated'.[34]

The immediate result of this suddenly found stability and haven of refuge was, however, *The Second Funeral of Napoleon*, published in January 1841. Home was not entirely what Thackeray desired. The article was a reconstruction of the reinterment of Napoleon at the Hôtel des Invalides in Paris on 15 December 1840. Thackeray wrote his little pamphlet almost immediately and published it with Hugh Cunningham in January 1841.[35] The isolation of the little volume, adrift in the marketplace and beyond the publishing structures of its day, is perhaps symbolic of the author's despair and loneliness. Gordon Ray comments that the essay is distinguished for a description of the family household, based on that of the Carmichael-Smyths. The emphasis upon the stability and virtue of the family unit contrasts the solitariness of the narrator, as it does the insidiousness of the City society in *The Great Hoggarty Diamond* and 'Notes on the North What-d'ye-Callem Election', both begun in September of that year.[36] However, the *Second Funeral* is about the collapse of an icon and the decay of the body's energies, the dissolution of identity, and the presence of the family serves only to further undermine the integrity of the authorial figure in the text. The journalist, Titmarsh, presides symbolically over the funeral of his own certainties (*his* is the 'Second Funeral'), and, more than anywhere else in his canon, Thackeray shows how the journal article can be a mediation between self and news and not a merely factual or historical record. The narrator ceases to be a contemporary historian, reporter, and political satirist, and becomes the outsider-observer,. an intriguing figure of isolation, as unmoved by the ceremony as the corpse itself.

In *The Second Funeral of Napoleon*, it is the narrator's exclusion from the sphere of domestic happiness which is important; he has become more introverted, the 'bachelor' Titmarsh. Thackeray's persona is not treated as a consistent character; in an earlier article, he is apparently married to a large woman and has several children, but here he is found addressing 'Dearest Amelia', a Miss Smith, who is cautiously unnamed in the opening line. The 'Smith', according to a letter written by Thackeray to Edward Fitzgerald, refers to his mother ('Smyth'),[37] but Samuel Titmarsh's wife in *The Great Hoggarty*

Diamond is called Mary Smith. Perhaps, however, some form of illicit liason might have suggested itself to the readership of the day. Thackeray thus assumed a playful bachelorhood, or perhaps even libertinism, in the midst of his enforced estrangement from his real wife.

The exalted position of the figurehead of Napoleon is deflated in the *Second Funeral*, as John Carey has remarked,[38] by the rather rough treatment which Thackeray gives the actual body, describing the 'corpse' with a deliberate and teasing restraint, remarking such details as 'his Imperial Majesty's brow was of a yellowish colour, which appearance was also visible about the orbits of the eyes'. Josephine, too, 'is dead now, and cold, poor creature'. The two great lovers are now corpses; desire is dead also. Whereas in 'Meditations at Versailles' Thackeray brought life back to the Court of Louis, on St Helena and returning to Paris he makes no attempt to revive the Emperor. Despite the great power of memory which Thackeray often invokes, the dead here are dead. The French ceremony of Napoleon's interment cannot and ought not to revive the Emperor's spirit; he must be confined to the annals of history and left there.

> Is it possible? can the Emperor forget? We don't like to break it to him, but has he forgotten all about the farm at Pizzo, and the garden of the Observatory? Yes, truly: there he lies on his golden shield, never stirring, never so much as lifting his eyelids, or opening his lips any wider.[39]

The parallelism at work in the article between Titmarsh and Napoleon is subtle and unobtrusive. Titmarsh is seen waking at the commencement of section three from the coldness of a night's sleep. He is placed in the same position of repose as the Emperor, seen lying in state at the end of the second part. The two 'bodies' arrive in Paris at the same time, but whilst Napoleon cannot live again, Titmarsh is undecided momentarily about his future. Section three, 'On the Funeral Ceremony', begins:

> Shall I tell you, my dear, that when François woke me at a very early hour on this eventful morning, while the keen stars were still glittering overhead, a half moon, as sharp as a razor, beaming in the frosty sky, and a wicked north wind blowing, that blew the blood out of one's fingers and froze your leg as you put it out of bed ... I felt myself, after imbibing the hot breakfast, so comfortable under three blankets and a mackintosh, that for at least a quarter-of-an-hour no man in Europe could say whether Titmarsh would or would not be present at the burial of the Emperor Napoleon. (XXII, 329)

Thackeray as a child, during his voyage to England from Calcutta, had seen Napoleon walking on St Helena; he had spoken on Napoleon at university.[40] Elsewhere in his writings, Napoleon becomes a significant icon, not just for his impact on Victorian culture, but as a shadow of a powerful personality – merging with Becky in an initial drawing in *Vanity Fair*, for example. Here, the resemblance works at a number of levels: as an image of greatness fallen, he suggests the vanity of the individual believing himself and his ideals invincible. The trauma of loss through which Thackeray passed is powerfully invoked in the image of a dead national idol.

Titmarsh is also placed in such a position to duplicate the argument that Thackeray is levelling at the glorification of greatness. The authoritative periodical voice (or, in this case, the narrative voice of a comic pamphlet) is exposed for what it is – not a distant, untouchable, unquestionable scholar, but 'a man and a brother'. Titmarsh acts as a foil for Thackeray's comic reduction of the greatness of Napoleon by revealing an honest human fallibility.

Titmarsh thus plays a dual role: as an integral figure in Thackeray's thesis and as an outside observer. Although the family described as it leaves the narrator's boarding-house is based on Thackeray's own, the narrator himself has no part within it. He is noticeably excluded from the family happiness. He travels with a 'companion', but this is a faceless co-traveller who quickly vanishes, and is only mentioned to preserve an authorial 'we' in the narrative (and also to displace the 'I'). The family is the 'very prettiest sight of the whole day', but it is just a 'sight', and Thackeray, as Titmarsh, has only his own thoughts for comfort. His self-projection is as an ageing man, cynical, unhappy, almost bitter. His sneering, though difficult for the innocent to understand, seems plain to him. 'Ah, my dear! you are young now and enthusiastic! and your Titmarsh is old, very old, sad, and grey-headed' (XXII, 327). He is in sharp contrast to the 'hale, handsome old lady of seventy' and the 'grandfather, spick and span, clean shaved ... walking as upright and solemn as may be, having his lady on his arm' (XXII, 330-31). Exhaustion is not necessarily part of ageing, but part of experience.

When the time for the ceremony arrives and the funeral cortège approaches, Titmarsh is seated in the church of Les Invalides, where all he can do is observe and be silent. He finds that the 'best and most solemn part of the show' is to be found in the objects around him, specifically in the 'long rows of dim ghostly-looking standards, captured in old days from the enemy' which hang from the roof 'with the glare of their original colours worn down by dust and time'. They belong to a past order of history, as far away as Thackeray's old self. They are the 'standards' of his magazinery, too: his hopes and dreams of writerly and family success. 'Ah Yellowplush! where are the days when you lived and laughed?' Thackeray asked of himself in a letter of May 1841.[41]

Images of death and decay surround the narrator. The simple and silent movements of the restless, waiting people as they stamp their feet and rub their hands in the cold imply their sympathetic relationship with their Emperor; 'we were frozen where we sat.' The crowd, Thackeray says, as at the coronation of Victoria and the hanging of Courvoisier, sought 'to pass away the weary time with the best amusements that will offer' and 'are jocular rather than solemn' on such occasions. They laugh at an old woman moved on from seat to seat, until she finally settles on one which nobody claims, a movement which Thackeray likens to the chicken at a pantomime which escapes its master and hops around the pit, cheered on until it is caught. She is another version of the Emperor and the writer: an outcast, an outsider, mocked and subsequently destroyed.

The beginning of the procession arrives, in the shape of incense-boys, priests, and bishops, and two bearers of candles held in enormous candlesticks, of which 'one was burning brightly, but the wind (that chartered libertine) had blown out the other'. Thackeray 'wondered to myself whether the reverend gentleman who carried the extinguished candle, felt disgusted, humiliated, mortified – perfectly conscious that the eyes of many thousands of people were bent upon that bit of refractory wax. We all of us looked at it with intense interest' (XXII, 345). The 'extinguished candle' is a metaphor for the dead hero, but, with a keen irony, it attracts greater attention than the actual body of Napoleon, and also, it might be added, than the actual person of the narrator. The candle-bearer is yet another alienated figure. The extinction is also a sexual one. The phallic candle is blown out by the 'libertine' wind, a suggestion of the sexual disease that affected Thackeray throughout his adult life and probably caused his premature death at 52. *The Second Funeral of Napoleon* is full of suggestive images, building upon the absurdity that Thackeray saw in the re-burial of the Emperor, and representing his own anxieties, at once displaced by comedy and journalism, and yet ever-present in the subjectivity of the narrator. Images of the solitary and world-weary traveller suggest that Titmarsh, too, has been dragged from his grave to be transported across the world and subjected to the ridicule of an ignoble show: one that displays the self to those who would read it. Self-mortification and self-abasement are given public exposure, but in such a way that enabled Thackeray to confront his own symbolic death in the very public world of the newspaper report.

The ending of the funeral day has a finality and a great loneliness about it. Despite the supposed presence of a second traveller with Titmarsh, the narrator appears to be more alone than ever as the crowds vanish home. Outside of Les Invalides, 'where thousands of people had been assembled ... the benches were now quite bare'. Thackeray suggests that the memories of the French people are not so deep or loyal as to keep them long from home. Even in France, families outweigh politics and ceremony. The funeral leaves only an image of the forgotten and abandoned:

> All the forty thousand people who covered the great stands before the Hôtel had gone away too. The Imperial Barge had been dragged up the river, and was lying lonely along the Quay, examined by some few shivering people on the shore. (XXII, 347)

This is the end of Carnival. Pleasure and sensuality, usually associated with Paris, are buried with Napoleon. Only an uncertain emptiness is left. There is one last comfort awaiting the narrator, however, when he returns to the boarding-house. He does not meet again with the happy family of the same building, but discovers 'that dinner was just ready'. A new appetite emerges to be exchanged symbolically with the sexual desires of the now decayed flesh. The bathos of this sitting down to dinner after the State funeral recalls the callous ending to 'A Gambler's Death' in the *Paris Sketch-Book*. It is Thackeray's great joke at the expense of the dead, and great honesty at the expense of the living. But here it is a comfort for the solitary narrator, and doubtless for the lonely Thackeray, to rejoin the home, whilst the implied human vanity of the dinner at Frascati's is missing.

As Thackeray came to identify more closely with his persona Michael Angelo Titmarsh, so the themes of his travel writing, as those of his fiction, came to reflect the contrast of the happy home with the solitary wanderer. Desire is translated into terms other than those associated with sexual exchange (prostitution, gambling), and established through images of eating and old age. One might argue that the symbolic codes of the Regency period – food, drink, gambling, women, which Benita Eisler in her recent biography of Lord Byron translates into restlessness, sensuality, melancholy, and exuberence[42] – were metamorphosing into 'safer' Victorian pursuits tinged with a longing for a freer moral climate (implicit but ambivalent in the warning to Pogson, with his volume of *Don Juan*). In 'A St Philip's Day at Paris', a day connected to a feast, Thackeray describes the male economy of pleasure, listing the miscellaneous and humble means by which men generate their own happiness:

> ... some men from reading Parliamentary debates; some from swinging on gates, or butterfly chasing; some, on the contrary, from political economy, from the study of the law, from the leading article of the Times newspaper; or from many other things equally strange.[43]

Such pastimes are timid compared to the great extremes of the Regency. Journalism, though, is pleasurable. The fear of squandering good feeling became very real to Thackeray after 1840. He told his mother in a letter of 20-21 August 1840, 'I find myself growing much more sentimental as I grow older', but adding, 'the world is not near such a bad one as some of your orthodox pretend.'[44] In his assessment of happiness, the contentment of man was becoming more important than the reason for his contentment – a viewpoint which would not have stood up to Thackeray's criticism a year earlier of jovial crowds at hangings.

> I saw a man to-day in the Champs Elysées – a large, fat man, with ear-rings and immense shirt-collar – a grandfather at least – walking placidly in the sunshine, sucking a stick of barley-sugar. He had sucked it in a beautiful conical way, and was examining its amber apex, glistening between his eye and the orb of day. He was showing his loyalty, in a word, to his King ... And why not?[45]

This tolerance towards mankind even stretches to the French king, Louis Philippe, scarcely thinkable in the *Paris Sketch-Book*. Yet it is a tolerance born out of a sense of suffering and personal loneliness. Louis Philippe, Thackeray says, 'is the wisest, the greatest – the most miserable man in Europe ... the sun, they say, is cold itself, and in the midst of its splendours, lonely'. As the crowds watch the King, greeted with silence on his balcony, withdraw into the palace, Thackeray comments 'it must be a sad life to stifle all day through, under this sickly mask of ceremony; to be lonely and yet never alone'.[46] Some months earlier, Thackeray had complained to his mother about the strain of nursing Isabella, who, in her worst moments, scarcely knew he was there or who he was.[47]

The sexual imagery here is as important as the journalism, however. Old age sucks its phallic barley-sugar and feels contented, having and enjoying. He is fulfilled in his familial role ('a grandfather *at least*'), and his King (the regent, the cone) is the totem of acknowledgement of this achievement. Moreover, he is bodily substantial, 'large', 'fat', 'immense', and not the wasted image of manhood that we see in the Titmarsh of the *Second Funeral*. It is in these images of manly satisfaction that Thackeray increasingly takes vicarious pleasure. The festivals about which he writes become only the background for such fantasies of male potency and omnipotence. But Thackeray/Titmarsh himself cannot indulge or be satisfied. Paris is no longer the place of erotic desire, but only a reflection of Thackeray's increasing sense of male marginalization. The self is 'stifled' and not released in the once pleasurable city of Paris. Loneliness and isolation replace the Bohemianism of a few years earlier, and the promise of family life now no longer attainable.

'Memorials of Gormandising' was originally intended as a longer work, and was advertised at the end of the first edition of *The Second Funeral of Napoleon*, which described as 'preparing for immediate publication Dinner Reminiscences, or the Young Gourmandizer's Guide at Paris, by Mr. M.A. Titmarsh'.[48] The association between the two projects is interesting and revealing. In 'Memorials of Gormandising', Thackeray used the comic persona of M.A. Titmarsh to explore the eating-houses of Paris and to examine the eating habits of England and France. His choice of title connects to the 'funerary' emblems of the *Second Funeral*, but is more celebratory than the 'reminiscences' of the original idea of a guidebook. 'Memorials' suggests both the departure of one age – the age of youth, of bachelorhood, of fine eating, of regency England – and the commemoration of that passing in the new age – a sense of honouring, toasting, carousing, not forgetting. Ironically, of course, Titmarsh's method of celebrating the good dinners he had with his friend in Paris is to go and have another good dinner! This is one pleasurable aspect of Thackeray's life which was not destroyed by the insanity of his wife, and indeed, it was a pleasure which was resurgent in his second bachelorhood and, as Carey suggests, in some ways assuaged his sexual appetite.[49]

Thackeray and Titmarsh, the solitary author and the solitary traveller, come very close together in 'Gormandising'. In his letters, the persona became an identifiable pseudonym, a method of distancing himself when having to talk about his personal life. His old comic characters, such as Yellowplush and

Gahagan, were becoming difficult to relate to. Titmarsh was a more mature and sombre character, who occupied a life similar to Thackeray's, but without the moral conscience. Bachelorhood becomes a focus of the 'Gormandising' essay, but not in an unhappy manner as in the *Second Funeral*, for instance. The 'gastronomic experiments' which Titmarsh sets out for the reader become the *raison d'être* of the solitary life. They are part of a strongly masculine world; a kind of male rejection of the increased attraction for domesticity in the culture of the 1840s and 1850s. They are also indication of the increasing commodification of capitalist culture. Food is not just for nourishment, but a pleasure in itself, and a luxury purchase, the possession of which indicates the gentility of the diner. In part, food also represents what Benjamin sees in capitalism as the desire for novelty.[50] Like the periodical, the next dinner is described by Thackeray as something to be memorable, to be historicized, to be purchased with care and thought and planning. Thackeray's love of eating is perhaps comparable to the jaunts that Dickens took with his friends. Thackeray sketched his popular rival's trip to Cornwall with Forster, Stanfield, and Maclise in 1842.[51] The bachelor world provides access to culture in a manner that the female-dominated domestic sphere prevents.

The family life comes to be seen as a repetitive and restricting life, where the Sunday roast mutton is served again and again throughout the week in a variety of forms: hot, cold, hashed, and then the joint of beef 'undergoes the same alternations of cookery, and disappears'. He says of London family life around the dining-table:

> You fancy it is virtuous and manly all this. Nonsense, my good sir; you are indifferent because you are ignorant, because your life is passed in a narrow circle of ideas, and because you are bigotedly blind and pompously callous to the beauties and excellencies beyond you.[52]

The dinner table, unlike the streets of Paris, is a place of companionship, of manliness. It is a refuge from the social world, the world of women and parties. Otherness is the family not the French. The mutual trust and open honesty of a good dinner is placed at the opposite pole from the affectation of the salon. The dinner table is also the place for the indolent man, the man who enjoys idleness, a vice that Thackeray criticized in himself. The public sphere of the dinner table is distinctly male, and perhaps represents an attempt to retain the coffee-house form of public discourse regretted by Habermas's history. The 'circle of ideas' is restrictive and repetitive; it requires the linear pageant of restaurant meals, of diversity, like the linear run of a magazine, to generate the excitement a man needs.

After a lengthy description of a meal enjoyed with his companion, Gustavus (a name no doubt intended to remind the reader of Sam Titmarsh's friend, Gus, in the *Hoggarty Diamond*, as well as referring to Thackeray's friend, Augustus Stevens – and also a return to a Classical age of male authority), Thackeray describes how the distant Paris street-hawkers cry out the names of the morning papers, and how the moon rises 'glittering over the tiles', illuminating 'two glasses of punch that two gentlemen in a small room of the Café Foy did ever and anon raise to their lips'. The men bask in the atmosphere; their closeness making conversation unnecessary:

> Both were silent; both happy; both were smoking cigars, – for both knew that the soothing plant of Cuba is sweeter to the philosopher after dinner than the prattle of all the women in the world.[53]

Again, the presence of the world of newspaper print (the hawkers' cries) is symbolic of its status as a bachelor pleasure. The comfort that the dinner table could offer was much more certain and, in a way, easier to find than the company of women for the married 'bachelor'. It was also morally acceptable. 'Let us appreciate the joys of idleness; let us give a loose to silence; and after having enjoyed this, the best dessert after a goodly dinner, at close of eve, saunter slowly home.' This is very much the central image of 'Memorials of Gormandising'. As such, it shows an avoidance or evasion of the family life, rather as the boarding-house in the *Second Funeral* functioned as a place of isolation for the narrator, a place where he remained outside of the social circle. The return home is left as late as possible, and made as slowly as possible, in order to prolong the outer life. But the walk home is solitary and not sullied by the search for prostitution or other metropolitan attractions. The Otherness of Paris has been replaced by a bachelorhood that maintains a decorous public image. It is 'silence' that is released after the dinner, and not sexual appetite.

'Memorials of Gormandising', however, despite these sombre indicators, is not a gloomy or despondent picture of life. It has far greater colour and humour than the articles for the Britannia, and less regret than the slightly earlier *Second Funeral*. It is a travel guide to good eating, turned moral essay.[54] Thackeray lists several restaurants, indicating their good and bad characteristics, and provides the novice traveller with a catalogue of menus at different prices. The article is very much a combination of Thackeray's personal love of food (which, unlike Meredith's, did not stretch to cookery[55]) with the periodical principle of the diffusion of knowledge. Where Thackeray earlier in his career used the menu to mock the magazine trademark of turning anything into 'useful information', here he creates a brilliant essay out of that very same ideology. The most ordinary subject becomes the correct topic for magazine discourse. And yet one might feel that Thackeray has hidden something in his determination to portray masculinity at this stage in his career. The Regency Rake's progress is now the travels of a Victorian foodie.

The article is comically moral; the individual, or a person 'in the middling classes of life', is taught that to overspend on something tasteless is a more heinous crime than to spend little on something plain, but honest. Similar criticism was levelled by Thackeray at the French government over their pasteboard and tinsel decorations in the *Second Funeral*. But it is also a symbolic argument reflecting Thackeray aesthetics of taste in painting and writing: honest and plain journalism, like the 'frisky Watteaus' he prefers to Reubens, have greater value (commercially?) than the pretensions of the Bulwer's and their sham self-importance.[56] The moral of the essay is illustrated by an anecdote about a bad dinner which Titmarsh and Gustavus are forced to endure at the behest of their friend, Captain Hopkinson. Titmarsh says, 'we had had for our three francs bad bread, bad meat, bad wine'. Hopkinson is mercilessly dropped from their list of acquaintances; 'how can you trust or be friendly with a man who deceives you in this miserable way?' The moral is: 'Avoid pretence; mistrust shabby eloquence; cut your coat according to your cloth; if you have but a few shillings in your pocket, aim only at those humble and honest meats which your small store will purchase.'[57]

But it is not a 'bad' dinner that is the offence, in Thackeray's eyes; good and bad remain part of the unavoidable substance of life, as they remain inseparable in the variety of Paris and the essence of human nature:

> A bad dinner does no harm to any human soul, and the philosopher partakes of such with easy resignation; but a bad and a dear dinner is enough to raise the anger of any man ...[58]

The economy of food further suggests its commodification.[59] The emphasis on money does, however, have more than comic and moral sides. Thackeray's complaints in his letters about his financial situation were still frequent in 1841. He still required that one literary success to secure his family's future: 'I make fine Alnaschar visions on the subject', he said in July 1840, 'but they all begin with 150£ in them'.[60]

Thackeray's love of Paris cannot be doubted.[61] As he says himself in 'Memorials of Gormandising', not without a degree of exaggeration and conceit to project a more worldly (and elderly) self-image for his persona:

> My good sir, what could we do without our Paris? I came here first in 1815 (when the Duke [of Wellington] and I were a good deal remarked by the inhabitants); I proposed but to stay a week; stopped three months, and have returned every year since.[62]

London gave him a 'grave thoughtful countenance'.[63] In Paris, 'my darling city improves ... with every visit, and has some new palace, or church, or statue, or gimcrack, to greet your eyes withal'.[64] The mixture of colonialism ('our') and sexual delight ('my darling') signifies the acquisitiveness and possessiveness that Thackeray and England felt in their relationships. But for Thackeray this mingling of bloods was under analysis and his sense of the alien world of Paris and of woman were merging in a manner he found difficult to integrate. In 'A Shrove Tuesday in Paris', he describes a festival which celebrates an excess of eating in preparation for a period of fasting. The significance of this is clear in his portrait of a 'grisette', Pauline, whom he recalls as making some shirts for him when at Paris some years previous. Pauline's prostitution is intellectualized and translated into an aesthetic judgement, such as he placed on Dickens' portrait of Nancy in 1839.

> A fierce, honest moralist might, to be sure, find a good deal to blame in Madame Pauline's conduct and life ... But to rightly judge the woman's character, we must take the good and the bad together ... Let us neither abuse her nor pity her too much, but look at the woman such as we find her, if we look at her at all.[65]

Pauline is also Paris. She is also writing, of a brisk and ephemeral sort. She is a sketch, and not a representative of high art. She is pleasure. She is morally questionable and yet she remains seductive. Her Otherness must also be accepted as present in all of us, though Thackeray cannot state this explicitly, and does not really attempt to do so until *Pendennis*. Nevertheless, Paris functions as the metaphor for our human frailty and moral failings. The seductive and sexual woman stands alongside the male against the family and the grandiose claims of permanency in art. The network of parallelism is complicated but revealing of the superstructure of Victorian culture. Thackeray writes:

> And if it be in writing, as in drawing, that a sketch taken from nature of a place never so humble or unpicturesque, has always a certain good in it that is not to be found in fanciful works of far greater pretension – in this manner poor Pauline's rude portrait may find a little favour in the eyes of the public. There are certain little features in the countenance which might, to be sure, be much prettier than they are; but it is best, after all, to take such things as we find them, nor, be they ever so ugly, has nature made them in vain.[66]

Having confronted the French and the seductions inherent in the French capital and its symbolic associations, Thackeray introduced a more complex discourse of evasion. Something of this, I think, was present also in his reconciliation of journalist and literary artist. In accepting both as part of an inherently male domain, albeit one fraught with obvious contradictions, he stood against the domesticating spirit of his age. But in maintaining a distance between sexuality and the family by locating the sexual drive in the bachelor figure and in the Public Sphere, he replicated those forces in his own culture that gradually subdued or neutered the sexual. The paradox of the sexual operating only outside of the family is thereafter a central tension in his fiction: Becky confronting Amelia, Arthur Pendennis confronting his twin magnets on the cover of *Pendennis*, Henry Esmond attracted to both Beatrix and Rachel. By so structuring these forces, and equating them to the binary of journalism/art, Thackeray makes of writing a public (the periodical) and private (the novel) face. The bachelor male and the family (associated with the female) thus come to occupy a further level of this binary opposition. Thackeray's loss of the second of these in the madness of his wife, and his later decline as a novelist which enforced his return to the periodical market-place in 1860, prevent any form of resolution between these oppositional forces in his work. France is lost, and becomes symbolic of loss. Although, after 1841, he continues to spend part of each year in Paris, there is no return to the exploration of the capital as a cultural mirror-image. Paris is always to be framed, and contained, by the literary (as in 'Dickens in France', 1842) or the magazine, as in the several *Punch* items. We see little else of 'my darling city'.

Notes

[1] Terry Eagleton, *Heathcliff and the Great Hunger* (London: Verso, 1995), 9.
[2] See Homi Bhabha in the foreword to Frantz Fanon, *Black Skin, White Masks* (London: Pluto Press, 1986), xvi; Firdous Azim, *The Colonial Rise of the Novel* (London: Routledge, 1993), 11-12.
[3] G.N. Ray, 'Thackeray and France', 47.
[4] Ibid., 75.
[5] See Ray's chronology of Thackeray's time abroad, compiled from the letters: ibid., 283-4.
[6] David Musselwhite, *Partings Welded Together: Politics and Desire in the Nineteenth Century English Novel* (London: Methuen, 1987), 130.
[7] *Letters*, II, 136, cited in Ray, *Uses*, 264.
[8] See, for instance, Dorothy Middleton, *Victorian Lady Travellers* (Chicago: Chicago University Press, 1982).
[9] See Thackeray's translations of French novels for reviews and uncompleted volume publications; Shillingsburg, *Pegasus*, 47, 57 (the review of Sue's *Mysteries of Paris* for the *Foreign Quarterly Review*, 31 (April 1843), 231-49, reveals just how much of this novel he knew well).
[10] Reynolds later operated on the darker side of English fiction with his reworking of Sue's epic, *The Mysteries of London*; regarding Thackeray, Edward Fitzgerald made an interesting comment in a letter to W.F. Pollock, 20 July 1839, about the *Memoirs of Grammont* (by Count Antony Hamilton), saying 'I have also heard Thackeray speak well of him: but he is naturally prejudiced in favour of the dirty and immoral', W.A. Wright (ed.), *More Letters of Edward Fitzgerald* (London: Macmillan, 1901). Is the 'he' Thackeray or Grammont? In either case, the comment suggests Fitzgerald's association of Thackeray with the immoral at the time he was writing the *Paris Sketch-Book*.
[11] Donald Hawes, 'Thackeray and French Literature in Perspective', *Studies in the Novel*, 13: 1-2 (Spring-Summer 1981), 14; see Thackeray's, *'Jérôme Paturot*. With Considerations of Novels in General. In a letter from M.A. Titmarsh', *Fraser's Magazine* (September 1843), and 'French Romancers on England', *Foreign Quarterly Review* (October 1843).
[12] Letter to Mrs Carmichael-Smyth, 1 June 1840; *Letters*, I, 448.

[13] His ambitions for periodical success in the field were finished when he failed to obtain the post of editor for the *Foreign Quarterly Review* in 1842, but he remained to write several articles for the paper.
[14] Ray, *Uses*, 183, 201; *Letters*, I, 358.
[15] John Buchanan-Brown, *The Illustrations of William Makepeace Thackeray* (London: David and Charles, 1979), 179 n.6; see comment in Ray, *Uses*, 172, on Thackeray's drawings. Thackeray later reversed the roles when he provided the letter-press for Louis Marvey's *Sketches after English Landscape Painters* (London: David Bogue, 1850).
[16] *Letters*, I, 409.
[17] The first travel review was of P.C. Scarlett's 'South America and the Pacific', *The Times*, 6 February 1838 (reprinted in Gulliver, 210-11); the first Paris article was 'Parisian Caricatures', *London and Westminster Review* (April 1839), which formed the chapter 'Caricatures and Lithography in Paris' of the *Paris Sketch-Book*; the *Corsair* and *Fraser* papers were published between August and December 1839.
[18] *Letters*, I, 327-29.
[19] See Ray, *Uses*, 252, 477n.
[20] 'Lord Lindsey's Travels in Egypt and the Holy Land', *The Times*, 28 September 1838; reprinted in Gulliver, 220.
[21] Tillotson and Hawes (eds), *Heritage*, 25; extracted from the *Spectator*, 18 July 1840, xiii, 689.
[22] Colby, *Canvass*, 37.
[23] See Thackeray's comments on travel writers like Victor Hugo making unacknowledged use of guidebooks, '*The Rhine*. By Victor Hugo', *Foreign Quarterly Review*, 29 (April 1842), 143, 'Travelling Romancers: Dumas on the Rhine', *Foreign Quarterly Review*, 30 (October 1842), 106-7, 'England. By Alfred Michiels', *Foreign Quarterly Review*, 33 (July 1844), 436.
[24] George Sand, *Lettres d'un Voyager* (Harmondsworth: Penguin, 1987), 43; Sand did not like tourists: she says elsewhere in the *Lettres* (published in the French press 1834-6, and collected as a volume in 1837), tourists 'are truly the scourge of our age, bent on altering with their presence the nature of all countries of the world and ruining with their idle curiosity and idiotic questions the pleasure of contemplative walkers' (p. 52).
[25] 'Travelling Romancers: Dumas on the Rhine', *Foreign Quarterly Review*, 30 (October 1842), 121.
[26] Chapter 62, 'Am Rhein', also describes the British traveller who has 'invaded Europe any time since the conclusion of the war' (*Works*, II, 292); the identification between Titmarsh and Napoleon in *The Second Funeral of Napoleon* (1841) adds an extra overtone to these parallels.
[27] 'An Invasion of France', *Works*, XVI, 1 [references in the text are to this edition].
[28] Carey, 121.

[29] This is paralleled in the portrayal of Becky Sharp as a mermaid in Chapter 64 of *Vanity Fair* (II, 316-17), and in the initial illustration to Chapter 44 (II, 91).
[30] Letter to Mrs Carmichael-Smyth, 6?-18 July 1840; *Letters*, I, 453; this was discussed in 'Going to See a Man Hanged'.
[31] The chapters written for the book are among the best: 'A Caution to Travellers', 'On Some French fashionable Novels', 'A Gambler's Death', 'Napoleon and his System', 'Beatrice Merger', 'The Case of Peytel', 'French Dramas and Melodramas', and 'Meditations at Versailles'.
[32] Ray, *Uses*, 172-3.
[33] See Chapter 6, below.
[34] Ray, *Uses*, 260.
[35] Shillingsburg, *Pegasus*, 44.
[36] Ray, *Uses*, 261-4.
[37] Letter to Fitzgerald, 10 Jan. 1841; *Letters*, II, 4.
[38] Carey, 123.
[39] *The Second Funeral of Napoleon*, *Works*, XXII, 333-4 [references in the text are to this edition].
[40] Ray, *Uses*, 66, 118.
[41] *Letters*, II, 22.
[42] Benita Eisler, *Byron: Child of Passion, Fool of Fame* (London: Hamish Hamilton, 1999), 5.
[43] 'A St Philip's Day at Paris', part 1, *Britannia*, 15 May 1841; reprinted in *The Works of William Makepeace Thackeray, with Biographical Introductions*, 13 vols (London: John Murray, 1913), XIII ('Ballads and Miscellanies'), 553 [hereafter, *Ballads*].
[44] *Letters*, I, 464.
[45] *Ballads*, 553.
[46] Ibid., 564-5.
[47] Letter to Mrs Carmichael-Smyth, 10 September 1840, *Letters*, I, 473.
[48] Printed in Melville, *Life*, 109.
[49] Carey, 84-5; Walter Bagehot discusses Thackeray's writings in terms of textuality and food, calling him 'the edited and illustrated edition of a great dinner' in a review of *Philip* for the *Spectator*, 9 August 1862; see Tillotson and Hawes (eds), *Heritage*, 306-7.
[50] See Brook Thomas, 'The New Historicism and Other Old Fashioned Topics', in H. Aram Veeser, *The New Historicism* (London: Routledge, 1989), 187.
[51] See Fred Kaplan, *Dickens: A Biography* (London: Hodder and Stoughton, 1988), illustration no. 34.
[52] 'Memorials of Gormandising', *Ballads*, 576.
[53] Ibid., 584.
[54] There is an echo of Thackeray's reading of the popular magazines like the *Town* here, that provided a guide to the gin-shops, tavern and free-and-easies of London.

[55] But see Thackeray's review of *Simpson's Cookery*, *National Standard*, 56 (25 January 1834).
[56] See Fisher, 'Aesthetics of the Mediocre', 65-82.
[57] 'Memorials of Gormandising', *Ballads*, 591.
[58] Ibid., 597.
[59] In 'Travelling Romancers: Dumas on the Rhine', *Foreign Quarterly Review*, 30 (October 1842), 105, Thackeray likens 'the race of cooks' to 'literary men', and that a popular novelist can 'make you forthwith a satisfactory dinner, dishing you up three hot volumes in a trice ... '; reprinted in Richard Pearson (ed.), *W.M. Thackeray: Early Travel Writings* (London: Routledge/Thoemmes Press, 1996).
[60] *Letters*, I, 459.
[61] For the argument on Thackeray's Francophobia, see Greig, *Thackeray*, 75-8; Carey, 120; Colby, *Canvass*, 37-41.
[62] 'Memorials of Gormandising', *Ballads*, 575.
[63] Letter to Mrs Carmichael-Smyth, 19 November 1839; *Letters*, I, 391-2.
[64] 'Memorials of Gormandising', *Ballads*, 575.
[65] 'Shrove Tuesday in Paris', *Ballads*, 569.
[66] Ibid., 572.

Chapter 6

The public and the press: journalistic authority, self-advertising, and the periodical commodity in social essays for *Fraser's Magazine* and *Punch*

The changing nature of literary production and the rise of mass periodical literature in the Victorian period transformed the relationships between author, publisher and public. For literary historians, this transformation ought to be a central factor in the study of nineteenth-century writers. The dearth of 'classic' literature in the 1830s has led to a neglect of a significant period in the development of English literature. But that very dearth is largely an indication of the need for writers to redefine the nature of their work in a period of immense upheaval. As Scott Bennett has described, the period from 1825 to 1845, and most specifically the 1830s, was 'the take-off period for the mass reading market'. The vital connection between the emerging industrialized capitalist economy and the periodical press is evident in Bennett's remark that 'the market for reading matter was one of the earliest consumer mass markets to develop, and it established itself primarily through serial publication'. He continues: 'Mass circulation journals became as central a feature of the industrialization and urbanization of Britain as did its coal, iron, and textile industries.'[1] The rise of the magazine, and the consolidation of the cultural importance of the newspaper, brought writers like Dickens and Thackeray, Jerrold and A'Beckett, Maginn and Lemon, to the forefront of literary experiment, whilst writers like Harrison Ainsworth, Bulwer-Lytton, the Countess of Blessington, Catherine Gore, G.P.R. James, G.W.M. Reynolds, and Frances Trollope could reach large popular markets with the serialization of their stories.

Recent literary criticism has begun to assess the Victorian self-analysis of the press. This work, however, tends to begin much later in the century with the magazine writers of New Journalism, or the contributors to the *Saturday Review* and the *Cornhill Magazine* in the late 1850s and 1860s. Certainly, the language of periodical criticism began to move towards more modern ideas at this time. James Fitzjames Stephen, for example, wrote an article entitled 'Journalism' for the *Cornhill Magazine*, just after Thackeray's editorship, in July 1862. In it, he provides a simple guide to newspaper and magazine writing, which suggests that, in his view, popular opinion was still unsophisticated in its attitude towards the press. 'Journalism,' he remarked, 'will, no doubt, occupy the first or one of the first places in any future literary history of the present times, for it is the most characteristic of all their [writers'] productions.'[2] His discussion of the press reminds us of just how advanced was Thackeray's critique of the periodical world. Despite *Pendennis* and *Punch*, and Thackeray's frequent analyses of the magazine and newspaper markets, Stephen still felt in 1862 that '[f]ew people have a definite notion of what a newspaper really is, of the different classes of persons who write it, and of the real extent of its influence on the course of affairs'.[3] Reflecting the growing sense of the capitalist nature of literary publication, again present in Thackeray's commentary, Stephen adds, 'a newspaper is beyond everything else a commercial undertaking'.[4]

The debate about the status of periodical literature was ever-present after Thackeray's engagement with the subject in 'The Dignity of Literature'. Indeed, even before this article, such self-analysis was a not infrequent feature of the magazines themselves. In criticism of sensation fiction in the 1860s (a genre denigrated as had been Newgate fiction in the 1830s), the 'dignity' and artistic merit of such popular fiction was questioned. Whilst Henry Silver, detailing the private conversations of *Punch* contributors around the dinner table, described the economic contest between Thackeray and Lemon, also in 1862.

> Thackeray thinks Freetrade is the right policy in literature and art – man takes his work where he's best paid for it ... Lemon thinks a Magazine should have a regular salaried staff of writers, and room for occasional outsiders. That would secure an evenness of quality.[5]

That the debate could continue this way between two old stalwarts of the periodical press as late as 1862 demonstrates just how uncertain the literary world was of the status and respectability of its product. In 1846, in one of his central statements on the professionalization of periodical writing, and dismissing calls for pensions for writers, Thackeray declared:

> Let men of letters stand for themselves. Everyday enlarges their market, and multiplies their clients. The most skilful and the most successful among the cultivators of light literature have such a hold upon the public feelings, and awaken such a sympathy, as men of the class never enjoyed until now ... I believe there never was a time when so much of the practically useful was written and read, and every branch of book-making pursued with an interest so eager.[6]

Fitzjames Stephen's article further suggests that, despite the controversies regarding the artistic merit of such publications, the media world was as fascinating to the Victorians as it is to us today. The claims being made for the press were perhaps exaggerated, but the popular impression was one of amazement at the technological advances in the creation of and the cultural dominance of the form. Thirty years after the boom really began, writers were still marvelling at – and perhaps by so doing they were still selling or advertising – their achievements. Whilst Thackeray was serializing *The Adventures of Philip* in the *Cornhill Magazine*, a novel about a foreign correspondent in the 1830s and early 1840s, Stephen's article was praising the very same role. The hyperbole is not unjustified.

> Every morning, it is said, a mass of print, containing as much matter as a thick octavo volume, is laid on our breakfast-tables. It contains an accurate report of speeches which were made some hours after we went to bed, and of the incidents which took place up to a late hour of the night; it gives us on the same day letters from persons specially employed for the purpose of writing them, about the Chinese, the Americans, the Italians, the enfranchisement of the Russian serfs, and scores of other subjects; and besides this, it puts before us a sort of photograph of one day's history of the nation in which we live, including not only its graver occupations, such as legislation and commerce, but every incident a little out of the common way brought to light by police courts or recorded by local newspapers. This goes on till at the end of the year its story is comprised in a book larger than all the classics and all the standard histories of the world put together.[7]

The role of the newspaper and magazine in telling the history of the nation is an important issue in Thackeray's writings. The 'realism' of journalism provokes his interrogation. In this chapter, I want to explore Thackeray's attitude towards 'journalism' as historical realism, his relationship with the main journals to which he contributed in the late 1830s and 1840s, his engagement with the media phenomenon, his view of the newspaper as a cultural signifier of his age, and his own notions of journalistic reporting. In particular, I want to demonstrate that he saw advertising and commodification as prevalent features of the new mass publishing industry and that his remarkable insights led to a profound ambivalence in his literary identity. The ideal of the man-of-letters and literary artist and the reality of working for a commercial industry produce a creative tension that, in turn, fosters Thackeray's desire to contribute and his guilt about his periodical writings. Nevertheless, Thackeray's belief in the value of literary journalism is surely apparent from the evidence that he spent almost fifteen years writing entirely within the periodical sector. Although many saw (and still see) the periodical as ephemeral, transient and 'low', Thackeray frequently argued that the journals of his day would form the historical sources of tomorrow. For this reason, a critical engagement with the press was essential; honesty, truth, 'realism', and knowledge were required in the periodicals if they were to become the Literature of tomorrow.

There is relatively little in the Thackeray canon which might immediately constitute journalism; however, there is much that tangentially engages with the spread of popular journalism and the role of the journalist in the new literary industry. This latter will be the subject of Chapter 7. Here, I am more interested in the concept of an age of journalism and how the literary writer positioned him or herself in response to this emerging culture of the contemporary. The notion of journalism as ephemera derives from the sense of the newspaper and magazine as providing information that is current rather than permanent, or a comedy which is transient and recyclable. Last week's newspaper has little to offer once yesterday has gone. However, it is a significant feature of the critical interest in journalism that it sought to transform this transience into permanence by interpreting periodicals as the repositories of history. Like vast museums of everything, the press gradually became the source for knowledge of the past, and more reliable than oral history or even the great retellings of history. With Hegel, Carlyle, Ranke, Macaulay and Acton, the nineteenth century has a reputation as being a period of historical interrogation; Ranke stands foremost as an historian who believed that archival sources should be the principal material for the historian and should drive historical narrative. His research, and that of his adherents, worked towards the gradual establishing of history as a scientific discipline.[8] It is no coincidence that the same period saw the emergence of the mass periodical. Even as early as 1840, critics were calling the magazine the purveyor of 'contemporary history', and, with its alignment to chronological time, its regularity in appearance, the magazine perpetuates the impression that it is part of history in the making. Margaret Beetham summarizes this view:

> Historians, including literary historians and critics, have long since recognised the special value of the periodical press in researching the recent past. Nineteenth-century magazines and newspapers are prime sources on economic, political and literary matters. However, a periodical is not a window onto the past or even a mirror of it. Each article, each periodical number, was and is part of a complex process in which writers, editors, publishers and readers engaged in trying to understand themselves and their society; that is, they struggled to make their world meaningful ... Those who owned, edited and wrote for the nineteenth-century periodical press had more power to define their world and 'make their meanings stick' than did their readers, whose most important power was the choice of whether to buy or not.[9]

This power of purchase was itself, however, a significant component in the chain of production. As Thackeray observed, the advertising function of journalism was geared towards attracting, pleasing, and stimulating, readerly desire. The 'commodity' and the 'historical repository' remained in tension when considering the symbolic value of the periodical. Thackeray, on his return to the journalistic world of London, and subject to the vagaries of editors and fluid contracts, began to observe the character of this new literary phenomenon and how far it could be described as providing an accurate portrait of his age. When he describes a sea-wreck from a newspaper article in the *Roundabout Papers*, he notes, '[h]ere, in a single column of newspaper, what strange, touching pictures do we find of seamen's dangers, vicissitudes, gallantry, generosity'.[10] The multiple associations borne out of the column of print elicit both the personal, emotive response and the detached historian's eye. Thackeray's journalism always contained this dualism of motive, this ambivalence of value.

There are three main journalistic articles by Thackeray in the late 1830s: a pair of investigations into popular print culture, 'Half-a-Crown's Worth of Cheap Knowledge' and 'Horae Catnachianae', and an account of a London hanging, 'Going to See a Man Hanged'. In the 1840s, there are the 'Letters from a Club Arm-Chair' sent out to India for publication in the *Calcutta Star*, and *Punch's* 'The Snobs of England', both of which, on one level, are parodies of journalistic reporting. Thackeray's many contributions to *Punch* are also of this type, though infrequently discussed. Week by week, they form a satirical response to current affairs ranging in subject matter from French politics and the Great Exhibition, to Cardinal Wiseman's views on acceptable reading matter. The papers which form 'Sketches and Travels in London', in particular, an account of emigrants sleeping rough at a railway station ('Waiting at the Station') and of family poverty and the pawnbroker's shop ('The Curate's Walk') are more overtly journalistic contributions to *Punch*. Such serious journalism indicates that in certain areas, Thackeray had strong social convictions and could express them in an unmediated arena more familiar to newspaper readers. It is always something of a surprise to read his comment in the *Roundabout Papers* dismissing G.H. Lewes's *Seaside Studies*: 'Go, Lewes, and clap a hideous sea-anemone into a glass; I will put a cabman under mine, and make a vivisection of a butcher.'[11] In the case of 'Going to See a Man Hanged', Thackeray thought enough of the sincerity of the piece to sign his own initials, 'W.M.T.', and stand personally before his public, as it were.

His examination of popular periodical and cheap book materials were articles most likely of his own suggestion and, unlike the foreign correspondence which was a regular journalistic employment, reveal Thackeray's own interests. The self-reflexivity they imply – his interest in media – further denotes a consistent consideration of industrial publishing through his career. If we place alongside these, his articles, 'A Brother of the Press on the History of a Literary Man, Laman Blanchard, and the Chances of the Literary Profession', 'On the Press and the Public', 'On Thunder and Small Beer' and 'The Dignity of Literature', we see a regular concern in his work to examine the writer's new situation. In comic terms, the *Punch* cartoons he drew of 'Author's Miseries' illustrate the problems and ironies of writing in the nineteenth century. 'Half-a-Crown's Worth of Cheap Knowledge' and 'Horae Catnachianae' are particularly signficant components of this theme.

Thackeray's journalism deals with social issues relating to class and poverty, but does so from the safe distance of the arm chair. However, unlike Disraeli, who put together his famous critique of industrialization in *Sybil: or, The Two Nations* (1845) from the contemporary government blue-books, Thackeray concerns himself with representation in the penny press and cheap publications of the day. He is not trying to simulate realism from fabricated knowledge. Indeed, even those articles which are derived from personal observation, such as 'Waiting at the Station', deal in fact with the awkwardness of class difference when confronting that which cannot really be known. The 'station' alluded to is as much the station in life of the figures described (and the persona describing) as a railway station. Thackeray is critical of writers like Bulwer-Lytton and, perhaps unfairly, Dickens, for writing to the fashions of the day and having little real knowledge of the class of persons depicted. Bulwer can write Silver Fork descriptions just as easily as Newgate fictions. 'Mr. Bulwer's low life, though very amusing, is altogether fanciful', he says.[12] Accurate portraits of the working classes are not to be found in the middle-class novelists:

> There is in some of these histories more fun – in all, more fancy and romance – than are ordinarily found in humble life; and we recommend the admirer of such scenes, if he would have an accurate notion of them, to obtain his knowledge at the fountain-head, and trust more to the people's descriptions of themselves, than to Bulwer's ingenious inconsistencies, and Dickens's startling, pleasing, unnatural caricatures.[13]

This middle-class simulacrum of a world of poverty, a class-mediated world, is romance. The plea for journalistic realism begins with analyses of the popular press of the late 1830s, and later focuses on the kind of journalistic reporting carried out by Henry Mayhew and the *Morning Chronicle* (another newspaper source). In his review of *Sybil* for the *Morning Chronicle*, Thackeray states that the 'whole cycle of labour' is 'a magnificent and untrodden field', but that the new industrial classes require, not Disraeli, but 'a Boz from among the miners or the manufactories to detail their ways of work and pleasure – to describe their feelings, interests, and lives, public and private'.[14] By 1850, Thackeray could appreciate Mayhew's reporting:

> A clever and earnest-minded writer gets a commission from the *Morning Chronicle* newspaper, and reports upon the state of our poor in London; he goes amongst labouring people and poor of all kinds – and brings back what? A picture of human life so wonderful, so awful, so piteous and pathetic, so exciting and terrible, that readers of romances own they never read anything like it; and that the griefs, struggles, strange adventures here depicted, exceed anything that any of us could imagine. Yes; and these wonders and terrors have been lying by your door and mine ever since we had a door of our own.

> We had but to go a hundred yards off and see for ourselves, but we never did.[15]

But for Thackeray, these 'travels into the poor man's country' are not the method. Thackeray discusses mediation and is not a hands-on investigative journalist. The *Roundabout Papers* are precisely that: meanders emanating from paper sources – a book read, a magazine article noted. His *Punch* articles usually derive their impetus from the news as reported in the daily press; he describes *Punch* as 'the father and protector of the press', a kind of overseer or watchdog, through its satire, of press intrusion and unfair practice.[16] Thackeray writes about writing; he critiques the representation of his world through media sources. His journalism takes place in the 'Club Arm-Chair' and not on the street. In 'Half-a-Crown', he explains:

> For those, then, though eager for knowledge regarding the habits of these people, are yet unwilling to brave the dangers which must be encountered in the search, there can scarcely be a better method of acquiring science than by such books as the fifteen penny publications above inscribed. If they do not give so lively a picture as that visible to the actual observers, they give, at least, a view more general. Long months' unremitting intercourse, and considerable expenditure, are necessary for him who wishes, with his proper eyes, to behold this enormous London world (for to call that 'the world' which is so registered in the *Court Guide* is sheer nonsense); by examining a heap of such papers, as these, he may know it, however, in a morning's reading. (307)

He goes on to add, with a touch of relief (that was not to be obtained in his commissioned travel guides to Ireland and Cairo):

> There is not much need, luckily, that a writer should be despatched expressly from the polite world to examine the doings of the world impolite. It has a literature its own ... (308)

The adjectives here are also indicative of the gulf between the classes and the consciousness of a difference that is designated in what amount to colonial terms, Thackeray famously referring to the 'aborigines of the Seven Dials' and the 'natives of Wapping', and the 'traveller' who explores this '*terra incognita*' (307).

The literature of this world, then, consists here of a series of fifteen periodicals, including the *Poor Man's Friend*, the *Penny Story-Teller*, the *Sporting World*, the *Fly*, and the *Town*, and, in 'Horae Catnachianae', the street ballads sold at Catnach's shop in Monmouth Street, Seven Dials. Both articles provide access to 'the nation's habits, opinions, likings and dislikings' ('Horae', 410). Also in each, Thackeray remarks on the lack of knowledge of this literature possessed by the readers of his own class, commenting in 'Half-a-Crown', 'few of them, we venture to say, have even heard of most of the above periodicals' (306). And yet, of the ballads, 'near a million copies of these works are published, purchased, and admired', and 'Fraser sells to his thousands, but Catnach to his hundreds of thousands' ('Horae', 410). Thackeray's articles are about revelation; revealing to a readership of *Fraser's Magazine*, a whole new body of texts that form an alternative history of England. In part, the essays are a warning; there is middle-class concern here that such histories are ignored at England's peril. The social problem novelists, and social investigators, such as Engels, de Toqueville, and Mayhew of the next decade, use the same tactics of surprise to carry their message to a skeptical readership. But Thackeray also has a genuine enthusiasm for his material. Not only is he conscious of the periodical press as the source for future historians, such as Beetham indicates are the cultural historians of the modern age, but he is also conscious of the contemporary press's advertisorial function in this light. Thackeray is both accepting and suspicious of this self-fashioning. Here, he establishes a complex intertextual relationship between the sources he is quoting and the periodical in which he is quoting such sources. This view frames the article, with the two following comments coming at the beginning and at the end of 'Horae Catnachianae' (the latter is an introduction to a sustained parody of Dickens' *Nicholas Nickleby* as an unnatural portrait of urban society, in contrast to the 'realism' of the 'popular poetry' cited from Catnach's).

> A file of penny newspapers, or a bundle of ballads, are not, to be sure, amongst the most dignified parts of the historical collection, but, nevertheless, they form some part in it; and as it may be pretty confidently predicted that many of the newspapers will cease to appear, and most of the songs will be forgotten, while *Fraser's Magazine* is still, under the guidance of our successors, the great instructor and entertainer of the present public, we feel, as it were, that we shall confer a benefit on posterity, in giving some brief account of the fugitive poetry of the year 1839; not to mention the actual good which the present subscriber to REGINA must derive from the perusal of the ensuing article. ('Horae', 407)[17]

The second comment reads:

> We can fancy, that after an interval of a couple of thousand years, or so, when some future historian shall describe the politics and the manners of this time, – we can fancy, we say, that he would put pen to paper in the following way: – 'There exists but few authentic documents to illustrate the state of English manners in the reign of Victoria; but, luckily, the name of *Fraser's Magazine* is still well known to us ... ' ('Horae', 420)

The self-reflexivity of these passages provides both a satirical comment on the self-aggrandizement of journals and journalism in the market-place and an acknowledgment that society views middle-class journals as being of more permanency than ephemeral popular writings. There is a class-consciousness here that is only half ironic. But there is recognition that periodicals provide the best access to history, that they are 'authentic' historical documents and of a value largely unrecognized amongst Thackeray's contemporaries. Ballads are, for Thackeray, part of the 'historical collection', part of the growing body of archival information that has passed to the twentieth century as a legacy of the Victorian mania for collecting. Thackeray reinvented the *National Standard* as 'the Museum' in 1860.[18]

Thackeray's awareness of the future use of the newspaper writing he produces is complex and ambivalent. He can be dismissive of the press; as, for instance, when he remarks on the fashionable society families 'covering up the window blinds of several houses in genteel quarters with the *Times* newspaper', as though its currency has been exchanged for more practical purpose as the wealthy go abroad for the summer.[19] But he believes in the continued legacy of the press. The point is made several times in similar fashion, but always with an interest in the marginal aspects of the periodical. In the *Irish Sketch-Book*, spending a rainy day reading the Dublin newspapers in 1843, he writes:

> Some hundred years hence, when students want to inform themselves of the history of the present day, and refer to files of the *Times* and *Chronicle* for the purpose, I think it is possible that they will consult, not so much those luminous and philosophical leading-articles which call our attention at present both by the majesty of their eloquence and the largeness of their type, but that they will turn to those parts of the journals into which information is squeezed in the smallest possible print: to the advertisements, namely, the law and police reports, and the instructive narratives supplied by that ill-used body of men who transcribe knowledge at the rate of a penny a line.[20]

History was also present in comic magazinery, such as Jerrold's series for *Punch*, *Mrs. Caudle's Curtain Lectures*. Reviewing these for the *Morning Chronicle*, Thackeray argues how

> ... a foreigner, or a student in the twentieth century, may get out of her lectures as accurate pictures of London life as we can out of the pictures of Hogarth ... The couple have become real living personages in history, like Queen Elizabeth, or Sancho Panza, or Parson Adams, or any other past character, who, false or real once, is only imaginary now, and for whose existence we have only the word of a book.[21]

The world is becoming textual in the new age of print; history is text and only knowable as text, a foreshadowing of the postmodern historicism of the late twentieth century.

Thackeray was not alone in such speculations, and reference has already been made to an article in the *Paris Literary Gazette* on advertising. The realism of the press was under scrutiny; its political bias, and the public's apparent ignorance of this, was frequently of concern. In 1839, the *London Saturday Journal*, a Catholic periodical, analysed the personal columns of the *Times* where tradesmen, governesses, and nurserymaids advertised their services, and described these as 'a sort of social mash-tun, where the bruised malt of human society is laid, to undergo the first process of being converted into liquor'.[22] The writer expressed a worry that 'if all materials for future history perished, except the advertising columns of the *Times*, what estimate would be formed of our social state' in '2555'?[23] Charles Clyatt, in an article entitled 'Contemporary History' in *Jerrold's Illuminated Magazine* in 1845, also voiced disquiet over the media's image of Victorian society:

> We fully admit the value of the 'contemporary history' which is shadowed forth in its legitimate place of record, the newspaper press; but yet everyone must acknowledge that party spirit gives such a colouring to the characters, opinions, and deeds, of the eminent man of the day, that plain people are likely to be considerably mystified if they resort to the odious process of comparison.[24]

The Whig *Morning Chronicle* and the Tory *Standard* will offer different portraits of Lord John Russell, Clyatt argues. The reader of the press, for the *London Saturday Journal* in 1840, requires a wide range of knowledge of 'political economy', 'moral philosophy', 'constitutional history and privilege', law, trade, and 'a Gibbon-like grasp of general history'.[25] The problems for the reader increase when Clyatt's further concerns are added. Journalistic sensationalism was rife, the English press having a taste for death, 'extraordinary births', lunacy, robbery, and murder, whilst 'penny-a-liners' gave 'a touch of the romantic to the most common-place event, so as to make it spicy and readable.' In a similar vein to Thackeray's caution, and the caution of the writer for the *London Saturday Journal*, Clyatt mused that 'a strange opinion might be formed in after times of the year 1845 if the writers upon the manner and spirit of the age were to drink too deeply from the sources of "Contemporary History"'. Nevertheless, beyond this 'embellishment', Clyatt found 'the daily press, generally speaking, furnishes the true record of facts'.[26] Thackeray's analyses, then, find a place in a wider context of self-reflexive debate, and, indeed, may well have helped to fuel that very debate.

Thackeray's analyses of the popular press in 'Half-a-Crown' reflect concerns that are current in much of his writing. His investigation wishes firstly to establish the political nature of the unstamped press, and comes to the conclusion that 'the people, for whose special benefit penny literature has been invented, do not care much for politics or instruction, but seek chiefly for amusement in exchange for their humble penny' (312). This was something he already knew from his experience on the *Constitutional* newspaper, which is also referred to here; such middle-class attempts at floating radical periodicals demonstrated how 'pure Radicalism is not the belief of the people'. The

Constitutional, and the *True Sun* (for which Dickens worked in the early 1830s), were 'as good as any other morning paper', but the former 'never had a thousand subscribers', and both failed (309).[27] Examining the political press, Thackeray finds the two he has bought for his half-crown are of different kinds; the *Poor Man's Friend* is a small and cynical publication, concerned more with the 'puffing' of another journal, the *London Dispatch*. Even amongst the popular press, commercial practices are uppermost. The *Moral Reformer*, a temperance magazine, presents a harrowing view of the poor, which Thackeray prints, and offers 'wholesome lessons', particularly to the middle-class reader (311). But, despite its work, Thackeray sees more of pleasure in the cheap publications than of politics. He continues by assessing publications which extract (plagiarise) war histories and general fiction or offer their own imitations of the best known authors (Dickens is imitated in the *Penny Story-Teller*, and in *Oliver Twiss*[28]). There are sporting magazines, including songs by A.W.N. Bayley, the original owner of the *National Standard*. The *Fly* is a satirical magazine of poor comedy and bad puns. Thackeray finds this an appalling rag; 'we scarcely ever have seen anything more witless and more blackguard than this *Fly*', and its coarse subject-matter make it 'inconceivably dirty' (318). The two most interesting papers are the *Penny Age*, and the *Town*, the latter, 'doubly valuable ... for it describes exactly that portion of the town of which no Christian ever heard until now' (321). These, and others, provide an alternative London to the one described in the middle-class periodicals, the lower-class 'fashionable amusements of the metropolis' (318). The world for the cheap entertainment guides consists of concerts in taverns ('the most select vocal establishments that we know of at present are the Eagle Tavern, City Road; the White Conduit; the Union Saloon, High Street, Shoreditch ... ', 319), the free-and-easies, the best barmaids, pawnbrokers, and tripesellers, and more. Thackeray finds the information fascinating; 'is there not a world of knowledge laid open to us?' he asks (320). The press itself carries all of the features of its middle-class counterpart; one paper has a medical adviser who answers readers' questions, another contains within its pages an analysis of 'the Puffing system' (321). The main difference is the level of obscenity and impropriety contained in the papers. In a comment which echoes his Preface to *Pendennis*, Thackeray says he has 'striven to tell the truth concerning every one of these newspapers, – though not, as we confess, in one or two instances, *the whole* truth' (325). The *Town*, the *Penny Age*, the *Fly*, and the *Shew-Up Chronicle*, contain 'ribaldry so infamous, obscenity so impudently blackguard and brazen, can hardly be conceived, and certainly never was printed until our day' (325). 'Our day' was supposed to demonstrate a spread of literacy, the 'March of Intellect', and other 'cant terms of the Radical spouters' (306), but, in fact, the devotion to pleasure and more immediate desires in the periodicals bought by the working classes produced in Thackeray a more cynical view. 'The popularity of the journals', he remarked, 'and their contents, are dismal indications indeed of the social conditions of the purchasers, who are to be found among all lower classes in

London' (325). A wider and wider audience is able to read these periodicals, and the industrialization of publishing makes them cheap enough to be affordable to many, but the quality of certain sections of the market, Thackeray concludes, has made immorality more accessible and more known.[29]

'Horae Catnachianae' is a different kind of article, in part used as a means of attacking the fiction of his middle-class contemporaries. The subheading reads 'A Dissertation on Ballads, with a few unnecessary remarks on Jonathan Wild, John Sheppard, Paul Clifford, and – Fagin, Esqrs.', and to these 'unnecessary remarks' is added a comic satire on Dickens' *Nicholas Nickleby* consisting of a 'translation' of a section of the book into correct English. A very funny piece of bravado, it shows the distance between Dickens and Thackeray even as early as 1839, and highlights the divergence of romance and realism at the time. That Thackeray could take issue with Dickens' grammar, for instance, also indicates what status the latter held in sections of the middle-class press. But it is the issue of 'copying nature' which is foremost in this essay; Thackeray argues that 'the sham low ... is altogether different from the honest, hearty vulgarity, which it pretends to represent', and the ballads he cites are more 'honest' than the comic grotesquery of Dickens. The reader is enjoined to access 'the real source' of information about the lower classes, present in the periodical-as-archive, and not the poor imitations made popular by the romancers of the day.

> Let him try, for instance, three numbers of the – twopenny newspaper: there is more information about thieves, ruffians, swindlers of both sexes, more real vulgarity, more tremendous slang, more unconscious, honest, blackguard NATURE, in fact, than Mr. Dickens will ever give to the public. ('Horae', 408)

Thackeray also attacks Dickens' imagination in 'Going to see a Man Hanged' in August 1840, but in this article he takes issue with a differently observed reality, rather than a textual one. In the crowds surrounding the scaffold, he observes a 'devil-may-care' prostitute, 'one that Cruikshank and Boz might have taken as a study for Nancy'. Thackeray saw a 'candour and simplicity' in the girl, 'something good' despite her behaving 'without a particle of modesty'. Thackeray turns the sight into a literary criticism:

> Boz, who knows life well, knows that his Miss Nancy is the most unreal fantastical personage possible; no more like a thief's mistress than one of Gesner's shepherdesses resembles a real country wench. He dare not tell the truth concerning such young ladies ... ; not being able to paint the whole portrait, he has no right to present one or two favourable points as characterizing the whole; and therefore, in fact, had better leave the picture alone altogether.[30]

The journal offers a space for Thackeray to engage with issues of realism, without altogether presenting an alternative truth. He rejects 'pictures quite untrue to nature',[31] a central tenet of his literary aesthetics which made him of interest to the Pre-Raphaelites in the late 1840s. In the 1830s, as he suggests in 'Half-a-Crown', he is unable to describe the 'whole portrait' of a salacious publication or a carefree prostitute.

The ballads described and printed in 'Horae Catnachianae' are interesting precursors of Thackeray's own periodical poetry for *Punch* in the 1840s. They are also important contributions to his sense of the lower-class urban 'real' and, thematically, to his conceptualization of gender and class relationships. He is, of course, being selective in his choice of materials to analyse; however, 'the sentimental and pathetic, the ludicrous and satirical, the political, the descriptive, and fashionable', such as he categorizes the ballads printed, are also elements of the fiction and criticism he produces for the periodicals. The ballads operate not unlike the purpose of *Punch* from its inception in 1841. The writers are 'chastising the follies, or chronicling in playful verse the events of the day' ('Horae', 409). Indeed, Thackeray even invokes his friend; the ballads provide 'Punch's humour, that lies not so much in the point of his replies as of his stick' ('Horae', 410).[32] There are ballads dealing with 'poachers, smugglers, and other evaders of the law', mockeries of policemen, comments on the state of the nation and the dissatisfaction of the poor, on the government, on drunkenness, the Reform Bill, fighting, soldiership, crime and 'Newgate songs', songs about seduction and abandonment (often relating to Irish subjects), and love songs and the sentimental ballad. The last song of the article is an analysis of good housekeeping and an explanation from 'The Pleasing Wife' to the 'Satisfied Husband' of how she spends the weekly wage.

The ballads attacking policemen, 'the devils blue' ('Horae', 412), who steal from the poor and violently arrest the drunken, are clearly an influence on Thackeray's own 'Ballads of Policeman X'. These latter assert the ordinary heroism of the police, the man 'passing on his beat, / Like a true and galliant feller', and objects to those 'abewsing and calling hout Poleece'.[33] The difference offers a perspective on Thackeray's class position and rejection of misrule and disorder. Elsewhere, Thackeray indicates his more Radical support of working-class suspicions regarding the Reform Bill, quoting their 'home truths' about it ('Horae', 412). Next, he discusses 'Newgate songs', 'some supposed to be written from prison, others from Botany Bay' ('Horae', 414), which clearly relate to *Catherine, A Story*, Thackeray's attack on Newgate fiction and narrated from prison, that began serialization in *Fraser's Magazine* the following month in May 1839. In the sentimental ballads there is a wealthy Irish landowner's daughter whose 'hair was black as a raven's feather' ('Horae', 415) and who may be echoed in the 1843 tale, *The Ravenswing*. Thackeray's consciousness of that shabby-genteel world he recreates in such stories as *The Bedford Row Conspiracy*, *The Great Hoggarty Diamond*, and *A Shabby Genteel Story*, finds a parallel in the worlds of the Betsys and Mary-Anns of the ballads. Indeed, his conceptualization of Becky

Sharp may originate here; the 'heroines' of these ballads interest him greatly, as, he comments, 'it is remarkable how in these ballads the ladies always take the initiative' in love ('Horae', 418). The ballads are a marginal but a valuable segment of the periodical press. 'A collection more curious', he says, 'cannot be imagined' ('Horae', 409). It is also worth remembering how much emphasis Trollope placed upon Thackeray's own compositions in this arena of literature, although he felt some were written to order.[34] Most significantly, they signify Thackeray's close reading of the culture of his day, and the detailed engagement he made with the periodical culture of all sections of his society. Thackeray knew the press very well indeed.

Politically, Thackeray was, like many of his class, worried about the possibilities of a revolution happening in England as in France.[35] But he translated this fear into a determination to see all humanity as equal and persisted with his critical openness by examining life from different angles. His exploration of popular periodicals should be read alongside that of his exploration of the territory of public hanging as reflecting an attempt to bring another class of life into the domains of a middle-class magazine. The reader of foreign correspondence and travel writings knew more of foreign races than their own.[36]

Probably Thackeray's most successful journalistic article was a social criticism of public hangings, 'Going to see a Man Hanged', *Fraser's Magazine*, August 1840. He had already attacked the process of capital punishment in his weekly column of Paris correspondence in the *Constitutional* and in an essay for *The Paris Sketch-Book*, 'The Case of Peytel', which appeared a month earlier in July 1840. The title of the article is another example of Thackeray's concern for 'the Man', his humanitarianism, and it is also taken from a comment made to him by a young girl at the event, 'We've koom to see the mon hanged'.[37] The description of the execution of Courvoisier which Thackeray attended with Richard Monckton Milnes in a crowd of 40,000 in front of Newgate prison, revealed the dichotomy between the attraction and excitement of a vast spectacle and the moral anxiety over the nature of such an attraction for the onlooker. Monckton Milnes was there, by all accounts, for the thrill.[38]

Thackeray's account of the event began with the walk to the scene at four o'clock on a beautiful London morning. The execution was at eight. Dickens was present at the hanging as well; Fred Kaplan relates how Dickens rented a room high in a building opposite the prison and stayed awake all night watching the gathering crowd.' In an interesting interplay of different points of view, Dickens and his friends saw Thackeray below them, his tall figure easily identifiable, but the noise of the crowd in the streets prevented the party from attracting Thackeray's attention.[39]

Thackeray's record of the hanging of Courvoisier was of a highly personal nature; it took his literary arguments about 'Newgate fiction' and such French writers as Petrus Borel and Alexander Dumas directly into everyday life (albeit extraordinary everyday life as hangings were not regular occurrences by the 1830s). He also announced that 'the writer has disregarded the magazine "We" altogether, and spoken face to face with the reader, recording every one of the impressions felt by him as honestly as he could'.[40] The confessional spirit was unusual for the press of the day and required an apology. Thackeray recreated the day he passed at the execution of Courvoisier, the thoughts that were impressed on his mind, and the conclusions that the events reaffirmed. He wrote as a spectator. He intended to question the public benefit of seeing an execution, and had thus to see one himself; his description tried to invoke as realistically as possible the emotions and sights which such an event brought to a man.[41] He was appalled, sickened, and closed his eyes at the moment of strangulation. The sight affected him for some days after, leaving him melancholy and distressed and unable to work.[42]

Thackeray's description of the crowd, taken from amongst the ordinary people themselves, gives the opposite impression to that of Dickens'. Dickens saw 'ribaldry, debauchery, levity, drunkenness, and flaunting vice in fifty other shapes'. He found his 'fellow-creatures' 'odious'.[43] Thackeray, however, described the 'mob' as 'extraordinarily gentle and good-humoured'; they were ordinary people – which made the spectacle all the more horrific. Thackeray considered the members of the 'gallery', perched, like Dickens, in the surrounding houses, as more disagreeable than the common man. These were paying for the privileged positions; the 'several tipsy, dissolute-looking young men, of the Dick Swiveller cast' and the 'many young dandies … with moustaches and cigars'.[44]

Thackeray's confessional tone acknowledged the excitement of the spectacle and the crowd, as well as the fear and terror of the hanging. He attacked the doubtful efficacy of public executions. The moral confusion that he experienced implicated himself in the whole process of retribution.[45] This implication, an enmeshing of himself within the forces of modern culture including those of commerce and business, is central to an understanding of Thackeray's irony. As a journalist, he refuses to set himself above his readers but to speak to them as an equal. The assumed authority of the magazine is not a licence to preach didactically, but to share a recognition of human weakness and the adaptations needed in order to survive in the rapid transformations of the modern age.

Punchinello, A Journal of Wit, Wisdom, and Romance, which ran for only one number, priced at 1d., on Saturday, 17 January 1846, and launched as a cheap rival to *Punch*, put the mood of the times into verse:

> This is indeed the age of publication,
> A printing mania sure hath seized the nation …

For the periodical, the railway speculation mania may have been exciting news, but investment in the print culture of the day although less talked about was more immediately relevant. *Punchinello* went the way of many such speculations: nothing could rival *Punch* in its own market.

For Thackeray, *Punch* was the perfect vehicle for extending and refining his critique of the press. Launched in 1841, *Punch* was both characteristic of its day and antipathetic to the growth in newspaper and magazine journalism.[46] *Punch* was a kind of mirror-image of the newspaper press, reflecting but reversing the tropes and techniques found there. It did not so much respond to the news, as to the way the news was reported in the regular daily press. It was more concerned with representation, with reading the newspapers, and with guarding the public against journalistic malpractice. It was established as a satire on the proliferation of newspapers in the 1830s, drawing on the experience of the journalist writers, such as Jerrold, Mayhew, Lemon, A'Beckett, and others who constituted its staff. Thackeray was a perfect kind of contributor; having worked for the press through much of the previous decade, and even with several of the *Punch* writers, and being himself acutely conscious of the tricks and turns of the profession, he was able to write parodies of press reporting swiftly and penetratingly to keep up with the weekly demands of the magazine. Many of his *Punch* contributions derive from stories in the press. Several also contain a self-referentiality which make the satire more subtle and complex.

In 'Titmarsh v. Tait' (*Punch*, 14 March 1846 – the same month as his 'Laman Blanchard' article appeared in *Fraser's Magazine*), for example, Thackeray writes as Michael Angelo Titmarsh, a persona associated with his work for *Fraser's* and used as a signature for his volume publications, but not connected with *Punch*. He begins, 'My Dear Mr. Punch, – You are acknowledged to be the censor of the age, and the father and protector of the press; in which character allow one of your warmest admirers to appeal to you for redress and protection.'[47] The appeal is against a suggestion in *Tait's Magazine*, in a review of Thackeray's travel book, *A Journey from Cornhill to Grand Cairo* (1846), that he was paid to advertise the Peninsular and Oriental Company on whose ship he was offered a place. Thackeray responds by rejecting the notion that a literary man should not be part of the more general trade and commerce of the day. As he argues in 'Laman Blanchard', a writer should be paid, and paid the going rate in whatever manner appropriate, in order to discharge his professional duties. He says of the 'professional man of letters' who thus abuses him,

> It is only literary men, nowadays, who commit this suicidal sort of impertinence; who sneak through the world ashamed of their calling, and show their independence by befouling the trade by which they live.[48]

Thackeray's lengthy defence of 'fleeting literature' in 'Laman Blanchard' makes the same point. This article derives from a biographical review of Blanchard's life written by Bulwer Lytton on the occasion of his suicide in 1846. Blanchard had worked with Thackeray for the *Constitutional* (where he was editor), and was a regular magazine professional. Bulwer had written to regret that Blanchard had wasted his talents writing popular magazinery and never fulfilled the promise he had by writing more as the literary artist. Thackeray rejected this snobbery, asserting 'let us take a stand at once ... why should not the day have its literature? why should not authors make light sketches? why should not the public be amused daily or frequently by kindly fictions?'[49] Blanchard is not to be viewed as an 'amateur martyr', Thackeray says, but as a hard-working professional feeding his family like everyone else. Of course, Thackeray might be accused of self-preservation; he had worked as just such a journalist for thirteen years when he published 'Laman Blanchard' and had not achieved the commercial success of Bulwer-Lytton. However, Thackeray remained faithful to this view of his profession even after the fame of *Vanity Fair* the following year.

Elsewhere in *Punch*, Thackeray responds to the journalistic ethos of the day. In 'Mr Snob's Remonstrance with Mr Smith' (*Punch*, 27 May 1848), he discusses a matter close to our own times: the press intrusion into royal privacy. Smith accuses Mr Snob at his club of disloyalty to the throne as a result of 'a previous letter of mine in this periodical'. Snob attacks, not the exposure of royal privacy *per se*, but the throne's own releasing of information about petty ceremonies that diminish the dignity of the crown. He asks:

> But if the privacy of Royalty is not to be intruded upon, why is it perpetually thrust in our faces? Why is that Court Newsman not stifled? I say that individual is one of the barbarous adjuncts of the Crown, whom we ought to abolish, and whom it is an honest man's duty to hoot off the stage. I say that it is monstrous, immodest, unseemly, that in our time such details should occupy great columns of the newspapers, as that of a Royal Christening, for instance, which appeared the other day ...[50]

Thackeray then cites a paragraph describing the clothes worn by the various Royal figures at the ceremony that reduces the event to a catalogue of fashions. He had mocked such Court Circular reporting since his days at the *National Standard*.

In 'Yesterday: A Tale of the Polish Ball' (*Punch*, 10 June 1848), Thackeray replies to a 'Morning Paper' paragraph reading:

> The absence of the Life Guards, being on duty against the mob, occasioned some disappointment to many of the fair fashionables at Willis's on Monday night.[51]

Coming so soon after the Kennington Common Chartist meetings in March, on which Thackeray reported for the *Morning Chronicle*, this paragraph was singularly insensitive, and Thackeray produced a comic tale in which Lionel of the Guards dies of pneumonia contracted whilst out on duty against the Chartists and his beloved Frederica dies of pining for her lover who fails to attend the Polish Ball at Almack's because of this patrol. The author declares, 'how much of this agony might have been spared if the odious Chartists would but have stayed at home ... '.[52] Again, the satire is aimed more at the newspaper concerned than at the subject of the tale. The comedy is in the newspaper's curious priorities and its melodramatic comment on the Chartist demonstrations ruining a night out at Willis's dance-rooms.

Thackeray's foreign correspondence for the *Calcutta Star*, published between September 1844 and August 1845 (with a gap between the first and May 1845 due to his Cairo journey), offers a similarly alternative version of regular journalism. Although the letters cover the news of the period, the relationship with France (embittered due to a pamphlet by the Prince of Joinville), Ireland and Catholicism, railways, and political figures such as Peel, Disraeli, Macaulay, and O'Connell, as well as another attack on public hangings, several of the letters also refer to the London press and act as advertisements for *Punch*. Thackeray remarks:

> There is (with respect be it spoken) a certain wholesome contempt for newspapers in this country, which renders the opinions of those publications of very little weight with the nation. They don't lead the public, it is only when they follow it, that their articles have any influence or echo.[53]

He looks at what the *Morning Chronicle*, the *Times*, the *Morning Post*, the *Globe*, and the *Standard* say about certain issues, and mentions articles in *Punch* (including his own 'Fat Contributor papers' and Jerrold's 'Mrs. Caudle'). The letters are another good example of the distance that exists in the newspapers between Thackeray's work, even when, as here, he is writing a regular column as a foreign reporter, and the work of the regular pressmen of the day. This is a form of defamiliarization. Thackeray can talk politics, but he never can quite be serious or refrain from that critical eye which mocks his fellow journalists. He offers a challenge to press identity and the identification with the conventions of the press. The self-promotional function is satirized by its very foregrounding ('My friend Punch ... '; 'the sale of *Punch* goes on increasing, and stupendously multiplying ... Rivals have appeared for a season but they die'[54]), and yet also functions as advertising. Such a paradox is central to Thackeray's periodical contributions.

When Thackeray's 'The Snobs of England. By One of Themselves' began their run in *Punch* on 28 February 1846, they did so as a combination of history, biography, travel-writing, burlesque, contemporary social observation, and news reporting. They were imbued also with the idea of themselves as a commodity within the product framework of *Punch* magazine and the context of the newspaper world of the 1840s. They emerged generically from earlier works of social observation, such as 'The Party at Willowford Hall. By One of the Guests', from the *Paris Literary Gazette*, the various descriptions of French characters in Thackeray's travel-writings, and the remarks on character types in paintings and on travelling tours, including the 'Fat Contributor' papers. More generally, they came from a recent writing tradition of verbal portraiture stretching from Hook's *Sayings and Doings*, *Sketches by Boz*, and R.H. Horne's *New Spirit of the Age* (1844).[55] Thackeray emphasized again the role of the journalist-observer as 'showing up' or identifying social types, in his remarks on this last author:

> ... all ranks and classes in the empire ... may find themselves caught, their bodies and souls turned inside out, so to speak, by this frightful observer, and confined to posterity in red calico.[56]

His series gained impetus (if it needed any) from a review of Catherine Gore's 'Silver-Fork' social observations, *Sketches of English Character* (1846).[57] Mrs Gore's sketches were collected from magazine ephemera and preserved as history, 'a tolerably faithful picture of Pall-mall in 1840', fashionable society in 'microcosm'.[58] In the same manner as Jeames de la Pluche used *Pelham* as a way into fashionable etiquette, so Mrs Gore's *Sketches* provide 'a good guide-book' to high society life, manners and customs, 'supposing that Pall-mall were the world'.[59] But, Thackeray sneers, 'if it be as here represented, the world is the most hollow, heartless, vulgar, brazen world, and those are luckiest who are out of it'.[60] As Thackeray told his readers of the 'Snob Papers' on 16 January 1847, two weeks after the commencement of his most famous novel, although the external, public life of the individual might be conventional, cautious, inscrutable, still 'each Bosom is a Booth in Vanity Fair'.[61]

'The Snobs of England' presents a demographic analysis of a cross-section of middle- and upper-middle-class society for posterity; the narrator, Mr Snob, identifies himself as an 'Historian of Snobs', a 'Snobographer', and 'your friend, historiographer and brother'.[62] The book is also about commodities – the glut of products fuelling the acquisitiveness of the Victorians – and how these define the individual or catagorize social types. Newspapers and magazines become important in this respect. They aid in the classification of an individual by indicating his taste in literature and identifying the media discourses he is exposed to. As with *Punch* itself, there is a close relationship between the 'Snob Papers' and the daily press, in both their description of the roles of newspapers in society, and the self-parodic traits of the series. The 'Snob Papers' expose the commodification of literature and characterize themselves as commodities useful to the purchaser. They are concerned with how facts reach the public and what those facts represent. In their more general targets, the 'Snob Papers' criticize the major institutions of the day – Royalty and the Aristocracy, the City, the Military, the Church, the Universities, political parties, the Club scene, and the literatii, as well as marriage and the family.[63]

The structure of 'The Snobs of England', whilst largely flexible, nevertheless suggests an interesting shift in Thackeray's focus over the year of their serialization. They were clearly designed as a long-running feature of *Punch*, consisting of short, single-page articles (chapters) which might be arranged around a satirical idea (a burlesque of the Court Guide, for instance), a character or characters (the 'Military Snobs', Lieutenant Grig and Lieutenant-General the Honourable Sir George Granby Tufto), or a short narrative (the fall of the 'Club Snob', Sackville Maine). The formula worked for single, self-contained chapters, for chapters linked by, for instance, place (Mr Snob's sojurn to the country house, the 'Evergreens', in 'A Visit to Some Country Snobs'), or for chapters more dependently arranged and linked by narrative suspense (such as the tale of Sackville Maine, Chapters 49-51 (Chapters 42-44 in the volume edition)). The first 24 parts (out of 52) have a greater immediacy and are more closely connected to the newspaper principles of *Punch*. They are more overtly political and thus deal more directly with the attitudes manifest in the daily press. Indeed, so bound to a discourse of contempraneousness are they that, when compiling the volume edition of 1848, Thackeray expunged those chapters which responded to the fall of the Peel ministry in June 1846 and the flogging to death of a soldier in Hounslow in July 1846.[64] The later 28 chapters have a more socially-based content, and deal with the everyday life and culture of the middle class. These consist of material more 'anecdotal and narrative'.[65]

One might characterize this change as a movement from newspaper-style to magazine-style – a movement which coincides with (and precipitates) the change of tone in *Punch* which led to an outburst from Jerrold and his seeking a journalistic news outlet in *Douglas Jerrold's Newspaper* of July 1846.[66] Thackeray's challenge to the Mr Punch stick came from his own more gentlemanly Mr Snob.

In Chapter 37 of the volume edition, 'Club Snobs' (Chapter 44, *Punch*, 2 January 1847), we are presented with a picture of newspapers as an important part of the Club-man's ritual evening. Whilst Jones pores over 'the last delicious novel or brilliant magazine', his fellow member at the 'Sarcophagus Club', Brown, 'that old newspaper-devouring miscreant', is up to his tricks.

> Old Brown, that selfish old reprobate for whom mere literature has no charms, [is] stretched on the best sofa, sitting on the second edition of *The Times*, having the *Morning Chronicle* between his knees, the *Herald* pushed in between his coat and waistcoat, the *Standard* under his left arm, the *Globe* under the other pinion, and the *Daily News* in perusal. 'I'll trouble you for *Punch*, Mr. Wiggins', says the unconscionable old gormandiser, interrupting our friend, who is laughing over the periodical in question.[67]

The attractiveness of the sub-newspaper *Punch*, which generates laughter in the inscribed reader, Wiggins, is clearly demonstrated in this passage. *Punch* has a distinct advantage over the squashed and rumpled hierarchy of the dailies. Indeed, the experience of reading *Punch* actually causes a moral change in Brown and the heart of Club-land, which the other papers could not effect. In the penultimate chapter of 'The Snobs of England', we learn that

'Gobemouche [i.e. Brown] does not take more than two papers at a time for his private reading'.[68]

The self-conscious narrator of the Snob papers, described by Charles Whibley,[69] has a physical presence in his world. The narrator is, in effect, in two places: externally observing in the fictional world, and behind the text as the writer at the *Punch* office receiving and answering correspondence from his readers. This exchange between 'author' and 'reader' alongside 'narrator' and 'character' further impresses upon the actual reader that we are all snobs so described. Playing out this letter-exchange in the public arena of the 'Snob Papers' themselves confuses the boundaries between fact and fiction, simultaneously reinforcing and paradoxically exploding the 'realism' of the journalistic voice.

Twice in the series we are presented with portraits of Mr Snob himself; these are self-parodic and contradictory, fancifully magnified and self-advertising. On 28 November 1846, he appears as:

> ... a quiet-looking young fellow, in a white top-coat, a crimson satin neckcloth, light blue trousers, with glossy tipped boots, and an emerald breast-pin.[70]

He intends to meet three young ladies who had written to him, and his dress is clearly designed to appeal to their sensibilities. He adds, 'I shall have a black crape round my white hat; and my usual bamboo cane with the richly gilt knob'. Mr Snob lacked moustaches with which to impress his female correspondents. On 19 December 1846, he was transformed into a fashionable man-about-town and 'flattered himself as he made a sensation as he strutted down Bittlestone Street with his richly gilt knobbed cane' on his way to a dinner engagement. Here he is

> ... a youth of an elegant appearance, in a neat evening-dress, whose trim whiskers indicated neatness, whose light step denoted activity ... and whose rich golden hair, curling down his shoulders, was set off by a perfectly new four-and-ninepenny silk hat ...[71]

Such is the prerogative of serial fiction. However, Mr Snob is used by Thackeray in the same manner as Titmarsh, whose private life intruded upon his critical articles to emphasize his ordinariness and satirize the pretensions of his profession. Mr Snob is genteel and fashionable; his persona is created with reference to various commodities which define him to an observer (and himself). He is capable of shaping himself to a provincial female audience and a male metropolitan one. The implication is, of course, that he is marked as a hypocrite and a snob, 'one of themselves', and one of us.

'The Snobs of England' carry on a dialogue with the *Punch* readership which begins by noting letters sent to the office by distressed parties upset at the portrayal of a particular class of people, or offering suggestions of types to be satirized. This is extended by printing a letter supposedly by three sisters in the North, 'from seventeen to two-and-twenty', who are anxious to know if they are snobs.[72] *Punch* represented itself as participating in the lives of its readers in a cultural and educational manner. As a cultural artefact – a saleable commodity – *Punch* could carry images of the City and of England to Northern provinces and abroad; 'something like a journal of the proceedings at the Evergreens may be interesting to those foreign readers of *Punch* who want to know the customs of an English gentleman's family and household'.[73] *Punch* had a cultural impact by subverting the values established in the conventional daily press. Mr Snob acknowledges, 'Already I'm told that, from some flippant and unguarded expressions considered derogatory to Baker Street and Harley Street, rents have fallen in these respectable quarters'.[74] The reporting of its own effects was peculiarly an act of social historiography. Certainly, whilst not affecting house-prices, Thackeray was investing a word of the English language ('snob') with a fresh resonance.[75]

The contemporary frame of reference in the 'Snob Papers' extends to advertisements for commodities in the newspapers – such as that for Mr. Eisenberg, Chiropodist.[76] The interaction of economic choices is interesting – commodities, particularly luxuries, show up the vainglorious side of Victorian life. In defence of the clergy, for instance, Thackeray asks teasingly:

> ... you who can't resist purchasing a chest of cigars, because they are so good; or an ormolu clock at Howell and James's, because it is such a bargain; or a box at the Opera, because Lablache and Grisi are divine in the Puritani; fancy how difficult it is for a parson to resist spending a half-crown when John Breakstone's family are without a loaf ...[77]

When arriving at Major Ponto's country residence, the 'Evergreens', in Mangelwurzelshire, Thackeray once again characterizes himself, as the narrator, in the role of Snob. He brings Mrs. Ponto 'a peace-offering ... viz., a cod and oysters from Grove's, in a hamper about the size of a coffin'. Whilst, having described the commodious artificiality of his bedroom in the house – 'the pen-wiper on the table was the imitation of a double dahlia; and there was accomodation for my watch in a sun-flower on the mantel-piece' – Thackeray breathes in 'such a delicious draught of country air as all the millefleurs of Mr Atkinson's shop cannot impart to any but the most expensive pocket-handkerchief'.[78] The satire creates a whole world of affected consumerism.

Thackeray attacked the vanity and doubtful morality attached to material objects and purchases, whilst his extensive introduction of commodities creates the texture of realism. The role of newspapers in this texture is, significantly, different. The periodical provides a signification of character, as does any other commodity in Thackeray's fiction, but the separate journals of the literary frame are also engaged critically as they are being transposed into a magazine which is itself a commodity and part of that literary frame and which thus possesses a vested interest. In other words, the periodicals are 'realistic' commodities and actual competitors of *Punch*. The satire contains a self-reflexive satire on the art of magazine self-advertising.

There are real and fictitious journals in 'The Snobs of England'. Those most frequently referred to amongst the genuine press are the *Court-Circular* (which includes reprints and gossip columns in the regular press), the *Morning Post*, the *Morning Herald*, and the *Standard* (these three parodied as Jenkins, Mrs Gamp, and Mrs Harris), the *Times*, the *Quarterly Review*, *Bell's Sporting Life*, and the *Gazette* (both for bankruptcies and military information).[79] The three fictional papers are the *Beadle*, the *Weekly Tomahawk*, and the *Jawborough Independent*.[80]

The level at which these papers are introduced varies. At times, Thackeray reflects upon the contemporary uses of newspapers. For instance, Jawkins at his Club has pretensions to political knowledge that he gets entirely from the Tory evening *Standard*. He talks politics in the City, returns to his club to pass on City information, and catches the last edition to update his erudition. Jawkins is described elsewhere as an MP and hence his dinners are announced in the *Morning Herald*.[81] Another Club reader is the wealthy East India Director, Goldmore, who arrives at the 'Conflagration Club' at four-thirty and reads the evening papers in the bow-window overlooking Pall Mall.[82] Elsewhere, Thackeray passes comments on the press more generally. He describes the 'Political Snob' of the Clubs 'who does not care so much for home politics, but is great upon foreign affairs ... It is for him the papers provide their foreign articles, at the expense of some ten thousand a-year each.'[83] Thackeray drew subject matter directly from the contemporary press, such as lead stories and advertisements; he drew from a variety of sources, on one occasion using the case of Rev D. French from 'one of the illustrated weekly papers'.[84] He would pass remarks also on the political bias of papers; during the Peel crisis in May 1846, the anti-free-trade supporters of Stanley and the Tory 'Country Party' attempted to reinvigorate 'the good old Tory times' with something of nostalgic despair.[85] Chief amongst these was Wilson's *Quarterly Review*, which Thackeray ironically describes as the 'dear old *Quarterly Review*, with its usual grace, and polite felicity of illustration'.[86] Pitying this group with *Punch*-like scorn, Thackeray commiserates with them: 'O poor dear bewildered old Quarterly! O Mrs. Gamp! O Mrs. Harris!'[87] The *Quarterly Review*, *Herald*, and *Standard*, are the frequent butts of Thackeray's jokes in the 'Snob Papers', the most cutting of which is probably the hit at Mrs. Gamp – after the close of the London season when the staid middle classes leave the City, the houses are shut up, 'and window blinds are pitilessly papered with the *Morning Herald*'.[88]

Old Jawkins' reading of the *Standard* and presence in the *Herald* classifies him in a particular social group: Tory Club and family, domestic man. Similarly, other characters are introduced by way of their newspaper affiliations. For example, 'Young Muscadel, that cheap dandy, is talking Fashion and Almack's out of the *Morning Post* ... '.[89] Captain Rag, 'devoted ... to billiards, steeple-chasing, and the turf', is recognised in *Bell's Life*;[90] and the Club Snobs, Spavin and Cockspur, 'growl together, in a corner, about sporting matters' and 'read *Bell's Life* (and a very pleasant paper too, with a great deal of erudition in the answers to correspondents)'.[91] Thus, the reporting of 'facts' in Thackeray's microcosm of fashionable society becomes significant as a register of the cultural ideologies at work in his day. Thackeray recognized that each newspaper or magazine had a market-ethos that singled out or appealed to (supply-demand) a section of society. This subset may be highly diverse (as with the readership of the *Post*), but there existed an essential characteristic which was revealed in their taste or acceptance of the discourse. He categorized the press into various indicators of human nature, and revealed how human society – the consumer, the reader – sought to possess a certain language, a particular system of knowledge, conforming to a newspaper's ideology, which might gain them an advantage in life. The press did not merely signify, it participated in the construction of identity and character. In this manner, periodicals could be important influences on the motivations of characters in Thackeray's fictional world.

Finally, then, these elements come together in a sustained attack on the *Court-Circular*: the diary and record of events in high society, and a sycophantic and undemocratic institution in Thackeray's opinion. In the chapter '"The Court Circular", and its Influence on Snobs', Thackeray voiced his concern and launched a tirade of invective against the newspaper columns of this kind.[92] The daily papers, whilst posturing towards politics and democracy, yet maintain the aristocratic hegemony via the near-worship of gentility and fashion. Thackeray's parody of a Court-Circular description of the dresses of Lady Snobky and her daughter shows the vacuity of this kind of commodity fetishism.

> *Costume de cour*, composed of a train of the most superb Pekin bandannas, elegantly trimmed with spangles, tin foil, and red-tape. Bodice and underdress of sky-blue velveteen, trimmed with *bouffants* and *noeuds* of bell-pulls. Stomacher, a muffin. Head-dress, a bird's nest, with a bird of paradise, over a rich brass knocker *en ferronière*. This splendid costume, by Madame Crinoline, of Regent Street, was the object of universal admiration.[93]

Thackeray's denunciation is uncompromising and honest. Moreover, he revealed the power of the papers to set fashions and trends. Continuing his criticism with a pertinent reference to Sarah Ellis's work, *The Women of England*, Thackeray cried:

> This is what you read. Oh, Mrs. Ellis! Oh, mothers, daughters, aunts, grandmothers of England, this is the sort of writing which is put in the newspapers for you! How can you help being the mothers, daughters, & c. of Snobs, so long as this balderdash is let before you?[94]

The influence on the public maintains social prejudices and inequalities. The *Court-Circular* is the epitome of the perhaps unconscious, perhaps cynical code of the press. It overbuilt the egotism of the upper-classes, Thackeray wrote, and inflated their self-importance; 'as long as a *Court-Circular* exists, how the deuce are people whose names are championed in it ever to believe themselves the equals of the cringing race which daily reads that abominable trash?'[95]

This attack provided the reader of *Punch* with an intimation of the subversive challenge implicit in 'The Snobs of England'. It is its own 'Peerage' – a *Court-Circular* of the middle and upper-middle classes in an alternative newspaper. The daily movements of the aristocracy, the reporting on the celebrities of the fashionable news of the present day – the structuring principle behind the *Court-Circular* – is adopted by Thackeray in his frame of reference to everyday events. However, he is at constant pains to remind the reader that his fictitious characters are not pleased to be set down and described in *Punch*. Appearing in 'The Snobs of England' is not quite the same as seeing your name in the *Post* or the *Herald*.

Thackeray's work for the periodicals of the early 1840s entered into a relationship with other newspapers and magazines of the time, drawing public attention to the textuality of life amidst this expanding cultural phenomenon of the press. As well as suiting his style and subject matter to the collective and editorial tone of the vehicle for which he was writing, he deliberately situated his articles within a complex framework of competing texts and discourses covering the literary ground between the *Quarterly Review* and the *Morning Post*. He made his readers aware of the associations between commodities and individuals. He created a surface reality which detailed modern fashions and opportunities (to buy, to be), whilst simultaneously puncturing that surface by making the reader recognize the processes constructing that apparent reality. Nevertheless, he strove throughout his work of this period for a greater degree of realism by shattering social illusions; he gave back to the authoritative, presumptuous, potentially manipulative voice of the journalist and critic, something of the genuine edge – the faults and vices, the hopes, wishes, and loves – of humanity. His periodical writings not only reported for posterity the condition of society in the 1840s, but also explored the media for presenting such information. He remained both a critic and a historian, yet problematized and thereby advanced the power, proficiency, and function of both of these roles within a new media and mediated context.

Notes

[1] Scott Bennett, 'Revolutions in Thought: serial publication and the mass market for reading', in J. Shattock and M. Wolff (eds), *The Victorian Periodical Press: Samplings and Soundings* (Leicester: Leicester University Press, 1982), 225-6.

[2] [James Fitzjames Stephen], 'Journalism', *Cornhill Magazine*, 6 (July 1862), 52.
[3] Ibid.
[4] Ibid., 53.
[5] Henry Silver's Diary for 1862, cited in R.G.G. Price, *A History of Punch* (London: Collins, 1957), 103.
[6] 'A Brother of the Press on the History of a Literary Man, Laman Blanchard, and the Chances of the Literary Profession', *Fraser's Magazine*, 33 (March 1846); *Works*, XXV, 87-100.
[7] Stephen, 'Journalism', 60.
[8] John Kenyon, *The History Men: The Historical Profession in England since the Renaissance*, second edition (London: Weidenfeld & Nicholson, 1993), 88ff.; John Lukacs, *Historical Consciousness, or the Remembered Past* (New York: Schocken Books, 1968/1985), xvi; Macaulay, probably the most popular historian of Thackeray's age, announced 'Facts are the mere dross of history', but he also saw the importance of integrating the ordinary with the famous, an historian 'must see ordinary men as they appear in their ordinary business and in their ordinary pleasures' (T.B. Macaulay, 'History', *Edinburgh Review* (May 1828), 10, 36).
[9] See Margaret Beetham, 'Towards a Theory of the Periodical as a Publishing Genre', in L. Brake, A. Jones, and L. Madden (eds), *Investigating Victorian Periodicals* (London: Macmillan, 1990), 20.
[10] 'On Ribbons', *Cornhill Magazine*, 1 (May 1860); *Works*, XXII, 26.
[11] 'Autour de mon Chapeau', *Cornhill Magazine*, 7 (February 1863); *Works*, XXII, 272.
[12] 'Half-a-Crown's Worth of Cheap Knowledge', *Fraser's Magazine*, 17 (March 1838); reprinted in Melville (ed.), *Stray Papers*, 307 [references in the text are to this edition].
[13] 'Horae Catnachianae', *Fraser's Magazine*, 19 (April 1839), 407 [references in the text are to this edition]; facsimile reprinted in Richard Pearson (ed.), *W.M. Thackeray: Early Fiction and Journalism* (London: Routledge/Thoemmes Press, 1996).
[14] 'Sybil. By Mr. Disraeli, M.P.', *Morning Chronicle* (13 May 1845); Ray, *Contributions*, 80; Henry Mayhew's series for the *Morning Chronicle* has elements of this.
[15] 'Waiting at the Station', *Punch* (9 March 1850); *Works*, XVI, 353; Thackeray knew Mayhew from his contributions to *Punch*.
[16] 'Titmarsh v. Tait', *Punch* (14 March 1846); *Works*, XXVI, 153.
[17] 'Regina' was the nickname that *Fraser's Magazine* cultivated as a corporate shorthand.
[18] The title given to an imaginary journal, based on Thackeray's first perodical, in *Lovel the Widower*, *Works*, XXIV, 18.
[19] 'Letters from a Club Arm-Chair', *Calcutta Star* (21 August 1845); reprinted in Summerfield, 230.
[20] *The Irish Sketch-Book*, *Works*, XVIII, 9.

[21] *Morning Chronicle* (26 December 1845); Ray, *Contributions*, 94-5; Thackeray described Jerrold as rivalling Dickens in this series in the *Calcutta Star* correspondence, 21 August 1845 (Summerfield, 233).
[22] *London Saturday Journal*, I (18 May 1839), 305.
[23] Ibid., 306-7.
[24] Charles Clyatt, 'Contemporary History', *The Illuminated Magazine*, 343; Jerrold, Thackeray's *Punch* colleague at this time, was also a prolific editor of his own newspapers and the comment here reflects his political consciousness and Radicalism, later a source of antagonism between the two writers. In October 1839, Thackeray wrote to John Mitchell Kemble suggesting an article entitled 'Contemporary History' on the different French and English newspaper reporting of the Napoleonic Wars; Harden, *Letters*, I, 54.
[25] 'Politics and Politicians', *London Saturday Journal*, 3 (18 January 1840), 33-5.
[26] Clyatt, 347, 343, 349, 346.
[27] Thackeray was still dealing with creditors for the *Constitutional* in 1838.
[28] *The Penny Story-Teller: Adapted for Family Reading and Amusement* began publication in October 1836; on 6 March 1839, it began printing extracts from *Nicholas Nickleby* 'for the amusement of such of our readers as have not the means of reading the original work' (75). Other periodicals also reprint Dickens; the *Fly* called him, 7 April 1838, 'unquestionably the most popular author of the present day', and had its own sub-editor called 'Buz'. It also reprinted Douglas Jerrold, to 'raise this popular writer still higher in public estimation' (10 March 1838).
[29] The *Fly* was not amused by Thackeray's criticisms and wrote a long critical review, no. 21 (17 March 1838), 82: '*Fraser's Magazine*: This scurrilous magazine has this month more than its usual quantum of slander. – The jealousy of the proprietors, it would appear, has been excited against the publications which cheaply disseminate knowledge among the people; hence the malicious article under the title of "Half-a-Crown's Worth of Cheap Knowledge," in which all the weekly Magazines of talent are slandered in a style, which could only proceed from the gin-excited imagination of the editor of "Fraser's Magazine." We can imagine the wily Fraser putting the half-crown into the Editor's hand, and directing him to purchase its worth of weekly periodicals; off starts the editor to Paternoster-Row, thinking to pocket the discount allowed by the wholesale publishers to the retail venders, to expend in his beloved fluid "blue ruin." On arriving at his destination he asked for the most popular magazines, and "The Town" and "The Fly" were handed to him, when imagine his chagrin on finding the discount was only allowed to the trade: back he trudged in (to use a newspaper phrase) the highest excitement, vowing vengeance against authors, publishers, and all; by the time, however, that he reached the Quadrant he became calmer, and was heard singing the following to the popular 'Air – Maid of Llangollen':

Tho' shabby my coat, and wretched my pate,
I see without envy the clever and great,
Contented and proud a hack writer to be,
Whilst the Conservative Lords smile sweetly on me.

My way up the Quadrant I cheerfully take,
To the shop where old Fraser the money does make.
And at eve I return with a heart full of glee,
For Conservative Peel will smile sweetly on me.

Melbourne's rich lord passes scornfully by,
But place ne'er can make him so happy as I,
But meaner than even the meanest I'll be,
Whilst Conservative asses smile sweetly on me.

Here he found himself at the door of Fraser the publisher, so using the cuff of his coat in the manner which, since the introduction of pocket-handkerchiefs, we had supposed had become obsolete, he presented himself before the publisher, who more than once has been horse-whipped as a publisher of lies, and more than once had a verdict returned against him as a malicious scandalizer. – This conscientious personage directed his shoeblack to show the editor up to the garret, where the article was concocted: but enough of this, suffice it for us to say that "censure from such a party is praise indeed ... "'

[30] 'Going to See a Man Hanged', *Fraser's Magazine*, 22 (August 1840); *Works*, XVI, 390-91.

[31] Ibid., 391.

[32] Thackeray may be recalling the popular satirical magazine, *Punch in London*, run by Jerrold earlier in the decade.

[33] 'The Ballad of Eliza Davis', *Works*, XXI, 258; 'The Organ-Boy's Appeal', *Works*, XXI, 282. Policemen X and Z25 appear in *Pendennis* and *Philip* to clear away the anatagonistic characters of Altamont and Hunt who are causing disturbances outside middle-class residences; *Works*, III, 422-3, *Works*, XI, 276-7.

[34] See the discussion of the ballads in Antony Trollope, *Thackeray* (London: Macmillan, 1879), chapter 8, 168-9 and ff.

[35] *Letters*, I, 411.

[36] For a discussion of this, see F.S. Schwarzbach, '"Terra Incognita": An Image of the City in English Literature, 1820-1855', *Prose Studies*, 5 (May 1982).

[37] *Works*, XIV, 396.

[38] James Pope-Hennessy, *Monckton Milnes: The Years of Promise, 1809-1851* (London: Constable, 1949), 130, describes how Milnes collected autographs and woodcuts of Courvoisier, as well as known hangmen, and occasionally livened up a Sunday morning 'by watching his guests recoil before a piece of

dried skin of a notorious murderer, which he kept pressed between the pages of some appropriate book'.
[39] Kaplan, *Dickens*, 198-200.
[40] *Works*, XIV, 393.
[41] Letter to Alexander Blackwood, 29 June 1840; *Letters*, I, 450-51.
[42] *Works*, XIV, 393-4; letter to Mrs. Carmichael-Smyth, 6?-18 July 1840, *Letters*, I, 453.
[43] Kaplan, 199.
[44] *Works*, XIV, 386, 388, 391.
[45] See John Reed's detailed discussion of Thackeray's attitude towards punishment, *Dickens and Thackeray: Punishment and Forgiveness* (Athens: Ohio State University Press, 1995).
[46] For the history of *Punch*, see M.H. Speilmann, *The History of 'Punch'* (London: Cassell, 1895), R.G.G. Price, *A History of 'Punch'* (London: Collins, 1957), Richard D. Altick, *Punch: The Lively Youth of a British Institution, 1841-1851* (Columbus: Ohio State University Press, 1997); see also W. Jerrold, *Douglas Jerrold and 'Punch'* (London: Macmillan, 1910), A. Mayhew, *A Jorum of 'Punch'* (London, 1899), A.W. A'Beckett, *The à Beckett's of 'Punch': Memories of Father and Sons* (Westminster: Constable, 1903).
[47] *Works*, XXVI, 153.
[48] Ibid., 154-5.
[49] 'Laman Blanchard', *Works*, XXV, 89.
[50] 'Mr. Snob's Remonstrance', *Works*, XXVI, 187.
[51] *Works*, XXVI, 190.
[52] Ibid., 193.
[53] Summerfield, 209.
[54] Ibid., 221, 233.
[55] John Sutherland (ed.), W.M. Thackeray, *The Book of Snobs* (New York: St. Martin's Press, 1978), 11, traces the title of the work to Sarah Ellis's *The Women of England* (1845-46); John W. Dodds, *The Age of Paradox: A Biography of England, 1841-1851* (London: Victor Gollancz, 1953), 71, discusses Ellis.
[56] *Morning Chronicle* (2 April 1844); Ray, *Contributions*, 15.
[57] *Morning Chronicle* (4 May 1846); Ray, *Contributions*, 140.
[58] Ibid., 140-41; see also Thackeray's attack on the lord-loving English in his review of Madame de Girardin, *Foreign Quarterly Review*, 32 (January 1842), 474-5.
[59] Ray, *Contributions*, 142.
[60] Ibid.
[61] 'Club Snobs', *Punch* (16 January 1847); *Works*, XIV, 169.
[62] 'On Some Country Snobs', *Punch* (31 October 1846), 'Some Continental Snobs', *Punch* (12 September 1846); *Works*, XIV, 119, 87.
[63] Ray, *Uses*, 350; Sutherland, *Snobs*, 11; Peters, 126-32.
[64] Sutherland, *Snobs*, 12, 20; Dodds, *Paradox*, 242, 251; the omitted chapters are nos. 17-23 in *Punch*, reprinted in *Works*, XXVI.

[65] Sutherland, *Snobs*, 12.
[66] Ibid., 17-18.
[67] 'Club Snobs', *Punch* (2 January 1847); *Works*, XIV, 161.
[68] 'Club Snobs', *Punch* (20 February 1847); *Works*, XIV, 194.
[69] Cited in J.Y.T. Greig, 'The Social Critic', in Alexander Welsh (ed.), *Thackeray: 20th Century Views* (New Jersey: Prentice-Hall, 1968), 43.
[70] 'Snobbium Gatherum', *Punch* (28 November 1846); *Works*, XIV, 138.
[71] 'Snobs and Marriage', *Punch* (19 December 1846); *Works*, XIV, 149.
[72] 'Snobbium Gatherum', *Punch* (28 November 1846); *Works*, XIV, 137-9.
[73] 'On Some Country Snobs', *Punch* (17 October 1846); *Works*, XIV, 109; there is also a hint here of the *Punch* satires on the visit of a group of Indians to London at this time, who were taken to Disraeli's house to sample an aristocrat's lifestyle.
[74] 'Party-Giving Snobs', *Punch* (2 August 1846); *Works*, XIV, 74.
[75] See Sutherland's etymology of 'snob'; Sutherland, *Snobs*, 235-7.
[76] 'On Clerical Snobs', *Punch* (16 May 1846); *Works*, XIV, 48; Sutherland, *Snobs*, 217.
[77] 'On Clerical Snobs', *Punch* (16 May 1846); *Works*, XIV, 9; and see Thackeray's tale, 'A Chest of Cigars', *New Monthly Magazine* (July 1845).
[78] 'On Some Country Snobs', *Punch* (3 October 1846); *Works*, XIV, 101; see Carey, 64.
[79] For examples, see (in order) *Works*, XIV, 85, 105, 122; 73, 167; 165-6; 41, 71; 29; 43, 170; 39; *Works*, XXVI, 324.
[80] See *Works*, XIV, 2, 90-1; *Works*, XXVI, 313.
[81] 'Club Snobs', *Punch* (9 January 1847); *Works*, XIV, 165-7.
[82] 'Snobs and Marriage', *Punch* (12 December 1846); *Works*, XIV, 146.
[83] 'Club Snobs', *Punch* (9 January 1847); *Works*, XIV, 167.
[84] 'On Clerical Snobs and Snobbishness', *Punch* (23 May 1846); *Works*, XIV, 50; Sutherland, *Snobs*, 217-18.
[85] *Works*, XXVI, 324; Sutherland, *Snobs*, 223.
[86] Ibid.
[87] Ibid.
[88] 'Party-Giving Snobs', *Punch* (22 August 1846); *Works*, XIV, 73; and see the *Calcutta Star*, above.
[89] 'Dinner-Giving Snobs Further Considered', *Punch* (5 September 1846); *Works*, XIV, 85.
[90] 'Military Snobs', *Punch* (9 May 1846); *Works*, XIV, 43.
[91] 'Club Snobs', *Punch*, (16 January 1847); *Works*, XIV, 170.
[92] *Punch* (28 March 1846); *Works*, XIV, 17-21.
[93] *Works*, XIV, 18; Sutherland, *Snobs*, 217, notes how close this description is to a *Morning Post* description of around the same date; see also Thackeray's parody in the review of Sir John Ross's travels in the *Paris Literary Gazette* (Chapter 2, above).
[94] *Works*, XIV, 18.
[95] Ibid., 19.

Chapter 7

Deconstructing the press: *Punch*, the journalistic persona, and the contributor of 'Fat'

Joseph Addison and Richard Steele, at the beginning of the eighteenth century, remarked on the significance of their magazines, the *Spectator* and the *Tatler*, as recorders of the manners and modes of their age; Johnson had admired the periodicals as a source of learning and a platform for teaching; Lamb unified his periodical work with his idiosyncratic self-consciousness; Hazlitt was keen to assess the periodicals as purveyors of a strata of high literature but was driven into them for money; and Scott had used them as sources and historical signifiers.[1] Thackeray became interested in the periodical as a literary commodity, as an expression of his own culture, and as an influence over the expanding reading public. More so than his predecessors, Thackeray was acutely self-conscious of being a journalist and magazine writer, and, from 1842 onwards, introduced a whole world of real and fictitious magazines and newspapers into his fiction as a way of examining the cultural impact of this literature. In addition, and with an eye to realism, he used these periodicals as devices in his fiction: as descriptive background, as part of characterization, and as narrative instruments. Further, Thackeray analysed the way people read, what they read, and how they read it. The magazine, society, and the individual become intrinsically linked in his work, not least because Thackeray was aware that future societies would access the two latter through contemporary magazines. Most importantly, Thackeray found it essential, during this period of energetic change in the very nature and format of literature, to explore what was meant by art, and the relationship between art and entertainment (or 'popular' and 'high' culture).

The image of the literary man was changing. When Thackeray read periodicals as a boy at Charterhouse school in the 1820s, he was accessing a period that saw a great renaissance in magazine writing, and an establishment of an essayist tradition that led back from Hazlitt, Lamb, and Leigh Hunt to Johnson, Fielding, and Dean Swift. These were the figures Thackeray returned to in his *Lectures on the English Humourists* in the early 1850s. Thackeray's entry into the world of London journalism must have been in stark contrast to the image of these men-of-letters. Above all else, the new world was dominated by profits and commercial activities that cut short his own venture into publishing with the *National Standard*. By 1840, Thackeray had a new sense of authorial identity; the leisured genius was replaced by the professional, the Romantic by the tradesman. It is interesting to recall his 1840 description of Henry Fielding, with whom he seems to closely identify at a moment of crisis in his own life. Thackeray is describing Fielding's early literary and legal apprenticeship in London, after having spent the vast part of his fortune:

> His days of trouble had now begun in earnest, and, indeed, he met them like a man. He wrote incessantly for the periodical works of the day, issued pamphlets, made translations, published journals and criticisms, turned his hand, in a word, to any work that offered, and lived as best he might. This indiscriminate literary labour, which obliges a man to scatter his intellects upon so many trifles, and provide weekly varieties as sets-off against the inevitable butcher's bills, has been the ruin of many a man of talent since Fielding's time, and it was lucky for this world and for him that at a time of life when his powers were at the highest, he procured a place which kept him beyond the reach of weekly want, and enabled him to gather his great intellects together and produce the greatest satire, and two of the most complete romances in our language ... When Harry Fielding was writing for the week's bread, we find style and sentiment both careless, and plots hastily worked off. How could he do otherwise? Mr. Snap, the bailiff, was waiting with a writ without, – his wife and little ones asking wistfully for bread within. Away, with all its imperfections on its head, the play or the pamphlet must go. Indeed, he would have been no honest man had he kept them longer on his hands, with such urgent demands upon him as he had. But as soon as he is put out of reach of this base kind of want, his whole style changes, and, instead of the reckless and slovenly hack-writer, we have one of the most minute and careful artists that ever lived.[2]

Thackeray's assessment of Fielding's life is astonishing for its similarities to his own, as reading Ray's biography will show. Caught in the industrial process of literary production, turning out sheets at a rate per line, having little success with volume publications like the *Paris Sketch-Book*, Thackeray must have wondered how writing could pay the bills. A few months earlier, he had written to his mother with some distress: ' ... please God, enable me to save for the little ones.'[3] The parallels in this Fielding review with the early part of Thackeray's professional life are striking. Indeed, there remains a critical consensus which views Thackeray as a hurried and rather casual writer, producing sheets of seemingly effortless fiction, scarcely planned, scarcely revised, scarcely even punctuated. This is far from being the case. But, coincidentally, this article was Thackeray's last piece of work for *The Times* and he was soon to 'procure a place' on *Punch* and establish a promising relationship with its publishers, Bradbury and Evans.

An important and recently formed figure to emerge in Thackeray's works at this time is the journalist. He had already created characters such as Yellowplush (the footman-writer), Titmarsh (the painter-critic), Gahagan (the braggard-autobiographer), all of who appeared on the frontispiece to the collected *Comic Tales and Sketches* in 1841. Perhaps this was a retrospect, a moving on; its timing is significant. And although he would continue with such personae – Fitzboodle, and Pendennis, for example, who are more literary figures, or men-of-letters – he would also create characters who are observers and commentators: the Fat Contributor, Mr Snob, Mr Spec, and Dr Solomon Pacifico. The 1840s also saw the creation of the foreign-journalist caricatures, the Frenchman, Gobemouche, the Irishman, Molony, the reports of the Arab, Hadjee Aboo Bosh, and the Crimean reporter, Mick, or 'Our Own Bashi-Bozouk'. These figures provide an important review of the new periodical field. They are ambivalent figures who are a direct result of the commercial press, transforming the everyday, the external, the raw material of life, into lucrative letterpress. They are another aspect of Thackeray himself; the journalist is neither man-of-letters nor literary artist, but is the mediator who converts reality into text. A journalist is not visible in the unsigned press with its corporate voice; and yet he is the essence of the daily periodical, the historian of contemporary history. Thackeray's narratives frequently deal with the ironies of the ordinary man who finds himself in a position of power, the middleman or middling-man who is at the centre. George Eliot made the study of provincial mediocrity and middle-of-the-road existence her forte. But for Thackeray, the middling men were at the heart of the established institutions of his time, and they were the powers in the press, that most powerful of new media.

Thackeray's 1840s work begins to deconstruct this figure. The journalistic identity is a problematic one as it assumes authority but sustains invisibility. The personalities 'seen' in the press are not those who write but are those of the fashionable or public world. Thackeray creates an opposition to this, a visible journalist, with faults and egotisms, who in fact often is incapable of reflecting the external world but only his internal emotions. This is an unpacking of the journalist persona. Thackeray's journalists tend to be individualists and independent of the corporate medium. But they are also dependent on this medium for their exposure. This central paradox finds its comic expression in the advertisorial function of the journalist's article. A 'puff' for *Punch* goes a long way to soothe contributor–publisher relations. Moreover, the newspaper and magazine of the 1840s was part of the economy of speculation and investment. The journalist, and the writer, was an individual speculator too. In several ways, Thackeray exposes the imposition made on a text to conform to a ready-made identity or family likeness.[4]

Although intending 'realism', the presentation of daily life in the middle-class newspapers was, for Thackeray and the *Punch* writers, snobbish, insincere, and untruthful. Where Thackeray's works are concerned with the everyday (for example, the social effects of railway speculation and the commercial exploitation of the public), the 'haut-ton' newspapers seized on sensationalistic stories about the wealthy and created heroes like corrupt George Hudson, the 'Railway King'.[5] Thackeray did not exonerate the world which created a market for such 'news'; but he points out simply the absurdities of a system whereby 'the fellow who comes to get a list of the company when you give a banquet or a dancing breakfast at Longueoreille House, gets money from the newspapers for performing that service'.[6] This fellow is 'Peter Jenkins', Douglas Jerrold's personification of the *Morning Post* created in *Punch* to satirize the world of fashionable news gossip, and to whose caricature Thackeray added several contributions.[7]

M.H. Spielmann and Richard Kelly provide full discussions of the Jenkins papers in *Punch*.[8] 'Jenkins' was a high society reporter (based on the *Post's* Rumsey Forster), who relished the names of grandees and the observances of upper-class society rather than substantial news. 'Lickspittleoff' was his Russian editor on the paper. Jenkins slavishly admired the aristocracy, and, in his *Court Circular*, gave out all the intelligence of their actions as though they comprised the world. He was marked by his affected and bad French. The *Post* retaliated against *Punch* and regularly criticized its writers; Thackeray received few good reviews of his writings for *Fraser's Magazine*, with the exception of the early 'Men and Coats'.[9]

The personification of the press was extended when *Punch* introduced two new characters, Mrs Gamp and Mrs Harris, as shorthand signifiers for the *Morning Herald* and the (evening) *Standard*. In November 1845, with *Martin Chuzzlewit* in serialization, *Punch* took these names from two characters in Dickens' novel – the first to suggest a gossipy, fussy, over-moral old woman, and the second to imply that the *Standard* was merely an echo of the *Herald*, a shadow, possibly even a figment of 'Mrs Gamp's' imagination. John Leech drew the characters as two old gossips 'in mop-cap and pattens'.[10] The *Herald* was considered a 'family' paper in early Victorian England; *Punch* was indicating that it was politically vacuous and frivolous. The *Standard*, *Punch* insinuated, was simply reprinting the morning news items from its fellow Tory paper and reiterating its editorial opinions.

There was some degree of political bias and self-defining in these attacks as well as a critique of newspaper reporting in general. Where Thackeray's *National Standard* had attacked its rivals, the *Literary Gazette* and *Athenaeum*, *Punch* was doing something of the same. Certainly, it ridiculed a variety of journals the contents of which it offered versions of in its own repertoire (such as art criticism, literature and political commentary). The *Standard* in its counter-attacks suggested that *Punch* simply reflected the voice of the Conservative *Times*, a view which *The Times* itself put forward in the 1890s.[11] Spielmann argues that *Punch* 'has always been above suspicion and above proof', since 'Democrat he was, and independent in his views';[12] but, it must be remarked that, with A'Beckett writing leader columns for *The Times*, there was inevitably some alliance of opinion. Further, *Punch* rarely attacked papers like the *Morning Chronicle* (for which Thackeray and Mayhew wrote; although Thackeray himself was not always uncritical, see his *Calcutta Star* items), the *Illustrated London News* (whose staff included A'Beckett and F.W.N. Bayley), and the *Daily News*, the venture of its own publishers. Other papers established by various team members – Jerrold's *Shilling Magazine* and *Weekly*, for instance – were left alone, too.

On the whole, although personal connections played some part, *Punch*'s and Thackeray's attacks on the press were in opposition to the techniques and the style of news reporting and the uncritical support of government opinion in several of the major daily papers. As Thackeray remarked in 'The Snobs of England', although *Punch* was 'eminently Conservative'; it remained on the side of the people and reform – at least, until democracy was won, then *Punch*

> ... will find himself in opposition as usual, and deploring the good old days and the advent of Radicalism along with poor old Mrs. Gamp and Mrs. Harris.[13]

Punch was against the politics, practices, and presumptions of the newspapers, rather than the newspapers' respective market positions. In any case, its real rivals were the comic magazines who imitated its contents, the *Great Gun* (1844-5) and the *Man in the Moon* (1847-9), amongst others.[14]

Thackeray's articles treating the character of the modern day journalist suggest that his interest in the 1840s moves away from anxieties about the death of the Romantic man-of-letters to a consideration of how the Victorian writer negotiated the terrain of contemporary journalism. Thackeray's view of the world is constructed and defined by the various magazine discourses of his day and the media through which those discourses are presented. He gradually absorbed the periodical world into his fictional world and generated a new relationship between the perceptions of his imagined 'reality' and the means through which those perceptions were expressed. In other words, by exploring the true nature of the daily and weekly press in his criticism and fiction, Thackeray generated a self-reflexivity that questioned the authoritativeness of the journalist and journalistic texts.

Thackeray's writings of the 1840s begin to be more overtly concerned with the popular trends in the reporting of current affairs. Although playing a minimal part in his work of the 1830s (except for where he was directly employed as a correspondent, such as for the *National Standard* and the *Constitutional*), a texture of contemporary references became a crucial feature in the 'realism' of his work after 1841. Indeed, one might see how the largely literary exercises of his early fiction are transformed into richly allusive and pertinent satires after his opening forays in *Punch*. In this shift, Thackeray's work mirrors the changing demands in the reading public characterized by the spread of newspapers.

Richard Altick's *The Presence of the Present* (1991), identifies many instances of contemporary referencing in the early to mid-Victorian novel.

The practice was widespread. One specific topic in Thackeray's writings may serve as an example: the spread of the railways throughout the early 1840s and the 'Railway Mania' and collapse in share-issues of 1845-7. Altick discusses descriptions in *Pendennis* and *The Newcomes*, as well as the story of Jeames de la Pluche in *Punch*, where Thackeray alludes to this subject.[15] In addition, references to the railway occur in other journalism from the early 1840s. Thackeray's response to the railways becomes political, economic, literary and travel-related, as he makes it a symbol of the condition of his age.

The topic was important to him; Thackeray lost £500 in the collapse of the share market for the 'sanguinary railroads'.[16] In 1845 and early 1846, Thackeray published a number of short pieces for *Punch* on the 'railway question' and drew the issues together in 'Jeames's Diary' (8 November 1845 to 7 February 1846). Several other single items also appeared.[17] Railway speculation provided Thackeray with a metaphor for worldly success through which he could show up human vanity and snobbery in his accustomed line. The stock-market gamble of Victorian city life replaced the 'rouge et noir' or card gambling of the Regency.[18] Everyone was involved; Dickens looked at the issues of railway building in *Dombey and Son* (1846-7), Jerrold cast Mr Caudle as a 'railway director' of the 'Eel-Pie Island Railway' in Lecture 33 of *Mrs. Caudle's Curtain Lectures* (1846). Bradbury and Evans's *Daily News*, edited by Dickens, was established in 1846 funded by 'railway money' from Joseph Paxton and having a 'Railway Editor'.[19] For Thackeray, *Jeames* involved 1840s financial speculation where the story of Yellowplush in the 1830s had involved the Regency gambling of Deuceace. Thackeray continued to use the card sharpers in his historical novels, *Barry Lyndon* and *Vanity Fair*; he also introduced other kinds of 'speculation' in the magazine-sting of *The Ravenswing*. Pluche's story reworks the rise and fall of fortune narratives of Stubbs and Cox, which enabled Thackeray to play out his comedies of the ordinary man adrift in aristocratic circumstances (at the opera, parading on horse-back, dining out). The themes of the crossing of class boundaries and the capitalist dream of the self-made man were persistent in Thackeray's fiction.[20]

The moral of the story of Jeames de la Pluche is an obvious one: it is not money that makes a gentleman (or a copy of *Pelham*) or brings true happiness. But the issue of gambling or speculation is more complex. Thackeray does not condemn or condone gambling; he accepts that the principles behind these are present in all walks of life. Marriage is a gamble, business consists of gambles, painting for popularity is a gamble (as is surely intended in Thackeray's description of the Royal Academy exhibition as 'May Gambols'), writing is a gamble. The process was not a terrible sin. As he noted in his defence of the Art Unions' picture lotteries in the *Pictorial Times*, 1 April 1843:

> An underwriter gambles when he insures a ship; calculating that he has a profit on the chances. A man gambles when he buys stock to

> sell afterwards, or a newspaper, or a house, or any other commodity upon which profit or loss may acrue.[21]

Thackeray's journalist of the later *Punch* period, Mr Spec,[22] plays on both the concept of the 'Spectator' and the 'Speculator'. As Jeames declares, 'Railway Spec is going on phamusly'.[23]

Thackeray's writings for this period bring together the growth of the railways and the spread of English commodities around the world. Indeed, everything seems commodified to Thackeray, including literature, the magazines, and his own writings. This is a crucial development in his work because it reveals how far he is aware of the periodical market as part of an economic system which influences what is produced. 'We are covering Europe with our railways, that we may sell our goods there', he remarked bluntly in one letter of foreign correspondence to the *Calcutta Star*.[24] In a review of Soulié's novel in the *Foreign Quarterly Review*, the railway becomes a comic 'conspiracy' against the French to prevent political warmongering agains English.

> It has been carried over to France by Englishmen. It has crept from Rouen to the gates of Paris; from Rouen it is striding towards the sea at Southampton; from Paris it is rushing towards the Belgian frontier and the channel. It is an English present. *Timete Danaos*: there is danger in the gift.[25]

The French will travel to London and realize that England is not the 'perfide Albion' that the French press likes to shout about. Speculation and the railroads, then, were useful metaphors for the fortunes and luck of life, as well as controlling forces behind his own writing practices and the mechanics of the periodical press. As Shillingsburg and others have pointed out, the hack-writer was constantly having to weigh up the labour spent on an article with the price it would fetch; Thackeray's unfinished or abandoned projects show how tricky this exchange of values could be. Indeed, each newspaper or magazine venture was a risk, as Thackeray knew only too well.

One of the more precious commodities of Thackeray's world was information. In fact, *Punch* might be said to offer alternative information on aspects of contemporary life, particularly to the economically-naïve public. In 'Jeames and the Time-Bargings', Thackeray exposed the rewards and pitfalls information could provide. Jeames's acquaintence, Frederick Timmins, a law student in London, meets his 'tumminus' in the 'time-bargings', as Jeames put it.[26] He is dealing in a kind of insider-trading. Receiving a hint that a certain group of shares will continue climbing in value after he himself has sold out, Timmins is persuaded to buy back heavily. The issue collapses, of course, and he loses, not only his money, but also his intended, Miss Mulligatawny, to Colonel Claw, the man who gave him the information. Investment in others' knowledge, as Thackeray indicated at the end of *The Great Hoggarty Diamond*, is a dangerous business. As he purchases an aristocratic pedigree, Jeames parenthetically confesses his doubts about facts in newspapers:

> I got from the Erald Hoffis (not the Mawning Erald – no, no, I'm not such a Mough as to go there for ackrit infamation) an account of my famly, my harms and pedigry.[27]

Thackeray, then, combined humorous attacks on contemporary journalistic practices with a moral commentary aimed at benefiting the ordinary reader. In an age where information was commodified, trusting to a newspaper was not without dangers.

Linked to this is Thackeray's criticism of the newspaper industry itself – the manner and morality by which journalism operated in the 1840s. The reporting of news was a booming business and editors and proprietors were continually seeking ways of attracting readers through more efficient and exotic methods of collecting information. The foreign correspondent was one such innovation. The mobile, local ('roving') reporter was another. This kind of close, hands-on observing and reporting was early developed by the social critics who travelled England compiling records of city life and people, as Dickens and Mayhew did. *Punch* and the *Illustrated London News*, with the immediacy of their response to daily events, helped to create this style of journalism.

The criticism of press intrusion into privacy, the 'danger of "being shown up"',[28] the reporter as observer-spy exposing secrets and circulating hidden knowledge in the public domain, was a fear of the early Victorians, if not generally acknowledged. Where one might see an honest connection between travel and news (the English explorer bringing back accounts of foreign peoples), one might also detect new forms of ideological control and cultural imperialism. Dickens' *Martin Chuzzlewit* (1843-4) contains an explicit attack on the American press (partly as a result of the American deriding of Dickens' calls for International Copyright Laws, against which the publishing houses of the New York journals had a vested interest).[29] In retaliation to the press hostility on the *American Notes* tour of 1842, Dickens had Martin Chuzzlewit arrive in New York to the greetings of newspaper-vendors:

> 'Here's this morning's New York Sewer!' cried one. 'Here's this morning's New York Stabber! Here's the New York Family Spy! Here's the New York Private Listener! here's the New York Peeper! Here's the New York Plunderer! Here's the New York Keyhole Reporter! Here's the New York Rowdy Journal! Here's all the New York papers!'[30]

The account of 'the wide-awake Sewer; always on the look-out' is elaborated by the description of Mrs. White's Ball, 'with the Sewer's own particulars of the private lives of all the ladies that was there!' and 'a whole column of New Yorkers to be shown up, and all their names printed!'[31]

In *Jeames's Diary*, Thackeray produced one of the earliest spoofs on newspaper reporting. The narrative followed a journalist on his chase to

Gretna Green of an 'ELOPEMENT IN HIGH LIFE'. This was the *Morning Tatler*'s 'ONLY AUTHENTIC ACCOUNT' of Jeames's bride-never-to-be, Lady Angelina's, elopement with Lieutenant George Granby Silvertop of the 150th Hussars.[32] The four newspaper reports interpolated into the tale are introduced by Jeames as 'the story of that ilorpmint I have no art to tell' (XV, 143). The first report tells of the wedding cancellation and describes the expensive preparations in a parody of the *Post*'s court guides. Jewels were bought 'from Messrs. Storr and Mortimer', cakes, carriages, liveries supplied, and the arrival of the Right Rev the Lord Bishop of Bullocksmithy is of less import than his 'staying at Milvert's' (XV, 143). Then follows a fictional representation of press harassment; Jims, 'of an Irish nation, a man of spirit and sinew, and Master of Arts of Trinity College, Dublin' (Irish journalists were commonplace in the press), joins a group of reporters making 'enquiries every ten minutes at the Earl's mansion in Hill Street', earning abuse from the distressed family. Later reports come from Newcastle and, finally, Gretna Green. These brief letters are concluded by a longer account of his confrontation with the groom outside a hotel in Whistlebinkie at midnight, entitled 'SHAMEFUL TREATMENT OF OUR REPORTER' (XV, 146).

Despite his argument that 'my employers were anxious to give the public every particular regarding an event so singular' (XV, 147), Jims is defeated by the voice of the incredulous ordinary man.

> And do you mean to say, sir, that you have dogged me all the way from London, and that my family affairs are to be published for the readers of the *Morning Tatler* newspaper? (XV, 147)

The exposure of Jims, the *Morning Tatler* reporter, is less sinister than Dickens' caricature. It is a jibe at the over-zealous enthusiasm of a journalist in carrying out what is seen as a dubious public benefit (and a great nuisance) in the name of 'duty'.

This account further defines Thackeray's attitude to a profession and a body of literature by which he was making a living. Unlike the dissolute art critic M.A. Titmarsh of the 1830s, whose critical status is problematized, Jims clearly represents a new breed of news-hound whom Thackeray disliked. Indeed, this is an attack on intrusive, gossipy reporting at its bluntest, rather than an attack on a specific target (although Thackeray probably had the *Morning Post* in mind as a model for his *Tatler*). As he remarked at the end of 'The Snobs of England', 'I am sick of Court Circulars. I loathe haut-ton intelligence ... A society that sets up to be polite, and ignores Arts and letters, I hold to be a Snobbish society.'[33]

Thackeray's next journalist, the 'Fat Contributor', brought to the magazine-reading public a middle-class world of travel and overseas commerce and established a discourse which mediated between the 'aristocratic' or artistic travel writer of several of Thackeray's reviews and the ordinary London-based reader. His papers examine comically the authority of the journalist and the reception, by the reader, of the magazine and the article. However, the Fat Contributor is an important figure, perhaps more so than Jeames de la Pluche, Yellowplush, Major Gahagan, or Barry Lyndon, because he represents an 'insider', belonging to the periodical world, like Titmarsh or Mr Snob. He is not the comic outsider writing-in. Created as a 'foreign correspondent' for *Punch* in August 1844 and contributing most of his pieces between then and October 1845, he provided Thackeray with a comic voice for new travel material (such as the Brighton journeys) and for a recasting of the material from the *Cornhill to Cairo* trip.[34] He is a mediation between the aristocratic world of the Grand Tour and the modern age of travel journalism, just as Thackeray manipulated his observations to suit the travel volume and the magazine markets.

The Fat Contributor – later referred to as, variously, 'Our Stout Contributor', 'Punch's Commissioner', 'the F.C.', 'le Gros Rédacteur', and 'Folkestone Canterbury' – earned his name by dint of his stoutness (although in the second paper he claimed to have slimmed down) and, more significantly though never stated, by being a contributor of 'fat' to the magazines. Thackeray devised these articles as satirical padding for *Punch*, thereby mocking the pervasive editorial practice of commissioning poor quality travel papers from amateurish third-rate writers. The Fat Contributor's lack of expertise and overbearing egotism provide one of the running jokes of his Eastern tour. Whilst stopping at various ports – Vigo, Malta, Oporto – his self-analysis, seasickness, and obsession with an attractive fellow passenger, contrive to make him miss all of the sights promised:

> I have missed what is said to be one of the most beautiful bays in the world ... [35]

As the *Punch* 'editors' note at the beginning of the series, 'there is not a word about the places visited by our friend, while there is a prodigious deal of information regarding himself'.[36]

The travels of Thackeray's fat journalist operate on a number of levels directly and indirectly related to his critique of the periodical press. The articles are parodic of the genre of travel writing, a comic guide to travelling abroad, a satire on the social world of English tourists, a reflection of England's trading and commercial domination, a deflation of Romance (the romance of travel and the exotic love-relationship discovered in another country), an essay on egotism, a series of observations on culture, a literary analysis of ways of looking, and a criticism of the kind of knowledge assumed and information given by the contemporary periodical press. The narrative develops either through a series of fragmented diary entries or as a short self-contained dissertation on an aspect of a place (for example, 'A Brighton Night's Entertainment', which described the Brighton theatre and a melodrama called 'The Warlock of the Glen'). Thackeray writes short sketches or observations, often illustrated by himself, and makes the letter press interact overtly with the drawings by a process of illustrating the text and commenting on the illustration. Finally, the Fat Contributor implicitly sees travel and places as raw material to be transformed into literary commodities for the magazines (i.e. *Punch*). The journalist is the inverse of the historical novelist or historian who uses the newspaper or magazine as a repository of source material to be transformed into narrative. Industry reverses the process, producing 'fat' from the substance of observable life. The Fat Contributor's words are currency.

The Fat Contributor is a traveller of the 'lion' sort, a generally unhelpful travelling companion who constantly boasts of his own experience and merits.[37]

> I have travelled like Benjamin Disraeli, Ulysses, Monckton Milnes, and the eminent sages of all time.[38]

> I roll like a ball – and possess a love of locomotion which would do credit to the leanest of travellers, George Borrow, Captain Clapperton, or Mungo Park.[39]

This lineage places him alongside a group of travel writers (of different cultural standing) suggesting a tradition of some importance. His actual status is not so ostentatious; his faults are absurdly inappropriate for his self-assumed role as a commentator on life and morality. For example, he confuses a footman with a lord (as Becky mistakes Sir Pitt for a servant): 'Such is life! and so may its most astute observers be sometimes deceived.'[40] As an educator of the public, assuming a social role, the Fat Contributor becomes almost afraid of the influence he might exert over his readers – another reference to the power of the press, paralleling the *Book of Snobs*. The people of Brighton write to complain of their negative portrayal in his *Punch* series (particularly worried are the boarding-house proprietors), and the Fat Contributor declares: 'And is it so? Is the power of the Commissioner's eye so fatal that it withers the object on which it falls?'[41] Journalism is portrayed as occupying a symbiotic relationship with business and commerce, as well as the trade of the Empire. The Brighton travel scenes demonstrate how newspaper reporting can affect tourism. The press is not to be ignored or taken lightly as a significant cultural development.

The Fat Contributor's depiction of 'the ship at sea' is a sketch 'taken under circumstances of great difficulty – over the engine-room – the funnel snorting, the ship's sides throbbing, as if in a fit of ague'.[42] The description externalises the Fat Contributor's sea-sickness, but it also represents the transforming of erotic desire into commercial text. The Fat Contributor admires his own 'masterpiece of perspective', and suggests that the Royal Academy should exhibit it, or 'Mr Moon' should publish it as 'a large five-guinea plate'. At the end of the description, the reader discovers the real reason behind the Fat Contributor's sketch:

> ... and far far away, on the quarter-deck, close by the helmsman, with the binnacle shining before his steadfast eyes, and the English flag streaming behind him – (it is a confounded head-wind) – you see – O my wildly beating, my too susceptible heart – you see DOLORES![43]

Dolores is the girl of the Fat Contributor's dreams who clearly has little interest in him and who, moreover, is presented unconsciously as a less than attractive proposition, a Spanish girl who tells jokes like Becky Sharp, eats more than the Fat Contributor himself, has a liking for 'onions and garlic', and is portrayed in what the narrator calls and unflattering 'sketch taken in rough weather'.[44] Her appetite mirrors the Fat Contributor's consumption of people: the fat he gains is the symbolic fat of writing. Sitting at the breakfast table, he watches others eat, and eavesdrops on their talk, remarking of a women pretentiously discoursing on the paintings of 'Ruben' at their meal:

> How little they knew that the fat gentleman opposite was the contributor of – ha! ha! My mind fills with a savage exultation every now and then, as, hearing a piece of folly, I say inwardly – 'Ha, my fine fellow! you are down.' The poor wretch goes pottering on with his dinner: he little knows he will be in *Punch* that day fortnight.[45]

This 'power' held in his 'possession', the Fat Contributor claims to 'wield ... justly'. 'It would,' he says, 'be death in the hands of the inexperienced to hold the thunderbolts of *Punch*.'[46] This is a parody of the authority of the 'Thunderer', *The Times*. But it also excites and enervates him. Of Dolores, the reader is cajoled into the position of voyeur and encouraged to observe 'by the aid of a microscope ... every lineament of her delicious countenance – every fold of the drapery which adorns her fair form', not for his own or universal benefit, but for the narrator's pleasure and, ultimately, for commercial gain. The magazine writer is a workman turning the fabric of the real world into fiction or satire for the market-place. Thackeray, too, was a 'Punch Commissioner'; collecting details to fill an article was the essential activity of the journalist.

The power to shape cultural fashions and to influence the behaviour of the public by means of a kind of literary spy is added to by the powerful persuasion over trade and commerce. Magazines were good selling agents of the products of others and of literary commodities. We might take one example where Thackeray sells an experience to several different publishers, and uses that incident to advertise his magazine.[47] His visit to the pyramids in 1844 provides an instance of multiple response. In his diary for 19 October 1844, Thackeray described good-humouredly how he climbed to the top of the largest of Cairo's pyramids and gave '3 cheers for Punch on the top'.[48] In *Cornhill to Cairo*, the pyramids look down on the 'trophies of peace' of English commerce rather than upon the centuries that Napoleon saw. Titmarsh declares that he will perform his cleansing ritual of thanksgiving at the foot of the monuments and 'pour out libations of bitter ale and Harvey sauce'. British exports characterize a new invasion of 'England in Egypt', an appropriation by British trade of a domain seized by Napoleon.[49] In the 'Fat Contributor Papers', the boorish English Patriot is hoisted up to the summit of the pyramid to 'perform' a 'duty'; he pastes a leaflet advertising *Punch* on the highest stone.

> We gave three immense cheers for *Punch*, which astonished the undiscovered mummies that lie darkling in tomb-chambers, and must have disturbed the broken-nosed old sphinx who has been crouched for thousands of years hard by.[50]

In this latter, we are reminded that *Punch* could disturb; it was a 'noise' abroad. Yet *Punch* is also implicated in Imperial penetration: '*Punch* in the East', a conqueror hoisting a standard over his dominions. One recalls the similar tone in Thackeray's article 'England' in the *Paris Literary Gazette* nine years earlier where 'the thirty centuries which look down from the pyramids on the name of Napoleon, may see Warren's Blacking inscribed underneath it'.[51] In the *Calcutta Star* of 7 May 1845, Thackeray mocked his *Punch* article, stating that he was present on the *Punch* tour of the East, but was not impressed by the Fat Contributor's joke: 'it seemed to me but a poor piece of ribaldry'.[52] But the most significant aspect of this passage is the symbolic uniting of commerce and the periodical: *Punch* is itself a commodity like Harvey sauce, exported and circulated around the world.

The 'Fat Contributor Papers' portray several scenes in which *Punch* plays the part of cultural imperialist and is held up as a standard of English mercantile pride, in a comic manner. *Punch's* foreign success is, like Thackeray's opportunity to travel across countries, bound up with the developments in transportation and the commercial aspirations of companies like the Peninsular and Oriental. The journey from *Cornhill to Cairo* was made possible by the sponsorship of the P & O Company.[53] The publicity they gained was not confined to the travel book, since they received mention in *Punch*, too.[54] One wonders whether, as was later suggested in 'A Plan for a Prize Novel' in which realism would be pushed to the extreme of mentioning real companies for a fee, Thackeray struck any deals early in his career.[55] As he remarked in 'Punch in the East':

> Pale ale is to be found universally throughout Turkey, Syria, Greece, and Egypt, and after a couple of foaming bottles of Bass, a man could eat a crocodile ...[56]

In Chapter 2 of '*Punch* in the East' – 'To the Editor of *Punch* (confidential)' – Thackeray describes the magazine as an exported commodity. This was an item of comic bravado akin to the moment in the *Tremendous Adventures of Major Gahagan* (1838) when the major is shot but saved by a copy of the *New Monthly Magazine* (in which it was published) under his tunic. The jokes from the 'noble miscellany' *Punch* have penetrated far into England's Middle Eastern territories. *Punch* gives out a jocular warning to *The Times* and the *Observer* whom the editor asks to 'acknowledge' the 'authority' of the satirical journal.[57] The Fat Contributor reports:

> At Malta the first greeting between Captain Tagus and some other captain in anchor-buttons, who came to hail him when we entered harbour, related to *Punch*. 'What's the news?' exclaimed the other Captain. 'Here's *Punch*,' was the immediate reply of Tagus, handing it out – and the other Captain's face was suffused with instant smiles as his enraptured eye glanced over some of the beauteous designs of Leech.[58]

Punch is enjoying a moment's arrogant self-advertisement here. Thackeray is also challenging the rights of the 'factual' daily and weekly newspapers and the high culture monthlies and quarterlies to be considered of more value than a comic. Ship's Captains read *Punch* for its commentary on contemporary events, rather as many social and cultural historians do today. Elsewhere in the series of papers, the Fat Contributor's own article in the July number is being read by the guests of the British hotel in Alexandria (they 'rushed upon it ... even more eagerly than on pale ale'[59]). The encomiums for the magazine become more and more exaggerated as the travels advance; the Fat Contributor claims that *Punch* exposed Russia's expansionist foreign policy, and that

> By it [*Punch*] we are enabled to counter-balance the influence of the French in Egypt; by it we are enabled to spread civilization over the vast Indian continent, to soothe the irritated feelings of the Sikhs, and keep the Burmese in good-humour.[60]

Punch, the Fat Contributor declares, holds sway over the 'intellect of the world' and must use its 'power' both 'wisely and gently'.[61] Thackeray undercuts this pan-*Punch*ism, at the end of his article by promising gifts to the editor and his family, if an advance is sent. At the end of the day, the journalist earns his living by writing and this trade is foremost in his mind.

The media, for Thackeray, is an enabling mechanism, it empowers. It also generates profit. These aspects of the press only emerged in any significant way during the 1830s and 1840s. But the media industry was very rapid in its expansion and very quick to catch up with other forms of production and commercial trade. By the second half of the 1840s, certain commercially successful properties, such as *Punch*, had amassed a popular readership abroad as well as at home. Thackeray's deliberate glibness regarding the availability and influence of *Punch* abroad signifies this growing trend, and disguises a more sincere concern that periodical power might be misused. As the Fat Contributor is placarding *Punch* on the pyramids – perhaps symbolic of the

English appropriation of Napoleon's domains through trade – and as the passengers on the voyage to the East are eagerly reading the latest 'news' from *Punch*, so Thackeray's eighteenth-century creation, *Barry Lyndon*, is using the press to further his exploitation of the unlucky Lady Lyndon. Also at the same moment, Thackeray was reviewing Disraeli's *Coningsby* for the *Pictorial Times*, 25 May 1844, and noting how 'every newspaper reader in the British Empire has perused the history of Mr. Rigby' (a character who writes 'slashing articles' for the magazines).[62] In the latter 1840s, Thackeray created a series of foreign journalists in *Punch* who provided a different view of the English at home for a fictitious, and comical, foreign press. He also created, as one of his last *Punch* offerings in 1854, a comic war correspondent, once again demonstrating his interest in the new evolutions of media reporting and the importance of the Crimean War in furthering the profession of the war correspondent.

I have discussed some of the foreign journalist figures elsewhere, and do not intend to expand on that discussion here.[63] However, it is worth reiterating the variety and pervasiveness of Thackeray's commentaries on the periodicals of his day through figures such as the fictitious journalists he invents as personae. Alongside the *Punch* team's creation of figures representative of the British press (Jenkins, Mrs Gamp), Thackeray adds caricatures such as Monsieur Gobemouche (whose name implies he has swallowed a fly, or is gullible), a French reporter who acts as London correspondent and sends absurd reports of English cultural mores he has misread. There is also Molony, an Irish journalist, and an Arab reporter, Aboo Ali Bosh. The main theme developed by Gobemouche and others is the unreliability of newspaper discourse. Although the principal source of current information, newspaper 'currency' was perhaps more financially connected than sometimes believed. Thackeray uses the foreign correspondent to demonstrate the possibility of misleading the public and to raise questions about the periodical text. In 'From the Own Correspondent of the Moniteur des Boulevards', *Punch*, 8 March 1851, he shows Gobemouche in a Leicester Square hotel analysing the contemporary affairs as reported in the English and Irish newspapers. Like the genuine foreign correspondent in Thackeray's own experience, the reports are compiled from texts obtained in the subject city; the circulated news is initially textual.

Gobemouche writes:

> For the present I have but the day's journal before me – reflex of daily opinion – and I read therein matter sufficient, indeed, for many a day's thought ... Were these facts not narrated in a newspaper, I should hesitate to believe them. But they are in print, and cause neither denial, nor surprise, nor indignation ... The shops are not closed; the tocsin is not sounding; the phlegmatic people are not in arms, but move with restless egoism on the affairs of their commerce. I feel that I am about to gaze on awful convulsions in the midst of a great, a doomed, a terrible people.[64]

The report reveals a number of carefully placed satires against the character of the French, their tendency to revolution as it was seen, and their view of the English. But it also mocks English complacency at the status of newspaper journalism in London. Elsewhere, Thackeray returns to his perennial concern about the status of the journalist himself, as writer. The paradigmatic shift in the nature of writing, from the intellectual and traditionalist genius to the commercial and industrial raconteur is signified in the signature of 'The French Conspiration', *Punch* (12 April 1851), where Gobemouche signs himself, 'man of letters, man of progress'.[65]

Thackeray's departure from *Punch* in 1851 seemed final, but he returned to write a series of satirical articles, which were printed on the first page of the magazine (showing again how highly he was regarded), relating accounts of the war in the Middle East. 'Important from the Seat of War! Letters from the East, by our own Bashi-Bozouk' were published in seven parts, 24 June, 1, 8, 15, 22, 29 July, and 5 August 1854. The series relates to the Crimean War which had begun in 1853, and which saw Britain siding with Turkey against Russian aggression. The most famous action was the siege of Sebastopol, a Russian naval fortress, by British and Turkish troops and ships, from late 1854 to September 1855. It has often been remarked how the use of the camera by British newspaper photographers in the Crimea helped to change the way newspapers acted as documentary and graphic repositories.[66] It was also the war in which the foreign war correspondent emerged, following closely with the troops.[67] Here, though, I want to discuss Thackeray's war journalist, who more explicitly suggests the imperial context of periodical news, as well as the self-interest to be promoted in the press.[68]

'Important from the Seat of War!: Letters from the East by Our Own Bashi-Bazouk', begins with a contextualization and a comment about the news in 1854. It advertises *Punch* and presents the magazine as a more accurate version of reality than its more serious daily rivals. The first letter establishes a whole range of important Thackerayan concerns about the press, and recapitulates several of the arguments he discussed in his novels and periodical essays. He had clearly not forgotten these in his three years' absence from the periodical pages. His journalist – whose only given name is 'Mick' – writes to *Punch* to ask for their help in publishing his war correspondence:

> Though your periodical is jocular in its nature and title, and occasionally trifling in its details, I am told that a good deal of truth lurks in its satire; indeed that much more of the commodity is to be found in your columns than in the broadsides of your gigantic contemporaries, who profess to supply only authentic information.[69]

He selects *Punch* for his letters,

> 1st, Because the Press though often misled is free in your country. And I desire the liberty of saying EVERYTHING, which I could not do in the *Journal des Debats* or the *Allgemeine Zeitung* ...[70]

The notion of inclusiveness is paralleled in the desire for sexual frankness in *Pendennis* and in the social totality of the other novels. But there is a more deliberate and immediate context here. Mick takes issue with the version of the war presented by *The Times* correspondent, and even tries to persuade the *Punch* editor that he saved this journalist's life and was indignant at the ingratitude he showed. The numbers of Russians reported as killed are exaggerated, he relays.

> Newspaper correspondents, I fully agree with my noble friends LORD SMOTHEREM and LORD BOTHEREM, in the House of Peers, are not to be relied upon, and ought to be put down. What the nation wants is TRUTH. Truth pure, Truth unadulterated, Truth gushing from the original tap, such as perhaps no other man in Europe but myself is in a condition to supply.[71]

The war, he argues, would never have happened if his advice had been taken. Like the Fat Contributor, and others, the journalist is the supplier of the commodity of 'truth', such as it is, for the daily newspaper reading market. For Mick, 'truth' is described in terms of its product quality.

Mick is derived from the early reports of the Crimean campaign then appearing in *The Times* by W.H. Russell.[72] Russell's work is normally seen as ground-breaking; his reports on the poor conditions in which the British army existed in camp and the dangerous lack of medical facilities and organization the army carried with it are cited as a demonstration of the freedom of the press and the power for good that the journalist possesses. A *Times* leader for 29 May 1854 declared, 'We can easily understand why a certain class of officers should like no tale told but their own; and why Government should wish a veil to be thrown over its possible neglects; but the people of England will look for safety in publicity rather than in concealment.'[73] Russell is seen as the campaigner for soldier's rights, and *The Times* supported him even in the face of government anger. Thackeray's critique is a complicated and inconsistent one, and its rationale is not certain. His work, however, deals much with the concept of 'publicity', and his *Punch* series began a month after this *Times* editorial (24 June 1854).

Russell's first letter to *The Times* was published on 15 March 1854. He had been despatched by the editor, William Delane, in February, with the intention of bypassing the normal method of reporting on wars (from official despatches) and providing 'a more comprehensive account of the coming campaign than any newspaper had ever attempted'.[74] Thackeray was present at Russell's farewell party at the Albion on 19 February, along with Dickens, Jerrold, Wilkie Collins, Mark Lemon, Shirley Brooks, Tom Taylor, and Albert Smith, making a substantial number of the *Punch* group.[75] Thackeray was further connected to the Crimean War through his assistance of Joseph Crowe, son of his old acquaintance and Paris correspondent, Eyre Evans Crowe, and brother of his secretary, the artist, Eyre Crowe. Crowe was sent out by the *Illustrated London News* as a war correspondent, along with others for the *Herald*, *Chronicle*, and *Daily News*, probably as a response to the excitement generated by Russell's reports.[76] The war was one of the most significant media events of the Victorian era, following the Great Exhibition of 1851.

Russell's accounts became a cultural phenomenon. He occupied a privileged position with the troops; E.L. Godkin of the *Daily News* complained that 'the *Times* correspondent receives rations for himself and three horses from the commissariat, by order of the home government'.[77] But his work was highly influential and the circulation of *The Times* was such that the information reached a considerable slice of the English middle class. Hankinson notes, 'Within a few weeks "Our Own Correspondent with the British troops at Gallipoli" was essential reading for all who would be well informed.'[78] The stories of the camp's daily existence and manoeuvres, made necessary partly due to the inactivity of the early months of war, were fascinating and novel to the public. This was new investigative journalism, similar in some ways to Mayhew's exposing of London poverty and labour that had recently appeared in the *Morning Chronicle*. Russell was forthright and determined. 'All that a newspaper correspondent wants is to see what is done, and to describe it to the best of his ability', he wrote.[79] His criticism stretched to both the official powers behind the army and, in certain ways, to the readership at home, who remained ignorant of the real state of affairs. On 19 August, he wrote:

> Just think of this, good people of England, who are sitting anxiously in your homes, day after day, expecting every morning to gladden your eyes with the sight of the announcement, in large type, of 'Fall of Sebastopol,' your Guards, your *corps d'elite*, the pride of your hearts, the delight of your eyes, these Anakim, whose stature, strength and massive bulk you exhibit to kingly visitors as no inapt symbols of your nation, have been so reduced by sickness, disease, and a depressing climate, that it was judged inexpedient to allow them to carry their own packs, or to permit them to march more than five miles a day, even though these packs were carried for them! Think of this, and then judge whether these men are fit in their present state to go to Sebastopol, or to attempt any great operation of war.[80]

More than the criticism of the English army command, this passage demonstrates Russell's grasp of the intense public interest and enthusiasm for his accounts. The serial suspense, 'day after day' generating its own tension, caused Thackeray to complain that the sales of serial novels would fall and that there was no writing against the excitement of the daily news.[81] He was publishing *The Newcomes* in serial parts.

Mick, our own Bashi-Bazouk, is clearly a parody of the dramatic life of *The Times*' Crimean correspondent. Lucy Brown suggests that the war correspondent was a unique figure in the newspapers, who required 'courage and enterprise' and 'often had a tendency towards self-dramatization'.[82] Although the first article is closely connected to *The Times* series and the daily reports from the Crimea, the tale quickly moves into the form of romance parody as Mick becomes involved in love rivalry and is eventually made Colonel of a regiment of vicious mercenaries called Bashi-Bazouks. Like the Fat Contributor papers, Mick's despatches are more concerned with his own affairs than affairs of state. He is a dislikable figure. He has fought for different sides in the conflict, suggesting his indifference to causes, and is now one of the Irish in the Turkish army. His presence in the army is explained by an earlier liaison in Russia at the time of Nicholas of Russia's attempted coup. He falls for Matilda Schouzoff, whose father is president of the Secret Correctional Police in Russia, and he evades a horsewhipping from the police for his behaviour by framing his rival, Count Tuffskin. He also avoids being sent to Siberia. He escapes Russia in the fourth letter by exchanging places on board ship with his Quaker friend, Dobkins, and fleeing to France to give Russian secrets to Napoleon III. Later, a newspaper report informs him that 'Dobkinski' took the Orthodox faith and married Matilda.

'Important from the Seat of War!' could not be further away from war journalism. This is the underside of Thackeray's imagination; he frequently has recourse to an aggressive, sexual energy in his work, which contrasts with the controlled and restrained realism of a novel like *The Newcomes*. As in *Catherine*, *Barry Lyndon*, and tales like *A Legend of the Rhine*, and *The Rose and the Ring* (which was published a year after 'Important from the Seat of War!'), his parodies tend towards the grotesque and engage with exaggerated villains of great potency and power. His narrator is the Becky puppet again. Mick is also a Major Gahagan derivative without the good-humoured heroics of the 1838 character. He is an exploiter of the war and of the people he associates with in the Crimea. Thackeray had not combined such material with a news report before. Here, the places and the events are real and form a frame that purports authenticity to enclose a tale that is clearly impossible or improbable. The exaggerated heroics of Mick, his high claims for his own version of the truth, and the subjective centralization that his lifestyle produces, are all extreme versions of the narratology of the war correspondent. Thackeray casts him as an adventurer, bringing back tall tales from exotic regions, such as explorers entertained the public with in the early days of print. By implication, the fashion for war coverage is simply an extension of the desire for romance and quixotism in the public's appetite. The war competes with the serial novel, because, ultimately, the news is fashioned in the same way. As the press developed, so the product became more sophisticated in its self-marketing and its ability to expand its market. If the serial novel borrowed the cheap format of the periodical, and the serialization of fiction in a newspaper had helped sales, by the 1850s, the newspapers were using the readerliness of the serial structure to make the news more commercial.

In the second half of 'Important from the Seat of War!', Mick continues his amorous campaigns in the Turkish army. The war image denotes the war of the sexes rather more than the nationalism behind the Crimean conflict. Indeed, Mick's apparent lack of national identity might be taken as a satire on the human aggression so based. Fleeing Russia, Mick disguises himself and joins the Turks. He is wanted for unspecified crimes in Ireland and England and is forced to change his allegiance.[83] A Turkish princess, the Princess Nijoona, is his next conquest, and he feels tempted by her palaces. But refusing to 'turn Turk', he finds himself hunted by her vengeance and is forced to fake his death at the siege of Silistria. The war provides him with the opportunity for several protean transformations. He is then made commander of a regiment of Bashi-Bazouks and tells of having to kill several of the 'officers' in order to assert his own command.

Mick's world is a primitive one. It is an exaggeration of the commercially competitive world in *The Newcomes*.[84] He kills his main rival in command and takes his possessions, spoils of war belonging to an Englishman, John Thomas Jones, who may or may not have been the man he killed. Encamped in the house of a Greek, he charms the ladies, especially the daughter of his elderly host, whilst robbing the old man of his food and bed. The sixth letter shows how he grows rich on the spoils he takes from those he kills (an officer of the Russian Hussars who has a cloak labelled 'Piccadilly'), and robs from Catholic churches and an Armenian convent. Finally, in the Fort of Arab Tabia, repelling waves of Russian assaults, he kills Tuffskin, who arrived in the infantry on the opposite side, and then receives a shoulder wound himself. Rhododactylos, the daughter of his Greek host, attends to him and he proposes marriage to her. The siege lifts and he tells Rhododactylos where he has hidden his fortune, only for her to steal it and elope with his aide-de-camp. A penniless adventurer, he now asks *Punch* to accept the bill he has drawn on their account, a final undermining of his authority – in Thackeray's version of the world, the penniless, the failed, are rarely given much voice.

Thackeray's war correspondent is a colourful caricature of a newly emerging press writer. He is not, though, an impartial figure, but is deeply involved in the war and in the emotions that sustain it. He uses the press as a means of promoting self-justification and of obtaining commercial gain. The spoils of war are textual as well as material treasure (indeed, one of his gains is a writing desk). Like the fictional reporters who turn observed human life into commercial product, Mick translates war into cash. Without political scruple or ideological cause, a figure of pure self-interest, he thus mirrors the newspaper correspondent who also remains an outsider. Russell and *The Times* were accused by some of revealing army secrets to the opposition (as Mick betrays the Russians).[85] Considering 'the crash of affairs' of Crimea, and the decline in sales of his works, Thackeray had proposed launching a journal to be entitled *Fair Play* in the 1850s,[86] a newspaper venture that suggests his attitude towards the press of the time. In the event, he decided that there were too many risks involved.

Thackeray was not, however, advocating a system of press censorship. His attitude towards the periodicals was more complicated. In his last two publications for *Punch*, 'Mr. Punch to an Eminent Personage' and 'A Second Letter to an Eminent Personage',[87] he took issue with Cardinal Wiseman's attacks on light, popular literature. The *Record* and the *Tablet*, two Catholic journals, printed Wiseman's lecture on current publishing tastes that called for an 'Index of Prohibited Books'. Thackeray defended the freedom of publishing, indicating that 'In our field the wholesome literature and the bad, the tares and the wheat, must grow up together.'[88] He was attacked in turn for his defence, and retaliated in the next number of *Punch*. 'When you propose, ever so politely, to gag the press of this country,' he wrote, 'we intend to be in a rage ... leave us and our liberty alone.'[89]

The journalist, as represented by Thackeray's fictitious depictions, is a complex and ambivalent figure. He is a new style of literary man, not a man-of-letters, nor a conscientious artist, but a necessary producer of popular print. He is a professional, but also a commercial practitioner. He has power and authority, but writes to make money. But he is a historian, a commentator on contemporary life, and an exposer of the ills of society. There are grand claims and sordid claims for his existence. His nature, for Thackeray, is a compound of the two. He is an exciting figure, who is often linked to sexual fulfilment and the pursuit of appetite and desire. Thackeray's revisiting of the figure in his novels (the press characters in *Pendennis*, the art critics in *The Newcomes*, the foreign correspondents in *Philip*) suggests how he maintained for Thackeray a potency that did not diminish. Journalism was always associated with Thackeray's own youth and sexual initiation. But the journalist is also a figure of guilt. He is the epitome of the commercial exploiter and the means of manipulating the image of others for personal profit. This attached the journalist to a network of social themes that Thackeray found uncomfortable. Within the literary world, the journalist was the most extreme product of Victorian capitalism and the industrialisation of literature. Framed by the corporate structure of the periodical, he could not however escape the fragmenting conflicts of race, class and gender that strained within his culture. The periodical promoted dissonance. It was one of the more commercially successful developments of the press in the latter half of Thackeray's career. And *Punch* itself, as Thackeray found, was a prime example of a 'Cave of *Dis*harmony'.

Notes

[1] George S. Marr, *Periodical Essayists of the Eighteenth-Century* (London: James Clarke, [1923]), 11ff.; James Boswell, *Life of Johnson*, ed. R.W. Chapman (Oxford: OUP, 1983), introduction (by Pat Rogers), and 86, 160-61, 226, 477; Charles Lamb, *Elia and the Last Essays of Elia*, ed. Jonathan Bate (Oxford: OUP, 1987), ix, xiii, xviii; William Hazlitt, *Selected Writings*, ed.

Ronald Blythe (Harmondsworth: Penguin, 1970), 9-10, 29; Walter Scott, *Waverley*, ed. Claire Lamont (Oxford: OUP, 1986), xviii, 7; *Thackerayana: Notes and Anecdotes* (London: Chatto and Windus, 1875), discusses the several eighteenth-century periodicals in Thackeray's library at his death (186-435), which included the *European Magazine*, 87 vols (1782-1825), *Gentleman's Magazine*, 142 vols (1731-1827), *Historical Register*, 24 vols (1714-1738), *Connoisseur* (1757-60), *Humourist* (1725, *Mirror* (1787), *Town and Country Magazine* (1769-73), and others (see Stonehouse, *Catalogue of the Library of W.M. Thackeray*, op.cit.).

[2] 'Fielding's Works', *Times*, 2 September 1840; *Stray Papers*, 107-8.

[3] Letter to Mrs Carmichael-Smyth, 11-15 February 1840; *Letters*, I, 421.

[4] See Julian Wolfreys' analysis of identity in *Deconstruction.Derrida* (London: Macmillan, 1998), 7-8.

[5] See Richard D. Altick, *The Presence of the Present: Topics of the Day in the Victorian Novel* (Columbus: Ohio State University Press, 1991), 604-6; Dodds, *Paradox*, 385-6.

[6] 'The Snobs of England: Chapter Last', *Punch* (27 February 1847); *Works*, XIV, 200.

[7] See 'Punch's Parting Tribute to Jenkins', *Punch* (16 September 1843), 'The Ducal Hat for Jenkins', *Punch* (13 January 1844), 'Gems from Jenkins', *Punch* (6 April 1844).

[8] Spielmann, 209-14; R. Kelly, *The Best of Mr. Punch: The Humorous Writings of Douglas Jerrold* (Knoxville, 1970), 20-21; and see Kelly, *Jerrold*, 112-13.

[9] Diary entry, 6 August 1841, Letters, II, 33.

[10] Spielmann, 211.

[11] Ibid., 212-13, 210.

[12] Ibid., 214.

[13] 'On Radical Snobs', *Punch* (8 August 1846); *Works*, XXVI, 334; Sutherland, *Snobs*, 88-9.

[14] Sullivan, *British Literary Magazines*, III, 505, 506 (see this whole section, 501-13).

[15] Altick, *Presence*, 183-5, 645.

[16] Letter to Sir James Tennent, 1-3 October 1846; *Letters*, II, 252; Norman Russell, *The Novelist and Mammon: Literary Responses to the World of Commerce in the Nineteenth Century* (Oxford: Clarendon, 1986), 169-73, discusses Thackeray and railway investment.

[17] See 'A Lucky Speculator' (2 August 1845), 'A Letters from "Jeames of Buckley Square"', signed 'Fitz-James de la Pluche' (16 August 1845), 'The Stags: a Drama of Today' (30 August 1845), 'Sonnick Sejested by Prince Halbert gratiously killing the Staggs at Sacks-Coburg-Gothy' (20 September 1845), 'A Seasonable Word on Railways. By Mr Punch' (4 October 1845), 'Jeames on the Time-Bargings' (1 November 1845), 'Jeames on the Gauge Question' (16 May 1846), 'Mr Jeames Again' (13 June 1846). Alongside these, there were articles which made mention of the railways, such as in 'Brighton in

1847' by the Fat Contributor, who, at the end of the piece, is startled on his horse by 'a bang, and a shriek, and a whizz' of a passing steam train (*Works*, XXVI, 140).

[18] See Donald Low's discussion of Fielding and Hogarth's artistic battles against the vice of gambling; *Thieves' Kitchen: The Regency Underworld* (Gloucester: Alan Sutton, 1987), 130-11.

[19] Kaplan, *Dickens*, 194-5; Spielmann, 84.

[20] In 1848-50, Thackeray provided Pendennis at the end of his novel with an independent fortune gained from selling land favourably to a railway franchise, dating the climax to *c*. 1844; Altick, *Presence*, 191.

[21] *Pictorial Times*, 1 (1 April 1843), 61-2.

[22] He first appeared as the failed historical painter, Alonzo Spec, in 'Mr Spec's Remonstrance', *Punch* (11 February 1843), but became a regular persona as the narrator of 'Sketches and Travels in London', *Punch* (20 November 1847-25 March 1848); Thackeray's *Punch* drawings were frequently signed with a tiny monogram of a pair of spectacles.

[23] *Works*, XV, 117.

[24] Summerfield, 216.

[25] 'French Romancers on England', *Foreign Quarterly Review*, 32 (October 1843), 246.

[26] *Works*, XV, 155.

[27] Ibid., 136-7.

[28] 'New Accounts of Paris', *Foreign Quarterly Review*, 32 (January 1844), 473.

[29] Kaplan, *Dickens*, 127-9.

[30] Charles Dickens, *Martin Chuzzlewit* (Oxford: OUP, 1951), Chapter 16, 255; while editor of the *Foreign Quarterly*, John Forster wrote a more liberal but still harsh account of the American newspapers, *Foreign Quarterly Review*, 30 (October 1842), 197-222.

[31] Dickens, *Chuzzlewit*, 255-6.

[32] *The Diary of C. Jeames de la Pluche, Esq.*, *Works*, XV, 143-7 [references in the text are to this edition].

[33] 'The Snobs of England: Chapter Last', *Punch* (24 February 1847); *Works*, XIV, 200.

[34] See 'Wanderings of Our Fat Contributor', *Punch* (3, 10, 17 August; 30 November; 7, 14 December 1844) (Brighton, Dover, Ostend, Antwerp, Brussels, and on voyage to Gibraltar); 'Punch in the East', *Punch* (11, 18, 25 January; 1, 8 February 1845) (Gibraltar, Malta, Athens, Constantinople, Alexandria, Cairo); 'Meditations in Solitude. By Our Stout Contributor', *Punch* (13 September 1845); 'Beulah Spa. By Punch's Commissioner', *Punch* (27 September 1845); 'Brighton', 'A Brighton Night's Entertainment', 'Meditations over Brighton', *Punch* (11, 18, 25 October 1845); 'Love Songs by the Fat Contributor', *Punch* (27 March, 15 June 1847); 'Brighton in 1847. By the F.C.', *Punch* (23, 30 October 1847); 'An Eastern Adventure of the Fat Contributor', *Punch's Pocket-Book for 1847* (a reprint of the Pyramid episode from 1845).

[35] 'Wanderings', *Punch* (7 December 1844); *Works*, XXVI, 95; the bay of Vigo is described in *Cornhill to Cairo*, *Works*, XII, 175.
[36] Ibid., 71.
[37] See the caricature in *Our Street* (1848), *Works*, XIII, 58; Thackeray praised Dickens in the *Calcutta Star* (21 August 1845), for avoiding art and antiques in his travel books and describing 'what he sees before him' (Summerfield, 233).
[38] 'Punch in the East', *Punch* (11 January 1845); *Works*, XXVI, 99.
[39] 'Wanderings', *Punch* (17 August 1844); *Works*, XXVI, 84.
[40] 'Wanderings', *Punch* (7 December 1844); *Works*, XXVI, 78; see Thackeray's comments on Victor Hugo as 'a most undeniable moi', 'The Rhine. By Victor Hugo', *Foreign Quarterly Review*, 29 (April 1842), 144-5.
[41] 'Meditations over Brighton', *Punch* (25 October 1845); *Works*, XXVI, 130.
[42] 'Wanderings', *Punch* (7 December 1844); *Works*, XXVI, 89.
[43] Ibid., 90.
[44] Ibid., 90-92.
[45] 'Wanderings', *Punch* (17 August 1844); *Works*, XXVI, 82.
[46] Ibid., 82.
[47] Peters, 123, contrasts the 'Fat Contributor Paper' on Athens with its counterpart in *Cornhill to Cairo*.
[48] *Letters*, II, 155.
[49] *Cornhill to Cairo*, *Works*, XII, 314; in the event, Titmarsh forgets this promise.
[50] 'Punch in the East', *Punch* (1, 8 February 1845); *Works*, XXVI, 114, 119.
[51] See Chapter 2, above.
[52] Summerfield, 214.
[53] Ray, *Uses*, 301; Peters, 113.
[54] 'Punch in the East', *Punch* (11 January 1845); *Works*, XXVI, 98.
[55] 'A Plan for a Prize Novel', *Punch* (22 February 1851); *Works*, XV, 94-7.
[56] 'Punch in the East', *Punch* (11 Janaury 1845); *Works*, XXVI, 99. See also the review of Puckler Muskau's *Egypt under Mehmet Ali*, *Morning Chronicle* (27 March 1845), where Thackeray again used the pyramids: 'We have heard of a pic-nic on top of the Great Pyramid, and one of the advertisements of the enterprising Mr Waghorn soothed the doubts of would-be pilgrims to the East, by the pleasant tidings that plenty of soda water would be found in the Desert!'; Ray, *Contributions*, 65.
[57] 'Punch in the East', *Punch* (18 January 1845); *Works*, XXVI, 106.
[58] Ibid., 104.
[59] Ibid., 105.
[60] Ibid., 106.
[61] Ibid.
[62] 'Literature – Coningsby; or the New Generation', *Pictorial Times*, 25 May 1844; *Stray Papers*, 222; Thackeray also reviewed *Coningsby* for the *Morning Chronicle* (13 May 1844), a review ironically referred to in the *Pictorial Times* item.

[63] See my chapter on 'Thackeray and *Punch* at the Great Exhibition: authority and ambivalence in verbal and visual caricatures' in Brian Maidment and Louise Purbrick (eds), *The Great Exhibition* (Manchester: Manchester University Press, forthcoming).
[64] *Punch* (8 March 1851).
[65] *Punch* (12 April 1851).
[66] See Petr Tausk, *A Short History of Press Photography* (Prague: International Organisation of Journalists, 1988), 34.
[67] The only other nineteenth-century example of a fictional war correspondent that I have found is Kipling's war artist, Dick Heldar, in *The Light that Failed* (1890).
[68] For a discussion of Thackeray and war, see John Peck, *War, the Army and Victorian Literature* (London: Macmillan, 1998), 48-70, where Peck (who is not aware of the Crimea articles) sees Thackeray as championing 'the rituals and conventions of a military code' no longer current, 49.
[69] *Punch* (24 June 1854).
[70] Ibid.
[71] Ibid.
[72] For a full account of Russell's Crimean correspondence, see Alan Hankinson, *Man of Wars: William Howard Russell of the Times* (London: Heinemann, 1982); a less hagiographic, though brief, account is in Brown, *Newspapers*, 234-5.
[73] Cited in Hankinson, *Man of Wars*, 59; and see also 55.
[74] Ibid., 47.
[75] Ibid., 48.
[76] Ibid., 56-7.
[77] Cited in Brown, *Newspapers*, 235.
[78] Hankinson, *Man of Wars*, 54.
[79] Ibid., 57.
[80] Ibid., 60.
[81] Peters, 235.
[82] Brown, *Newspapers*, 216.
[83] The British army in the Victorian period was suspected of harbouring criminals and had a poor reputation until the last decade of the century; Hankinson, *Man of Wars*, 46.
[84] See Chapter 8, below; 'If a better place than yours presents itself just beyond your neighbour, elbow him and take it' (*Works*, V, 86).
[85] Russell notes how General Sir George Brown and other officers disliked his work and told him that the Russians regularly used his Gallipoli letters; Hankinson, *Man of Wars*, 58.
[86] Letter to Mrs. Carmichael-Smyth, 2 February 1855; *Letters*, III, 415.
[87] *Punch* (16 September 1854), 110-11; *Punch* (23 September 1854), 113-14.
[88] *Punch* (16 September 1854), 111.
[89] *Punch* (23 September 1854), 113.

Chapter 8

Mediahood and manhood in *Pendennis*

Pendennis is a novel about maturity. Its central concern is with the growth of the writer and the man into a respectable middle-class novelist and husband, negotiating the various influences and temptations encountered in early life and manhood. The pressures upon the central hero are economic as well as sexual. The prostitution of the self as writer and the prostitution of the self as man are closely entwined; Pendennis must rise above the common experience of journalistic and sexual excitement in order to establish himself as a writer and gentleman of integrity. '*Pendennis* is about the artist as well as the man, or rather, about the artist *as* man.'[1] The novel is generically a *bildungsroman*, tracing the spiritual development of the central subject, but places this firmly against the material world that he inhabits. Early critics saw the book as continuing the social satire Thackeray created in *Vanity Fair*: another journey through the stalls, but this time located in the male world of clubs, taverns and business of the contemporary 1830s and 1840s, rather than the more female world of Amelia and Becky.[2]

Pen moves through a Fieldingesque structure of learning; like Tom Jones, he travels from country-house gentility to city rakishness, becoming a 'jaded and selfish worldling'[3] before finding salvation through the love of the sister-figure, Laura. In the first half of the book, Pendennis encounters the 'country' love of the low-class actress, the Fotheringay, and the upper-class 'actress', Blanche Amory, who introduce him to his own shallowness and the shallowness of others. The second half repeats the experience in the city, this time with Pen considering a mercenary marriage to a Blanche he no longer cares for, and subsequently a second low-class match with the naïve Fanny Bolton. At the end of the novel, he returns home to penitence, and to discover the love of Laura that waits for him. The ending is not quite so straightforward in its sentiment; Laura has given up the love of Pen's friend Warrington, who himself is trapped in a loveless early marriage, and accepts Pen as a solid second choice.

It is not so much the manhood of the central character, however, with which I intend to deal here. It is more with another of the book's main themes, the manhood of the media, or, rather, the author's negotiation of the transforming periodical market-place. Several critics have commented on the novel's representation of the world of writers and journalists; indeed, in its day, the novel was criticized for what was seen as a negative portrait of the writer's profession. Dickens thought it in poor taste,[4] and there is no doubt that Thackeray's reputation amongst the writers of his own 'trade' was ambivalent (he fell out with Douglas Jerrold, Dickens and the young Edmund Yates).[5] Mark Cronin has argued plausibly that Dickens' non-portrayal of the writing community in *David Copperfield* was deliberate; 'Dickens' silence about the writing life was a response and "protest" to Thackeray's effusiveness.'[6] The two authors offer 'competing depictions of the artist as hero'.[7] Indeed, Pendennis's own autobiographical novel, his romantic *Walter Lorraine*, might be taken as Thackeray's interactive critique of Dickens' and others' approaches to heroic self-fashioning.[8]

However, Thackeray's community of writers is also an historical one. It, like Pen himself, is in transition and flux. As I have been arguing in this book, Thackeray's anxieties about the nature of the writer's calling are focused on the marginal line between the penny-a-line, earn-as-you-write, periodical world, and the romantic notions of writerly power and authority held at the beginning of the century and located in the figure of the man-of-letters. Thackeray's understanding of the publishing industry, however, was not as simplistic or binary as this. He explored all of the nuances of authorship, all of the different forms of contribution that were abundant in the mid-nineteenth-century market. Indeed, he had practised a good many of them himself in his developing career. And while it is tempting to see the post-*Vanity Fair* novels as representing Thackeray's final transformation from magazine man to 'genuine' author, the novels themselves remain closely tied to the periodical world from which they emerge. This is not just part of the serial publishing process to which they (with the exception of *Esmond*) belonged. As Robert Colby points out, *Pendennis* 'is the culminating novel of "the Punch connexion", just as *Barry Lyndon* had marked the zenith of his career with "F[raser's] a magazine of wit"'.[9] Bradbury and Evans, the publishers of both *Pendennis* and *Punch*, were keen to make the connection themselves on the front cover of the novel, by announcing the author as also the author of *The Book of Snobs*, a recent *Punch* serial.[10]

The novel moves beyond such a straightforward identification, however. Its immediate milieu is more the period prior to Thackeray's involvement with *Punch*, the 1830s. As Pendennis contemplates his future direction, strolling through London and gazing in the shop windows at the publishers' commodities, he is discovered in Paternoster Row beside St Paul's Churchyard, significantly the place where Thackeray began *his* career, and where the *National Standard* had its office:

> Many a poor devil before him has trodden those flags, with similar cares and anxieties at his heels, his bread and his fame dependent upon the sentence of his magnanimous patrons of the Row. Pen looked at all the wonders of all the shops; and the strange variety of literature which they exhibit. In this were displayed black-letter volumes and books in the clear pale types of Aldus and Elzevir: in

> the next you might see the *Penny Horrific Register*, the *Halfpenny Annals of Crime*, and *History of the Most Celebrated Murderers of all Countries*, *The Raff's Magazine*, *The Larky Swell*, and other publications of the penny press; whilst at the next window, portraits of ill-favoured individuals, with facsimiles of the venerated signatures of the Reverend Grimes Wapshot, the Reverend Elias Howle, and the works written and the sermons preached by them, showed the British Dissenter where he could find mental pabulum ... Scarce an opinion but has its expositor and is place of exhibition in this peaceful old Paternoster Row, under the toll of the bells of St. Paul. (III, 349)

The books described form part of a new world of literary commodification; they are an early example of the niche marketing of literature. The shops have to attract their patrons and purchasers, and they appeal now to the man on the street. The establishments of Bacon and Bungay, the rival publishers based on the real competition of Colburn and Bentley, are opposite each other and symbolize the advertising function of the literary shop. Both appeal to a sense of nostalgia in the onlooker, and mirror such traits in Pendennis and certainly in Thackeray. In order to give sense to the modern market, to provide its place within an historical continuity with that past age of letters, Thackeray portrays this as part of the firms' self-imaging. There is irony here; is the literary link a genuine continuity of writerly community? Or simply a modern marketing design?

> Bacon's shop was an ancient low-browed building, with a few of the books published by the firm displayed in the windows, under a bust of my Lord of Verulam [i.e. Francis Bacon], and the name of Mr. Bacon in brass on the private door. Exactly opposite to Bacon's house was that of Mr. Bungay, which was newly painted and elaborately decorated in the style of the seventeenth century, so that you might have fancied stately Mr. Evelyn passing over the threshold, or curious Mr. Pepys examining the books in the window. (III, 349)

The 'newly painted' mock antiquity of Bungay's shop, and the self-styled ancestry of Bacon's, provide an awkward version of the historical process which signifies rupture as much as continuity. Whilst Pen becomes attracted to the possibilities of his own place in this literary heritage, the novelist undermines the certainty of the value of such a tradition. The literary past becomes a commodity, of use in the present as an advertisement for a publisher's respectability and integrity. Once again we are in a world of image-makers.

The number of *Pendennis* in which this description appears is constructed around a detailed portrayal of the literary world. Number 10 (August 1848) appeared just before Thackeray's illness caused a three-month hiatus in publication, following Number 11 (September 1848). The number demonstrates ambivalence towards the writing profession, just as the contrasting characters of Pen and Warrington suggest different sides to Thackeray's own literary identity, or the self-identity he had constructed. Pen is the would-be writer-as-artist, Warrington the satisfied and professional periodicals man. If the beginning of the number describes the Inns of Court in relation to the literary heritage existing there (the world of letters), the end of the number portrays the editor of the *Pall Mall Gazette*, on which Pen has found employment during the number, writing the magazine's prospectus for Mr. Bungay, the proprietor, from a cell in the Fleet debtor's prison (the modern world). Throughout the number, alongside the shops discussed above, we are also shown the commercial rivalry which drives the development of the press at this period, and which is further based around the binary of Bacon and Bungay. The irony throughout questions the nature of the periodical world into which Pen is drawn. Can his integrity be maintained or advanced in such an environment of competition?

Originally partners (like Colburn and Bentley), Bacon and Bungay have come to signify the rapacious capitalist ethos, like Osborne and Sedley in *Vanity Fair*. Friendship and co-operation becomes business rivalry as enterprises mature and the two men engage in a 'furious war' of publications. Warrington tells Pendennis that 'no sooner does one bring out a book of travels, or poems, a magazine or periodical, quarterly, or monthly, or weekly, or annual, but the rival is in the field with something similar' (III, 352). Bungay has the *Londoner* to Bacon's *Westminster Magazine*, and 'Bungay is publishing his *Pall Mall Gazette* as a counterpoise to Bacon's *Whitehall Review*' (III, 352). The significance of the publishers' activities is to demonstrate the marginalization of the writer from the genesis of a new journal. The impetus for literary production is not individual genius but corporate competitiveness. This modernity is contrasted to the literary heritage that is present in the writers' surroundings (a different, but similar, heritage to that promoted by Bacon and Bungay).

Pendennis and Warrington live in chambers in the Inns of Court, a male bachelor region populated with a variety of social classes and professions. For Pendennis-the-narrator, the Inns have a literary charm that sets his response to them apart from that of his legal colleagues. His delight is genuine, but the nostalgia is balanced by a later recognition of the commercial potential of such sentiment.

> ... those venerable Inns which have the Lamb and Flag and the Winged Horse for their ensigns, have attractions for persons who inhabit them, and a share of rough comforts and freedom, which men always remember with pleasure. I don't know whether the student of law permits himself the refreshment of enthusiasm, or indulges in poetical reminiscences as he passes by historical chambers ... but the man of letters can't but love the place which has been inhabited by so many of his brethren, or peopled by their creations as real to us at this day as the authors whose children they were – and Sir Roger de

> Coverley walking in the Temple Garden, and discoursing with Mr. Spectator about the beauties in hoops and patches who are sauntering over the grass, is just as lively a figure to me as old Samuel Johnson rolling through the fog with the Scotch gentleman at his heels on their way to Dr. Goldsmith's chambers in Brick Court; or Harry Fielding, with inked ruffles and a wet towel round his head, dashing off articles at midnight for the *Covent Garden Journal*, while the printer's boy is asleep in the passage. (III, 319-20)

Pen's own printer's boy appears in Chapter 31, 'In which the Printer's Devil Comes to the Door', at the end of this number. The passage perhaps brings out connections with Thackeray's own 'Mr Spec' papers in *Punch*, and even, in part, the historical period of *Barry Lyndon* in *Fraser's Magazine*. But most importantly, it establishes Thackeray's own literary antecedents – Fielding, also a magazine writer, and the 'journalism' of Addison and Steele – and introduces the ideal of the 'man of letters', momentarily recreating the myth.[11] However, it also challenges our perception of reality by blurring the ontological levels between fictional characters and historical personages. The use of the past is as inspiration, 'refreshment'; this balances the use of the past for commercial purposes by the publishers. One might wish to register Thackeray's own use of the past against these two oppositions; does it represent inspiration or trade? This dialectic runs throughout the theme of writing and publishing in the novel.

In relation to this, one might consider the tension between public and private spheres as outlined by Jürgen Habermas. Habermas locates the emergence of a popular public sphere in the beginning decades of the nineteenth century, alongside a shift in the public debating arena from the coffee-house culture of the eighteenth century to the printed newspaper reports of the nineteenth. Debating citizens, he remarks, become consumers, and the effect on the public sphere is to elevate 'publicity' over the merely 'public'.[12] In some ways, Thackeray can be seen throughout his writings of the 1840s, in particular, to be exposing the private face of the public press. He is interested in the 'real' figures behind the headlines: the Shandons and the Finucanes, the Bacons and the Bungays. Where the newspapers of the Victorian period projected themselves as the signifiers of civilization, 'that life without them would be barbaric',[13] Thackeray tries to suggest the advertisorial and commercial practice of this self-image. Certainly, the newspapers and journalists of *Pendennis* stand in a position of ambivalence, part of the transparent binary of the text manifest even in the cover-page illustration of Pen's tug-of-war with the forces of seduction and domesticity, replicating Becky and Amelia, journalism and art.

The twinned newspapers, the *Dawn* and the *Day*, described in Number 10, are another good example of these forces at work. They offer an ironic contrast to the uplifting histories of the eighteenth-century 'men of letters'. Mr Hoolan and Mr Doolan are the comic rival proprietors, thumbnail caricatures of the more developed Bacon and Bungay. The papers are part of the culture of the 'Back Kitchen', a 'house of entertainment' (III, 334).

> Doolan's paper, the *Dawn*, was lying on the table much bestained by porter, and cheek by jowl with Hoolan's paper, which we shall call the *Day*; the *Dawn* was liberal – the *Day* was ultra-Conservative. (III, 335)

The newspapers engage in a war of words over their reporting techniques, 'newspaper rows' one reporter calls them in friendly conversation with his rival. Thackeray provides an example, read out by Warrington, of a leading article in the *Dawn*. It is typical of the press competition of the period, and similar to Thackeray's own leader items in the *National Standard*. Newspapers create their self-identities in relation to each other, and exist in a symbiotic relationship within the market-place, 'cheek by jowl'. *Pendennis* is a novel of spinning coins, where value might be found on either side, but neither side can exist without its counterpart and counterpoint. The *Dawn*'s editorial presents its own brand of truth in opposition to that of the *Day*'s, and without any other basis or reality. They are simply political opponents in textual combat.

> As rogues of note in former days who had some wicked work to perform, – an enemy to put out of the way, a quantity of false coin to be passed ... employed a professional perjurer or assassin to do the work, which they were themselves too notorious or too cowardly to execute; our notorious contemporary, the *Day*, engages smashers out of doors to utter forgeries against individuals, and calls in auxiliary cut-throats to murder the reputation of those who offend him. A black-vizarded ruffian (whom we will unmask), who signs the forged name of Trefoil, is at present one of the chief bravoes and bullies in our contemporary's establishment ... The charge which he has brought against Lord Bangbanagher, because he is a Liberal Irish peer ... is, etc ... (III, 336)

The style of the editorial is mocked, too. Shandon, the author, writes it in two hours, we are informed, from his station in the debtors' prison. In the media world of the 1830s and 1840s, anonymity preserves authority, and Thackeray's novel aims to remind the reader of the ordinary person who claims such authorial power. Of course, the debate cannot remain within the realm of the press alone. Thackeray uses *Pendennis* to explore various kinds of writerly power, just as he examines the power relations within class and gender. I do not intend to reopen gender issues here, but it is worth noting that the balance of narratorial power between Pendennis and Laura offers another binary that is both self-sustaining and destabilizing.[14]

As Lyn Pykett has pointed out, the central discourse in the study of periodicals is a search for totality and mastery, to understand the magazine or journal as a whole.[15] However, the nature of the magazine is to fragment; it is a miscellaneous collection of disparate elements from salaried staff and external contributors, which is assembled as a whole rather than is naturally homogeneous. The editorial function in any magazine is thus to hold together this collection, and its advertisorial dimension fulfils this goal by fostering a corporate identity for the magazine which encompasses and even extends beyond any individual contribution. *Punch* magazine is a brilliant example, producing a dynamic and immediate image that IS *Punch*, Mr Punch himself. Thackeray certainly is aware of the tendency of journals to promote themselves; Pykett describes the magazine as 'a means of constructing opinion and identity' in Victorian culture,[16] something which Thackeray was investigating, I would argue, from the inception of the mass press in the 1830s.

Anonymity is an important component of the corporate image of a magazine. Although most frequently defended as a means of promoting open opinion and debate, and a protection against libel, anonymity was certainly useful in the media war as a means of creating wholeness in a journal. In-house dissent was more easily kept in-house where the journal maintained a united front. Thus, Thackeray might complain about the *Punch* reporting on the Great Exhibition, and announce his near resignation over the event, but his own variant versions of the Exhibition reportage continued to sit alongside a host of generally anonymous contributions.[17] Aled Jones notes that the subject of anonymity was controversial in the Victorian period. 'Defended by some,' he writes, 'as "the life and soul of journalism", anonymously published articles were held to remove authorial vanity from the newspaper and, in consequence, to enable readers to judge those articles by their contents rather than their signatures.'[18] Laurel Brake adds to this by contending that the convention of anonymity helped writers to work across a number of magazines and newspapers simultaneously, without being perceived as busy hack-writers.[19] As Jones puts it, the system 'served to protect the identities of a network of writers who contributed, often simultaneously, to monthly, weekly and daily periodicals, ensuring a degree of continuity of style and content between what were otherwise perceived to be distinct media forms'.[20] Certainly, Thackeray contributed to *Fraser's Magazine*, *The Times*, the *British and Foreign Review*, *Britannia*, the *Corsair*, and jobbed on the *Morning Advertiser*, all at around the same time in 1838-9. In 1843-4, he was working for *Punch*, the *Pictorial Times*, the *Calcutta Star*, the *Foreign Quarterly Review*, and the *Morning Chronicle*, simultaneously. As we see in the figures of Captain Shandon, and subsequently, Warrington and Pendennis himself, this was by no means unusual.

However, as I suggested in Chapter 2, anonymity could, in fact, be a problem for a writer. Thackeray found means to extend his personae across periodical boundaries, and even into volume publication – the Wagstaffs and Titmarsh appear in more than one media form – as a means of sustaining publicity. It is also true that he produced a vast body of marginal material that he never saw fit to collect into his 1857 *Miscellanies*, and which was never incorporated into the posthumous twenty-four volumes of his works. My own reprinting of *Paris Literary Gazette* items here (see Appendix 1) resurrects a little more of this marginal and semi-anonymous corpus, but one assumes that it is by no means yet exhausted.

In *Pendennis*, Pen recapitulates these autobiographical reminiscences of the extensive publishing demanded of a labouring periodicals man. In Number 11, for instance, Thackeray describes the breach between the public image of the *Pall Mall Gazette* and the reality behind. He does this initially in terms of authorship and anonymity.

> It was generally stated, that an influential political party supported the paper; and great names were cited amongst the contributors to its columns. Was there any foundation for these rumours? We are not at liberty to say whether they were well or ill founded; but this much we may divulge, that an article upon foreign policy, which was generally attributed to a noble lord, whose connexion with the Foreign Office is very well known, was in reality composed by Captain Shandon, in the parlour of the "Bear and Staff" public-house ... and that a series of papers on finance questions, which were universally supposed to be written by a great statesman of the House of Commons, were in reality composed by Mr. George Warrington of the Upper Temple. (III, 385)

The public sphere for Thackeray is an illusion fostered in the press and it self-generates the confidence in its own production. The public is happy to accept the image of authority behind which the tavern writers hide. Rumours are 'generally stated' and 'universally supposed' to be true; the newspaper needs only to carry off the performance to assert its veracity. The same section of the novel describes the sub-editor, Jack Finucane, who creates the fashionable news columns from a variety of other papers, including the Scottish and Irish provincial press. 'With an eagle eye,' we are told, 'he scanned all the paragraphs of all the newspapers which had anything to do with the world of fashion over which he presided' (III, 387). Pen finds the discrepancy palpable between Finucane's subject matter and his personal appearance; he is found 'with a plate of meat from the cook-shop, and a glass of porter from the public-house, for his meal, recounting the feasts of the great, as if he had been present at them' (III, 387). That 'as if' locates the vanities of the publishing world, and the world of readers who suppose their print to represent authority.

In the department of critical reviewing, Pendennis also generates his own self-image of knowledge and wisdom. Like the self-criticism Thackeray levelled at himself in *Lovel the Widower* for his work on the *National Standard*, Pendennis assumes the airs of a scholar in order to pass judgement on writings about which he knows nothing. 'The courage of young critics is prodigious', Thackeray remarks (III, 389). Pendennis would have 'signified his august approval' of Macaulay or Herschel, if asked, 'as if the critic had been their born superior and indulgent master and patron' (III, 389). He reads general information in the British Museum and astonishes his mother and himself at the range of his learning, all of which is a sham. His 'authority' is part of the convention of newspaper discourse; anonymity assists in the fostering of such power. Thackeray mocks both Pen's audacity and the media world in which it is generated; the periodical press exists as a separate sphere even from the genuine intellectual research presented in the volumes of the day. Pen 'would not have hesitated, at twenty-four hours' notice, to pass an opinion upon the greatest scholars, or to give a judgement upon the *Encyclopaedia*,' we are warned (III, 389).

The collective identity of the magazine, then – its public face – operates to advertise the integrity and authority of the words it prints because it covers the disparate reality beneath. This process, of course, has its parallel elsewhere, in Thackeray's creation of the self-promoting Becky Sharp or the media construction of the 'Ravenswing'. In *Pendennis*, the self-fashioning belongs, not to the female siren, but to the text itself; reality is caught in a bind between textual authenticity and media fabrication. It beggars the question, how real is the realist text; how textual is any text? If the historical Joseph Addison is as real as his character Sir Roger de Coverley, is this a justification for the 'reality' of Pendennis, or an ironic denial of his truthfulness?

The magazine, the *Pall Mall Gazette*, epitomizes the problems of textuality and history. Unlike such fictional representatives of the media as the *Lady's Lute* or the *Museum*,[21] both of which are based on the *National Standard*, the *Pall Mall Gazette* is difficult to place in Thackeray's personal history. It is not a parody, in the same vein as these latter, or a pastiche, as the *Dawn* and the *Day*. It has a reality, but it is not like anything for which Thackeray contributed.[22] It is political and literary; more like a newspaper than a magazine, and yet it is a 'gazette', and written in opposition to a 'Review', and as such appears of more literary substance than a newspaper. The prospectus describes it as a Conservative organ for the middle classes, for 'the gentlemen of England'. However, it is not above trade and, significantly courts the business of commercial interest: '[Shandon] pointed out delicately to advertisers that there would be no such medium as the *Pall Mall Gazette* for giving publicity to their sales ... ' (III, 358). The central irony in the *Gazette's* portrayal, however, is, like Pen's personal status in the novel, its desire to remain aloof from the working-class sources of its current productivity. In other words, the magazine snobbishly rejects the industrial world that has in fact pervaded literary production. With this in mind, Thackeray opens Shandon's prospectus (and Number 11) with a diatribe against the industrial masses:

> ... the time had come at last when it was necessary for the gentlemen of England to band together in defence of their common rights and their glorious order, menaced on all sides by foreign revolutions, by intestine radicalism, by the artful calumnies of mill-owners and cotton-lords, and the stupid hostility of the masses whom they gulled and led. (III, 355)

The defining of gentlemanliness as an essentially middle-class quality is one of the central tenets of the book, and locks into a contemporary cultural debate that leads to Dickens' *Great Expectations*. Although Thackeray is unhappy about the relationship between the classes here, and ironic in his tone of Shandon's Prospectus (written from the Fleet debtors' prison and inherently manipulative and untruthful), his eventual line is to reaffirm the nature of gentlemanliness as incorporating the values of his own class. The irony remains a problem, however. As with other aspects to the novel, there are always two sides competing equally for voice.

Thackeray's portrayal of the press, just around the corner from Shandon's current abode, demonstrates the extent to which industrialization permeates the writing process. In the previous number (Number 10), Pen and Warrington traverse the Strand, discovering a female presence there – not the usual prostitutes who habitually walk the Strand, but the personification of the press as an industrial empire and queen. The sexual subtext is present, however, and returns us again to the ambivalence of journalism as both literary modernity and erotic permissiveness.

> They were passing through the Strand as they talked, and by a newspaper office, which was all lighted up and bright. Reporters were coming out of the place, or rushing up to it in cabs; there were lamps burning in the editors' rooms, and above where the compositors were at work: the windows of the building were in a blaze of gas.
>
> 'Look at that, Pen,' Warrington said. 'There she is – the great engine – she never sleeps. She has her ambassadors in every quarter of the world – her couriers upon every road. Her officers march along with armies, and her envoy walks into statesmen's cabinets. They are ubiquitous.' (III, 339-40)

The industrial process is present in the demands placed upon authorship, too. The debate between Pen and Warrington in Chapter 32 (Number 11), exposes the dilemmas of the would-be artist/poet (Pen) and the cynical literary hack (Warrington) in their relationships with the new market-place. Pen tries to maintain his desire to write as a man of letters, a genius of a previous age, whilst Warrington has already abandoned what he sees as illusions, at least for himself. Warrington does, however, retain some hope for Pen – whilst telling him he is good enough 'to write a magazine article, and turn out a pretty copy of verses', he also recognises that Pen has 'got the sacred flame – a little of the real poetical fire' (III, 345, 344). Pendennis objects to the trade in literary flesh, and criticizes the publishers' role; 'No man shall tell me that a man of genius, as Shandon is, ought to be driven by such a vulgar slave-driver, as yonder Mr. Bungay ... who fattens on the profits of the other's brains, and enriches himself out of his journeyman's labour' (III, 362). Warrington, on the other hand, sees nothing despicable about making money through writing. His language is, perhaps, a little harsher than Thackeray's, but the point is largely the same as has been made elsewhere by Thackeray in his magazine writings.

> What is it you want? Do you want a body of capitalists that shall be forced to purchase the works of all authors, who may present themselves, manuscript in hand? Everybody who writes his epic, every driveller who can or can't spell, and produces his novel or his tragedy, – are they all to come and find a bag of sovereigns in exchange for their worthless reams of paper? Who is to settle what is good or bad, saleable or otherwise? Will you give the buyer leave, in fine, to purchase or not? ... Rags are not a proof of genius; whereas capital is absolute, as times go, and is perforce the bargain-master. It has a right to deal with the literary inventor as with any other ... I may have my own ideas of the value of my Pegasus, and think him the most wonderful of animals; but the dealer has a right to his opinion, too, and may want a lady's horse, or a cob for a heavy, timid rider, or a sound hack for the road, and my beast won't suit him. (III, 363)

Craig Howes sees Warrington's view as essentially Thackeray's, similar in kind to the statements he made in his essay on 'Laman Blanchard' in 1846. Howes suggests that Thackeray believed 'most writing is mechanical and commonplace', and that writers were being marginalized from the production of literature during the commercial period of the 1840s. Howes comments, 'The goal is production, and writers are small cogs in the machine who become increasingly alienated from their labor as the machine's other servants – editors, compositors, and printers – transform words into commodities ...'[23] However, Thackeray did also occupy other such roles and so the argument here needs qualifying. The remarks made by Thackeray in Numbers 10 and 11 of *Pendennis* sparked a row in the press about the nature of the literary profession, and earned Thackeray the criticism of Dickens and others. As Howes notes, Thackeray's initial response was an indignant reply to an article in the *Morning Chronicle*, entitled 'The Dignity of Literature'. This famous statement of art in the commercial world did not endear Thackeray further to his literary colleagues. But Howes also suggests that in Number 12, Chapter 41, which deals with the reworking of Pen's autobiographical novel, *Walter Lorraine*, Thackeray qualifies his views and capitulates somewhat, accepting the presence of artistic genius, and 'a union between the emotional and the market'.[24] The views of Pen and Warrington merge, he argues, but the novel maintains the critique of absurd artistic ego and 'the grindingly commonplace operations of the literary marketplace'; in effect, 'art's creative dimension adapts itself to survive with integrity in the world of commerce'.[25]

Howes' argument provides a rationale for what he and other critics have seen as a falling-off of Thackeray's work in the later novels. *Henry Esmond*, he says, is written to conform to the Bulwer-Lytton view of art as standing beyond modes of production, economics and business, and possessing a genius of its own. Therefore it attempts to affirm the Pendennis view at the expense of the more critical Warrington. The narrative voice becomes more digressive and less certain as it struggles with the paradoxes of production. However, the idea ignores the market forces surrounding a volume novel. This was bound into the Circulating Library system with a force that suggests the serial form was, in some ways, more liberating for certain kinds of writers.[26] Although Trollope found *Esmond* the most artistically satisfying of Thackeray's works[27] – and he was never a supporter of piece-meal serial writing – Thackeray never wrote fiction in that manner again.

In my view, it was not so much a determined change in aesthetic direction that altered Thackeray's writing, but the loss of the immediate stimulation of the periodical press. Clearly, Thackeray did deliberately leave *Punch* and the periodicals in the late 1840s. His last contributions to the *Morning Chronicle* were in 1848, and he wrote for no other magazine except *Punch*, from which he finally resigned in 1851. Apart from the occasional paper for *Punch*, *Fraser's Magazine* and *The Times* during the 1850s, he did not return to magazinery until 1860 when the *Cornhill Magazine* was launched. However, in *The Newcomes*, he found his subject matter in the reminiscences of his days of writing art criticism in the 1830s and early 1840s, and, of course, returned to his role as foreign correspondent in *The Adventures of Philip* in 1860.

Pendennis may foreground the theme of personal maturity, and it may suggest an over ripening. But it is also very much about class, and the clash of class forces in 1848. Read alongside the industrial novels of the period, such as *Mary Barton* or *Shirley*, it does not on the surface appear to tackle such issues. But if we recall Charlotte Brontë's dedication of *Jane Eyre* to Thackeray – not as the erstwhile seducer of governesses and the possessor of a mad wife as is usually stressed, but as what Brontë calls the 'first social regenerator of the day'[28] – we might wish to look more closely into the novel as a translator of class tensions into market forces. *Pendennis* certainly deals with the tendency of the aristocracy and the middle classes to exploit the poor. Pen's attitude towards Fanny Bolton provides a genderized version of class exploitation, which initially does not display much credit in Pen's behaviour, and demonstrates also the class isolation of Laura and his mother.

Prior to writing *Pendennis*, Thackeray was asked by the *Morning Chronicle* to provide a journalistic report of the meeting of Chartists on Kennington Common in London.[29] For four years he had written book reviews for the newspaper on a variety of subjects, but mostly of contemporary fiction. It is not certain how much journalism he contributed to the newspaper, and, indeed, these may be the only examples (they are verified by references in the letters), but they remain unusual productions from Thackeray's pen at this stage in his career. In fact, he had written little purely journalistic material.

The tone of Thackeray's two reports is mildly facetious, deprecating the theatrical extremes of the meeting (flying the tricolour on the 'platform for the principal performers', for instance[30]) and applauding the common sense of the masses gathered (they later pelt the tricolour with mud after the main speakers have left). He adds an ironic note surrounding the expected violence of the meeting: little happened beyond 'a baker's shop in the neighbourhood was rifled of some bread and flour by a gang of desperadoes'.[31] Like Dickens' portrait of Slackbridge in *Hard Times*, Thackeray's summary of the speeches by G.W.M. Reynolds, a Mr Williams and a Mr Sharp, hints at their inflammatory rhetoric. Williams, for example, 'regretted some disgraceful persons were encouraged by the police to commit plunder' at the previous week's meeting in Trafalgar Square, and 'had no hesitation in stating that the police were at the bottom of it'.[32] In 'Chartist Meeting', there is a more distinct tone of mockery at the Chartist delegation's account of their meeting with French Republicans in Paris. One speaker, Mr McGrath, 'proceeded to entertain the meeting with a few lively horrors, in which a rusty old guillotine was made to perform the principal part, and which he produced as a specimen of the ex-King's cruelty, but the description was rather over-charged, and what was intended to excite a thrill ended in a titter'.[33] But the reports offer a basically factual account of what was said – Reynolds, for instance, attacked the expense of upholding the Monarchy compared to the cost of the American President who 'did the work for £5000 a year'.[34] Nevertheless, the relationship between the middle and working classes is a notable theme. 'The middle classes were the enemies of the working classes,' Williams is reported as saying, 'and they were beginning to see the evil of that state of things.'[35]

In *Pendennis*, the class theme revolves around Pen's exploitation of Fanny Bolton, the daughter of a housekeeper. In Number 15, Chapters 45-7 (April 1850), Thackeray explored the interrelatedness of class and, using Pen's near sexual exploitation of Fanny, satirizes the complacency of those who do not recognize the presence of class difference. Thackeray is not promoting this difference, but he will not ignore it either. And it is clearly Pen who comes out the worst for his failure to realize his own class faults. The number brings middle-class Pen together with the aristocratic Henry Foker and then with the working-class Fanny to show up his pretensions to treat all classes equally. Although in society, all classes are mixed, Pen aligns himself with the upper classes and either mocks (as he does in his imitation of Captain Costigan) or abuses the working classes.

The narrator's sweeping descriptions of London join together all manner of people: 'Editors of newspapers, Covent Garden market-people, night cabmen and coffee-sellers, chimney-sweeps, and gentlemen and ladies of fashion who frequent balls ... ' (IV, 80). Such people are present in the night streets of London and at Vauxhall Gardens, where Pen meets Fanny in a dangerous tryst that involves his sexual temptation. Pen, we are told, is an observer of people, 'Mr. Pen said that anthropology was his favourite pursuit', and this is initially established as a cross-class empathy and compassion. 'Of this sympathy with all conditions of men, Arthur often boasted' is Thackeray's ironic comment (IV, 88). But Pen finds himself drawn to Foker for his aristocratic connections whilst he treats Fanny with a sense of his own power over her. When with Foker, Pen is 'dazzled and blinded' by his friend, and 'could see no more faults in [him] than in the sun ... ' (IV, 80). This, in turn, leads to displays that gain the mockery of others: 'And as he spoke, flinging himself into an absurd theatrical attitude, the men in the cab-stand in Piccadilly wondered and grinned at the antics of the two young swells' (IV, 81). In this number, Pen tells Foker of his intention of marrying Blanche Amory for her money, and, although Foker notes she has little, Pen translates this into a magnanimous acceptance on his part that he would be happy in 'a snug little house somewhere off Belgravia', hardly much of a sacrifice (IV, 82). One chapter later, he is flirting with Fanny in Vauxhall.

Barbara Hardy has described the Vauxhall passage in *Pendennis* as 'more sinister and sexually suggestive' than that in *Vanity Fair*.[36] Indeed, the Gardens have declined further across the four decades between the periods of the novels, and Thackray's scenes indicate this. Hardy focuses on Pen's greater knowledge of the world and Fanny's innocence that sharpens the sexual tension in the scene. It is certainly a physically close one and Thackeray was pushing at the limits of permissibility as 'people were pushing and squeezing there beside and behind them' and forcing bodily contact of which they are both conscious (IV, 97). But in addition to this 'seduction of a poor virgin',[37] Pen is titillated by the power that his class position affords him. The tension in the scene is part of the tension in the book as a whole. Pen's desires and his constraints are not of the same source: whatever 'Mr. Pen would have liked to do, he behaved honestly, and like a man' (IV, 99). Over the next two chapters of the novel, Pen tries and fails to defeat his desire for Fanny. He laughs at his attraction to her and tours the sights of London in an attempt to banish his thoughts. Fanny's mother, Mrs. Bolton, and her music teacher, Mr Bows, show their suspicions that Pen means to seduce and abandon Fanny, but her mother is also flattered at the attentions and does noting to discourage Pen. Fanny, too, is a complex set of cultural conditionings. In contrast to Pen's knowledge of the promiscuous journalistic world, Fanny is familiar with the world of 'the circulating library' romances. But the world is not one that warns her of the dangers of a Pen:

> Periodical literature had not reached the height which it has attained subsequently, and the girls of Fanny's generation were not enabled to purchase sixteen pages of excitement for a penny, rich with histories of crime, murder, oppressed virtue, and the heartless seductions of the aristocracy ... (IV, 105)

The irony is partly against the decline in a standard of publishing taste, and the rise of the 'penny dreadfuls', but it is also interesting that the narratives referred to implicate Pen in a similar 'heartless seduction'. Reynolds was a writer of such sensational romances, and *The Mysteries of London* was appearing at the time of Thackeray's writing.[38] Thackeray aims to show how Pen more realistically *does not* seduce Fanny, but the tensions and intentions remain. He is, as Trollope says, 'weak, and selfish, and untrustworthy',[39] but his weaknesses are also compounded by the social class structure of the day.

Pen is representative of a new middle class rejecting what it is trying to climb away from and desiring what it can see within reach higher up. He is a flux, a confluence of what Raymond Williams called residual and emergent cultural trends. It is Mr Bows who finally articulates the true nature of Pen's relationship with Fanny and exposes the class conflict underpinning the previous scenes. Bows confronts Pen, declaring:

> ... you came to steal a pretty girl's heart away, and to ruin it, and to spurn it afterwards, Mr. Arthur Pendennis. That's what the world makes of you young dandies, you gentlemen of fashion, you high and mighty aristocrats that trample upon the people. It's sport to you, but what is it to the poor, think you; the toys of your pleasures, whom you play with and whom you fling into the streets when you are tired? I know your order, sir ... You must have your pleasures, and the people of course must pay for them. What are we made for, but for that? (IV, 123-4)

Pendennis's reply to Bows is defensive and carries some truth in it: 'to a man who has to work for his bread as much as you do,' he says, 'how can you talk about aristocrats tyrannizing over people?' (IV, 124). But Pen is also aware of the power he has and his indulgence over Fanny. Bows rejects his arguments that they are still 'romantic young fellows'; Pen has to accept his responsibilities and the cultural changes that have transformed class and gender relations. As Bows remarks, 'times are changed', and you cannot act as though they have not (IV, 124).

Pendennis, then, is a novel about maturity, but it about the maturity of the Victorian age as much as the growth of a single central character. The confrontation between Pen and Bows takes place 'In or Near the Temple Garden', a chapter-title replete with symbolic connections. Chapter 49 begins with an evocation of place – of Sir Roger de Coveley and Mr Spectator, Johnson and Goldsmith and the Mitre Inn. Pen and the narrator imagine the lineage of men of letters to which Pen fancies he belongs. But 'times have changed'. Pen writes for the *Gazette* and has launched his fashionable romance, *Walter Lorraine*. He may dream himself a heritage, but the real nature of contemporary publishing is concealed behind the façade of an illusory place of worship. Bows provides the opposition. He suggests that Fanny has been influenced in her class-susceptibility by romances; she 'has heated her little brain with novels ... and she scarcely sees that she treads on a kitchen floor' (IV, 124). But the novel she has just finished, we are told, is *Walter Lorraine*, which she had borrowed from a circulating library. She has learned nothing from the book, except to resent her own station. Thackeray entwines the class issue with the love-plot here; Fanny reacts to the book as to a simple romance:

> '*Walter Lorraine*,' Fanny sighed out. 'How I do *hate* that Neara – Naera – I don't know the pronunciation. And how I love Leonora; and Walter, oh, how dear he is!' (IV, 121)

The reduction of the narrative of *Pendennis* to a romance plot (with Naera as Blanche Amory, Leonora as Laura, and Walter as Pen) suggests something of the betrayal of realist art that condemns Pen as a writer. The commercial exploitation of the public by the publisher becomes entangled in the sexual exploitation of a young girl by the dandy. There are parallels here to Gaskell's *Mary Barton* (1848), where Harry Carson toys with the naïve Mary. But Thackeray's social critique is more subtle because it implicates the writer. Pen is not *directly* responsible for Fanny's innocent reading errors; nor is she to blame for desiring betterment. But the commercial system led Pen to rewrite his autobiographical novel and transform it into a popular bestseller. The industry fuels the desires of the market, however naïve or wrong-headed they might be. Thackeray is conscious of the decisions that a writer makes and of the compromises he is forced to make. The impact of these forces on the readership, on society, on intimate relationships of the time, show how much Thackeray thought about the consequences of writing. The insidious complexity of the commercial relationships of the 1840s, the complete implication of all in the system, the impossibility of escape from the mechanics of production, all combine to generate Thackeray's deep anxiety and ambivalence about the state of literature in his day. Pen, then, acts as a symbolic figure of transition. He characterizes the change in times, and through him Thackeray insists that innocence is no longer possible or believable. The encompassing class issues of the late 1840s pervade *Pendennis*, and have a more direct expression in contemporary works for *Punch*, such as 'The Curate's Walk' and 'Waiting at the Station', the *Morning Chronicle* articles on the Chartist meetings, and the Christmas book, *Our Street* (1848). But *Pendennis* is also able to suggest the complexities of class relations and their inextricability from the discourses of the popular print of the times. The writer, even with good intentions, cannot be absolved.

Pendennis is a novel which itself crosses the class barriers. It is both 'serious' and 'intellectual' in its designs, but represents an attempt to popularize the novel in the field attained by, not just Dickens, but Reynolds and other sensation writers. Moreover, the serial's affinity with the popular magazine is self-evident. Thackeray's text imitates the magazine in that it offers a diverse panorama of contemporary social life, controlled by an 'editorial' voice that shapes the material from a future vantage point, and it remains self-referential in that it contains allusions to the textual world that surrounds it: both to the world of volume publication (*Walter Lorraine*, amongst others) and the world of the newspaper and magazine. It takes less than a page for us to discover the world of newspapers when we enter the novel. Major Pendennis sits to breakfast at his club in Pall Mall (echoing the magazine later to be Pen's springboard), and waits for 'his toast and his hot newspaper' (III, 2), and, after reading his daily letters, 'took his breakfast and looked over the paper, the gazette [another echo], the births and deaths, and the fashionable intelligence, to see that his name was down among the guests at my Lord So-and-so's fete ... ' (III, 3). The Major takes the paper as a means of self-fashioning and uses it as a mirror for his own sense of social eminence. It offers confirmation of his identity and not a direct channel to contemporary history. There is an obvious contrast with Pen's early reading described in the novel's third chapter. This is all book-based, and very much in the style of the man of letters, but is also a muddied set of texts reflecting country taste and popular commercial fiction: Inchbald's *Theatre* and White's *Farriery*, a set of French novels, and Hakluyt, Hobbes, and Chaucer (the first three of which clearly hint at the affair with the actress, the Fotheringay, which will be Pen's first love relationship).

The *Pall Mall Gazette*, then, in many ways, offers a consummation of Pen's acceptance of the Major's social world. But it is the reader, and not the writer, who can create identity in the periodical text. Pen has to step outside of the magazine, with *Walter Lorraine*, in order to explore his sense of self-worth, just as Thackeray does with the novel as a whole. Pen's periodical productions – his verses in the 'Poet's Corner' of the *County Chronicle* (paralleling Thackeray's first publications in the *Western Luminary*) – attempt a shaping of the self, but falsify and distort, and are only a part of his 'infancy' (III, 28). If we look to the final chapter, it is the periodical press that retains a presence over Pen-the-novelist. The press, in the form of 'the *Chatteris Champion, Clavering Agriculturist, and Baymouth Fisherman* ... so eligible a medium for advertisements' (IV, 404), announces Pen's decision to stand down as a Parliamentary candidate and to marry Laura instead. In the final paragraph, we are given yet another parallel to the 'Laman Blanchard' essay, in that Thackeray places the journalist Warrington above the 'genius' Pen: 'If Mr. Pen's works have procured him more reputation than has been acquired by his abler friend, whom no one knows, George [Warrington] lives contented without the fame ... We own, and see daily [in the press?], how the false and worthless live and prosper, while the good are called away ... ' (IV, 423).

Pen's arrival in the columns of fashionable intelligence – albeit, and ironically, in Chatteris and not London – transforms him into a figure not unlike his uncle, the Major. However, he retains a value as a productive writer. Warrington remains outside of the public sphere in his ironic absence as the journalist-writer. In his biographical history, Thackeray leaves Warrington behind as he moves away from the role of magazine writer for a time. But there is a self-knowledge behind the final portrait of the two writers – the two personalities – the two Thackerays – which suggests he is not wholly satisfied in the triumph of art over ephemera. 'People in the big-book interest', he wrote in 'Laman Blanchard', ' ... cry out against the fashion of fugitive literature', adding, 'Why should not the day have its literature?'[40] If we reconsider the front-page illustration to the novel, we remark that Pen actually gains both the siren of fame and wealth *and* of domestic happiness and tranquillity. He has merged the two rather than defeated the immoral for the moral. This is Thackeray's message in *Pendennis*; his novel is not positing Victorian middle-class domesticity over material gain, but showing how the ordinary man, the 'whole man', desires both. But in Warrington he presents us with a figure who gains neither. He 'lives alone' and writes in obscurity. Thackeray's representation of the world of media journalism, then, is as a loss. Pen's success is qualified by the greater value in its own terms of the 'lesser' world lost. Which, then, is the defining figure? The shaper of the press, who writes and produces, the 'prose labourer' (III, 363)? Or the image created by the press, the subject of the media – the pen – who attains recognition by entering the public sphere of textuality?

Notes

[1] Juliet McMaster, *Thackeray: The Major Novels* (Manchester: Manchester University Press, 1971), 77.
[2] Colby, *Canvass*, 277.
[3] *Pendennis, Works*, IV, 85 [references in the text are to this edition].
[4] Grahame Smith, *Charles Dickens: A Literary Life* (London: Macmillan, 1996), 15-16.
[5] See P.D. Edwards, *Dickens's 'Young Men': George Augustus Sala, Edmund Yates and the World of Victorian Journalism* (Aldershot: Ashgate, 1997).
[6] Mark Cronin, 'The Rake, The Writer, and The Stranger: Textual Relations between *Pendennis* and *David Copperfield*', *Dickens Studies Annual*, 24 (1996), 216.
[7] Ibid.
[8] Robert Colby notes the market-driven nature of Pen's novel; Colby, *Canvass*, 288.
[9] Ibid., 305.
[10] Ibid., 274.
[11] See Thackeray's identification with Fielding, discussed above in Chapter 7.
[12] Habermas, 55-6, 84-5, 195.
[13] Aled Jones, *Powers of the Press*, 29.
[14] See Ina Ferris, 'The Demystification of Laura Pendennis', *Studies in the Novel*, 13 (1981), 122-32, which traces her character through *Pendennis, The Newcomes*, and *Philip*.
[15] Lyn Pykett, 'Reading the Periodical Press: Text and Context', in L. Brake, A. Jones, and L. Madden (eds), *Investigating Victorian Journalism* (London: Macmillan, 1990), 3-18.
[16] Ibid., 6.
[17] Letter to F.M. Evans, 24 March 1855; *Letters*, IV, 431-3.
[18] Jones, *Powers of the Press*, 119-20.
[19] Brake, *Subjugated Knowledges*, 11.
[20] Jones, *Powers of the Press*, 121.

[21] See 'Miss Tickletoby's Lectures on English History', *Punch* (2 July-1 October 1842); *Lovel the Widower*, *Cornhill Magazine* (January-June 1860); *Works*, XXVI, 4; *Works*, XXIV, 18.
[22] The influence of Thackeray's work is felt in the establishment of a real *Pall Mall Gazette* by George Smith (proprietor of the *Cornhill Magazine*) in 1863.
[23] Craig Howes, '*Pendennis* and the Controversy on the "Dignity of Literature"', *Nineteenth-Century Literature*, 41 (1986-7), 280.
[24] Howes, 293.
[25] Ibid., 294, 291.
[26] See, for instance, the study of *Esmond* in N.N. Feltes, *Modes of Production of Victorian Novels* (Chicago: University of Chicago Press, 1986) and J.A. Sutherland, *Victorian Novelists and Publishers* (Chicago: University of Chicago Press, 1976).
[27] Trollope, *Thackeray*, 122.
[28] Charlotte Brontë, *Jane Eyre: An Autobiography*, ed. Q.D. Leavis (Harmondsworth: Penguin, 1966), 36.
[29] 'Meeting on Kennington Common', *Morning Chronicle* (14 March 1848), and 'Chartist Meeting', *Morning Chronicle* (15 March 1848); reprinted in Ray, *Contributions*, 192-8 and 198-201.
[30] Ray, *Contributions*, 195.
[31] Ibid., 194.
[32] Ibid., 196.
[33] Ibid., 200-201.
[34] Ibid.
[35] Ibid.
[36] Hardy, *Exposure*, 134.
[37] Ibid., 136.
[38] Tillotson, *Novels of the 1840s*, 31; G.W.M. Reynolds, *The Mysteries of the Court of London* (1848-56).
[39] Trollope, *Thackeray*, 109.
[40] 'Laman Blanchard', *Works*, XXV, 88-9.

Chapter 9

Warring spirits: *Cornhill's* 'Notch on the Axe' and Dickens' sensational *All the Year Round*

It is an interesting but little remarked feature of Thackeray's career that it ended almost back where it began, editing a literary magazine on the fringes of the City. Whilst many of his earlier contemporaries, Dickens, Ainsworth, Jerrold, A'Beckett, the Mayhews, found a regular and relatively lucrative additional role as newspaper or magazine editors to supplement the writer's income, Thackeray only twice took the editor's chair. In 1833, he began his professional literary career as proprietor and editor of the *National Standard*. From the end of 1859 until March 1862 (the year before he died), he was appointed editor of the *Cornhill Magazine*, a new venture launched by his then publisher, George Smith.[1] The roundabout ride had gone full circle. The *National Standard* was published from St Paul's Churchyard, in the shadows of the dome, and clinging to the end of Grub/Fleet Street; the Cornhill symbolized commercial success and banking respectability and Thackeray had used it as his imaginative starting-point for a journey to Grand Cairo in his travel book of 1846, a year of economic boom.[2] The intervening thirty years had taken Thackeray and Victorian Britain a long way. He had written a significant proportion of the *National Standard* himself, assisted by a sub-editor and some scissors and paste; the *Cornhill* boasted a wealth of writers including Anthony Trollope, G.A. Sala, G.H. Lewes, George Eliot, John Ruskin, Harriet Beecher Stowe, Charles Lever, and Alfred Tennyson. Under Thackeray, the *National Standard*, a weekly, failed after just ten months; the *Cornhill* began with a circulation of 110,000 copies and settled down to a regular 80,000 per month.

The *Cornhill Magazine* is notable in Thackeray's career for a number of reasons. In 1859, when he became involved in the planning for the first number for January 1860, it was eight years since he had left the team of writers on *Punch*, and he had not since been associated with a magazine or newspaper. For most of the 1850s, he had built his reputation as a novelist with three major novels – in volume-form, *The History of Henry Esmond* (1852), and two large 24-part free-standing serials, *The Newcomes* (1853-5) and *The Virginians* (1857-8). He had also undertaken lecture tours of Britain and America, with *The English Humourists of the Eighteenth Century* and *The*

Four Georges (subsequently published in the *Cornhill*). Only very occasionally had he published magazine or newspaper items. N.N. Feltes has argued that Thackeray, under the guidance of Smith, was reconstructing himself as a historian-novelist and putting behind himself the journalistic reputation which was the foundation of his fame.[3] Despite the successive increases in print runs for these novels, however, *The Virginians* was not a commercial or critical triumph.[4] Critics have long argued that Thackeray's later completed novels, *The Virginians* and *The Adventures of Philip* (1861-2), show a marked deterioration in his powers to sustain the reader's interest, and they remain out of print as second-favourites to the racier narratives of Trollope and the sensation school of novelists from the same period. In several ways, this view reflects precisely the literary battle that Thackeray was fighting during the last years of his life. The realist, ironist, humanist, and subjectivist, was losing out to the demand for mystery, murder, middle-class madness and the cliff-hanger ending.

One might look briefly at *The Virginians* to see the problem. Thackeray's story of near-identical American twins, moving between England and Virginia during the second half of the eighteenth century, caught up in love and domestic battles, asserting themselves against the prejudices of the English society which considers them savages, one failing as a playwright, the other succeeding alongside General Wolfe, and finally fighting on opposite sides in the War of Independence, continually negates its own drama. Thackeray consciously eschews sensationalism – although he does get drawn into a historian's fascination for the details of battles and national political motivations – and collapses his broad canvas into the domestic drawing-room and George Warrington's subjective musings. Dickens' version of eighteenth-century revolution, English international relations, and identical character doubles in *A Tale of Two Cities* (1859) (echoed again in the 'savage' twins of *The Mystery of Edwin Drood* (1870)), or Collins' identical doubles in *The Woman in White* (1859-60) and *Armadale* (1864-6), transpose these ideas to the fiction of sensation where they originated and have continued to work well.

The *Cornhill Magazine*, then, represents a return into the stimulating and aggressive world of journalism that Thackeray had left behind in 1851. In part, it provided Thackeray with a forum for a sustained attack on the new school of sensation writers, headed, predictably, by Dickens and his weekly magazine, launched in 1859, *All the Year Round*. Thackeray saw the 'new' school of sensation fiction as, in fact, a continuation of the earlier school of 'Newgate' fiction which he parodied in the 1830s and 1840s.

Critics of the periodical press and of Thackeray usually wish to see the *Cornhill* as a highbrow literary magazine, and forerunner of the *Pall Mall Gazette* (which took its title from Thackeray's fictitious journal in *Pendennis*, *The Newcomes* and *Philip*), *Temple Bar* (edited by Sala from 1860-63), the *St. Paul's Magazine* (set up by Trollope to rival Smith's publication), and *Belgravia* (established by the sensation writer Mary Braddon using the pen-name of Captain Shandon, Thackeray's editor of the *Pall Mall Gazette*!).[5] Thackeray wrote, 'the Magazine must bear my *cachet* you see and be a man of the world Magazine'.[6] Its success certainly helped to create that tradition. But in its opening days, competing as a magazine for fiction and poetry, as well as articles of general interest, its eye, or at least its editor's eye, seems to have been on its most obvious popular rival, *All the Year Round*. Thackeray always watched what Dickens was doing; the incident with Yates in 1857 which became the Garrick Affair (where Dickens supported Yates) only served to heighten their rivalry at this time.[7] Is it mere coincidence that *The Virginians* and *A Tale of Two Cities* bear surface similarities; or that *The Adventures of Philip* should adopt a central character with the same personal name as the central figure in *Great Expectations*, which began serialization a few weeks earlier?[8] Indeed, Thackeray's opening serial in the *Cornhill*, *Lovel the Widower* (1860), opens with a direct echo of *David Copperfield*, 'Who shall be the hero of this tale?', and goes on to separate their authorial sensibilities with, 'Not I who write it'.[9]

It might be remarked that Thackeray's decision to accept the post of editor and contributor on the *Cornhill Magazine* gave him the opportunity to revitalize his career, and that he intended to do that by a re-immersion in the periodical world. He described it as moving 'out of novel-spinning and back into the world'.[10] When outside of this world, writing his serial novels of contemporary life, Thackeray always turned to it for inspiration: *Pendennis* we have already discussed; *The Newcomes* focuses on Clive Newcome and a group of aspiring artists, and contains portraits of art critics and magazine men drawn from Thackeray's experiences as an art critic (Michael Angelo Titmarsh) for *Fraser's Magazine* and elsewhere in the 1830s and early 1840s; *Philip* introduces the world of the foreign correspondent and again returns us to the same period and Thackeray's own work as Paris correspondent and travel writer and critic. Now, in 1860, Thackeray would redefine his own writings alongside those of his contemporaries in the magazine world. In a contrapuntal movement to his earlier refashioning as a historian, his identity would be reforged inside the periodical world that created him.

Thackeray's main contributions to the *Cornhill Magazine* are *Lovel the Widower*, in six parts from January to June 1860, *The Adventures of Philip*, January 1861 to August 1862, and the *Roundabout Papers*, almost-monthly essays, 34 in total, the last one appearing in November 1863, a month before he died. Thackeray was editor until March 1862, when he resigned due to disagreements over editorial policy, but he continued as a contributor until his sudden death in December 1863.[11] *Denis Duval*, an unfinished novel left in manuscript, was published posthumously in the *Cornhill*, March-June 1864. 'The Notch on the Axe', the *Roundabout Paper* which lends its title to this chapter and which will be discussed below, was different from the others in that it appeared in three parts over three months (April-June 1862), is more distinctly an extended fictional story, and was written in the month immediately following his resignation as editor. *The Adventures of Philip* succeeded Trollope's *Framley Parsonage* and was followed by Eliot's *Romola*. Harriet Beecher Stowe's *Agnes of Sorrento*, another historical novel like Eliot's, ran simultaneously. Fiction in Dickens' *All the Year Round* was represented at this time by Collins' *The Woman in White*, followed by *Great Expectations*, Bulwer-Lytton's *A Strange Story*, and Collins' *No Name*.

The *Roundabout Papers* provided Thackeray with a regular forum for his meditations on a wide range of subjects. Several of the papers find their starting place in texts taken from the media, such as the third paper, 'On Ribbons' (in the fourth number of the *Cornhill*, April 1860), which extracts newspaper accounts of the heroism of merchant seamen during ship fires and storms. As Thackeray remarks, '[h]ere, in a single column of a newspaper, what strange, touching pictures do we find of seamen's dangers, vicissitudes, gallantry, generosity!'[12] These papers are, in effect, a return to the occasional periodical articles of the 1830s and 1840s, such as 'Half-a-Crown's Worth of Cheap Knowledge' or 'Going to See a Man Hanged'. But they also function as editorials for the new *Cornhill*, helping to define its identity in the marketplace. They bear many similarities with the 'Our Leader' items, and other editorials, written for the *National Standard* in 1833-4.[13] Although Thackeray himself, and subsequent critics, aligned the papers with Montaigne's *Essays*,[14] or Lamb's *Essays of Elia*,[15] they are also highly contextualized and part of a process of marketing. Edgar Harden has noted how the essays probably provided the editor (Thackeray, initially) with pages that might be reduced or extended should the issue have overrun or fallen short of its word length.[16] The digressive and meandering structure enabled the writer to cut or extend the essay as required. I shall talk about their defining role for the *Cornhill* in a moment, but first I want to consider their redefining of Thackeray himself and *his* relationship with the periodical press.

The title of the *Roundabout Papers* is pregnant with suggestive allusions. It does not just refer to the discursive style that Thackeray adopts, as is usually accepted. The roundabout also returns Thackeray to his first days as a writer and editor. It is suggestive of the fairground and *Vanity Fair*, of a world of pleasure (the themes of idleness, childhood play, and the pleasure of just passing the time in leisurely activity, are often invoked in the papers). We recall the chapter in *Vanity Fair* entitled, 'A Roundabout chapter between London and Hampshire' (Chapter 44). *Punch* is present too, in its 'Spec' paper, 'A Roundabout Ride', from March 1848. The essayist's meditative titles for the papers, 'On ... ' this and 'On ... ' that, recall further Proser and Spec articles in *Punch*, as well as *The Book of Snobs*. The tradition invoked is not just that of Montaigne, but also of Thackeray's own periodical contributions (a device we have already seen Thackeray use in order to generate coherence across his miscellaneous magazine publications). The motion implicit in the title, that of a circular returning upon the self, provides a good analogy to the 'bundle of egotisms', the papers, which centre on the subjective 'I'.[17] Thackeray comments how 'that right line "I" is the very shortest, simplest, straightforwardest means of communication between us, and stands for what it is worth and no more.'[18] It contrasts with the Dickensian narrative trajectory, the quickly propelled forward motion of the sensation serial.

The contemporary counterpart of Thackeray's papers are, of course, Dickens' *The Uncommercial Traveller* articles for *All the Year Round*. Their notion of travelling is distinctly away from the self, or, rather, externalizing aspects of the self and the conscious memory. Although, Dickens might sit in a carriage and take a flight of fancy across continents, which eventually leads back to himself,[19] the overall effect is of a loss of self, a forgetting; whereas, for Thackeray, the self remains foregrounded. It is interesting how both writers feature the commercial in their imaginative structure for their essays. Dickens' 'uncommercial' writer travels without the intention of doing trade or business, but for reasons nobly associated in Romantic thought with the integration or wholeness of the self. However, his essays are obviously commercial money-spinners. Thackeray posits the notion of the roundabout: an activity paid for and undertaken for momentary pleasure and not necessarily invested in for profit. *His* commercial activity is avowedly commercial, but a self-denigrating one, as if the writer remains unsure of the value of his work. We find a return here to the tensions of old in Thackeray's writings between the defining of art as unrelated to commerce and the sense that writing in the industrial world is a trade. Indeed, in the first *Roundabout Paper*, 'On a Lazy Idle Boy', Thackeray brings together the erotic desire implicit in reading – 'the appetite for novels' – and the mercantile practice of writing, 'the demand being what we know it is, the merchant must supply it, as he will supply saddles and pale ale for Bombay and Calcutta'.[20] Moreover, the paper characterizes the *Cornhill* itself as a ship, and the readers as 'fellow-travellers', but one rather more for passengers and pleasures than trade.

The imaginative return to earlier periodical arguments provides the key to Thackeray's reconstruction of his authorial identity in 1860. It is not, in fact, a retreat into the past, but it is a reconsideration of the past in the context of the present. Catherine Peters is very unfair to Thackeray when she describes the *Roundabout Papers* as providing 'a very powerful flavour of an "old codger" of the 1860s, looking back over a half-century which has seen tremendous and only half-understood changes'.[21] After all, Thackeray was only 49, and had been representing himself in the magazines as an older and more experienced man since he was 22 (in reviews for the *National Standard*, for instance). The public liked authority in its journalism, and Thackeray was adept at providing, and exploding, the illusion of this. His writings deconstruct the media voice.

Lovel the Widower is a short novella that carefully examines this very process of self-analysis and re-identification, and symbolically positions the new Thackeray in relation to his own past selves. It was a reworking of a play, *The Wolves and the Lamb*, originally written in 1854 and never performed.[22] Thackeray refers to such literary rejection in the serial itself (as he had in the failed dramatist's career of George Warrington and his version of *Pocahontas* – a popular American dramatic subject – in *The Virginians*), by having Charles Batchelor, the semi-autobiographical narrator of the story, mention his 'tragedy' that never seems to get written, as well as his previous plays 'of which envious managers never could be got to see the merit' (XXIV, 122). The play, then, is transformed into a new commodity, a magazine serial in six parts, just as the author moves from novelist (/playwright) to periodicals man. I have mentioned how the opening reminds the reader of *David Copperfield*, Dickens' most autobiographical work. There are also many allusions to *Hamlet* throughout, intertextualizing the introspection of the narrator, but also an echo of *Copperfield*.[23] More generally, the structure of the story consists of two central figures: Batchelor, the narrator, who is ever-present, and Lovel, his old school-friend, who barely appears and remains an often absent figure at his business in the City. Batchelor never married, after the failure of an affair of the heart with Glorvina O'D[owd], a character from *Vanity Fair*.[24] Lovel's hated first wife has died and his household is now controlled by two domineering mothers and a group of empowered servants. Several of the male characters in the story, including Batchelor, are in love with the governess, a lower-class girl, Elizabeth Prior. Batchelor, for whom she represents a link to his younger days, proposes to her, but she sees him as an older father-figure. When her past as a ballet-dancer is exposed, however, she seizes the opportunity to marry Lovel, who is an equal age to Batchelor. As characters, Batchelor represents the unrooted and largely uncategorized writer, whilst Lovel is the wealthy, home-owning respectable city gentleman. Batchelor talks to servants and nobility alike; Lovel retains his sense of class difference until his elevation of Elizabeth. One might be tempted to read this dualism as Lovel (whose name unites love and novel) representing all of those things from which Batchelor/Thackeray (effectively a batchelor since his wife's insanity) is now excluded. Jilted by wife-art in the 1830s and forced into the world of journalism, Thackeray had now been jilted a second time by novelist-art and returns again to the peripatetic batchelorhood of journalism. The axes of love/sex–novelist/journalist we have seen in Thackeray's work before.[25]

The tale does more than symbolically feature this reorientation. In the first part of the story, published in the first number of the *Cornhill Magazine*, Batchelor tells something of his past life, and dwells on his purchase of a magazine, the *Museum*, and his work as editor and reviewer. The magazine is described as a purchase or business venture, an 'eligible literary property'. But the main thrust of the passage is a reconsideration of the past: the magazine being a thinly disguised version of the *National Standard*.[26] This was the only other time that Thackeray had acted as an editor, now he was returning to that world.

> I dare say I gave myself airs as editor of that confounded *Museum*, and proposed to educate the public taste, to diffuse morality and sound literature throughout the nation, and to pocket a liberal salary in return for my services. I dare say I printed my own sonnets, my own tragedy, my own verses … I dare say I wrote satirical articles, in which I piqued myself upon the fineness of my own wit, and

> criticisms, got up for the nonce out of encyclopaedias and biographical dictionaries; so that I would be actually astounded at my own knowledge. I dare say I made a gaby of myself to the world: pray, my good friend, hast thou never done likewise? If thou hast never been a fool, be sure thou wilt never be a wise man. (XXIV, 18)

The Museum operates as an indicator of the changes that had taken place in the periodical industry between 1833 and 1860. The philosophy behind the magazine – education, morality, taste – is tempered by the sense of the author's earnings and his effrontery, his putting up of a front. This public-spiritedness has failed periodical literature. The *Cornhill Magazine* will be run differently; one might see an implicit self-advertisement here, that the *Cornhill* is modern and not a museum-piece. It shares the characteristics of modern journalism. But the tension at the centre of this reminiscence does actually pervade Thackeray's late work too; indeed, of course, here it is manifested in the structure of his reminiscence. The integrity of the writer remains in question throughout; can an artist be a tradesman?

The character of Slumley, the editor of the *Swell* newspaper, is another backward glance at his apprenticeship. Living on the first floor of Batchelor's lodgings, Slumley 'wrote for a paper printed at our office' (XXIV, 19). Both writers receive proof-sheets for correction brought by the printer's boy. The boy, Dick Bedford, is later the self-taught intellectual head servant of Lovel's household, and a suitor for Elizabeth, presumably having benefited from his early contact with the writers, and is furthermore a contributor with 'A Voice from the Basement' for the *Putney Herald and Mortlake Monitor* (XXIV, 56). Slumley's paper recalls in brief the newspapers of *The Ravenswing* (*Fraser's Magazine*, 1843), and Elizabeth's career as a ballet-dancer is a further echo of this (indeed, Sir George Thrum, a character from *The Ravenswing* is mentioned later, and Captain Fitzboodle is a friend of Batchelor's; *Philip* also contains allusions to this story, see below). The paper 'used to make direful attacks upon individual reputations; and you would find theatre and opera people most curiously praised and assaulted in the *Swell*' (XXIV, 12). As in earlier portrayals of the press, the *Swell* emulates the kind of paper whose text is riddled with self-interest. The media creates and destroys personalities or identities. It is significant that, at a time when Thackeray is returning to a direct engagement with the media, he reminds his readers of this modern phenomenon. The press can be corrupt, but has power; at the beginning of *Lovel*, he reminds us of 'the advertising-puffers' and their 'silly baits to catch an unsuspecting public' (XXIV, 6). The newspapers do not offer a truthful reflection of life in their contents, but they do so obliquely in their methodologies or mediation. Thackeray ironically passes over Slumley's life, suggesting: '[y]ou see it is "an insult to literature" to say that there are disreputable and dishonest persons who write in newspapers' (XXIV, 12).

Lovel the Widower, then, revisits the debates about 'truth' or realism and about the integrity of the writer and his relationship to the mediated discourse of the periodical press. The commercial world makes the writer's artistic integrity, as well as his moral integrity, more problematic. For example, Batchelor's review of his own career (in part, Thackeray's) demonstrates the untrustworthy nature of authorship, not necessarily of writing itself, but of the motivations behind it which potentially undermine its meaning. Leaving university with debts to his name, Batchelor is saved by Lovel, who lends him money. He then 'engaged in literary pursuits ... became connected with a literary periodical' and 'imposed myself upon the public as a good classical scholar' (XXIV, 17).[27] The purpose of writing becomes intimately connected with money, as it did in Thackeray's life after the loss of his income in 1833. The publications he produces are scoffed at by the mature writer, but gained public approval in their day: 'my "Translations from the Greek, " my "Poems by Beta," and my articles in the paper of which I was part proprietor for several years, have had their little success in their day' (XXIV, 17). These are the periodical days of the early 1830s when hack-work offered itself more freely for the hopeful writer, and clearly contrast with the kind of reputation which the *Cornhill* intended to establish and represent. The media of the 1860s was, on the surface at least, more responsible and more professional than its predecessors. As Thackeray noted in the first *Roundabout Paper* (this same week):

> ... our *Cornhill Magazine* owners strive to provide thee with facts as well as fiction; and though it does not become them to brag of their Ordinary, at least they invite thee to a table where thou shalt sit in good company ... that account of China is told by the man of all the empire most likely to know of what he speaks [Sir John Bowring]...[28]

Thackeray's comment here stresses first-hand knowledge and not the dilettantism of his early life. *Lovel the Widower*, in one sense, functions as a subtle advertisement for the *Cornhill*. However, it also continues to problematize periodical discourse. Batchelor is paying his debts to Lovel '[b]y laborious instalments' (XXIV, 17), just as the transformation of play into serial is a trade of instalments.

Realism, too, becomes a mercantile and profit making aesthetic. There are plenty of echoes of earlier works here, particularly of the 'Fat Contributor Papers' in *Punch*. At the beginning of the tale, Batchelor confesses that part of the reason for his current work of fiction is to exact revenge against Lovel's first wife and her mother (XXIV, 6). By representing her in fiction, he can satirize her behaviour: 'Here you are, do you hear? Here you shall be shown up.' This school of realism is, though, of a past age also. The 'advertising-puffers', who once wanted novels of high life based on originals and would sell them by inviting readers to guess the true identities of the characters, have now renounced that 'stale stratagem' (XXIV, 6). But his initial admission and this subsequent denial is intended itself as a satirical lure to the reader, whom Thackeray knows *will* wish to guess identities. The paradox of the narrative is spelled out to the 'candid public', that 'though it is all true, there is not a word of truth in it' (XXIV, 6). This phrase appears to refer to a notion that here is a story that is 'true' to the spirit of human nature, that characters are true-to-life, but which does not contain real people or originals and real incidents. However, this itself is open to question; there may be a fictitious narrator attacking fictitious friends' ex-wives, but there are also a lot of allusions to Thackeray's own life and career here (and one might think of the Brookfields even). This unreliability is present elsewhere. Not only does writing for money disrupt authoritative meaning, but it brings an element of mistrust into the discourse of love. When Batchelor finally accepts the loss of Elizabeth and makes clear to her the death of his love, he says

> ... I can't give a better proof of my utter indifference about the matter, than the fact that I wrote two or three copies of verses descriptive of my despair. They appeared, you may perhaps remember, in one of the annuals of those days, and were generally attributed to one of the most sentimental of our young poets. I remember the reviews said they were 'replete with emotion,' 'full of passionate and earnest feeling,' and so forth. Feeling, indeed! – ha! ha! 'Passionate outbursts of a grief-stricken heart!' Passionate scrapings of a fiddlestick, my good friend ... Despair is perfectly compatible with a good dinner, I promise you. (XXIV, 110)

Writing becomes a process of transforming feeling into text, and the very process reveals a loss of or distancing from the original thought/self. The sentimental album of verses symbolically exchanges genuine feeling for the literary commodity. Thackeray always criticized the poor quality of verses in these productions (here, he says, '"Lonely" of course rhymes with "only," and "gushes" with "blushes" ... ', and so on, XXIV, 110[29]), and the hint again here is a further return to his journalism of the 1830s. But he is also showing how the industrial processes of writing have led to the commodification of texts; formulae pervade published texts and make truth less accessible. This is his argument against sensation fiction and the tendency towards the sensational generally.

Lovel the Widower contains many interesting episodes and ideas. It is an experimental work, but in a style that Thackeray did not pursue further. Nevertheless, it is important as his initial statement about returning to work for the periodical press in a new era of publishing taste. Representation, spying/seeing, and the magnet of the sensational, are marginal but essential themes of the story, and relate the work to his other writings for the *Cornhill Magazine*.[30] Newspapers surround the text; Mrs Lovel's death in Naples is announced in the newspapers and Batchelor is 'not a little scared to read' the information (XXIV, 23).[31] He knows how upset his friend will be. The totemizing of her harp, described in Gothic terms as being covered in a leather shroud like the dead woman's skin, is defeated by the remarriage of Lovel, but not before a harp string twangs at the crucial moment of his declaration of love for Elizabeth (XXIV, 23, 122).[32] Such minor intrusions of the sensation genre provide an effect of bathos clearly intended to poke fun at the current fashion. The newspapers are implicated here, too. As Dick Bedford closes up the house, Shrublands, one evening, he remarks to the narrator,

> Come to see all safe for the night, sir, and the windows closed before you turn in ... Best not to leave 'em open even if you are asleep inside – catch cold – many bad people about. Remember Bromley murder! – Enter at French windows – you cry out – cut your throat – and there's a fine paragraph for the papers next morning! (XXIV, 56)

Everyone is thinking of murders and the terrific. The story has the air of a Collins novel, focusing on a middle-class household and the many tensions and stories hidden in its depths. But Thackeray will not maintain the tricks of the suspense writers in exposing the secrets he describes. Early in the story, he observes, 'in this little chapter, there are some little mysteries propounded, upon which, were I not above any such artifice, I might easily leave the reader to ponder for a month' (XXIV, 20). This technique of anti-suspense is present throughout *The Adventures of Philip*, too, as Thackeray constantly reassures his readers of the eventual happy outcome of the story. Despite this, however, Thackeray binds together the notion of the sensational with the writer's assertion of self. Batchelor's moment of mock heroic selfhood, defending Dick Bedford and Lizzie from the physical presence of Lady Baker's footman, Bulkeley, sees him take up a paper knife as a weapon to threaten the bully.

> ... there was a fine shining dagger on the table, used for the cutting open of reviews and magazines, I seized and brandished this weapon, and I dare say would have sheathed it in the giant's bloated corpus, had he made any movement towards me. (XXIV, 91)

Reading a review a few hours later, Batchelor is again confronted by Bulkeley's threat, '[b]ut I poise my paper-cutter, and he retires growling' (XXIV, 96). The symbolism is carefully poised, too; the moment is simultaneously parodic and revealing. The instruments of publishing, in this case of reading, are involved as the accessories of sensation. The endowing of the ordinary periodical accoutrement with the symbolic weight of a popular genre threatens to destabilize the genteel world of reading. Batchelor, in his youth, reads 'elegant literature'; his world, like Thackeray's, was that of the eighteenth-century man-of-letters. But such a world is no longer viable; the writer/reader is inexorably drawn into the sensationalist's perception of reality. Thackeray can take his stand against the invader, and repel the 'bloated corpus' of sensation fiction with his magazine cutter, but the act itself taints him with that very style he seeks to debase.

Whilst the sensational is both mocked and an invader, so too is realism a problem for the literary tradesman. It is with subtle irony that Thackeray has the lodging house of his early days (those 1830s journalistic days) now occupied by a seedy café, the *Café des Ambassadeurs*, paradoxically frequented by low-looking characters, and a photographer's studio. In a parody of Thackeray's own aims at realistic representation, the photographer's *charge-d'affairs* calls out to him, 'Step in, and 'ave it done. Your correct likeness, only one shilling' (XXIV, 25). Realism and commerce meet in the shilling portraitist.

Throughout the *Roundabout Papers* and *The Adventures of Philip*, this tension exists between the aesthetic of the real and the fascination of the sensational. In some ways, the interface is an 1860s version of the repulsion/fascination theme that Thackeray correlates with sexual women (Becky Sharp) and journalism earlier in his career. Once again, this theme is complicated by the process of textual mediation that Thackeray consciously exploits and critiques. Thackeray must use the tricks of his profession, even though their very presence in the text undermines the thesis of realism he wishes to employ. It is a very postmodern perception of the problems of artifice and authentic representation.

Before I discuss Thackeray's tale 'The Notch on the Axe', I must tease out further the connections between sensationalism and realism in the fiction of the day, and Thackeray's discussion of this in the *Roundabout Papers*. When Thackeray began the *Cornhill Magazine*, the literary sensation of the day was undoubtedly Wilkie Collins' *The Woman in White*. This novel, published in *All the Year Round* (26 November 1859 – 25 August 1860), brought a new Gothic sensibility to the Victorian middle-class household both in its subject matter and in its appeal to modern readers. Thackeray might have had reservations about its narrative techniques, but he sat up all night to finish the story.[33] In a *Roundabout Paper*, 'De Finibus', *The Woman in White* is one of his chosen entertaining novels, 'the thrilling "Woman in White" … gave me amusement from morning till sunset' and becomes familiarly referred to as 'the *W. in W.*'.[34] Elsewhere, he calls it, 'the cold-shudder-inspiring "Woman in White"'.[35] His reaction is the same as his earlier response to popular romances: 'read we must, and in spite of ourselves'.[36]

Collins set in motion a trend for sensation fiction which saw Dickens write his darker cliff-hanger, *Great Expectations*, and Bulwer's return to occult fiction with *A Strange Story* (*All the Year Round*, 10 August 1861 – 8 March 1862). Mary Braddon's *Lady Audley's Secret* appeared in 1862 and Thackeray saw a performance of a play (by George Roberts) based on the book at the St James's Theatre on 28 April 1863.[37] When *The Adventures of Philip* commenced in January 1861, *Great Expectations* had reached Chapter 8, and yet Thackeray's novel was to see out the whole of Bulwer's text and the first 'scene' of Collins' *No Name*, such was the difference between the weekly and the monthly serial. I have discussed the portrayal of the newspaper world in *Philip* already; here, I want to concentrate on the novel's relationship to sensation fiction and 'The Notch on the Axe'.

Firstly, though, it is worth noting a connection to *Lovel the Widower*. Thackeray echoes his earlier tale in the first number. There are references to

Hamlet again, amongst the dismal ornaments of Dr Firmin's house. The death of Philip's mother has left behind 'a harp smothered in a leather bag in the corner'; whilst 'everybody's face seemed scared and pale in the great looking-glasses, which reflected you over and over again into the distance, so that you seemed to twinkle off right through the Albany into Piccadilly'.[38] The novel once again betrays its conscious self-referentiality and is thereby linked to the themes of the preceding work. But the novel's scope is far greater than that of *Lovel*, and Thackeray is clearly attempting to give his fiction an imaginative leap by boldly declaring his resistance to new literary fashions. Where Dickens' Philip Pirrip is metamorphosed into the metaphor of a 'Pip', a seed in readiness to grow whichever way mind and culture will take it, Thackeray's Philip stubbornly resists such transformation. Throughout the novel, Philip is an irritant and, as the subtitle intimates ('The Adventures of Philip on his way through the world, showing who robbed him, who helped him, and who passed him by') lacking in the self-analysis of a Pendennis or a Batchelor. He is spoilt and boyish, brash and even violent. But he is also unrelentingly honest and never hides his true feelings, even when this costs him friendships and fortunes that might have been gained through sycophancy or flattery. He is more of a solid 'Fact' than an adapting and changing body like Pip. However, this intransigence is certainly not evolved or naturalistic.

The narrative, too, might be seen as an expression of Thackeray's dislike of the sensation romance. At the opening of the story, the narrator describes a scene between Dr Firmin and his son, Philip, in which

> The old man glared at the young one, who calmly looked his father in the face. Wicked rage and hate seemed to flash from the doctor's eyes, and anon came a look of wild pitiful supplication towards the guest, which was most painful to bear. In the midst of what dark family mystery was I? What meant this cruel spectacle of the father's terrified anger, and the son's scorn? (X, 111)

The 'mystery' is established in the usual sensation manner; it is the middle-class family torn apart by dark secrets. However, Thackeray destroys any suspense that this might generate by, a few pages later, offering the reader a glimpse of the ending of the novel, the future to which the central characters will be propelled. The tale will be an ordinary one and will end in an ordinary and not an extraordinary fashion. This is only the first instalment of the novel and Thackeray has already told his readers the ending! It is a putting of extraordinary faith in the power of his telling of the tale to maintain reader interest. But it is also, more directly, a critique of the artificial methods of suspense used by Dickens and Collins. Having begun to describe Philip's schooldays, the narrator suddenly drags the reader back into his own present:

> He [Philip] with whom we have mainly to do is a gentleman of mature age now walking the street with boys of his own. He is not going to perish in the last chapter of these memoirs – to die of

> consumption with his love weeping by his bedside, or to blow his brains out in despair, because she has been married to his rival, or killed out of a gig, or otherwise done for in the last chapter but one. No, no; we will have no dismal endings. Philip Firmin is well and hearty at this minute, owes no man a shilling, and can enjoy his glass of port in perfect comfort. So, my dear miss, if you want a pulmonary romance, the present won't suit you. So, young gentleman, if you are for melancholy, despair, and sardonic satire, please to call at some other shop. That Philip shall have his trials is a matter of course – may they be interesting, though they do not end dismally. (X, 116)[39]

This rejection of the artificial and the narrative of readerly suspense is central to Thackeray's continued striving for realism. It helped to establish a binary in writing between the romance and nineteenth-century forms of realism. The evasion of the sensational happens explicitly in places. When General Baynes and Colonel Bunch and their wives argue over Philip's marriage to Charlotte Baynes, and nearly fight a duel, Thackeray notes how they had all been 'sitting over a powder-magazine' but never realized, and he would have depicted the fight, '[w]ere your humble servant anxious to harrow his reader's feelings, or display his own graphical powers … ' (XI, 113). He wishes neither and the occasion passes from melodrama to a realism based on parody.

The influence of the realist aesthetic, and possibly of Thackeray's approach, can be found in the preface and design of Collins' novel, *No Name*, which commenced two months before the end of *Philip*. Collins declared that he wished throughout 'a resolute adherence … to the truth as it is in Nature'. The design suggests a conscious decision to switch 'sides' – indeed, in 1864, a few months after Thackeray's death, Collins moved to the *Cornhill Magazine* and published *Armadale* (November 1864 to June 1866). In *No Name*, he declares,

> … it will be seen that the narrative related in these pages has been constructed on a plan, which differs from the plan followed in my last novel [*The Woman in White*], and in some other of my works published at an earlier date. The only Secret contained in this book, is revealed midway in the first volume. From that point, all the main events of the story are purposely foreshadowed, before they take place – my present design being to rouse the reader's interest in following the train of circumstances by which these foreseen events are brought about. In trying this new ground, I am not turning my back in doubt on the ground which I have passed over already. My one object in following a new course, is to enlarge the range of my studies in the art of writing fiction, and to vary the form in which I can make my appeal to the reader, as attractively as I can.[40]

The narrative of *No Name* has some similarities to *Philip*, in that it stems from a father's near-bigamy. Vanstone Senior's first marriage was made in haste as a young man and collapsed, but his relationship with his second 'wife' began outside of wedlock, producing two daughters, until the first wife died. Vanstone then marries his wife to legitimize the union, but is killed in a train accident before his will can be amended, and his wife dies from shock-induced complications to her late pregnancy, thus disinheriting the children who, in law, have 'No Name'. *Philip* also develops from bigamy. As with *Lovel the Widower*, Thackeray once again returns to an old piece of writing, the unfinished *A Shabby Genteel Story*, serialized in *Fraser's Magazine* in 1841, and cut short by the suicide attempt and mental collapse of his wife. Caroline Gann, a lower-class girl, is seduced into a false marriage by Brandon; in *Philip*, Brandon, now Dr George Brand Firmin, is married again to a wealthy heiress, Louisa Ringwood, deceased at the start of the novel. Mrs Brandon's claims on Firmin are revealed, thus creating a tug-of-war over Philip's legitimacy and inheritance by the family of his second wife. When Firmin proves his son's legitimacy and the sham nature of the first marriage, he also reveals that he has already spent Philip's inheritance, thus forcing him, like the Vanstone daughters, to make his own way in the world. Thackeray constructs the parent–child relationship as an inescapable bond of influence which affects the subsequent generation; for Philip, '[h]is father was his fate ... and there were no means of averting it' (XI, 251). But the parent is no guardian or guide; here, the doctor is a leech, drawing money from his child like blood from a patient (XI, 250). Collins' plot is more typically sensational, despite its plea for a 'natural' and organic plot. It is more formulaic in its division of good daughter/bad daughter. But it is interesting how the two texts overlap from their writers' given niches: Collins adapts a model of realism, whilst Thackeray once again confronts the invading motifs of the sensational. In Thackeray's text, the chloroforming of Tufton Hunt in the second volume is only one example, for instance, of an infiltration of medical discourse more usually found in the sensation genre.

Once again the theme of the past asserting its influence on the present is located in the text. It is almost as if Thackeray directly returned to the magazine writings of the 1830s and 1840s in order to consummate the redefinition of the self in the periodical market-place. As he comments in 'Notes of a Week's Holiday', '[a] man can be alive in 1860 and 1830 at the same time, don't you see? Bodily, I may be in 1860, inert, silent, torpid; but in the spirit I am walking about in 1828, let us say; – in a blue dress-coat and brass buttons ... '.[41] Sir George Thrum, from *The Ravenswing*, appears yet again (as in *Lovel*), this time as the music teacher of the Ringwoods, and Philip meets the Ravenswing herself, thinking her a fallen woman (XI, 229, 216). But it is the whole imaginative return to the beginnings of his career that is again central to the narrator's engagement with the world. The writer's history is text. He writes:

> Every man who lives by his pen, if by chance he looks back at his writings of former years, lives in the past again. Our griefs, our pleasures, our youth, our sorrows, our dear, dear friends, resuscitate.

> How we tingle with shame over some of those fine passages! How dreary are those disinterred jokes! (XI, 130-31)

The act of narrative, for Thackeray, is always closely associated with memory. His earliest substantial novels, *Catherine*, *Barry Lyndon* and *Vanity Fair*, were all historical novels, and, although closer to its origins, *Pendennis* (1848-50) was set back in the world of the 1830s and early 1840s. *The Newcomes* and *Philip* both return to this world, and the chronic distance gradually increases. Like the Dickens of 'The Haunted Man', Thackeray is reaching for an understanding of the self through a confrontation with the past. Comically likening the writer to a dentist, and about to put his main characters through the pain of drawing their teeth (that is, recalling painful moments in their lives), he says meditatively, '[a]nd yet they remain, they remain and throb in after life, those wounds of early days...So have we all suffered...and years and years, maybe, after, as you think of it, the smart is renewed, and the dismal tragedy enacts itself over again' (XI, 49-50).

Commentators have considered *Philip* a painful return for Thackeray to the point of his wife's debilitating collapse and the end of his married life. Certainly, the resurrection of *A Shabby Genteel Story* connotes this. A note by Thackeray in the 1857 volume of *Miscellanies* where the tale was reprinted, states how the 'tale was interrupted at a sad period of the writer's own life ... the memory of past is renewed as he looks at it ... '.[42] But Thackeray in 1857 was already engaged in extending a footnote of *Henry Esmond* into *The Virginians* and fulfilling an idea expressed in a letter to George Smith some years earlier.[43] Continuity is a significant feature of Thackeray's writings. However in 1857 he had decided that '[i]t is best to leave the sketch, as it was ... '.[44] *Philip* then is a kind of bigamous text, simultaneously wedded to an earlier age, and now also joined to the revitalized Thackeray of the 1860s magazine world.

Thackeray's redefining of a new authorial identity for himself in the *Cornhill Magazine* was a complex process. It involved a sense of the cultural psychology of authorship: the contemporary meaning of what it was to be a writer. But it also involved a re-examination of the author's own past, his life and career, and the continuing authorial persona built up across the decades in the magazines and serial novels. In the first year of the *Cornhill Magazine*, Thackeray introduced a whole range of figures from his earlier writings; not merely characters and narrators, or scenes and memories, but phrases and ideas. He gives the impression, above all, of a textual self mediated through the periodicals and newspapers of the mid-nineteenth century. The image of the writer is a construct of several things: the critics' responses to his writings,[45] of readers' responses, of the relationship with other rival periodicals and writers. The writer's identity thus comes to be restructured alongside the journal through which his voice is mediated. No longer independent, as he was in the novels of the 1850s, Thackeray returns to the public sphere where texts are always relative to each other, in constant comparison and intertextual relation, and where the authorial ego becomes text, becomes the magazine.

Thackeray perhaps found this return a difficult one to make. He brought his past into the present in an attempt to establish a coherent corpus for the self, a continuity. But the schism between the periodical world of the 1830s and that of the 1860s was widening, and Thackeray's writings give the impression of a writer trying both to adapt and to remain the same through confrontation. If Thackeray saw a parallel between Newgate fiction and sensation fiction which helped him to conceptualize his reaction to the latter – just as *Catherine* had defined itself in opposition to the popular crime novels of Ainsworth, Bulwer and Dickens – he was caught up in a more problematic paradox between his mature realism and the desire to involve fascinating components of sensationalism.

'The Notch on the Axe' represents this schism most clearly. Significantly, it was published immediately after Thackeray's resignation as editor of the *Cornhill* and hence at that moment when his newly defined self struck for a regaining of independence from the mediating product of the magazine. Significantly, too, it is an assumption of the serial form, a three-part *Roundabout Paper* and a disruption of the usual style and content. The serial breaks replicate the sensational suspense-narratives of the current fashionable genre of Sensation fiction; they force the reader of the *Roundabout Papers* to experience the genre itself in this parodic form. The story is structured around a narrator who listens to a tale told him by Pinto, a Count Fosco-type of dominating personality, who is also part of the tradition of Thackerayan braggadoccios and charlatans, Major Gahagan, Barry Lyndon, and even George Brand Firmin. The parody itself bridges the distance in time between the Newgate fiction of the 1830s and 1840s and the modern sensation writings. It suggests how the modern genre is not so much a new vogue as the recasting of an old one. Thackeray's last unfinished novel, *Denis Duval*, appears to be in this style too, invoking the military picaresque novels of a Lever.[46]

The parody is a form of literary criticism for Thackeray, and in this way it bridges such time gaps too. It returns the reader of Thackeray to the mocking satires on Bulwer-Lytton's works, such as 'Epistles to the Literati. No. XIII. Ch–s Y-ll-wpl-sh, Esq. To Sir Edward Lytton Bulwer, Bart.', *Fraser's Magazine* (January 1840) and 'Punch's Prize Novelists', *Punch* (3 April – 9 October 1847). Here again Bulwer-Lytton is the main target of his satire. Interestingly, though, Thackeray compounds two Bulwer novels in his narrative: the contemporary *A Strange Story*, which had ended the previous month in *All the Year Round*, and the earlier *Zanoni* (1845), also bridging the time period. Both of these novels involve the occult and Rosicrucianism; 'Dat vich ve call a Rosicrucian by any other name vil smell as sweet', he jokes.[47]

'The Notch on the Axe' also involves a bewildering concoction of spiritualism, mediumship, and mesmerism. The narrator is held in thrall by the conversation of his 'friend' the Count de Pinto, who tells him about a guillotine with a notch in its blade that he was shown in the back of a shop. A headless man, a ghost, emerges and Pinto recounts the tale of his beheading, in which he played a part. This is the Chevalier Goby de Mouchy, who, as a member of a secret freemasonry sect, gives away the secret rules to Pinto's beloved, Blanche de Bechamel. She dies suddenly and de Mouchy is placed in a trance by Pinto and led to his death at the guillotine. The story over, Pinto uses a spirit hand (of the narrator's grandmother) called up from beyond the veil to sign a cheque in payment for a trinket bought from the narrator. The narrator tries to bank the cheque, but it is refused, until the hand reappears and blackmails the clerk into paying! The narrator then awakens from a dream, the trinket, a snuff-box, is still on his table, 'and by its side one of those awful – those admirable – sensation novels, which I had been reading, and which are full of delicious wonder'.[48] He adds, 'If the fashion for sensation novels goes on, I tell you I will write one in fifty volumes', and, with a wink at the power of such fiction, he feels 'rather sorry to lose' his mysterious adventurer, Pinto.[49]

The tale parodies the sensation genre by running through the various fashions in the popular varieties of the form. It incorporates the occult, ghosts, levitation, spiritualism, mediumship, the elixir of life, human immortality, table-tapping and spirit manifestations, metaphysical discussion and Rosicrucianism, mesmerism, trances and control through will-power. The tale draws explicit comparison to the fashion for such materials in the periodicals of the 1860s, including an article published in the *Cornhill Magazine* itself. Mocking the superficiality of sensation metaphysics, Thackeray writes:

> Is life a dream? Are dreams facts? Is sleeping being really awake? I don't know. I tell you I am puzzled. I have read 'The Woman in White,' 'The Strange Story' – not to mention that story 'Stranger than Fiction' in the *Cornhill Magazine* – that story for which THREE credible witnesses are ready to vouch. I have had messages from the dead; and not only from the dead, but from people who never existed at all. I own I am in a state of much bewilderment: but, if you please, will proceed with my simple, my artless story.[50]

The reference to an article in the *Cornhill Magazine* helps to contextualize Thackeray's parody further. This piece, a description of a séance attended by the author of the article, purported to raise a debate about such phenomena as are seen at seances by asserting how 'real' they appeared to be. The seance was run by D.D. Home, the Victorian spiritualist, and featured the usual rappings, music and noises, and ectoplasmic manifestations. The whole topic was a popular one; Dickens mocked it in 'Well-Authenticated Rappings', Browning in 'Mr. Sludge, the Medium'. *All the Year Round* covered the subject several times, including in an article entitled 'Strange but True'.[51]

For the *Cornhill* to intervene in the spirit world was perhaps unusual. Thackeray, as editor, added a disclaimer to the front page of the article, demonstrating how cautious the magazine had to be towards such a topic.[52] Later in the magazine, FitzJames Stephen published two articles, on 'Spiritualism' and 'Superstition', which had to dismiss correspondents' views that in publishing the earlier article, the *Cornhill* was accepting the arguments for the existence of spirits. Stephen sets out to rubbish such views.[53]

Thackeray's writings then, the development of his realist aesthetic at this stage in his career, were closely related to the developments in other genres of fiction and even in the whole anti-materialist backlash against the evolutionary scientists. But Thackeray also interestingly occupies a position that refuses either end of the binary scale. In a late *Roundabout Paper*, 'Autour de Mon Chapeau', he refers to G.H. Lewes's recent *Seaside Studies*, which, influencing George Eliot of course, insists on a close objective analysis of natural phenomena as the basis for truth. 'Go, Lewes,' Thackeray cries, 'and clap a hideous sea-anemone into a glass: I will put a cabman under mine, and make a vivisection of a butcher.'[54] For Thackeray, people are more important and more complex. Indeed, as we have seen, it is the subjective self that sits at the centre of his writings, albeit a mediated subjectivity.

Bulwer-Lytton's *A Strange Story* is at the centre of the parody in 'A Notch on the Axe'. Pinto is a parody of Bulwer's central character, Margrave, who professes to great age and wisdom and has lived beyond man's lifespan through the possession of an elixir of life. During the novel, he has run short of the liquid and seeks to recreate it with the help of the narrator, Dr Allan Fenwick, a materialist and, later, Margrave's enemy. The control of the mind of Dr Fenwick's beloved, Lilian Ashleigh, even forcing her into a sleepwalking trance, also occurs in the novel. Thackeray parodies a number of characteristics and scenes directly. Pinto looks 'more than a hundred' and 'may be a thousand years old for what I know'.[55] He is a figure of memory, living simultaneously in the historical past (talking of historical figures he knew) and the present, not unlike Thackeray's own projection of himself at this period. He 'spoke all languages with an accent equally foreign'[56] and hence mocks the conventional alien nature of the sensation protagonist (Count Fosco, for instance). His great age is comically exaggerated in the details of his false appurtenances: he has false teeth, a glass eye, false hair, and even a wooden leg. This in itself recalls one of Thackeray's first braggard/narrators: Augustus Wagstaff from the *Paris Literary Gazette*. The boredom the narrator feels at hearing Pinto's endless metaphysical speculations is one of Thackeray's usual criticisms of Bulwer's style. Pinto takes his elixir in the presence of the narrator, 'a light green and violet flame flickering round the neck of the phial',[57] and, in a parody of a scene in *A Strange Story* where Sir Philip Derval renders the doctor unconscious, the narrator sees Pinto levitate to the ceiling and grin down on him, an effect attributed by Pinto to the fumes of his medicine. The hypnotic control of Lilian in Bulwer's story, in which she is entranced and forced to sleepwalk under Margrave's power, is replicated in the sleepwalk of Goby de Mouchy to his death. Both central characters are all-powerful, omniscient figures, who know the inner thoughts of their 'victims'.

On one level, then, 'The Notch on the Axe' is a critical parody of Bulwer's current fiction, and of sensation fiction more generally. It occupies a place in Thackeray's defining of his aesthetic practices and seeks to parody romance in order to further the growing assertion that realism was the most important form of narrative fiction. However, it also occupies a more symbolic position in Thackeray's writings for the *Cornhill Magazine*. Coming immediately after his resignation of the editorship, it suggests a further reassessment of the role of the writer himself. I would contend that the story functions also as a comic problematization of the mediated voice of the periodical, and a consideration of Thackeray's own status as essayist-journalist in the magazine.

The role of the Count de Pinto in the story is one which parallels Thackeray's own as the authoritative voice in the *Roundabout Papers* themselves and, indeed, more widely in his fiction. Pinto interprets signs, the 'notch' or damage on the blade of the guillotine, just as Thackeray does, for instance with his meditation on the chalk-mark on his own door.[58] Both present the reader with an interpretation which seeks to be taken as authoritative, but which is deeply subjective. They are mediators of meaning in their texts. Thackeray brings together questions of subjectivity, authority, and personality – common themes in his works. As he admits in the *Roundabout Papers,* it is his 'sensibility' that produces his writing and also gains him critics. The unifying principle throughout his works is his ego, his personality. The digressive and discursive style of his writings subjugates plot to exegesis and analysis. Thus it is that Thackeray has to assert a desire to break from his usual approach and write a novel which is all plot. Certainly, until the arrival of the sensation novel as a 'serious' form in the 1860s, such 'popular' plot-based romances had never been considered intellectual or artistic. Indeed, the several references to Ann Radcliffe in the *Roundabout Papers* may be taken as indicative of Thackeray's belief that intellectual Gothic is possible but is not like the present publications. He notes that 'our novels are but for a season', i.e. transcient and fashionable, and, unlike Radcliffe's *Mysteries of Udolpho,* Sue's *Mysteries of Paris* have 'ceased to frighten'.[59]

Throughout 'The Notch on the Axe', there are allusions which connect the story to other *Roundabout Papers* and other of Thackeray's texts. For example, the narrator/Thackeray 'under the influence of that astounding MEDIUM into whose hands I had fallen', thinks himself 'sleep-walking' or even writing as he sleep-walks.[60] In 'On Some Late Great Victories', a paper which is all about the success of the first six numbers of the *Cornhill Magazine*, Thackeray mocks a newspaper report of his presence at a boxing-match, saying that if he had been there 'I must have walked to the station in my sleep, paid three guineas in a profound fit of mental abstraction, and returned to bed unconscious'.[61] The narrator is present at Pinto's chambers in Shepherd's Inn because the Count has told him that 'I could give you the clue to the mystery of the Two Children in Black', a running joke in the second *Roundabout Paper*.[62] There is also an allusion to the story of Judith and Holofernes, a statue of which Goby de Mouchy sees as he enters Guillotin's house prior to his own decapitation. Thackeray draw an illustration for this in *Philip*, and the scene between Mrs Brandon and Tufton Hunt where she administers the chloroform makes specific allusion to it as well (XI, 254, 271). The effect of these references is to make the story part of the texture of the *Roundabout Papers* as a whole; it is both discreet parody and part of a continuity of theme and style. This is, of course, part of Thackeray's art. Indeed, in 'De Finibus', a *Roundabout Paper* written to coincide with the end of the run of *Philip*, and which followed 'The Notch on the Axe', Thackeray says of his central characters from his novels, Pendennis, Clive Newcome, and Philip Firmin, 'some folks are utterly tired of you, and say, "What a poverty of friends that man has! He is always asking us to meet those Pendennises, Newcomes, and so forth. Why does he not introduce us to some new characters? ... "'.[63] This interplay between texts helps to cement together Thackeray's authorial identity and generate a corporate coherence for the *Cornhill Magazine*.

In addition to these general allusions, Pinto projects elements of Thackeray's authorial persona. He is able to range across history as a repository of memories and histories. His interest, like Thackeray's, is in biography and he introduces the narrator to his anecdotes of Joshua Reynolds and Oliver Goldsmith, figures of Queen Anne's reign, and Napoleon – all characters significant enough in Thackeray's own studies. (At this period, Thackeray was building his house at 2 Palace Green, Kensington, in the Queen Anne style.) Pinto is also adept at narrative digression, like Thackeray. His self-absorbed reminiscences are a parody of Thackeray's own, and the narrator finds his concentration drifting away from his companion after 'he had been carrying on for about fifty-seven minutes; and I don't like a man to have *all* the talk to himself'.[64]

If Pinto is meant to represent a version of Thackeray, then what of Goby de Mouchy? This is an interesting figure, as he is himself an echo of an earlier Thackeray character. 'Gobemouche' is a journalist-reporter for French newspapers in several sketches published in *Punch* in the late 1840s. As such, he was an exposer of secrets, whereas here he is murdered for speaking out about the secrets of the Rosicrucian brotherhood to which he belongs. It is the woman, Blanche, who is his downfall – unable to keep the secret he confides to her. But Goby de Mouchy might be seen as a representative of an older order of truth and writing. For Thackeray, the periodical in the 1860s has changed from the newspapers and magazines to which he contributed in his earlier career. Here, he symbolizes the death of such designs behind journalism as a revealer of the truth. The true meaning of the 'notch' on the axe blade is the loss of honesty and objectivity in the press. This is a consistent theme throughout the *Roundabout Papers*, as I have endeavoured to demonstrate. 'The Notch on the Axe' is about power, authority, control, and the manipulation of an audience. As such, it reflects once more Thackeray's genuine concerns with the sensationalization of the press and its mediation of the world through its desires for profit and sales. That he is part of this world, too, makes his concerns all the more self-reflexive and ambivalent. The story is not just a critique of Bulwer's work, it is also an imaginative engagement with his own. Pinto is the reverse of Thackeray's authorial and authoritative discourse. As with the characters in *Lovel the Widower*, Thackeray is both Pinto and the nameless narrator. The mediation of the story is a complex one.

The Roundabout Papers offer a final glimpse into Thackeray's continued association with the mid-nineteenth-century periodical press. His return to the magazine fold is a significant one. It demonstrates how difficult it was at the time for a writer to remain independent of the publishing houses and their modern print vehicles, the modern media. Although Thackeray could write that it was the age of steam which heralded social change in the Victorian period, he still remarks the print age as significant: 'gunpowder and printing tended to modernise the world. But your railroad starts the new era, and we of a certain age belong to the new time and the old one.'[65] The newspaper and magazine become the real inspirations behind the discourses on life that form the *Roundabout* meditations. Although Thackeray recasts the focus of the titles to suggest an essayist's eclecticism, many of the papers begin and end with reference to the published press. 'On Ribbons' begins with news reports of the bravery of merchant seamen; 'Dessein's' with *The Times*' complaints against the cost of the hotel; 'On a Pear-tree' with the *Saturday Review's* notice of the imprisonment of a friend; 'On Screens in Dining-rooms' with the *Saturday Review's* attacks on the *Cornhill* proprietor. Many more papers contain several references to the magazine world of the period and make comments on the views of the world presented by writers in other magazine stables.

The newspaper is a pervasive influence in Thackeray's life, and it constantly punctuates his surroundings. 'A news-boy had stopped in his walk', he begins 'On Some Late Great Victories', 'and was reading aloud the journal which it was his duty to deliver'.[66] The enraptured audience of an orange-girl and a young crossing-sweeper show just how penetrating newsprint had become. Thackeray's concerns for the effects of such mediated versions of reality stretch into the future and the continued growth of print culture. As he demonstrates in 'Strange to Say on Club Paper', the interpretation placed upon the world by the press was often not for the truth but for the story. This *Roundabout Paper* comments on a notice of a death in the *Observer*, which announces that the will and testament of the late Lord Clyde was 'strange to say' written on paper from the Athenaeum club. The newspaper's intimation is that Clyde had stolen the notepaper, and was therefore questionable as a gentleman. Thackeray, also a member of the club, points out, however, that Clyde's solicitor was a club member too and had drafted a will whilst at the club and sent it for Clyde's signature. The explanation is an innocent one; the newspaper had little interest in such innocence. The media signifier 'strangeness' was permeating social discourse and casting doubt on the innocence of man. For the purveyor of periodicals, the middle-class home was a seed-bed of corrupt desires and activities, the darker side of mankind was emerging. However, for Thackeray, this kind of attitude, is a modern and mercantile phenomenon. 'There is an enjoyment of life in these young bucks of 1823,' he says of *Tom and Jerry*, 'which contrasts strangely with our feelings of 1860'.[67] The press has not so much enlightened us, and enriched our world-view, as made the world strange to those who believe its textual representation to be unmediated by the power of popular journalism.

Notes

[1] For a brief history of the *Cornhill Magazine*, see Ray, *Wisdom*, 293-321; Andrew Blake, *Reading Victorian Fiction* (London: Macmillan, 1989), 88-96; Walter E. Houghton (ed.), *The Wellesley Index to Victorian Periodicals, 1824-1900* (Toronto: Routledge and Kegan Paul, 1966-89), I, 321-4, (listings, 325-415).
[2] Thackeray described it as having 'a sound of jollity and abundance about it'; letter to George Smith, 4 October 1859; *Letters*, IV, 156; Ray, *Wisdom*, 294.
[3] N.N. Feltes, *Modes of Production*, 28-9.
[4] On print runs of Thackeray's novels, see Shillingsburg, *Pegasus*, 75-7, which shows that *Pendennis* and *The Newcomes* were his largest selling works.
[5] Solveig C. Robinson, 'Editing Belgravia: M.E. Braddon's Defense of "Light Literature"', *Victorian Periodicals Review*, 28: 2 (Summer 1995), 109-22.
[6] Letter to George Smith, 7 September 1859; *Letters*, IV, 150.
[7] Edwards, *Dickens's "Young Men"*, 59-68.
[8] A letter to Smith shows that they had discussed the coincidence, Thackeray deciding 'as the posters are out, let Philip stand – and see if we can't make a good fight against tother Philip'; letter to George Smith, December 1860; Edgar F. Harden, *The Letters and Private Papers of William Makepeace Thackeray: A Supplement*, 2 vols (New York/London: Garland, 1994), II, 1007.
[9] *Lovel the Widower, Works*, XXIV, 3 [references in the text are to this edition].
[10] Ray, *Wisdom*, 296.
[11] Ibid., 320-21.
[12] *Works*, XXII, 26.
[13] In 'On Two Children in Black', for instance, a reader-friend is pleased to note that Thackeray had 'left off that Roundabout business', *Works*, XXII, 10, an echo of the *National Standard* reader who complained of the magazine's tone; *National Standard*, 50 (14 December 1833)
[14] Ibid., 8, 10, which talks of the essays being collected as a volume in the future (this is only the third).
[15] Peters, 263.
[16] Harden, *Serial Fiction*, 220-21.
[17] *Works*, XXII, 10.
[18] Ibid.

[19] See 'Travelling Abroad', *The Uncommercial Traveller*; D. Pascoe (ed.), Charles Dickens, *Selected Journalism, 1850-1870* (London: Penguin, 1997), 193-203.
[20] *Works*, XXII, 6.
[21] Peters, 264.
[22] Ray, *Wisdom*, 234-5; Harden, *Serial Fiction*, 220.
[23] See Valerie L. Gager, *Shakespeare and Dickens: The dynamics of influence* (Cambridge: CUP, 1996), 226-9, which discusses the pervasive influence of *Hamlet* on *David Copperfield*.
[24] This event provides a covert identification of Batchelor with Major Dobbin who rejects Glorvina in the earlier novel.
[25] Lovel is also the name of Scott's character in *The Antiquary* (1816), where he represents youth in contrast to the Antiquary's age; this novel is also about the power of the past to invoke meaning in the present. Scott notes in this novel, however, that 'Lovel' is a common fictional name for a Romantic hero (35), such as in Clara Reeve's *The Old English Baron* (1777), 378, n.35.21; Walter Scott, *The Antiquary*, ed. David Hewitt (London: Penguin, 1998).
[26] Gulliver, 45, suggests that the name derives from a review in the *National Standard*, 53 (4 January 1834) of a periodical entitled the *Lady's Magazine and Museum*.
[27] The periodical here might be the *Original* (1832) (see Appendix 2).
[28] 'On a Lazy Idle Boy', *Works*, XXII, 6-7.
[29] See, for example, his reviews of the annuals for *The Times* (2 November 1838) and *Fraser's Magazine* (January 1839).
[30] Andrew Blake describes Trollope's *Framley Parsonage* (*Cornhill Magazine*, January 1860–April 1861) and its 'mutuality of concern with the rest of the magazine's contents', 90; he links the themes of love and marriage to other articles in the *Cornhill*, including Thackeray's *Four Georges* and a series called 'Bird's-eye View of Society' (which he erroneously attributes to Thackeray, but was actually by Richard Doyle); whilst Blake is correct to maintain this intertextual exchange, his use of the *Four Georges* shows the pitfalls of the approach as these lectures were written as early as 1855; Edgar Harden, *Thackeray's English Humourists and Four Georges* (Newark: University of Delaware Press, 1985), 132-3.
[31] This is reminiscent of the comment at the end of *Catherine: A Story* that we are all destined to end our days as newspaper print, announcing our death.
[32] See also the background of Thackeray's illustrations, 23, 116; this image reappears in *Philip* (see below).
[33] Robert Ashley, *Wilkie Collins* (London: Arthur Baker, 1952), 59.
[34] *Works*, XXII, 227.
[35] 'On Two Papers I Intended to Write', *Works*, XXII, 138.
[36] 'Thieves' Literature of France' (review of Eugène Sue, *Les Mystères de Paris*), *Foreign Quarterly Review*, 31 (April 1843), 233.
[37] Diary for 1863; *Letters*, IV, 411.

[38] *The Adventures of Philip*, *Works*, X, 119 [references in the text are to this edition].
[39] Later, *Works*, XI, 47, he writes, 'I tell you they are married; and don't want to make any mysteries about the business. I disdain that sort of artifice. In the days of the old three-volume novels, didn't you always look at the end ... '. *Philip* does not have a triple-decker ending, however, and continues through marriage to the birth of children (*Works*, XI, 182).
[40] W. Wilkie Collins, *No Name* (Oxford: OUP, 1986), 5-6.
[41] *Works*, XXII, 164.
[42] *Works*, X, ix.
[43] Harden, *Serial Fiction*, 138.
[44] *Works*, X, ix.
[45] See, for instance, in 'Thorns in the Cushion', *Cornhill Magazine*, 2 (July 1860).
[46] 'De Finibus', *Works*, XXII, 228.
[47] *Works*, XXII, 216.
[48] Ibid., 222.
[49] Ibid.
[50] Ibid., 205.
[51] Robert Bell, 'Stranger than Fiction', *Cornhill Magazine*, 2 (August 1860), 211-24; [Anon.], 'Strange but True', *All the Year Round*, 16 (August 1862).
[52] Thackeray notes that 'readers are ... free to give or withhold their belief', 'Stranger than Fiction', ibid., 211.
[53] J. Fitzjames Stephen, 'Superstition', *Cornhill Magazine*, 5 (May 1862), 537-49; J. Fitzjames Stephen, 'Spiritualism', *Cornhill Magazine*, 7 (June 1863), 706-19.
[54] *Works*, XXII, 272.
[55] Ibid., 202.
[56] Ibid.
[57] Ibid., 203.
[58] 'On a Chalk-Mark on the Door', *Cornhill Magazine*, 3 (April 1861).
[59] 'On a Peal of Bells', *Works*, XXII, 236.
[60] *Works*, XXII, 206.
[61] Ibid., 30.
[62] Ibid., 204.
[63] Ibid., 223-4.
[64] Ibid., 213.
[65] 'De Juventute', *Works*, XXII, 64.
[66] *Works*, XXII, 29 (and illustrated, 30).
[67] 'De Juventute', *Works*, XXII, 73.

Appendix 1: Three contributions to the *Paris Literary Gazette*, 1835

The following three items appeared in the *Paris Literary Gazette* in 1835 and have never before been reprinted. They are important Thackeray publications as they demonstrate the development of his periodical writings towards the more mature later writings. Augustus Wagstaff is a forerunner of Charles Yellowplush in that he is both comic reviewer and narrator. Whilst 'The Party at Willowford Hall' is clearly an early version of *Mrs. Perkins's Ball* and *The Book of Snobs*.

1. *Paris Literary Gazette*, 4 (17 November 1835), 52-4.
'Narrative of a Second Voyage in Search of a North-West Passage, and of a Residence in the Arctic Regions during the Years 1829, 1830, 1831, 1832, and 1833, by Sir John Ross, C.B.K., S.A.K., C.S. Captain of the Royal navy, etc.'
Letter from Augustus Wagstaff, Esq., on Captain Ross's Second Voyage.
(To the Editor of the *Paris Literary Gazette*)

Respected Sir –
When you were polite enough to desire for your new journal some contributions from the insignificant pen of Augustus Wagstaff, you added, I recollect an opinion regarding my merits as a critic, which my known modesty will forbid me here to mention.

I confess that I expected to have commenced my labours in your journal, either with a profound metaphysical paper, or a touching article in poetry, or a brilliant historical essay; – why, then, did you (entertaining those sentiments regarding me which you have been so pleased to express) send me the unfortunate book which figures at the head of this letter?

Sir, I occasionally read the *Morning Chronicle* newspaper; I have perused Lord Brougham's last article in the *Edinburgh*; I have actually read Mrs. Trollope's new novels; but I declare to you, that Sir John Ross's work, in desperate and undeviating dullness, infinitely exceeds then all three. On the members of my household it has acted like a dose of laudanum. Since its perusal, Mrs. Wagstaff has been in a perpetual doze; – that most lively of women lies in a state of torpidity, which astonishes her servants, accustomed to her eloquence, and her husband, who misses cruelly that ceaseless flow of language, for which you know she was remarkable.

All that I can gather from this bulky volume is, that Sir John Ross, like that king of France recorded by the poet, who 'with twenty thousand men, marched up the hill – and then marched down again,' has been to the North Pole, and has come back again; that he has planted his Majesty's flag upon several islands and tracts of land, the possession of which no monarch in Europe will be such a fool as to dispute; and that the end of his labours, and the glorious reward of his exertions has been – 'permission to dedicate his work to his majesty, and to add the name of William IV. to the magnetic pole!'

Can anything be handsomer on the king's part than this glorious permission? And the further insistence of liberality recorded by Sir John; who, when he applied for this glorious privilege, was desired by the king to write on the chart, not only the august names of William and Adelaide, but those of all the other kings and queens of Europe! So that the magnetic pole will be the most aristocratic spot in the world – as full of kings and queens as a fairy tale.

And though it be true that this, the only discovery of the expedition, was not discovered by Captain Ross, yet, as he says with justice, he was a very few hundred miles off from the spot, he *might* have discovered it had he been there: he was at the head of the whole business, and therefore must have the credit of it. Lieutenant Cassio, when in a state of intoxication, justly asks, 'Shall not a lieutenant go to heaven before an ensign?' How much more, then, must a post-captain be preferred to a commander? The glory of this business entirely appertains to Sir John Ross, and not to Commander Ross, his nephew, who happened to be on the spot when the discovery was made, and who by chance was the first person to ascertain it.

Well, then, Sir John Ross, C.B., K.S.A., K.C.S., etc., Captain in the Royal Navy, the man who did *not* discover the magnetic pole, has given to the world five hundred pages, which contain the history of his virtues and those of his crew. When the men are ill, the captain comments on it. He mentions the sailor's disease, his name and qualities, the remedies employed, the manner in which they acted, and so forth. He describes the state of the weather with the eloquence of a watchman of old; he shows how the crew learnt their catechism, and how they ate their dinner; how it agreed with them, and of what it consisted; how pleasant it is to be on the ice for one's amusement, and how unpleasant to stay there for four years; how the Esquimaux eat blubber, and how they are partial to a jovial glass of train oil; how the men of the Victory took salmon, and shot walruses, and saw polar foxes and polar bears – to which latter animal the gallant knight himself, in his portrait, has no small resemblance. However, comparisons are odious; and I have no right to say that an honourable gentleman and a brave officer is like a polar bear, or any other animal; but I may say, and keep within the limits of politeness, that the captain is a polar BORE, and one of the largest of the specimens ever known in England.

I do not, of course, allude to him as a man, but an author. Now, would it not be more economical, and quite as instructing, to do those travels in Mr. Colburne's back shop? Should that enlightened publisher be inclined to close with the proposition, I can only say, that Augustus Wagstaff is ready, at three months notice, to make a book twice as amusing as the captain's, and equally edifying. My men shall eat twice as much blubber as Captain Ross's, and say their catechism after the fashion of his excellent mariners; and as for the discoveries – why they are, as Sir John says, a mere bagatelle. How can a man discover a thing when he's not near it?

Mrs. Wagstaff, half asleep, as I told you, unfortunately let a large paper of notes fall into the fire, and thus I am deprived of some of the tit-bits of which I intended to dish up an article; so that I can only dip at a venture into the book, and pick up such stray morsels as may be likely to suit the reader's palate.

[Extract from Jan. 28th, when a raven was shot; concludes:]

'In other days, or minds more deeply tinctured with poetry or superstition, I know not what mental misery might not have followed an act so sacrilegious.'

But no; our ancient mariner is not like Coleridge's; it would be unjust to charge him with superstition, and certainly absurd to accuse him of poetry.

'Jan. 30 – Proceeding to the Esquimaux village, we met the wooden-legged man coming alone towards the ship, with a present of an arrow, and with the intention of informing us that Otookiu was sick. We found him with a swelled face.' [Extract continues briefly]

Such, in fact, was the awful dearth of news in this book, that we really hailed with delight the little incident of the wooden-legged man, and felt a tender sympathy for Otookins and his swelled face. If the reader has, by perusing the above extract of the diary, been worked up, like ourselves, to a painful state of excitement, he will be glad to peruse the diary of Feb. 1.

'There was another arrival of Esquimaux on the first day of the new month, with wives and children, and we bought from them dresses. *The man with the swelled face was better*, and brought a bow which he had promised to give us […] one of the women had an ornament on her head, consisting of the head of an owl, with some ermine skins. The temperature was minus 25 degrees, and the day so cloudy, that none of the expected occultations in Taurus could be observed, nor any of the moon-cultivating stars.'

But what are the occultations in Taurus, or the moon-cultivating stars, to the cure of the man with the face, or to the appearance of the lovely and interesting girl whose costume is here touchingly described by the captain? I suppose the Esquimaux Court Journal must have contained a blazing paragraph on the business: – 'Yesterday some of our fashionables were invited to a party, by the commander of the English ship stationed here, and a repast consisting of all the delicacies of the season was provided by the hospitable captain. The train-oil went gaily round, and dancing was kept up to a late hour. Among the most "distinguies toilettes" we remarked the elegant "toque d'hibou," worn by the Hon. Miss R-z-x-g-f-uk, and the beautiful nose-ring of double teeth, *sported* by the *dashing* young Bl-gx-ck. As a novelty, we observed a "queue de sauman," which is worn over the left eye, and gives a particularly arch appearance to the fair wearer. The lovely Z-gl-sh had a necklace of seals *intestines*, one end of which she kept continually in her fascinating mouth – "Why do you wear that necklace?" said Bl-gch. "Because I chews it," was the lovely creature's ready and elegant reply.

Our gentlemen vied with each other in bolting slices of blubber to the King of England's good health – and much curiosity was excited concerning the Prince of Whales.'

It appears that the gallant captain possessed the most fascinating manners, for we learn that –

'A complete female dress had been made ready as a present for me […] In return, I presented this generous lady with a silk handkerchief; being the article, of all that I had shown her, which attracted her chief admiration.'

When captain Sir John Ross, C.B., K.S.A., K.S., etc., was attired in this garment he must have looked perfectly killing. It is a pity he had not been drawn in it, instead of the unmeaning fur-collared coat, which in his portraits, he is made to wear; but of course when he waited on his majesty after his arrival in England, he sported this graceful and becoming costume.

Another fact is also to be observed, with regard to the excellent discoverer, that he has an eye for science, and another for the main chances; witness the silk handerchief which he gives in exchange for the costly and becoming fur gowns; and for the following bargain for fish.

[Extract.]

It was a hard bargain, no doubt – a thousand pounds of salmon for three big knives! But the captain had a conscience, it appears, and did not know what a small sum he was offering.

We extract the whole business of salmon eating, which must greatly edify the English public.

[Extract is a discourse on varied eating habits of man, and the Esquimaux consumption of extraordinary quantities of salmon; concludes:]

'In this way they proceeded till the whole stock of fish was consumed. One of them, afterwards eating the scraps on one of our plates, where there chanced to be some lemon juice, made wry faces, to the great amusement and laughter of the rest. Man seems a laughing animal, as he has been termed, even where he approaches as nearly as he can to his inferiors of four legs.'

And now, Sir, having brought you well through this meal, I leave you at full liberty to *digest* it.

A.W.

2. ***Paris Literary Gazette*****, 8 (15 December 1835), 116-17.**
'A Passage in the Life of Augustus Wagstaff'

When I lost my nose at the battle of Bundlecund, I gave up all claims to be considered a handsome man. The previous poking out of an eye at Futtyghur was a trifle, for I had a very handsome glass one blown by a travelling chokeybader or tinker, which quite cut out the other ball in lustre, expression and general appearance. In fact, it had always been said that my eyes were of too light a colour, being of a greyish green hue, much like the garden fruit called a gooseberry in England; so I had the sham one made of a beautiful black, and black it is to the present hour.

But still I don't know – although, as I say, with but one eye, a stiff knee (shattered by the bursting of a baggage waggon at the affair of Ferruckabad), and a large piece of sticking-plaster covering the spot where once had grown a goodly nose, there *was* a something about me which won the hearts of the dear creatures, as the following adventure will fully prove.

When I left the Honourable Company's service, and retired in half-pay (which, with the little pensions for my hurts makes me tolerably comfortable), I took up my abode in the romantic little village of Stoke Pogis. If you look in the Gazetteer you will see that it is beautifully situated in the fens of Lincolnshire; a coach was within seven miles of the place; there is a church, a reading-room, fourteen public-houses, and a flourishing population of about four hundred souls.

It was there that I became acquainted with Lady Barbara O'Grady, and her two lovely girls, Miss Wilhelmina and Miss Arabella.

Her ladyship was the thirteenth daughter of the Earl of Fitz-Ague; and not being provided by fortune with the means for keeping up her dignity and her exalted name, she had returned to this tranquil village, where she lived in pleasant retirement, occupying a cottage sweetly situated opposite the independent burying-ground. Here might her ladyship be daily seen, sauntering in the little gravel walk, which surrounded her cottage and garden, while her blooming daughters lolled at the parlour window, and bestowed smiles, as tokens of acquaintance, on the passers by.

I need not say that I was one of the happy individuals, who, very speedily after my arrival at Stoke Pogis, made Burying Ground-lane my favourite promenade. Lady Barbara was a widow of forty or thereabouts. She was taller than the generality of women; about five foot nine, I should think, without her shoes, which the cobbler told me were the largest in the parish; had a cheek which would have shamed the rose in hue, or even the red cabbage; and hair of the brightest possible auburn.

As for her daughters, surely, as Burke says, 'there never lighted on the earth two more delightful visions.' Miss Bell had her mother's smile, her golden locks, her commanding figure; and Miss Will, pale and black-haired, who, though her form was not so perfect as her sister's (she was slightly crooked, and wore a steel spit down her poor back), had a genius such as seldom falls to mortals' lot, which manifested itself in every thought and word, and which pervaded her whole frame, from her eyes to the very hump on her back.

Like Othello, the story of the dangers I had run, of my feats in the field or on the eminent deadly breach, made a speedy and favourable impression on the hearts of these ladies.

'Oh Captain Wagstaff,' said Lady Bab, as one day we had been reading the delightful tale of the gentle Desdemona, 'was it not a beautiful stroke of nature in our immortal poet, to have made the simple and delicate being bestow her affections on the stern soldier, who had no attractions but his courage, no charms but his scars?'

'Madam,' said I, 'Othello, being a black-amoor, was doubtless no beauty; and I never heard that a slash across a man's face was considered as pretty as a dimple; but I perfectly agree with your ladyship in thinking, that a soldier is what a woman loves best.'

'Yes, truly,' said she, sighing; 'and she glories, Captain, in her husband's scars. Think you I would have married my O'Grady, had he not been a soldier like yourself. Yes, he was a soldier, a brave soldier; and the veterans of the Clonakilty volunteers still drop a tear when they speak of the untimely doom of their ensign.'

Here the poor thing paused, and wiped away a tear or two. I thought, as I took her hand in mine, and pressed it to my lips, that I had never felt a harder or seen a bigger one. But what matter, said I inwardly, how the hand is, if the heart is in the right place.

'Your feelings do you honour, Lady Bab,' said I, 'and I would weep with you, but that my eyes are dried for many a year' – indeed since I had the accident with one of them, I have never shed a single tear with the other; and to cry with a glass eye is, of course, out of the question.

A great deal more conversation of the like affecting description followed this pathetic burst of her ladyship.

'He was a happy man, madam,' said I, 'Mick O'Grady, to have won such a prize as your ladyship; and blessed will be the person who is destined to stand in his shoes.'

Here Lady Bab sighed, and looked down at her own.

'Yes, Captain,' responded she, ''tis a vulgar error to suppose that the heart once stricken can never recover again; on the contrary, the long habit of happiness cannot so easily be broken through; and those who, like myself, with my blessed Mick, have enjoyed such perfect bliss in the nuptial tie, are not loth to a second marriage, when they see one of their choice.'

'If Ensign O'Grady is a saint, madam,' said I politely, 'you, at least, are an angel, so that you were a well-matched couple any-how.'

And with this I left her.

The next day I had a long and delicious morning's confab with Miss Will, who was as sentimental as her mother.

'You have seen, Captain Wagstaff,' sighed she, 'the dark-eyed beauties of the Eastern climes! did no dusky daughter of Cashmere, no sun-burnt maiden of

Korasan, fix the glances of that roving eye, or melt the icicle of that cruel heart?'

'Oh, Miss Will,' I cried, 'the daughters of Cashmere had no more effect on my natural eye than on my artificial one; and as for my heart, you would surely never suppose that an ignorant black woman, worshipping Mahomet and Juggernaut, eating ghee, and wearing large brass nose-rings, could gain the affections of a Christian soldier and gentleman.'

'They were haply, then, engaged in some other and fairer quarter,' said she, blushing.

'If I might venture to tell you the history, Miss Will O'Grady,' said I, 'you would, I think, pity me and appreciate me,' and then I poured into her ear all the soft things I could think of; and indeed they came to me pretty easily, seeing that I had repeated them all to Lady Bab the morning before.

* * * * * * * * * * * * * * * *

I may be said to be absolutely ugly, said I to myself as I strolled home, and yet, could the handsomest dog in England carry on a love-match with more irresistible skill? Now came a series of civilities on the part of this worthy family; my cover was always laid for dinner, and there were regularly crumpets for tea; in fact, everything was done which could fix my fancy or tickle my palate.

But it was not enough that two ladies in one house should fall in love with me; my cup of happiness was not yet full. It actually came to pass that Miss Bell followed the example of her mother and sister, and became desperately enamoured of one of the modestest and plainest of men.

I became aware of this fact by a very simple and touching incident. One evening, on my departure, Miss Bell presented me with a paper of those delicate cakes called macaroons, which were, and are to this day, the objects of my particular esteem. As I was munching the last of them some few days after, I chanced to look at the paper in which they had been enveloped, and there I saw written in her well-known hand,

Arabella O'Grady.
Arabel – Augustus.
Arabella Wagstaff!

It was too true! I was left to choose any one member of this accomplished family, and was as puzzled to decide as an ass would be between *three* bundles of hay. Never mind, I thought, Lady Bab has still a knife and fork for me at dinner, and a hot crumpet for tea; why should I interrupt the harmony of the charming circle by removing from it one of its members.

So, being perfectly contented with the actual state of things, I determined to let well alone.

Lady Bab never thought it necessary to breathe a word to her daughters concerning her *penchant* for me, nor did the young ladies mention a syllable of their own amours to each other or to their mamma.

Could a half-pay lieutenant be in a more charming situation?

But this Elysian and romantic state of things could not be expected to last long: one unfortunate day, about Christmas time, brought no less than three visitors to the cottage in Burying-ground Lane. There were the Honourable Ulick O'Toole, her ladyship's brother, a lieutenant in the navy, who had retired on a wooden leg and a pension after Lord Howe's action; Michael, Lady Bab's oldest son, settled in the paternal estate at Clonakilty, near Cork; and Samuel Fitz-Ague O'Grady, head clerk to Higgs, Biggs, and Blatherwick, the eminent solicitors.

Well, you may be sure that there was a grand carousel at the cottage, in honour of the arrival of these gentlemen; and, as may naturally be supposed, I, Augustus Wagstaff, was not omitted in the invitations to dinner.

After partaking of one of the most delightful turkies into which I ever had the good fortune to stick a fork, whilst the Port was gaily traversing the polished and hospitable mahogany, Lady Bab said to her brother, 'I am glad, dear Ulick, that you should know this gentleman, Captain Wagstaff, of the 120th regiment of Bengal Infantry, for he is likely soon to become a member of our family.'

Miss Bell blushed, and Miss Will cast her eyes to the ground, and Sam O'Grady, the lawyer, squeezed my hand affectionately. I saw that my time was come, and that now or never I was bound to make my retreat.

'I don't know, gentlemen,' said I, 'how to express my sense of the kindness with which Lady Barbara and her two charming daughters have ever received me. As for being a member of her family, if friendly feeling on my part, and affectionate hospitality on hers, can cause a relationship, I am already most closely bound to you. I never can sufficiently thank her, or the lovely girls, for the care with which they have watched over a poor fellow whose limbs and whose health have been cruelly treated in the service of his country – '

'Dear Captain Wagstaff,' said the three ladies in a breath.

'*I*, I say, can never sufficiently thank them, but there is one who will. My wife, gentlemen, my excellent wife, whom I left behind me in India, has long been made aware of the friendship I have received in this house, and will feel it from the bottom of her soul.'

Here Lady Bab screamed and fainted; the young ladies gave way to an agony of sobs; and I thought it wise to leave them in this pathetic situation, determining to quit Stoke Pogis at the earliest opportunity.

But the next morning at breakfast, I received, at intervals of about a quarter of an hour, the three following notes.

'Sir, – You cannot expect that your base conduct to my sister, the Lady Barbara O'Grady, can be passed over unnoticed by her brother. I demand from you satisfaction, and beg to know when and where you are willing to meet your humble servant,

ULICK O'TOOLE.

'Mr. O'Grady has been informed by his sister, Miss Arabella O'Grady, of the infamous manner in which you have deceived her, and expects from you either instant marriage, or complete satisfaction. Mr. O'Grady begs you will state at what time, and with what weapons, you propose to meet him.'

Sir, – Your conduct to Miss Wilhelmina O'Grady, my sister, has been so infamous, that it leaves me only one course to pursue. I have commissioned my friend, Major Black, to wait on you, and demand that reparation which is due to an injured lady, and to your obedient servant,

SAMUEL O'GRADY

* * * * * * * * * * * * * * *

I trembled when I thought at how dear a price I must pay for my dinners and my propensity to small talk.

'What,' said I to my friend Mahony of the Royal Irish, 'what shall I do in this business? – must I marry Bell, and Will, and Lady Bab – I, who have a wife living – or must I fight the whole squad of kinsmen?'

'It appears,' said he, 'that the three gentlemen know as little of each other's notes, as the ladies do of each other's amours. Accept all three challenges, and we will carry you through the affair as well as may be.'

So I wrote a circular, and accepted the cartel of each. The next morning we were to meet in a field at a short distance from the village.

The morning came. I and my second arrived early on the ground, where, however, we found the old lieutenant had preceded us, pistols in hand.

But presently appeared Sam with his weapons of war, who was speedily followed by Mick, armed to the teeth, and ready to do battle.

The brothers stared, amazed at each other, not knowing why there was so numerous a family attendance.

'Gentlemen,' said I, 'I lost my nose at Bundlecund, my eye at Futtyghur, and my knee was fractured by the blowing up of a baggage-waggon at the affair of Ferruckabad. These will prove to you that I am not averse to fighting, and not exactly fit for making love. But if, in spite of all, your relations *will* fall in love with me, how can I help it?' – And, indeed, how could I?

So the three Irish heroes consulted a while with their seconds, retired, and left me master of the field.

And whenever I am again called upon to fight three men, may I be equally victorious.

A.W.

3. *Paris Literary Gazette*, 9 (22 December 1835), 141-2.
'The Party at Willowford Hall: By One of the Guests'

Country parties at this time of the year are proverbially stupid; at least for us of the *beau sexe*: for the men have not yet had time to get tired of their fox-hunting; and mammas, suffering still from the fatigues of the last 'season', are extra cross with their poor unmarried daughters. Heigho! And I'm sure we can't help it.

There is no walking out: for who can move with any degree of grace in spring-clogs? and as for music and drawing, one can't always be singing 'Tu ch'accendi', and etching Vale Crucis Abbey by moonlight. I have just hit on a plan *pour me disennuyer un peu*, which is, gentle Editor, to give you from time to time some short account of our party here – their characters, plans, and proceedings. I make no apology for taking this liberty with my host and friends; for the practice is too common to need one. As Lord Ashenhunt says every day after dinner, if one can't take liberties with one's friends, who the plague *can* one take liberties with? At least I shall be on my guard about family secrets – though, of course, if they come to my ear they are no longer so: and I shall endeavour not to be too scandalous – for a lady.

To begin with my host. Sir Thomas Smith Willowford is his name. How he came by that name is another thing. His godfathers, I believe, are only answerable for the Thomas Smith portion of it; and the other, they *do* say, was – what do you think? – *bought*. How bought? you will ask. Why, thus the tale goes. That Mrs. Thomas Smith – Mrs. Ex-Thomas Smith, I should say – who is ambitious as Lady Macbeth herself, never ceased twitting her poor husband with his plebian patronymic till he had consented to change it; and that, to bring this about without exciting the ridicule of the world in general – and their *friends* in particular – he entered into a compact with the late Sir Hugh Willowford, then at the last stage of penury and a galloping consumption, by which he undertook to redeem the Willowford estate from three generations of mortgages, and pay down the sum of five thousand pounds, on condition that Sir Hugh would leave him the said estate, with a proviso that he, Smith, should adopt the family name and quarter the Willowford arms in his escutcheon. But people are so very censorious: for my part, I don't believe a word of it. Then, *they say*, Sir Thomas only keeps his fox hounds to oblige his lady, and that it is absolutely *Mazeppaizing* every time he goes out with them, which he is obliged to do about four times a week – bye days exclusive.

But it is time I spoke more particularly of his lady, who is indeed, as the worthy knight says, his better half; or, as the wits at the covert side describe it, his *three-quarters*. With tolerable parts (for the wife of a country squire), and an agreeable person (for a married woman), she might make a very respectable figure in the world. But she is totally uneducated – in the *beau monde*, I mean – and unfortunately for her own, and her husband's peace, she aspires to be a universal genius, a sort of *Admirable Crichtoness*; proposes *bouts rimés* instead of short whist, and is at this moment engaged on an Essay on the life and times of Offa, King of Mercia, by which she hopes to gain celebrity and the Lord Mayor's prize for the best production on that interesting and recondite subject. She has a daughter, who resembles herself – in all her bad points – who doats [*sic*] on philosophy and hates men, performs on an electric machine instead of a pianoforte, looks at the moon through a telescope, and reads latin gravestones.

But enough of the ladies. Our men are both more numerous and more agreeable. First there is young Henry * * * * – but why do I say *first*? And why not write his name in full. Poor Henry! Oh, Mr. Editor, what a shame it is that younger brothers should always be so very fascinating, and Messieurs les frères ainées such horrid bores! How *do* you account for it? Is it that nature tried her 'prentice hand' on the latter, and exerted her finished skill on the others? Heigho! But it's of no use complaining, for mammas are incorrigible. No sooner do they spy one out with a bevy of Mister Henries, or Mister Charleses, or Mister Herberts, but we are assailed with maternal frowns and almost annihilated with maternal scowls.

One of the greatest *characters* at present at Willowford Hall is Mr. Colon, the punctuator of a great book establishment. Lady Willowford became acquainted with *him* through the publication of her last volume of *Sonnets on Various Subjects*, which, bye the bye, didn't *give away* nearly so well as was expected – nay, they do say, that the poor lady, to obtain readers at all, was obliged to make it a class-book at her charity-school; and an anecdote is in circulation in the neighbouring village, that one of the little girls was found crying and being asked if she was afraid of a beating, said 'No: she didn't care about being beaten, but what she was afraid of was being obliged to learn one of Mrs. Willowford's *Various Subjects*.' But to return to our punctuator. Of course, Mr. Editor, you know what a punctuator is: some of your readers may not. I will inform them. He is a gentleman whose business it is to point the manuscripts (lamentably in want of it sometimes?) of amateur authors and authoresses who are not acquainted with the mysteries of commas and semicolons. But our friend is not a punctuator merely – he is an enthusiast. No branch of literature in his opinion (for he dignifies his occupation with that name) is of equal importance, or requires greater genius. 'Ah, Miss – ,' said he to me at breakfast the other morning, 'there are few people in the world who can appreciate the beauties of a finished punctuation. Stops, Miss, are the jewels on which the watch turns. Without them its movements would be abrupt and deceptive. Look at our great poets, Shakespeare, Milton, and the rest; how often has the alteration or omission of a single point altered or mystified the sublimest passages! I am at this moment engaged in a very important and voluminous work – an Essay on the genius and stops of Shakespeare. Bye the bye, talking of essays, have you seen my great work, the Essay on the Antiquity and Importance of the Comma? Permit me to present you with a copy of it. But, as I was saying, there are few, very few, who can feel the beauties of a finished punctuation! Men nowadays seem to think that if they hit on a new idea or pourtray [*sic*] a new character, they have done everything: but how mistaken! The first thing I look to in a new book is the stops: if those are defective, the author is ruined in my eyes forever. 'What do you think of Eugene Aram?' I was once asked. 'Bad,' said I. 'Well, but you must allow the apostrophe to the stars to be sublime.' Sublime! said he yes – if it hadn't been for that semicolon. The fellow laughed, Miss! Will you believe it, the fellow laughed in my face! But I had my revenge.' What! did you call him out, said I? 'No, Ma'am: but I cut up one of his books in the *European, Asiatic, African, American, and Australian Quarterly*.' I could not help smiling at the punctuator's ardour. 'You laugh, too,' said the stopper. Yes, said I; but you can't call me out, and I don't write books for my friends to review in the Quarterlies. This brought Mr. Colon to his good humour again. 'Ah, Miss,' said he, 'I see you are a wag – excuse the word – I don't know the French for it – but depend on it what I say is true: we are fallen on degenerate days: our authors have all of them the same fault – *they don't know how to stop*.'

The next – but stay, I have no room for any *next*; and perhaps I have already exceeded the limits of your patience. If you have any desire to be further acquainted with the *Party at Willowford Hall*, you have only to say so, and you shall hear again from.

ONE OF THE GUESTS.

Appendix 2: Thackeray's contributions to the *Original*, 1832

The following list of contributions to the short-lived comic miscellany, *The Original* (1832), edited by William John Thoms and Henry Plunkett Grattan (Henry Willoughby Grattan Plunkett), may well be Thackeray's. The pieces are in a similar vein to those of the *Western Luminary, The Snob* and *The Gownsman* and, like several of these, are signed 'T.'

The editors of *The Original* have some possible connections with Thackeray. William John Thoms (1803-85) (whose name might suggest him as author of the 'T.' articles) was an antiquarian with interests in European romances. He published a small number of poems in *The Original*, signed 'WJT', of a lyrical and serious style. Between 1827 and 1828, he produced an edition of *Early English Prose Romances* and followed this in 1834 with *Lays and Legends of Various Nations*. A learned and earnest writer, he was yet able to capitalize on market opportunities in publishing, analysing the country's royal institutions in *The Book of the Court* (1838) to coincide with the accession of the new Queen. He had his greatest impact in 1848, when he hit upon the idea for, and, aided by Charles Wentworth Dilke, founded and edited, *Notes and Queries*. Thoms produced 'A Chapter on Clowns' for *Bentley's* in 1838, but this was far more learned and historical and less literary than *The Original* article 'Chapters on Court Fools' (see no. 15 and below).

Henry Plunkett Grattan was a minor dramatist of the 1830s and 1840s. He wrote several plays for Covent Garden, including one based on a series of Cruikshank designs and another co-authored with Mark Lemon. He contributed (as 'Fusbos') to the early numbers of *Punch*, and then set up a rival comic magazine, *The Squib*, in 1842. *The Squib* was very much a *Punch* imitator, containing some very Thackerayan items (for instance, 'Hints for Modern Authors: By One of the Rejected'). Gratton's wife was a Covent Garden actress, whose name constantly appears in the magazine's Drama columns. It is conceivable that Gratton knew Jerrold and A'Beckett in the publishing world of 1832, when all three were launching rival comic rags (*The Original, Figaro in London,* and *Punch in London*).

Internal evidence is strong for the attribution of the 'T.' articles to Thackeray. For instance, one item is a translation from Anacreon, and, although such translations were popular as magazine fillers at this time, Thackeray had translated Anacreon for the *Western Luminary* and *The Gownsman*. Moreover, Pendennis is described as translating 'Anacreon's Odes' and as contributing a poem, 'To a Tear', in his early youthful scribblings (*Pendennis*, Chapter 3). Harold Gulliver identified 'To a Tear' with the verse 'The Tear', signed 'T.', in the *Western Luminary* (paralleled to the *County Chronicle* in which Pen publishes his juvenilia), but there is an unsigned poem in *The Original* entitled 'To a Tear' ('Pure, silent messenger of sympathy!'); see no. 9, below. Futhermore, there is a short story in *The Original*, no. 6 (7 April 1832), 81-3, entitled 'Boarding-House Bores: From Mrs. Lavinia Lettsom to the Editor of the Original', signed 'Letitia Lettsom', which also sounds Thackerayan. This coincides with Thackeray's letter to Fitzgerald, noting his own 'fictitious and poetical forehead', and comes shortly after Thackeray's renewed friendship with William Garrow Lettsom (his co-editor on the *Gownsman*) in Weimar in 1830-31. Lettsom was attached to the suite of an English Minister at Weimar and later became Queen Victoria's *Chargé d'Affaires* in Uruguay. Thackeray had a knack of utilizing friends' names in his magazinery (for example, his 'brave Augustus', and the various patronyms of Fitzgerald), and this may well be another such instance. Finally, one item listed here is an 'epigram', of which, again, Thackeray contributed many in his undergraduate days.

In addition to this evidence, the subject matter of several of the items is typical of Thackeray's early work. The sonnet, 'The Witch' (no. 10), is a comic verse about the poet, on a dark night, coming across a broom-sticked witch, only to discover, through her broad and deflationary Cockney, that she is 'the voman, Sir, vot sweeps this crossing': a situation similar to that in 'Miss Shum's Husband', one of the first *Yellowplush* tales. 'The Man-at Arms' (no. 11) is a comic poem about one Serjeant Simkins, whilst 'The Leviathan' (no. 18) refers to the Margate steam-boat. 'The Darby Day' tale (no. 14) is a precursor of the 'Stubbs' and 'Cox' kind of rise and fall of fortune narratives, about Joseph Stumpkins and Jemima Flytrap. The article 'A Chapter on Court Fools' (no. 15) contains several references to Addison and Walter Scott, and notes 'That there are as many fools as men in the world, we may readily concede, when we consider that every man carries a fool within himself'. Finally, 'A Romance of Real Life, by George Robins' (no. 17), is a clever undercutting of the Romance genre, as well as a hit at the disguising of advertisements within fiction to pay for the publication – suggested by Thackeray in 'A Plan for a Prize Novel' in *Punch*. Thackeray refers to George Robins (an auctioneer and apparently a notorious liar) in the *Irish Sketch-Book* (1843). There is also an unsigned comic item on the need for literary critics to analyse the artistic merits of advertisements in the *Paris Literary Gazette*, no. 9 (22 December 1835), 141, which might indicate Thackeray's closer association with that magazine.

1. 'To Sybil' ('I gave to thee a rose, fresh budding'), signed 'T.'; no. 4 (24 March 1832), 51.

2. 'Boarding-House Bores: From Mrs. Lavinia Lettsom to the Editor of the Original', signed 'Letitia Lettsom'; no. 6 (7 April 1832), 81-3.

3. 'Original Sonnets. No. 2. AIR.' ('Oh! to be borne upon the wings o' the wind'), signed 'T.'; no. 6 (7 April 1832), 85.

4. 'The Chinaman's Lament; or, The Tail Cut Short' ('Malediction severe on the severing knife'), signed 'T.'; no. 6 (7 April 1832), 89.

5. 'Original Sonnet. No. 3. FIRE.' ('Had I been doomed upon the earth to dwell'), signed 'T.'; no. 7 (14 April 1832), 98.

6. 'Epigram upon Epigrams' ('Epigrams, like pins, conjoin't'), signed 'T.'; no. 7 (14 April 1832), 111.

7. 'The Unlucky Emigrant', signed 'T.'; no. 8 (21 April 1832), 117.

8. 'Epigram' ('Tom, you're the biggest fool I know'), signed 'T.'; no. 8 (21 April 1832), 127.

9. 'To a Tear' ('Pure, silent messenger of sympathy!'), unsigned; no. 10 (5 May 1832), 149.

10. 'Very Original Sonnet. No. 7. The Witch' ('Midnight it was, and desolate the street'), signed 'T.'; no. 12 (19 May 1832).

11. 'Very Original Sonnet. No. 9. The Man-at-Arms' ('"A gallant knight came pricking o'er the plain"'), signed 'T.'; no. 14 (2 June 1832), 215.

12. 'On Phrenology and Science in General, From a Member of the Motcombe-cum-Stoke Mechanics Institution', signed 'Jeremiah Bumpus'; no. 16 (16 June 1832), 243.

13. 'Anacreontic' ('Love, the youthful poet's dream'), signed 'T.'; no. 16 (16 June 1832), 244.

14. 'The Darby Day; or, An Exquisite at Epsom', signed 'T.'; no. 17 (23 June 1832), 259-60.

15. 'Chapters on Court Fools. Ch. 1. On Folly in General – And Fools in Particular', signed 'T.' and '(To be Continued)'; no. 17 (23 June 1832), 260-62.

16. 'Very Original Sonnets. No. 11. The Alchymist' ('I saw a follower of the mystic art'), signed 'T.'; no. 17 (23 June 1832), 265.

17. 'A Romance of Real Life, by George Robins, Esq.', unsigned; no. 18 (30 June 1832).

18. 'Very Original Sonnet. No. 14. The Leviathan' ('Slow roll'd the waters, by a ripple curl'd'), signed 'T.'; no. 21 (21 July 1832).

The Original ceased publication with no. 22 (28 July 1832). Thackeray was mostly in London during the months of these *Original* contributions, exercising his 'fictitious and poetical forehead', working as a law clerk in the Temple, and visiting the House of Commons for the readings of the Reform Bill. He was also, according to his diary, preparing to buy a newspaper (which plan collapsed) and being introduced to the literary world by William Maginn. (An article, signed 'G.C.', in *The Original*, no. 18 (30 June 1832), is entitled 'Some Account of the Death of Morgan O'Doherty: Late Ensign and Adjutant of the 46th Regiment' – Morgan O'Doherty was the pseudonym of Maginn in *Blackwood's*, in the 1820s, and, at this period, in *Fraser's* (and also used in the 1820s by J.G. Lockhart and W.H. Forbes in *Blackwood's*).

On 19 June 1832, Thackeray travelled down to the Bullers' house in the West Country to help with the hustings for his friend's Parliamentary election. He came into his patrimony on 18 July 1832, leaving for Bonchurch, Isle of White, and then, 31 July, sailing for France. This may well explain the lack of 'T.'s contributions to *The Original* in July 1832: the last few pieces had been written, perhaps, in advance of his departure with Buller in mid-June.

Appendix 3: Thackeray's contributions to the *National Standard*, 1833-4

The standard editions for Thackeray's publications from the *National Standard* remain W.T. Spencer, *Mr. Thackeray's Writings for the 'National Standard' and 'Constitutional'* (London, 1899), George Saintsbury, *Works* (Oxford edition), Vol. I, and the fragments and edited versions of articles in Harold Gulliver, *Thackeray's Literary Apprenticeship* (Georgia, 1934). The fullest account and analysis of the magazine is Donald Hawes, 'Thackeray and the "National Standard"', *Review of English Studies*, 23 (1972), 35-51. All of these works fall short of a detailed assessment of precisely what Thackeray wrote for his journal, but all suggest that Thackeray wrote much of it (see Peters, 61). Although external evidence for identifying Thackeray's contributions scarcely exists (indeed, Spencer and Gulliver use only internal evidence to support their reprintings), Thackeray's style and opinions are usually recognizable. The following list is, I hope, a comprehensive and reliable index to the extensive range of Thackeray's writings over the period 1833-4, and shows, more than hitherto has been apparent, the enormous range of his reading at this early date.

I have omitted those short and edited columns on 'Drama', 'Fine Arts' and 'Literary Intelligence' which Thackeray may have had a hand in, unless they are of some length and detail. I work on the supposition that, as the evidence of his letters suggests, Thackeray was working extensively to secure the success of his paper during the period of its survival; I do not believe that Maginn had much, if any, direct hand in the writing of the paper. Several fictional items, signed 'S.', initially seemed to me to be early versions of later known Thackeray works ['Snob'?]; however, 'S.' is referred to in the 'Notes to Correspondents' for no. 47 (23 November 1833), and requested to send more material; Thackeray may have unconsciously recalled these slight narratives when he came to work on his later fiction.

Thackeray took over the editorship of the *National Standard* from no. 19 (11 May 1833); the first six items may be his contributions to earlier numbers. I have omitted a system of 'poss.' or 'prob.' contributions as all of the items are included without external evidence, except for the story, 'The Devil's Wager' and the four items of Paris Correspondence.

Volume 1

No. 9 (2 March 1833):

1. 'Original Correspondence: Letter to the editor of the "National Standard"', signed 'Kitty Anti-Brady'; 134-5.

No. 10 (9 March 1833):
1. 'Original Paper: The Importance of Dress', 149-51.

No. 11 (16 March 1833):
1. 'Varieties', [verse] 'Love in the Kitchen' ('Do you ever think of me, love?'), 175; this was supposedly extracted from the *Licensed Victuallers' Magazine* (reviewed, no. 10, 148-9)

No. 18 (4 May 1833):
1. 'Louis Philippe' (and woodcut), 273.
2. *History of Europe during the French Revolution*, Archibald Alison, 2 vols. Blackwood, 1833, 273-9.
3. 'Drama', includes a review of Taglioni in *Flore et Zephyr*, 286-8.

No. 19 (11 May 1833):
1. 'Address', 289.
2. 'Mr. [John] Braham: Sonnet. By W. Wordsworth', 289.
3. *Biographical Sketch of Joseph Napoleon Bonaparte, Count de Surveilliers*. Ridgway, 1833, 290-91.
4. [G.P.R. James], *Mary of Burgundy; or, the Revolt of Ghent*. Longman & Co., 1833, 291-2.
5. *Observations on the Greenwich Railway, in a Letter Addressed to Subscribers*. By an Inhabitant of Greenwich. Ridgway, 1833, 292-3.
6. *French Revolution* [second notice, see above], 294-7.
7. 'Original Communications: Parliamentary Portraits; no. 1 (Whig) Lord Althorp', 297-8.
8. 'Original Poetry. "The Field-Marshall" (from the German of Ernst Moritz Arndt)', 298.
9. 'Our Olden Authors: Thomas Randolph' [ex-Trinity College, Cambridge poet, b. 1605], 298-9.
10. 'Fine Arts – The Somerset House Exhibition', 299.
11. 'New Publications', 299.

No. 20 (18 May 1833):
1. 'N.M. Rothschild, Esq.' (and woodcut), 305.
2. *Lucien Greville*. By a Cornet in the East India Company's Service. Saunders & Otley, 1833, 307-8.
3. *Poor Laws and Paupers Illustrated. 1. The Parish; A Tale*. By Harriet Martineau. London, 1833, 309-11.
4. *Fragments of Voyages and Travels*. By Captain Basil Hall. London: 1833; pp. 311-13.
5. *Observations on Impediments of Speech ... In a Letter Addressed to T.J. Pettigrew, Esq.* London: 1833, 313-14.
6. 'Hymn – Comfort in the Storm' ('Awakened from his troubled sleep'), 316.
7. 'Fine Arts – The Somerset House Exhibition', 316-17.

No. 21 (25 May 1833):
1. 'London Characters' (and woodcut), 321.
2. *Characteristics of Goethe* ... By Sarah Austin London: 1833, 322-3.
3. *Eben Erskine; or, The Traveller*. By John Galt. London: 1833, 323-5.
4. *Narrative of a Residence at the Court of London*. By Richard Rush, Esq. London: 1833, 325-7. [review referred to in no. 32.]
5. *Rejected Addresses*, Smith Brothers. Illustrations by G. Cruikshank 18th edition; reprinted, London: 1833, 328-30.
6. *Kidd's Picturesque Pocket Companion to the Isle of Wight* [no details], 331.
7. 'Drama', 332-4.

No. 22 (1 June 1833):
1. [Theodore Hook], *The Parson's Daughter*. Bentley. London: 1833, 337-8.
2. *Works of Lord Byron*. Vol. XVII. Murray, 1833, 338-40.
3. *Memoires of the Duchess d'Abrantes (Madame Junot)*, Vol. V (1833) Bentley, 340-22.
4. *Barbadoes, and Other Poems*. By M.J. Chapman, Esq. Fraser: 1833, 342-3.
5. *Eben Erskine* [second notice; see above], 343-5.
6. 'A[lfred]. Bunn' (and woodcut), 345.

No. 23 (8 June 1833):
1. [Frances Trollope], *The Abbess; a Romance*. London: 1833. Whittaker & Co., 355-6.
2. *Characteristics of Goethe* [second notice, see above], 356-7.
3. *Sketches of Canada and the United States*. By W.L. MacKenzie. Wilson. London: 1833, 357-8.
4. [Frances Trollope], *The Mother's Manual*. Treuttel and Wurtz. London: 1833, 358.
5. *An Historical and Topographical Guide to the Isle of Wight* ... By W.C.F.G. Sheridan. Mitchell. London: 1833, 359-60.
6. *He Would be Married: A Comedy, in Three Acts*. By George Geast. London: 1833, 360-61.
7. 'Love in Fetters; a Tottenham-Court-Road Ditty' (and woodcut), 362.
8. 'Fine Arts – The Byron Gallery. Chalon's *Maid of Athens*', 364.

No. 24 (15 June 1833):
1. *The Young Enthusiast in Humble Life. A Simple Story*. London: 1833. Fraser, 369-70.
2. [Edward Bulwer-Lytton], *Godolphin*. London: 1833. Bentley, 370-73.
3. *Rhymes and Rhapsodies*. By R.F. Williams. London: 1833. Fraser, 373-4.
4. *The Parson's Daughter* [second notice, see above], 374-6.
5. *Woman; The Angel of Life: A Poem*. By Robert Montgomery. London: 1833, 376-7.
6. 'Drama – Covent Garden' (and woodcut), signed 'GAMMA', 380-81.
7. 'Drama – King Bunn's Proclamation', 381-2.

No. 25 (22 June 1833):
1. *Romances of the Chivalric Ages. The Pilgrim Brothers*. London: 1833. Bull, 385-6.
2. *Narrative of a Voyage to Patagonia and Terra del Fuego, through the Straits of Magellan* ... By John MacDowall, R.N. Renshaw and Rush. London: 1833, 386-9.
3. *Godolphin* [second notice, see above], 389-93.
4. 'Petrus Laureus' (and woodcut), 395.
5. 'Bunniana: *Poems*. By Alfred Bunn (London, 1816)', 395-7.
6. 'Drama', 398.

No. 26 (29 June 1833):
1. *Criminal Law; Being a Commentary on Bentham on Death Punishment*. By Henry Bartlett Andrews. Render, Ridgeway, Chappell. London: 1833, 405-7 [review referred to in no. 42]
2. *Poetical Works of Sir Walter Scott*, Vol. III. London: 1833, 407-8.
3. *The Life of William Roscoe; by his son, Henry Roscoe*. Cadell, London; Blackwood, Edinburgh: 1833, 409.
4. *Romances of Chivalric Ages* [second notice, see above], 410-11.
5. 'Paris Correspondence', dated '22 June 1833' (and woodcut), 412-13.

Volume 2
No. 27 (6 July 1833):
1. 'Address', 1. [announces reversion from 2 columns to 3]
2. *Memoirs of the Court of King Charles the First*. By Lucy Aikin. London: 1833. Longman & Co., 1-3.
3. *Delaware; or, the Ruined Family. A Tale*. Edinburgh: Cadell; London: Whittaker & Co. 1833, 3-5.
4. *Sharpe's Peerage of the British Empire* ... 'Two thick Vols' Sharp. London: 1833, 5-6. [further extracts appear from this work in several following numbers]
5. *The Repealers: a Novel*. By the Countess of Blessington. London: 1833. Bentley, 6-7.
6. 'Paris Correspondence', dated '29 June 1833' (and woodcut), 10-11.

No. 28 (13 July 1833):
1. *Narrative of the Expedition to Portugal in 1832*. By George Lloyd Hodges, Esq., Late Colonel in the Service of Her Most Faithful Majesty the Queen of Portugal. London: 1833. Fraser, 17-18.
2. *Taxation of the British Empire*. By R. Montgomery Martin. London: 1833. Wilson, 20.
3. *Memoirs of Mrs. Inchbald; including her Familiar Correspondence with the most distinguished Persons of her Time* ... Edited by James Boaden, Esq. London: 1833. Bentley, 20-22.

4. *A Popular History of Priestcraft in all Ages and Nations*. By William Howitt. London: 1833. Wilson, 22-4.
5. *An Encyclopaedia of Cottage, Farm, and Villa Architecture*. By F.C. Loudon. Twelve Parts. London: 1833. Longman & Co., 24.
6. 'The Charruas – Paris Correspondence', dated '5 June [a misprint for July] 1833' (and woodcut), 28-9.

No. 29 (20 July 1833):
1. *Dramatic Scenes from Real Life*. By Lady Morgan. London: 1833. Saunders & Otley, 36-8.
2. *Waltzburg. A Tale of the Sixteenth Century*. London: 1833. Whittaker & Co., 38-9. [This review contains a reference to Michael Angelo Taylor (1757-1834)]
3. 'Paris Correspondence', dated '13 July 1833' (and woodcut), 42-3.

No. 30 (27 July 1833):
1. *England and the English*. By Edward Lytton Bulwer, Esq. M.P. London: 1833. Bentley, 49-51.
2. [Some short reviews of French books are published in this number, following Thackeray's return from Paris, 51, 54-5.]
3. 'The History of the Fish', translated from the French of G. Pauthier (from a Sanskrit original) (and woodcut), 56-7.
3. 'Science and Art – Description of the Salt Mines of Wieliezka [From the French]', 59-61.

No. 31 (3 August 1833):
1. *Great Britain in 1833*. By Baron D'Haussez, Ex-minister of Marine under Charles X. London: 1833. Bentley, 65-8. [referred to in no. 44.]
2. 'Original Poetry – Song. By a literary man to his wife. AIR – When in death I shall calm recline ('When to jail I shall once be sent'), 74.

No. 32 (10 August 1833):
1. *Men and Manners in America*. By the Author of "Cyril Hornton" & C. London: Cadell; Edinburgh: Blackwood, 1833, 77-9. [refers to review of Rush, no. 21.]
2. 'Foreign Article': *Struensee; ou la Reine et la Favori*. Par Fournia et Augusto Arnould. 'Struensee; or the Queen and the Favourite.' Paris: 1833. Dupont, 82-3.
3. 'The Devil's Wager', 85-6 [continued in No. 34].
4. 'Awful Business – Suicide of Mr. Dilke', 86.
5. 'Drama – Parisian Theatricals', 88.

No. 33 (16 August 1833):
1. [E. Bulwer-Lytton], *Eugene Aram; a Tragedy* [*New Monthly Magazine*, August 1, 1833], 93-4.

2. *Men and Manners in America* [second notice, see above], 94-5.
3. *Sir Guy de Lusignan. A Tale of Italy*. By F. Cornelia Knight, Authoress of 'Dinarbas', 'Marcus Flaminius', 'Latium', & c. London: 1833. Saunders & Otley, 95.
4. *Exposition of the False Medium and Barriers excluding Men of Genius from the Public*. London: 1833. Wilson, 95-7 [this is the third notice, the previous being mostly extracts only, see pp. 24, 71-2].
5. *Santa Maura. A Fragment. In Two Cantos*. By Nugent Taylor, Esq., a Minor. London: 1833. Chapple, 97-8.
6. 'Foreign Article. *Le Nepénthes. Contes Nouvelles et Critiques*. (Paris: L'Advocat, 1833)', 100-101.
7. 'Drama – Vauxhall', 103-4 [includes comic mock-speech by Master of Ceremonies].

No. 34 (24 August 1833):
1. *Mémoires du Marechal Ney, Duc d'Elchingen, Prince de la Moscowa. Publies par sa Famille*. 2 tom. Londres: 1833. Bull, 109-10.
2. *Romances of Chivalric Ages* [third notice, mostly extracts, see above], 110-12.
3. *Men and Manners in America* [third notice, mostly extracts, see above], 112-15.
4. 'The Devil's Wager' (continued), 121-2.

No. 35 (31 August 1833):
1. 'Our Leader', 125.
2. *Notre Dame; A Tale of the Ancient Régime*. From the French of Victor Hugo ... By the Translator of Thierry's 'History of the Conquest of England by the Normans' ... London: 1833. Wilson, 126-30.
3. *Davenant; or the Escape. An Historical tale*. London: 1833. Whittaker & Co., 130-31.
4. *Musings and Prosings*. By Thomas Haynes Bayly. Boulogne: 1833, 131-2.
5. *An Answer to a Pamphlet entitled Observations on the Rejected Local Courts' Jurisdiction Bill*. Richards: 1833, 134.
6. 'Foreign Article. *Mémoires de Mademoiselle Arvillion, Première Femme de Chambre de L'Imperatrice, sur la Vie privée de Joséphine, sa Famille et sa Cour*. (Paris: L'Advocat, 1833)', 135-7.

No. 36 (7 September 1833):
1. *Phoenician Ireland*. Auctore Doctore Joachimo Laurentio Villanueva ... Translated by Henry O'Brian ... Author of the Prize Essay upon the Round Towers of Ireland. London: Longman; Dublin: R.M. Timms, 1833, 141-3.
2. *An Address to the Subscribers to the Windsor and Eton Public Library and Reading Room*. By Sir J.F.W. Herschel, K.G.H. London: 1833. Smith, Elder & Co., 143-4.
3. *My Sketchbook*. By George Cruikshank. Nos 1 & 2. London: 1833, 150-51.

No. 37 (14 September 1833):
1. 'Solitude in September', 157.
2. *The Book of the Seasons; or, the Calendar of Nature*. By William Howitt. Second Edition. London: 1833. Bentley, 161-3.
3. *Men and Manners in America* [fourth notice, see above], 163-4.
4. *The Philoctetes of Sophocles.* By G. Burges, A.M., Trinity College, Cambridge. London: 1833. Longman, Whittaker & Baldwin, 166. [referred to in no. 39.]
5. *Rosine Laural. A Novel*. By R. Smith Esq. In 2 Vols. 8vo. London: 1833. A K Newman, 166-7.
6. 'Original Pieces: Scene from an Unpublished Tragedy', 168.

No. 38 (21 September 1833):
1. 'Messrs. Hall and Allan's Work', 173.
2. *The Headsman; or, the Abbaye des Vignerons. A Tale*. By the Author of 'The Bravo', & c. Three Vols. London: 1833. Bentley, 174-7.
3. *The Yeoman's Daughter; or, a Domestic Drama, in Two Acts.* By T.J. Serle, author of 'The Merchant of London', & c. Duncombe, 178-9.
4. *A Treatise on the Physiology and Diseases of the Eye, together with Remarks on the Preservation of Sight, and on Spectacles, Reading Glasses, & c.* By John Harrison Curtis, Esq. London: 1833. Longman & co., 179-80. [refers to reviewers adopting spectacles sooner than others (WMT replacing his monocle?); and see no. 40.]
5. *The Russian Catechism: with Explanatory Notes*. Published by Authority. London: 1833. Effingham Wilson, 181. [referred to in no. 39.]
6. *The Hangman and the Judge*. By Edward Gibbon Wakefield, Esq. London: 1833, 181.
7. *Europe during the Middle Ages; Being the Forty-Fifth Volume of Lardner's Cabinet Cyclopaedia.* London: 1833. Longman & Co. '[BOUGHT]', 181-3.

No. 39 (28 September 1833):
1. 'Literary Gazette – Athenaeum – National Standard', 189.
2. *The Autobiography of John Galt.* Two Vols. 8vo. London: 1833. Cochrane and M'Crone, 190-93.
3. *The United States of North America.* By Achille Murat. 1833, 195-6.
4. 'Original Correspondence. Burges v. "The National Standard"', 197. [Burges complains about the review in no. 37; the writer stands by his review as he knows the author (both Burges and Thackeray were Trinity men).]
5. 'Original Correspondence. Russian catechism: To the Editor of "The National Standard"', 197-8. [complaint and response about the review in no. 38.]
6. 'Fine Arts – The National Gallery', 199.

No. 40 (5 October 1833):
1. '"A Fog is on the centre of the town"', 205.

2. Galt's *Autobiography* [second notice, see above], 206-8.
3. *The Book of the Seasons* [second notice, see above], 208-10.
4. *Twenty Minutes' Advice on the Eyes, and the Means of Preserving the Sight.* By a Retired Oculist, of many years' active practice. pp.59. London: 1833. Kidd, 210. [reviewer notes he burns the midnight oil for the sake of his readers, and discusses spectacles; and see no. 38.]
5. 'Periodicals', 211-15 [reprints, 213-14, the *Cambrian and Caledonian Quarterly's* praise of the *National Standard*, and defends the *Standard's* selling of advertising space (see Gulliver)]

No. 41 (12 October 1833):
1. 'Puffing and Fishing', 221.
2. *The Library of Entertaining Knowledge: Vegetable Substances: Materials of Manufactures.* London: 1833. Knight, 222. [facetious review.]
3. Galt's *Autobiography* [third notice, see above], 222-4.
4. *Poor Laws and Paupers Illustrated. II. The Hamlets; a Tale.* By Harriet Martineau. London: 1833. C. Fox, 224-5.
5. 'Original Papers. A Tale of Wonder', 228-9.
6. 'Drama. Drury Lane', 233. [verse parody of an address by the actress Miss Taylor.]
7. 'NOTICE EXTRAORDINARY', 235. [The *National Standard* is to be translated into the language of 'Timbuctoo' and published there and in London simultaneously.]

No. 42 (19 October 1833):
1. 'Ourselves and Our Correspondents', 237.
2. Reviews of the Annuals: '*The Oriental Annual*; *Fisher's Drawing-Room Scrap-Book*; *The Landscape Annual* (T. Roscoe); *The Landscape Annual* (W. Westall); *The Comic Offering*', 238-47.
3. *The Toilette of Health, and Dressing-Room Companion.* London: 1833. Griffiths, 248.
4. *The National Drama; or, The Histrionic War of the Majors and Minors.* London: 1833. Muers, 247-8. [facetious review.]
5. 'The Periodicals', 248-9. [refers to Harriet Martineau and reviewer's comments on capital punishment, see no. 26.]
6. 'Original Correspondence. To the Editor of the "National Standard"', 249-50. [another letter from Burges and another response, see nos. 37 and 39.]

No. 43 (26 October 1833):
1. 'Our Own Leader', 253.
2. *The Heiress. A Novel.* in 3 vols. London: 1833. Bentley, 256-8.
3. *Excursions in New South Wales* ... By Lieutenant Breton, R.N. London: 1833. Bentley, 260-61.
4. *The Law relating to the Purchase of Government Annuities.* By John Tidd Pratt, Esq. London: 1833. Shaw and Sons, 258-9. [facetious review.]

5. *A Vision of Death's Destruction and Miscellaneous Poems*. By T.J. Ouseley. London: Longman & Co.; Leicester: Combe, 259.
[Other short reviews, 262-3, may also be by Thackeray.]

No. 44 (2 November 1833):
1. 'A Lecture on Humbug', 269.
2. *Tom Cringle's Log*. 2 Vols. Edinburgh, Blackwood; London, Cadell. 1833, 270-72.
3. *Traits and Traditions of Portugal, collected during a residence in that country*. By Miss Pardoe. Two Vols. London: 1833. Sauders and Otley, 272-4.
4. *The United States of North America*. By Achille Murat. London: 1833. Wilson [Concluding Notice, see above], 274-5. [mock Murat's belief that the Law is always right: 'He thinks nothing of the fable of the boy and the frogs.']
5. *The New-Year's Gift, and Juvenile Souvenir*. Edited by Mrs Aleric Watts. London: 1834. Longman & Co., 276-7. [facetiously refers to Martineau and Malthus.]
6. 'The Periodicals', 277-80. [refers to his review of Baron D'Haussez in no. 31.]

No. 45 (9 November 1833):
1. 'The Pope and the National Standard', 285.
2. Reviews of the Annuals: '*Forget-me-Not; a Christmas, New Year's & Birthday Present*, ed. by Frederick Shoberl; *The Amulet*, ed. by S.C. Hall; *Heath's Picturesque Drawing Annual* ... Engravings from Drawings by Clarkson Stanfield. By Leitch Ritchie; *Friendship's Offering and Writer's Wreath* [includes 'My Baptismal Birth Day' by Coleridge], 286-9.
3. *Scott's Works* – 'Marmion', 289-90.
4. 'The Periodicals', 291-4. [reviews the *Foreign Quarterly Review* and the need to know foreign literature.]
5. 'Original Papers. Recollections by an Old Fool', signed 'AN OLD FOOL', 294-6.

No. 46 (16 November 1833):
1. 'Mrs Yates's "Grace Hustley"', 301.
2. *Trevelyan*. By the Author of "A Marriage in High Life." Three volumes. London: 1833. Bentley, 302-3.
3. *The Keepsake for 1834*. Edited by Frederick Mansel Reynolds. London: Longman & Co., 303-5.
4. *Tracts and Traditions of Portugal* [second notice, see above], 305-7.
5. *Maxims of Sir Peter Laurie, Knt*. Lord Mayor of London. London: 1833, 307-8.
6. 'Original Correspondence. To the Editor of the "National Standard"', 313. [complains about a review on page 277.]

No. 47 (23 November 1833):
1. 'Weekly Chronicle', 317-18. [Some passages from this series, and the sections following, sound distinctly Thackerayan, with references to Napoleon's statue in the Place Vendôme (see 'Paris Correspondence'), Hood's *Annual*, Alfred Bunn, Disraeli, Bulwer and velvet trousers; the format gave the writer the opportunity to discourse on a variety of contemporary topics.]
2. *Biographical and Critical History of the Last Fifty Years*. By Allan Cunningham, 318-19.
3. *Peter Simple*. By Captain Marryat. 3 vols. 8vo. London: 1833. Sauders and Otley, 319-20.
4. *Christ Crucified; An Epic Poem, in Twelve Books*. By William Ellis Wall, MA, of Trinity College, Oxford. Oxford, 1833, 320-21.
5. *The American Comic Almanack*. 1834. New York: D. Felt. Boston: C. Ellms, 321-2.
6. *The Art of Polite Correspondence. English and German Perfected*. Leipsic and London: Schloss, 323.
7. *Lives of the British Admirals*. By R. Southey. London: 1833. Longman & Co., 324-6.
8. 'Sonnet to Harriet Martineau. By Lord Brougham' ('Most lovers on a lady's sylph-like form'), 330.

No. 48 (30 November 1833):
1. 'Our Leader', 333.
2. 'Weekly Chronicle', 334-5.
3. *Dilemmas of Pride*. By the Author of "First Love". Three Volumes. London: 1833. Bull & Churton, 335-6.
4. *Southey's Lives* [second notice, see above], 336-8.
5. *Heath's Book of Beauty*. London: 1834, 338.
6. *Margaret Carnegie: a Tale*. By the Viscount Castlereagh, 338-9.
7. *Christ Crucified* [Second notice, see above], 340-41.
8. *Lectures on the History and Principles of Painting*. By T. Phillips. London: 1833. Longman, 341-2.
9. 'Original Papers', 'History of Crakatuk', a translation from the German of Hoffmann (continued below), 342-4.

No. 49 (7 December 1833):
1. 'Fudge – Fudge – Fudge', 349.
2. [Theodore Hook], *Love and Pride*. By the Author of 'Sayings and Doings' & c. London: Whittaker & Co., 350-52.
3. *The Comic Annual*. By Thomas Hood, Esq. London: 1834. Tilt, 352-4.
2. *The Flash Mirror; or, Kiddy's Cabinet*. 12mo. London: publisher unknown, 354-5.
3. *The Club; or, a Gray Cap for a Green Head*. By James Puckle. London: 1733. Reprint: 1834. Tait, 355-6.

4. *Songs of the Loire, and Other Poems*. London: 1834. Baldwin & Cradock, 356-7.
5. 'Original Papers: The History of Crakatuk. From the German of Hoffmann. [Continued from our last]', 360-61.

No. 50 (14 December 1833):
1. 'National Standard Office', 365-6.
2. *Gale Middleton; a Story of the Present Day*. By the Author of "Brambletye House". 3 vols. London: 1833. Bentley, 367-70.
3. *Stories of the Study*. By John Galt. 3 vols. London: 1833. Cochrane and McCrone, 371-3.
4. *Random Rhymes; or Lays of London*. London. Willoughby, 373-4.
5. *Turner's Annual Tour: – Wanderings by the Seine*. By Leitch Ritchie, esq. London: 1834. Longman & Co., 374.
6. 'Original Correspondence', 377. [Letter is critical of the magazine's recent 'trash', editor responds.]

No. 51 (21 December 1833):
1. 'Importance at Home and Abroad', 381.
2. *Pilgrim's Progress; Metrically Condensed*. By Thomas Dibdin. London: 1833. Harding & King, 382-3.
3. *The Dark Lady of Doona*. By the Author of 'Stories of Waterloo'. London: 1833. Smith, Elder & Co., 383-5.
4. *The Story Without an End. Translated from the German*. By Sarah Austin. London: 1834. Effingham Wilson, 385-6.
5. *Love and Pride*. By T. Hook [second notice, see above], 386-8.
6. *Indiana*. Par George Sand. Bruxelles: 1833, 388-9.
7. *Lives and Exploits of English Highwaymen, Pirates, and Robbers*. By C. Whitehead, Esq. London: 1834. Bull & Churton, 389-90.
8. *Barnadiston; a Tale of the Seventeenth Century*. London: 1833. Saunders & Otley, 390-92.
9. *England and America*. Two vols. London: 1833. R. Bentley, 392-3.

No. 52 (28 December 1833):
1. 'Address', 397.
2. *Cecil Hyde; a Novel*. 2 vols. London: 1834. Saunders & Otley, 398-400.
3. *Lives and Exploits of English Highwaymen* [second notice, see above], 400-403.
4. *England and America*. 2 vols. London: 1833. Bentley, 403-6. [second notice; first notice in no. 51 consists of extracts only; refers to 'the tribe of Trollopes'.]
5. *Forty Years' Residence in America; or, the Doctrine of a Particular Providence, exemplified in the Life of Grant Thorburn, (the original Lawrie Todd,) Seedsman, of New York*. London: 1834. Fraser, 406-8.
6. *Indiana*. Par George Sand [second notice, see above], 408-9.

7. 'Notices to Correspondents', 411.

Volume 3
No. 53 (4 January 1834):
[Renamed *The National Standard, and Literary Representative*]
1. 'Melancholy State of the Year 7834', 1.
2. *The Black Watch*. By the Author of 'Domince's Legacy'. London: 1834. Bentley, 2-5.
3. *The Coquette*. By the Author of 'Miserrimus'. London: 1834. Hookham, 5-6. [The subsequent reviews for this number are all short and consist mostly of extracts – a result of Thackeray being 'left ... to do all the work' by his assistant, James Hume (Letter to Mrs. Carmichael-Smyth, December 1833)]
4. *Retrospect in the Proceedings in the Prosecution of Rex v. Woolcombe at the Suit of Vice-Admiral Sir Edward Codrington*. London: 1833, 7.
5. *Memorials of a Tour in Greece*. By R.M. Milnes. London: 1833. Moxon, 7.
6. *Thoughts of the Church Establishment*. By a Layman. London: Hatchard; Hurst. 1833, 8.
7. 'The Periodicals', 9-10 [includes the *Lady's Magazine and Museum*].
8. 'Original Papers. King Odo's Wedding', 11-12.
9. 'Science and Art – On the Existence of Sensation after Decapitation', 14.
10. 'Drama – Drury Lane – The Olympic', 15.

No. 54 (11 January 1833):
1. *The Works of Robert Burns; With his Life*. By Allan Cunningham. London: 1834. Cochrane and M'Crone, 17-19.
2. *Memorials of a Tour in Greece* [second notice, see above], 19-21.
3. *Kay's Travels and Researches in Caffraria*. London: 1833. Mason, 21-3.
4. *The East India Sketch-Book*. London: 1833. Bentley, 23-4.
5. *A Tableau of French Literature during the Eighteenth Century*. By M. de Barante. London: 1833. Smith & Elder, 24-5.
6. *Zara; or, the Black Death. A Poem of the Sea*. By the Author of 'Naufragus'. London: 1833. Whittaker and Co., 25.
7. 'Music', 29.
8. 'Drama', 29-30. [refers to Jerrold's *The Wedding Gown*, reviewed in no. 56.]

No. 55 (18 January 1834):
1. *The Year. A Poem*. By Thomas Albin, Jun. London: 1833. Baldwin and Cradock, 33-5.
2. *The Baboo, and other Tales, descriptive of Society in India*. Two volumes. London: 1834. Smith, Elder & Co., 35-6.
3. *Social Evils, and their Remedies*. By Chas. B. Tayler. No. II. *The Lady and the Lady's Maid*. London: 1834. Smith & Elder, 36-7.
4. *The Stoic; or, Memoirs of Eurysthenes the Athenian*. By Jane Kinderley Stanford. London: 1834. Smith & Elder, 37-8.

5. *Sketches and Eccentricities of Col. David Crockett, of West Tennessee.* London: 1834. O. Rich, 38.
6. *Francis Berrian, or the Mexican Patriot.* By Mr Flint. 3 Vols. London. Newman & Co., 38-42.
7. 'Original Papers': 'The Devil to Pay – A Sketch', signed 'T.M.', 43-4.
8. 'Original Papers': 'Father Gahagan's Exhortation', 44.
9. 'Original Poetry': 'Song. I met her in the early month', signed 'T.M.', 45.
10. 'Drama', 46.

No. 56 (25 January 1834):
1. *Adam, the Gardener.* By Charles Cowden Clarke. London: 1834. Effingham Wilson, 49-52.
2. *The Wedding Gown; a Comedy, in Two Acts.* By Douglas Jerrold. London: 1834. Miller, Henrietta-street, Covent Garden, 52-4. [referred to in no. 54.]
3. *Cambridge Quarterly Review.* No. III. Tilt: London; Hatfield: Cambridge, 54-5.
4. *The Pirate's Bride; a Story of the Levant.* By Semloh. London: 1834. Dalton, 55-6.
5. *Medical Quarterly Review.* Souter, 56.
6. *Simpson's Cookery, Improved and Modernized. The Complete Modern Cook.* By Henderson William Brand, of the Kitchen of his late Majesty George the Fourth … London: Baldwin and Cradock, 56-7.
7. *The Baboo, and other Tales* [second notice, see above], 57-9.
8. 'Drama': 'Plays and Play-Bills', signed '∅', 62.
9. 'Original Correspondence': 'Mr. O'Brien and the *Athenaeum*', 62-3.

No. 57 (1 February 1834):
1. *Faust; a Dramatic Poem.* By Goëthe. Translated into English Prose by A. Hayward, esq. London: 1834. Moxon, 65-7.
2. *Aurungzebe; or, a tale of Alraschid.* London: 1833. Cochrane & M'Crone, 67-9.
3. *The Romance of History. England.* By H. Neele. London: 1833. Bull and Churton, 69-70.
4. *Colton's Tour of the American Lakes and among the Indians.* London: 1833. Westley and Davis, 70-72.
5. 'Periodicals', 72-5. [refers to *Fraser's Magazine*; *The Lady's Magazine*.]
6. 'Original Papers': 'The Minstrel's Curse', 75.
7. *Étude sur Mirabeau.* Par Victor Hugo. [Paris, 1834.], signed '∅', 75-6.

Selected Bibliography

There is no modern edition of Thackeray's works and little to choose between the extant editions. My reference edition is therefore: *The Works of William Makepeace Thackeray*, 26 vols (London: Smith, Elder and Co., 1894-6).

A'Beckett, A.W., *The à Beckett's of 'Punch': Memories of Father and Sons* (Westminster: Constable, 1903)

Altick, R.D., *The English Common Reader: A Social History of the Mass Reading Public, 1800-1900* (Chicago: University of Chicago Press, 1957)

Altick, R.D., *The Presence of the Present: Topics of the Day in the Victorian Novel* (Columbus: Ohio State University Press, 1991)

Altick, R.D., *Punch: The Lively Youth of a British Institution, 1841-1851* (Columbus: Ohio State University Press, 1997)

Altinel, A. S., *Thackeray and the Problem of Realism* (New York: Peter Lang, 1986)

[Anon.], 'Strange but True', *All the Year Round*, 16 (August 1862)

Ashley, R., *Wilkie Collins* (London: Arthur Baker, 1952)

Aspinall, A., *Politics and the Press, c.1780-1850* (London: Home and Van Thal, 1949)

Azim, F., *The Colonial Rise of the Novel* (London: Routledge, 1993)

Baker, J., 'Thackeray's Recantation', *PMLA*, 77 (1962), 586-94, retitled 'The Adventures of Philip' in A. Welsh (ed.) *Thackeray: A Collection of Critical Essays* (New Jersey: Prentice-Hall, 1968)

Bell, R., 'Stranger than Fiction', *Cornhill Magazine*, 2 (August 1860), 211-24

Blake, A., *Reading Victorian Fiction* (London: Macmillan, 1989)

Brake, L., 'Production of Meaning in Periodical Studies: Versions of the English Review', *Victorial Periodicals Review*, 24: 4 (Winter 1991), 163-70

Brake, L., *Subjugated Knowledges: Journalism, Gender, and Literature in the Nineteenth Century* (London: Macmillan, 1994)

Brake, L., A. Jones, and L. Madden (eds), *Investigating Victorian Journalism* (London: Macmillan, 1990)

Brown, L., *Victorian News and Newspapers* (Oxford: Oxford University Press, 1985)

Buchanan-Brown, J., *The Illustrations of William Makepeace Thackeray* (London: David and Charles, 1979)

Carey, J., *Thackeray: Prodigal Genius* (London: Faber & Faber, 1977)

Chittick, K., *Dickens and the 1830s* (Cambridge: Cambridge University Press, 1990)

Clarke, M.M., *Thackeray and Women* (DeKalb: Northern Illinois University Press, 1995)

Colby, R.A., *Thackeray's Canvass of Humanity: An Author and his Public* (Columbus: Ohio State University Press, 1979)

Collins, P., *Dickens and Crime* (London: Macmillan, 1962)

Collins, P. (ed.), *Thackeray: Interviews and Recollections*, 2 vols (London: Macmillan, 1983)

Cranfield, G.A., *The Press and Society: From Caxton to Northcliffe* (London: Longman, 1978)

Cronin, M., 'The Rake, The Writer, and The Stranger: Textual Relations between *Pendennis* and *David Copperfield*', *Dickens Studies Annual*, 24 (1996)

Cross, N., *The Common Writer: Life in Nineteenth Century Grub Street* (Cambridge: Cambridge University Press, 1985)

Crowe, E., *With Thackeray in America* (London: Routledge/Thoemmes Press, 1996)

Dodds, J.W., *The Age of Paradox: A Biography of England, 1841-1851* (London: Victor Gollancz, 1953)

Eagleton, T., *Heathcliff and the Great Hunger* (London: Verso, 1995)

Edwards, P.D., *Dickens's 'Young Men': George Augustus Sala, Edmund Yates and the World of Victorian Journalism* (Aldershot: Ashgate, 1997)

Eigner, E.M. and G.J. Worth (eds), *Victorian Criticism of the Novel* (Cambridge: Cambridge University Press, 1985)

Elwin, W., 'Thackeray in Search of a Profession', *Monthly Review*, 17 (October 1904), 88-105.

Erickson, L., *The Economy of Literary Form: English Literature and the Industrialization of Publishing, 1800-1850* (Baltimore: Johns Hopkins University, 1996)

Fanon, F., *Black Skin, White Masks* (London: Pluto Press,1986)

Fasick, L., 'Thackeray's Treatment of Writing and Painting', *Nineteenth Century Literature*, 47 (1992-3), 72-90

Feltes, N.N., *Modes of Production of Victorian Novels* (Chicago: University of Chicago Press, 1986)

Ferris, I., 'The Demystification of Laura Pendennis', *Studies in the Novel*, 13 (1981), 122-32

Fisher, J.K., 'The Aesthetics of the Mediocre: Thackeray and the Visual Arts', *Victorian Studies*, 26 (1983), 65-82

Fox-Bourne, H.R., *English Newspapers: Chapters in the History of Journalism*, 2 vols (London: Chatto and Windus, 1887)

Gager, V.L., *Shakespeare and Dickens: The dynamics of influence* (Cambridge: Cambridge University Press, 1996)

Garnett, R. (ed.), [W.M. Thackeray], *The New Sketch Book, Essays Collected from the 'Foreign Quarterly Review'* (London: Alston Rivers, 1906)

Gillett, P., *The Victorian Painter's World* (Gloucester: Alan Sutton, 1990)

Gilmour, R., *The Idea of the Gentleman in the Victorian Novel* (London: Allen & Unwin, 1981)

Graham, W., *English Literary Periodicals* (New York: Thomas Nelson, 1930)

Grant, J., *The Newspaper Press: Its Origins – Progress – and Present Position*, 3 vols (London: Tinsley Brothers, 1871-2)

Greig, J.Y.T., *Thackeray: A Reconsideration* (Oxford: Oxford University Press, 1950)

Guivarc'h, J., 'Deux Journalistes Anglais de Paris en 1835 (George W.M. Reynolds et W.M.T.)', *Etudes Anglaises*, 28 (1975), 203-12

Gulliver, H.S., *Thackeray's Literary Apprenticeship: A Study of the Early Newspaper and Magazine Work of W.M. Thackeray* (Georgia: Valdosta, 1934)

Habermas, J., *The Structural Transformation of the Public Sphere: An Inquiry into a Category of Bourgeois Society* (Cambridge: Polity Press, 1989)

Hall, D., *Fixing Patriarchy: Feminism and Mid-Victorian Male Novelists* (London: Macmillan, 1996)

Hankinson, A., *Man of Wars: William Howard Russell of the Times* (London: Heinemann, 1982)

Harden, E.F., *The Emergence of Thackeray's Serial Fiction* (London: George Prior, 1979)

Harden, E.F., *Thackeray's English Humourists and Four Georges* (Newark: University of Delaware Press, 1985)

Harden, E.F., *A Checklist of Contributions by W.M. Thackeray to Newspapers, Periodicals, Books, and Serial Part Issues, 1828-1864* (Victoria: University of Victoria, 1996)

Harden, E.F., *Thackeray the Writer: From Journalism to 'Vanity Fair'* (London: Macmillan, 1998)

Harden, E.F. (ed.), *The Letters and Private Papers of William Makepeace Thackeray: A Supplement*, 2 vols (New York/London: Garland, 1994)

Hardy, B., *The Exposure of Luxury: Radical Themes in Thackeray* (Pittsburgh: University of Pittsburgh Press, 1972)

Hawes, D., 'Thackeray and the "National Standard"', *Review of English Studies*, 23 (1972), 35-51

Hawes, D., 'Thackeray and French Literature in Perspective', *Studies in the Novel*, 13: 1-2 (Spring–Summer 1981), 5-20

Hazlitt, W., 'The Periodical Press', *Edinburgh Review*, 38 (May 1823)

Hickson, W.E., 'Reduction, or Abolition, of the Stamp Duty on Newspapers', *London Review*, 2 (January 1836), 336-55

Hickson, W.E., 'Proposed Reduction of the Stamp Duty on Newspapers', *London and Westminster Review*, 25 (April – July 1836), 264-70

Hindley, D. and G., *Advertising in Victorian England, 1837-1901* (London, 1972)

Hollingsworth, K., *The Newgate Novel, 1830-1847: Bulwer, Ainsworth, and Thackeray* (Detroit: Wayne State University Press, 1963)

Houghton, W.E. (ed.), *The Wellesley Index to Victorian Periodicals, 1824-1900*, 5 vols (Toronto: Routledge, 1966-89)

Howes, C., '*Pendennis* and the Controversy on the "Dignity of Literature"', *Nineteenth-Century Literature*, 41 (1986-7), 269-98

Hudson, D., *Thomas Barnes of 'The Times'*, With Critical Essays edited by Harold Child (Cambridge: Cambridge University Press, 1944)

Hughes, L.K., and M. Lund, 'Textual/sexual pleasure and serial publication', in John D. Jordan and Robert L. Patten (eds), *Literature in the Marketplace: Nineteenth century British Publishing and Reading Practices* (Cambridge: Cambridge University Press, 1995)

Humpherys, A., 'Thackeray the Novelist of Society', in J. Shattock (ed.), *Dickens and Other Victorians: Essays in Honour of Philip Collins* (London: Macmillan, 1988), 185-201

Jadwin, L., 'The Seductiveness of Female Duplicity in *Vanity Fair*', *Studies in English Literature*, 32 (1992), 663-84.

James, L., *Fiction for the Working Man, 1830-1850: A Study of the Literature Produced for the Working Classes in Early Victorian Urban England* (Oxford: Oxford University Press, 1963)

James, L., *Print and the People, 1819-1851* (London: Allen Lane, 1976)

Jerrold, D., *Men of Character* (London, 1838)

Jerrold, W., *Reminiscences of Father Prout* (London: 1876)

Jerrold, W., *Douglas Jerrold and 'Punch'* (London: Macmillan, 1910)

Johnson, C.P., *The Early Writings of William Makepeace Thackeray* (London: Elliot Stock, 1888)

Jones, A., *Powers of the Press: Newspapers, Power, and the Public in Nineteenth Century England* (Aldershot: Scolar Press, 1996)

Kaplan, F., *Dickens: A Biography* (London: Hodder and Stoughton, 1988)

Kelly, R., *The Best of Mr. Punch: The Humorous Writings of Douglas Jerrold* (Knoxville, 1970)

Kelly, R.M., *Douglas Jerrold* (New York: Twayne, 1972)

Kenyon, J., *The History Men: The Historical Profession in England since the Renaissance*, second edition (London: Weidenfeld & Nicholson, 1993)

Kiely, R., 'Victorian Harlequin: The Function of Humour in Thackeray's Critical and Miscellaneous Prose' in Harry Levin (ed.), *Veins of Humour* (Cambridge, Mass.: Harvard University Press, 1972)

Loofbourow, J., *Thackeray and the Form of Fiction* (Princeton: Princeton University Press, 1964)

Lougy, R.E., 'The Dynamics of Exile and Desire: Narrative Form and Meaning in Thackeray's *Notes of a Journey from Cornhill to Grand Cairo*', *Modern Language Quarterly*, 50 (1989), 227-47

Lukacs, J., *Historical Consciousness, or the Remembered Past* (New York: Schocken Books, 1968/1985)

Lund, M., *Reading Thackeray* (Detroit: Wayne State University Press, 1988)

Marr, G.S., *Periodical Essayists of the Eighteenth-Century* (London: James Clarke, [1923])

Maurice, C., 'Miroirs de *Vanity Fair*', *Etudes Anglaises*, 45: 4 (1992), 424-31

Mayhew, A., *A Jorum of 'Punch'* (London, 1899)

McMaster, J., *Thackeray: The Major Novels* (Manchester: Manchester University Press, 1971)

McMaster, J., 'Funeral Baked Meats: Thackeray's Last Novel', *Studies in the Novel*, 13 (1981), 133-55

McMaster, R.D., *Thackeray's Cultural Frame of Reference: Allusion in 'The Newcomes'* (London: Macmillan, 1991)

Melville, L. (ed.), *Stray Papers By William Makepeace Thackeray, Being Stories, Reviews, Verses and Sketches (1821-1847)* (London: Hutchinson, 1901)

Melville, L., *The Life of William Makepeace Thackeray* (London: Caxton, 1906)

Middleton, D., *Victorian Lady Travellers* (Chicago: Chicago University Press, 1982)

Miller, A.H., *Novels Behind Glass: Commodity Culture and Victorian Narrative* (Cambridge: Cambridge University Press, 1995)

Mudge, I.G. and M.E. Sears, *A Thackeray Dictionary* (London: Routledge, 1910)

Musselwhite, D., *Partings Welded Together: Politics and Desire in the Nineteenth Century English Novel* (London: Methuen, 1987)

Pantuckova, L., *W.M. Thackeray as a Critic of Literature*, *Brno Studies in English*, 10-11 (Brno: Universita J.E. Purkyne, 1972)

Pearson, R., 'W.M. Thackeray: An Uncollected Paris Letter from the *Constitutional* (1836-37)', *Notes and Queries*, 238:4 (December 1993), 474-7.

Pearson, R., '"The public likes light literature and we write it": W.M.Thackeray and the Periodical Press, 1833-46' (PhD thesis, University of Manchester, 1994)

Pearson, R., 'Thackeray and *Punch* at the Great Exhibition: authority and ambivalence in verbal and visual caricatures', in Brian Maidment and Louise Purbrick (eds), *The Great Exhibition of 1851* (Manchester: Manchester University Press, forthcoming)

Pearson, R. (ed.), *W.M. Thackeray: Early Fiction and Journalism* (London: Routledge/Thoemmes Press, 1996)

Pearson, R. (ed.), *W.M. Thackeray: Early Travel Writings* (London: Routledge/Thoemmes Press, 1996)

Peck, J., 'Racism in the Mid-Victorian Novel: Thackeray's *Philip*' in Gary Day (ed.), *Varieties of Victorianism: The Uses of a Past* (Macmillan, 1998)

Peck, J., *War, the Army and Victorian Literature* (London: Macmillan, 1998)

Peters, C., *Thackeray's Universe: Shifting Worlds of Imagination and Reality* (London: Faber and Faber, 1987)

Pope-Hennessy, J., *Monckton Milnes: The Years of Promise, 1809-1851* (London: Constable, 1949)

Prawer, S.S., *Israel at Vanity Fair: Jews and Judaism in the Writings of W.M. Thackeray* (Leiden, New York: E. Brill, 1992)

Prawer, S.S., *Breeches and Metaphysics: Thackeray's German Discourse* (Oxford: Legenda, 1997)

Price, R.G.G., *A History of Punch* (London: Collins, 1957)

Pykett, L., 'The Real versus the Ideal: Theories of Fiction in Periodicals, 1850-1870', *Victorian Periodicals Review*, 15 (Spring 1982), 63-74

Ray, G.N., 'Thackeray and France: Being an Account of the part played by Thackeray's life in France and his reading of French Literature in the Formation of his Mind and Art', PhD thesis (Harvard University, 1940)

Ray, G.N., *W.M. Thackeray: the Uses of Adversity (1811-1846)* and *The Age of Wisdom (1847-1863)* (New York: McGraw-Hill, 1955, 1958)

Ray, G.N. (ed.), *The Letters and Private Papers of W.M. Thackeray*, 4 vols (Cambridge, Mass.: Harvard University Press, 1945-6)

Ray, G.N. (ed.), *W.M. Thackeray: Contributions to the 'Morning Chronicle'* (Urbana: University of Illinois Press, 1955)

Reed, J., *Dickens and Thackeray: Punishment and Forgiveness* (Athens: Ohio State University Press, 1995)

Roberts, H.E., '"The Sentiment of Reality": Thackeray's Art Criticism', *Studies in the Novel*, 13: 1-2 (Spring–Summer 1981), 21-39

Robinson, S.C., 'Editing Belgravia: M.E. Braddon's Defense of "Light Literature"', *Victorian Periodicals Review*, 28: 2 (Summer 1995), 109-22

Rosa, M.W., *The Silver-Fork School: Novels of Fashion Preceding 'Vanity Fair'* (New York: Columbia University Press, 1936)

Russell, N., *The Novelist and Mammon: Literary responses to the World of Commerce in the Nineteenth Century* (Oxford: Clarendon, 1986)

Saintsbury, G. (ed.), *Works of William Makepeace Thackeray*, 17 vols (London: Oxford University Press, [1908]).

Schwarzbach, F.S., '"Terra Incognita": An Image of the City in English Literature, 1820-1855', *Prose Studies*, 5 (May 1982)

Segel, E.T., 'Thackeray's Journalism: Apprenticeship for Writer and Reader', *Victorian Newsletter*, 57 (1980), 22-7

Shattock, J., *Politics and Reviewers: The Edinburgh and the Quarterly in the early Victorian age* (Leicester: Leicester University Press, 1989)

Shattock, J. and M. Wolff (eds), *The Victorian Periodical Press: Samplings and Soundings* (Leicester: Leicester University Press, 1982)

Shillingsburg, P.L., *Pegasus in Harness: Victorian Publishing and W.M. Thackeray* (Charlottesville: University Press of Virginia, 1992)

Smith, G., *Charles Dickens: A Literary Life* (London: Macmillan, 1996)

Speilmann, M.H., *The History of 'Punch'* (London: Cassell, 1895)

Spencer, W.T., *Mr. Thackeray's Writings for the 'National Standard' and 'Constitutional'* (London: W.T. Spencer, 1899)

Stein, R.L., *Victoria's Year: English Literature and Culture, 1837-1838* (Oxford: Oxf6rd University Press, 1987)

Stephen, J. Fitzjames, 'Superstition', *Cornhill Magazine*, 5 (May 1862), 537-49

Stephen, J. Fitzjames, 'Journalism', *Cornhill Magazine*, 6 (July 1862)

Stephen, J. Fitzjames, 'Spiritualism', *Cornhill Magazine*, 7 (June 1863), 706-19

Stevenson, L., *The Showman of Vanity Fair: The Life of William Makepeace Thackeray* (London: Chapman & Hall, 1947)

Stonehouse, J.H. (ed.), *A Catalogue of the Library of William Makepeace Thackeray* (London: Piccadilly Fountain Press, 1935)

Sullivan, A. (ed.), *British Literary Magazines, Vol. II: The Romantic Age, 1789-1836*; *Vol. III: The Victorian and Edwardian Age, 1837-1913* (Westport, CT.: Greenwood Press, 1983, 1984)

Summerfield, H. (ed.), 'Letters from the Club Arm-Chair: William Makepeace Thackeray', *Nineteenth-Century Fiction*, 18 (December 1963), 205-33

Sutherland, J., 'Thackeray as Victorian Racist', *Essays in Criticism*, 20 (1970), 441-5

Sutherland, J., *Thackeray at Work* (London: Athlone Press, 1974)

Sutherland, J., *Victorian Novelists and Publishers* (London: Athlone Press, 1976)

Sutherland, J. (ed.), W.M. Thackeray, *The Book of Snobs* (New York: St Martin's Press, 1978)

Thackerayana: Notes and Anecdotes (London: Chatto and Windus, 1875)

Thomas, B., 'The New Historicism and Other Old Fashioned Topics', in H. Aram Veeser, *The New Historicism* (London: Routledge, 1989)

Thomas, D.S., *Thackeray and Slavery* (Athens: Ohio University Press, 1993)

Thompson, J.B., *Ideology and Modern Culture* (Cambridge: Polity Press, 1990)

Thrall, M., *Rebellious Fraser's: Nol Yorke's Magazine in the Days of Maginn, Thackeray, and Carlyle* (New York: Columbia University Press, 1934)

Tillotson, G., *Thackeray the Novelist* (Cambridge: Cambridge University Press, 1954; London: Methuen, 1963)

Tillotson, G. and D. Hawes (eds), *Thackeray: The Critical Heritage* (Routledge and Kegan Paul, 1968)

Tillotson, K., *Novels of the Eighteen-Forties* (Oxford: Clarendon, 1954)

Trollope, A., *Thackeray* (London: Macmillan, 1879)

Wadsworth, A.P., 'Newspaper Circulations, 1800-1954', *Transactions of the Manchester Statisticals Society*, 1954-5

Ward, M.C., 'Preparing for the National Gallery: the Art Criticism of William Hazlitt and P.G. Patmore', *Victorian Periodicals Review*, 23: 3 (Fall, 1990), 104-10

Weiner, J.H. (ed.), *Innovators and Preachers: The Role of the Editor in Victorian England* (Westport, CT.: Greenwood Press, 1985)

Welsh, A. (ed.), *Thackeray: Twentieth-Century Views* (New Jersey: Prentice-Hall, 1968)

White, B.A., 'Douglas Jerrold's "Q" papers in "Punch"', *Victorian Periodicals Review*, 15 (1982)

White, E.M., 'Thackeray's Contributions to "Fraser's Magazine"', *Studies in Bibliography*, 19 (1966), 67-84

Wicke, J., *Advertising Fictions: Literature, Advertisement, and Social Reading* (New York: Columbia University Press, 1988)

Winegarner, L., 'Thackeray's Contributions to the "British and Foreign Review"', *Journal of English and German Philology*, 47 (1948), 237-45

Wolfreys, J., *Deconstruction.Derrida* (London: Macmillan, 1998)

Index